THE MAQĀM BOOK

The Maqām Book

A Doorway to Arab Scales and Modes

David Muallem

Translated by Yoram Arnon

OR-TAV MUSIC PUBLICATIONS

Kfar Sava, Israel

(מוסיקה בין מזרח ומערב)
(Music Between East & West)

David Muallem

Edited by Yosef Zucker

Translation from the Hebrew text: Yoram Arnon

Musical examples prepared by Yosef Zucker

Cover design: Dilek Muallem dilekmuallem@gmail.com

Cover illustration: Djālghī Baghdād (Ensemble Baghdad)

Painting by Shlomo Kedourie, used by permission

Photo of author: Necmi Aydin aydinnecmi@yahoo.com

Accompanying CD:

Qānūn: Abraham Salman

29111

ISBN 978-965-505-053-0

Printed in Israel, 2010

OR-TAV Music Publications

P.O.B. 1126, Kfar Sava 44110 Israel

Tel. +972-9-767-9869 Fax. +972-9-766-2855

E-mail: info@ortav.com www.ortav.com

David Muallem

Tel. +972-3-699-1331 Fax. +972-3-699-1294

Email: david@musicdm.com www.musicdm.com

For my grandchildren,
Bar, Tom, Guy, and Jan Rast,
without whom there would be no purpose for writing this book;

For my daughters in law, Efrat and Dilek,
and my sons, Dror and Yinon,
without whom I would not have the motivation to write it;

And for my dear wife,
Janet,
without whose support, help, advice, and love,
it would have been impossible to begin or finish this project.

March 2010

TABLE OF CONTENTS

AUDIO TRACKS
(listen online or download from www.ortav.com/audio/maqam)

The Adjam Family of Maqāmāt

1. Maqām ʿAdjam
2. Maqām ʿAdjam ʿUshayrān
3. Maqām Djahārkāh
4. Maqām Shawq-Afzā
5. Maqām Sūzdalāra

The Nahawand Family of Maqāmāt

6. Maqām Nahawand
7. Maqām Faraḥ-Fazā
8. Maqām ʿUshshāq Miṣrī
9. Maqām Nahawand Muraṣṣaʿ
10. Maqām Sulṭānī-Yakāh

The Kurd Family of Maqāmāt

11. Maqām Kurd
12. Maqām Ḥidjāz-Kār-Kurd
13. Maqām Lāmī
14. Maqām Lāmī (additional performance)

The Nawā-Athar Family of Maqāmāt

15. Maqām Nawā-Athar
16. Maqām Nakrīz

The Ḥidjāz Family of Maqāmāt

17. Maqām Ḥidjāz
18. Maqām Ḥidjāz-Humayūn
19. Maqām Ḥidjāz-Kār
20. Maqām Shadd-ʿArabān
21. Maqām Zandjarān or Zank-Kalā

The Rāst Family of Maqāmāt

22. Maqām Rāst
23. Maqām Sūznāk
24. Maqām Māhūr
25. Maqām Dalanshīn
26. Maqām Yakāh

The Bayāt Family of Maqāmāt

27. Maqām Bayāt
28. Maqām Bayāt Shūrī
29. Maqām Ḥusaynī
30. Maqām Muḥayyar

The Sīkāh Family of Maqāmāt

31. Maqām Sīkāh
32. Maqām Huzām
33. Maqām Awshār
34. Maqām ʿIrāq
35. Maqām Bastah-Nikār
36. Maqām Awdj
37. Maqām Mustaʿār

Maqāmāt that Do Not Belong to a Family

38. Maqām Ṣabā
39. Maqām Mukhālaf

TRANSLITERATION OF ARABIC WORDS AND NAMES

ʾ	ء	gh	غ
b	ب	f	ف
t	ت	q	ق
th	ث	k	ك
dj	ج	l	ل
ḥ	ح	m	م
kh	خ	n	ن
d	د	h	ه
dh	ذ	w	و
r	ر	y	ي
z	ز	**Diphthongs**	
s	س	ay	يْ
sh	ش	aw	وْ
ṣ	ص	**Long Vowels**	
ḍ	ض	ā	ا ,ى
ṭ	ط	ī	ي
ẓ	ظ	ū	و
ʿ	ع		

PITCH AND OCTAVE REGISTER INDICATIONS

This book uses the following system to indicate note pitches and their specific octave registers:

When referring to a note without regard to its octave register, the note appears as a capital letter (with an accidental when required) without any number next to it (e.g., G, A, B♭, E𝄳).

When referring to a note with a specific octave register, the note appears with a number that indicates its specific octave register in the Arab two-octave system (e.g., G1, A2, B♭1, E𝄳2), according to the following system:

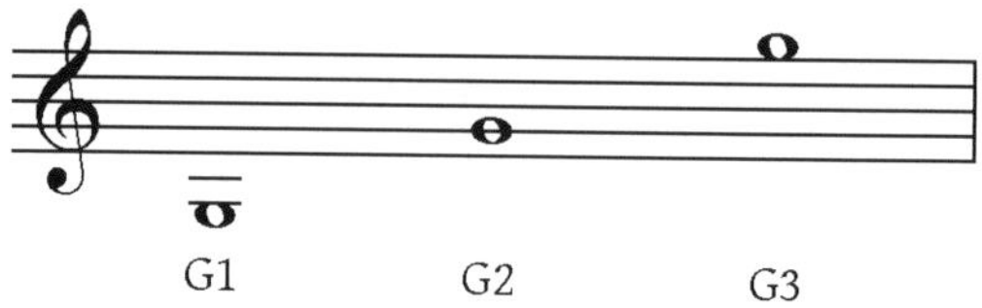

See also p. 60.

ACKNOWLEDGEMENTS

I THANK the Land of the Two Rivers, Iraq, where I was born and raised, for nourishing me with the best of the Arab classical tradition that has flourished there from days forgotten.

I thank the legendary Iraqi ensemble djālghī baghdād, who, for me, symbolizes the unique musical culture that has evolved there over generations, for nurturing me and endowing me with handfuls of inspiration.

I bow my head with respect for my late grandfather, Shimon, father of my father, a teacher and cantor, of whom it is said, had a full command of the maqāmāt. I thank him for teaching me how to recognize by ear dozens of maqāmāt, when I was yet a child seated at his feet, not even knowing what a musical scale was.

I express my deepest gratitude to my late mother, Sabiha, who, even when we were starving and penniless, sent me as a child to study the violin with a teacher whose fee was as high as the pension she was receiving since my father had died.

And to my late oldest sister, Tikva Agasi, a linguist and Arab history scholar, who ever since I was a child showed me the way, teaching and guiding, correcting and adding. To her I dedicate the Arab proverb: "The person who teaches me even one letter, is the one whose slave I will be forever." Tikva passed away on April 4, 2008, about two years after the publication of the Hebrew edition of this book. May God rest her soul.

I take off my hat before all the wonderful musicians who are the pillars of Iraqi music, both old and modern, from whom I learned so much: to the al-Kuwaytī brothers – Ṣalāḥ, the violinist, and Dā'ūd, the 'ūd player – both composers and performers; to Dā'ūd Akram, a violinist and composer, Yosef Pataw, the sanṭūr player, and Ṣalāḥ Shmuel, the djūzah player – members of the famous djālghī baghdād ensemble; to the late Menashe Tsadik, my compassionate friend; to Selim al-Nur, also known as Shlomo Ziv-Li, an engineer who in the weekly group lessons in which I participated revealed to us the wonderful structures of Arab music; to Abraham Salman, the renowned qānūn player, who contributed to this book the musical examples that appear in the attached CD; and to many, many others.

I thank all my beloved student friends at the Ethnic Music School at Bar Ilan University, who, during the many years spent with them, have helped me formulate the theory I present in this book, and whose need for an accessible source of information about Arab music was my inspiration to write.

I am grateful to all those angels who stood by me during the process of writing the Hebrew version of this book and contributed to it: firstly, to Prof. Taiseer Elias, a musician and musicologist, a unique scholar of Arab music, who, even before I ever told anyone about my intention to write this book, was my guiding light, and later when he knew, went over the manuscript and toiled on it as if it was his own; to Prof. Ami Maayani, then the head of the Music Academy at the Tel Aviv University, who did not stop grieving over the fact that he had no knowledge of the music of the East, but when going over the manuscript, has taught me that musicians are musicians, whatever their language; to Dr. Amatzia Bar-Yosef, a lecturer on Arab musical culture, who went twice over the manuscript and made valuable contributions; to Liora Ziv-Li, a pianist and teacher, who guided me through the field of European music, a path that I treaded if not securely, then at least without stumbling; and last but not least, to Prof. Dalia Cohen, a thinker and innovator, who even before I entrusted her with the final manuscript, had already known with certainty what mistakes she would find in it and all the important features I omitted – and indeed she was right.

I thank Prof. Sasson Somech of Tel Aviv University, recipient of the Israel Prize, who opened for me those small loopholes, through which I managed to squeeze, and to Dr. Yael Shai, the supervisor of musical education at the Ministry of Education, for her support and encouragement.

Special thanks go out to the translator of this book, Yoram Arnon, who being a musician and ethnomusicologist, did not only translate, but also corrected and advised (and listened), and has produced an excellent translation; and to my publisher, Yosef Zucker, who toiled over the technical work of this publication and with his skillfulness, produced such a magnificent result.

Finally, I thank myself for being patient with them all.

David Muallem
March 2010

FOREWORD

THE MUSICAL SCALE AND ITS SIGNIFICANCE

Dalia Cohen[1]

THE TERM *scale* is one of the fundamental terms that are used when teaching music. Yet, what is a scale? What is music?

Generally speaking, we can say that music is manifested in experiences that are derived from the organization of sounds, and that it serves as a function of a tremendous variety of human activities. Musics that differ in style, that is, in their rules of organization, produce various experiences. What are we organizing? When the subject is music, this is not a simple question. Other arts are also associated with experiences that are the consequence of rules of organization. However, in all arts, except for music, we know what we are organizing: in painting – colors and forms, in dancing – body movements, in literature – words and ideas. In these arts, the material that we organize is familiar to us and even arouses other experiences that are not related to art. However, in music, this is not the case. One of the common answers to the question of what we are organizing in music, and particularly in scales, is "notes." Yet, what are notes? What are their characteristics?

The Basic Parameters

ANY SOUND – whether a musical sound, human speech, an animal sound, a sound produced by a natural inanimate object or by a man-made one – can be described by using four parameters, or basic characteristics:

1. **Pitch:** Not all sounds have a distinct pitch; for example, most of the consonants we use in speech, such as *sh*, *s*, and *t*, and most of the sounds we hear in day-to-day life do not have a definite pitch. A sound that has a definite pitch is called a *musical tone*[2] or a *note*, and a sound that has an indefinite pitch is called noise. A *melody* refers only to musical notes, that is, to sounds that have a definite pitch.

2. **Duration:** *Duration* is the length of time between the onsets of consecutive sound events that are clearly distinct from one another. This parameter is one of the manifestations of "time," which makes possible measurable and complex organization.

3. **Intensity:** This characteristic is familiar to us from day-to-day life.

4. **Timbre.** This is a complex term, which is more easily defined by using negatives: Timbre is the characteristic

1 Dalia Cohen is Professor Emeritus at the Department of Musicology, the Hebrew University, and at the Jerusalem Academy of Music and Dance. She has been researching the nature of music from various complementing aspects: theory, practice, musical education, and more. She has published many books and articles on these topics.

2 Because the word *tone* has many different meanings and refers to various properties, here we shall use the word *note*.

that distinguishes between sounds and is not pitch, duration, or intensity. Timbre is most easily apparent in different instruments, as they are distinguished by their timbre. Thus, the timbre of a melody produced by singing, that is, by a human voice, is different from the timbre of the same melody when it is played on the piano; moreover, we can sing in different timbres.

All the components of musical organization are the result of the organization of these four parameters. The first two parameters are perceived by us in an accurate quantitative way and they are the ones that supply most of the complex organizations that we are not familiar with from day-to-day life. Pitch determines intervals (between pitches), scales, chords, etc., and duration determines rhythms (relations between durations), beats, meter, and tempo. Thus, a *melody* is defined by combining intervals, scales, rhythms, meters, etc. Unlike these two parameters, we are familiar with intensity from experiences unrelated to music and it cannot be defined in an accurate quantitative way. In terms of organization, its role is mainly to serve the other parameters, by emphasizing or softening them, as well as to take part in defining the rhythmic organization. Nevertheless, intensity itself and its variations influence our experiences.

Organizing timbre is not simple, because it is almost impossible to arrange it on a simple scale of "more than" or "less than," even though it is the only parameter that has an autonomous meaning out of context. Phonemes are differentiated from one another mainly in terms of timbre.

It should be noted that though we produce sounds with definite pitch with our voice, almost all components derived from pitch (collections of intervals, scales, etc.) were chosen by humans and differ from one culture to another. Moreover, they were established by means of measurements on musical instruments invented by people. Thus, even the musical "raw material" is man-made.

Therefore, music is considered the most abstract of all arts. Nevertheless, this does not mean that these "learned" components are arbitrary. They are significant for the various types of organization and therefore for the types of experiences. These components are defined mostly by aesthetic preferences of certain types of experiences made by a culture or a historical period.

Where do these four parameters come from? Do they represent the only means of describing sounds?

Stages in the Description of Sounds

TODAY, WE IDENTIFY three stages in the description of sounds. The description we discussed in the previous section is the second stage, the middle one.

1. **The acoustic stage:** The external physical stimulus causes us to sense a sound. The acoustic stimulus that is perceived by the ear is described by physical phenomena: frequency (of oscillation, or periodic vibrations) of air particles, the amplitude of the vibrations, various combinations of the vibrations (taking their phases into account), and more.

2. **The psychoacoustic stage:** In this stage, we interpret the acoustic stimuli in terms of the four psychoacoustic parameters: pitch, duration, intensity, and timbre.[3] This stage defines the hearing characteristics that are common to all human beings (e.g., the smallest pitch difference we can perceive and the conditions that bring about a definite pitch), because of the properties of the organs that take part in the hearing process (the ear and its various parts, the nerves, etc.)

3. **The cognitive stage:** This stage, obtained from our brain activity, consists of *selecting* the specific components of music. This stage comprises the collection of available intervals and the types of scales, rhythms, and meters, and it represents the diversity of various styles while it is continuously subjected to the constraints of the psychoacoustic stage. There are also cognitive constraints.

The rules of organization at the cognitive stage can be described as a hierarchical framework in which each level affects the next level, starting with the raw material (the entire collection of notes and intervals that were selected

3 We will not go into detail here about the interesting relationship between the two stages. We merely mention that we can compare the sound parameters to visual parameters relating to the psychophysical stage – various colors of various intensities and various forms – which are the interpretation of the physical stimuli caused by the electromagnetic vibrations perceived by the eye.

for a certain style and from them scales are formed), followed by rules of composition, the musical piece itself (which exemplifies one of the realizations of the raw material and the rules of composition), the performance (any performance is one of the realizations of the raw material and the rules of composition), and the perception and listening process, which is affected by the individual characteristics of the performer (such as age, cultural background, and musical knowledge). So what is style?

Manifestations of Style

STYLE IS determined by characteristics that are common to a group of musical pieces as compared to another group of pieces. These characteristics can refer to rules of organization (e.g., a melismatic style vs. a syllabic one, rhythmic vs. non-rhythmic, homophonic vs. polyphonic) or to the types of experiences that are the result of the various organization processes, which represent aesthetic preferences (such as an excited style vs. a calm one, static vs. dynamic, clear vs. unclear).

We can also talk about a "stylistic framework," which describes an extra-musical factor that is common to a group of musical pieces that share the same style. These frameworks may be very narrow, or very wide, such as a Western style vs. an Eastern style. When examining the Western style, we can refer to the framework of a historical period (Baroque style vs. Renaissance style), or to the framework of a composer's pieces (Bach style vs. Mozart style). We can also talk about the framework of function, such as lamentation music vs. dance music. The actual framework can say something about the culture itself. For example, the frameworks of the historical period and the composer, which are so important in Western music, are sometimes negligible in other musics. Frameworks also determine at which level of the hierarchical organization the change of style is most apparent. For example, musical rules of organization of various cultures are differentiated at the most basic level of the raw material, while different historical periods sometimes share the same raw material but differ in their rules of composition.

How do we perceive various styles?

Schemata and the Way We Perceive Them

WHEN WE HEAR a certain style of music as children, our brain unconsciously formulates various rules of organization that are termed *schemata*. Schemata link events and arouse expectations concerning the continuation of the progression, which may or may not be fulfilled, and sometimes an intentional deviation from expectations might occur. Various styles are based on arrays of different schemata (e.g., scales, rhythms, chords, and harmonic patterns). When we hear a musical piece, we continuously refer to schemata that were formed in our mind. Our mind "wants" to know which schemata elicit the events that occur in the musical piece we hear. Sometimes the answer is quite simple, but sometimes the composer intentionally obscures the schemata, and this creates a feeling of uncertainty, which becomes an important characteristic of the style of the piece. Yet, what if we are completely unfamiliar with the schemes? For example, if an Arab person who never listened to Western music, and therefore does not have any schemata of harmony in his mind (not even unconsciously), would listen to a piece that is based mostly on harmonic patterns, it would all sound the same to him. Similarly, a non-Arab person who does not have schemata of maqāmāt (which are the subject of the present book) in his mind would not respond to changes that are considered significant by an Arab listener.

These culture-specific schemata are "learned" schemata (but they are not necessarily arbitrary). Alongside these schemata, we find "natural" schemata, which are significant for our experiences and represent rules of organization that are not culture-specific because we are familiar with them from areas other than music; for example, the curves of change (contours) of various parameters (ascending/descending, convex/concave, zigzag/unchanging, and various combinations), deviations from anticipated events, and various cognitive operations, such as inversion, enlargement and contraction, repositions, and more.

The subject of the present book refers to schemata of scales in Arab music, which are an essential part in the definition of the maqām, which represents an "Arab modal framework." The framework of the maqām and the schemata of mīzān (which represent principles of predefined drumming patterns) form the basis for Arab music theory.

Scales and Modal Frameworks

A *SCALE* is a sequence of notes that are arranged according to pitch and have a certain hierarchy with reference to the *tonic note*. In tonal music, scales form the main pool of notes. In the course of a musical piece there may, of course, be changes in the tonal center.[4] Quantitatively, a scale can be described in terms of the sizes of the intervals between each pair of consecutive notes in the scale, or in terms of the intervals between each note in the scale and the tonic. In Western music, both methods are common, while in non-Western music, the first method is the most common one.

Scales represent important "learned" schemata that are the result of the pitch parameter and serve to distinguish between cultures. These schemata have many quantitative realizations, which differ in their level of coherence, and this affects the possibilities of organization of the notes of the scale and its intervals – simple/complex, short-term/long-term, and clear/unclear organizations. In non-Western music, the modal framework comprises a group of modes, while each mode represents a group of melodies that are considered similar. The term *mode* comes from the Classical Greek *modus*. Each culture has a different name for its modal framework: in Arab music, it is named *maqām*, in India, *raga*; in Persian music, *dastgāh*; in Indonesia, *pathet*; and in Jewish music, *shteyger*. Each modal framework is characterized by various musical elements and sometimes even by extra-musical elements, such as the preferred time of performance and the *ethos*,[5] so that in all of them, the modal framework is a scale and other factors. Only in Western music, starting in the seventeenth century, they are characterized solely by their scales. The number of modes was narrowed down to just two: the major (which consists of a major third and a major sixth) and the minor (which consists of a minor third and a minor sixth), so they can be contrasted with each other. The scales are defined exclusively by a sequence of seven notes in one octave; therefore, changing their register (higher or lower) does not change the scale.

Other cultures feature a profusion of scales, their scales are not as abstract, and there are conventional limitations on how they are realized. Modal frameworks from different cultures differ in the "additions" that accompany the scale, in the level of abstractness of scales, in the number of their notes, in the level of coherence that is apparent in the types of intervals between consecutive notes, and more. All these influence the rules of organization of a particular style and the resulting experiences.[6]

Scale Systems and Operations for Forming Scales

WE CAN THINK of scales as the result of a variety of structures and processes. Firstly, as was said above, they usually represent a selection of notes out of hierarchical systems of notes, and the collection of scale notes includes some hierarchy (e.g., the "tonic note"). The widest systems (in each modal framework there is only one) include all the notes and intervals that were "selected" for that particular framework. This array includes notes that are "foreign" to the scale (in Western music, they are named *chromatic notes*) that serve to emphasize the notes of the scale, similar to the way dissonances emphasize consonances. The intervals between consecutive notes of the scale are the result of combining the small intervals between notes of the wider system.

For example, in Western music, scales are the result of *shifting* or *repositioning* the tonic in the cyclical diatonic system, resulting in seven notes for each cycle (as it is represented by the white keys on the piano) and this in turn is the result of the widest system, which consists of 12 notes (including the black keys). The intervals between consecutive notes in the system of 12 notes are only semitones, while the intervals between consecutive notes in the diatonic system and in its scales are of two kinds: a major second, which consists of a whole tone, and a minor second, which consists of a semitone. The diatonic system that was selected in the West represents one arrangement of these two types of seconds out of three alternatives,[7] and it was proven that the system selected in the West is the most coherent one.

In Arab music, since the nineteenth century and probably even a little before, the widest array of notes consists of

4 This is the case in Western music. In Arab music, in contrast, the modulation is mainly between the various scales.

5 *Ethos* is a Greek term; it is parallel to the Indian *rasa* and the Arab *ta'thīr*.

6 It should be noted that we do not discuss here in detail the important relation between rules of organization and experiences.

7 In Indian music, all three alternatives are used, in addition to many other scales that are the result of other systems.

24 notes to an octave, in intervals of quartertones. In the 1932 Cairo Congress of Arab Music, it was decided that these intervals are equal. From these intervals, five different seconds are formed, and from these, many scalar systems and specific scales are formed.

In the time of the theoretician Ṣafī al-Dīn al-Urmawī (the thirteenth century), the widest system was formed by dividing the octave into 17 parts of two sizes (as opposed to one size in Western music), and by combining these parts, five types of seconds were formed (as opposed to two types in Western music). In classical Indian music, the octave is divided into 22 unequal parts (named *śruti*, which means "hearing"), and by combining these, three basic seconds were formed, each consisting of two, three or four śruti.

Another method for forming scales, which is related to the above method, is by combining small groups of notes that form parts of the scale: tetrachords – consisting of four notes, trichords – three notes, and pentachords – five notes. In Classical Greece, theoreticians referred to two forms of combining three types of tetrachords.[8] Ṣafī al-Dīn's theory suggests five sizes of seconds and groups of tetrachords and pentachords, each composed of two or three types of seconds. All together, his theory suggests 12 types of pentachords and seven tetrachords, and by combining these, 84 scales can be formed. Out of these, the 12 most important scales were selected.

In India, in the modern period (from the end of the seventeenth century), there is a clear distinction between North Indian and South Indian music. Each has a different extensive system, from which scales are formed by combining two tetrachords. In South Indian music, there are 12 possibilities for the first tetrachord and six for the second tetrachord, forming all together 72 scales. In North Indian music, there are eight possibilities for the first tetrachord and four for the second tetrachord, forming all together 32 scales, which are classified according to certain criteria. Some of these scales can be viewed as being formed by repositioning the tonic in various scalar systems. It is interesting to note that Ravi Shankar, the famous sitar player, added three more scales (with a diminished fifth), which were admitted into the collection of recognized scales.

Scales can also be formed by using *alteration* – that is, changing some notes of a certain scale in order to form another scale. A familiar example from Western music is the formation of two scales – the harmonic minor and the melodic minor – by applying alteration to the natural minor scale. In Arab music, as will be discussed in this book, the scale of maqām Huzām is the result of alterations in the scale of Sīkāh. In Classical India (around 1000 AD), theoreticians formed many scalar systems out of a basic scalar system by means of alterations. Each of these scalar systems could be used to form various other scales by repositioning the tonic. In theory, there were 12 forms of alteration (lowering or raising a number of śruti), and seven of these were considered important.

Another process that was hinted above, but was not mentioned by name, is *screening.* Out of any wide system, narrower systems can be formed by a process of screening. Thus, for example, by screening the system of 12 notes, we can form three systems of seven notes, and by screening the system of seven notes that was selected in Western music, we can, theoretically, form 15 pentatonic systems, which in turn can generate, by repositioning the tonic, 75 different scales.

These pentatonic systems can be classified into three possible basic structures: (1) a system that is composed of a duchord (two consecutive notes) and a trichord; (2) a system that is composed of a tetrachord and a "spread" triad (e.g., C–D–E–F–A–C–D . . .); and (3) a combination of a pentachord and a fourth. If we ignore microtonality, we can see that the two last possibilities do not exist in reality, and the five systems that are generated by the first possibility are the common ones. Theoretically, each system can generate five scales by repositioning the tonic, but in practice, less repositions are used. Out of the five systems, the one that is known as "the Chinese system" (which is represented by the black keys on the piano) is theoretically the most coherent one.

Up until now, we have not paid attention to the phenomenon of *cyclicality*, which has great significance in systems of Western music. Cyclicality is most apparent with reference to register or octave position. In Western music, scales are not dependent on the register, that is, the octave in which they are played. This is not always evident in other musics. For example, in the tuning of the instruments of the *gamelan* (The Indonesian orchestras), we often find different intonations in different octaves. In Arab music, there are sometimes significant changes in the pitches of notes in

8 Each of these consisted of two sizes of seconds: big and small; very big and small; very very big and very very small. Several theories suggested accurate measurements of the various sizes of seconds.

different octaves. For example, in the scale of maqām Ṣabā, the octave note is diminished, and in many other cases, a description of a scale of a maqām must refer to two octaves.

Another common cyclicality (in Western music and much earlier, in ancient Chinese music) generates a scale based on a sequence of fifths. In ancient China, theoreticians were aware of the fact that a sequence of "natural" fifths (as they appear in the overtone series that constitute most notes) would not result in returning to the initial note, as is the case with equal temperament (in which B sharp = C), because a natural fifth is slightly larger than an equal-tempered fifth, and after 12 steps, the difference amounts to almost an eighth of a tone, which is a significant difference.

Tessitura (the range with reference to the tonic note) can also become a factor in the characterization of a scale. For example, in the medieval modes, there was a differentiation between the Dorian mode and the Hypodorian mode (in the latter, the melody descends below the tonic note). Such a systematic differentiation is noticeable in the Chinese theory of scales.

"Modulation" of scales is one of the important methods of composition. It can serve as one of the means of forming a superstructure in which the melody moves away from the primary scale and its tonic and later returns to it. Modulation facilitates an important point of reference and has different manifestations in various cultures. In Western music, most modulations are of the same scale to different tonal centers, while in other musical cultures, most modulations are to different scales.

We can see, therefore, that scales are formed by a variety of processes: cyclicality, screening, shifting the tonic, alterations, combining small units, modulations, and more. In various cultures, we can find different manifestations of all of these processes, resulting in the formation of various types of scales, which affect the possibilities of musical organization and the types of experiences we undergo. To the aforementioned factors, we must add the quantitative aspect, which is a very significant factor in the characterization of the organization.

Summary of the Unique Characteristics of the System of Western Music

1. The Western system features only one cyclical diatonic system consisting of seven notes (with minimum asymmetry). Most other cultures feature many scalar systems [9]

2. The system of seven notes is derived from the system of 12 notes, which is a kind of an optimum that is attained in-between a profusion – which can result in the division of the octave into 72 parts (in the Neo-Byzantine music theory) – and a scarcity

3. Many musical components are characterized by binary contrasts: there are two types of seconds (major and minor – as opposed to many types in other systems); two primary scales (major and minor – so they can be contrasted); in terms of rhythmic organization: two types of beats (accented and unaccented – as opposed to many types in other musical cultures – an abundance related to the timbre of drumming); mostly two types of meter (duple and triple – as opposed to many types in other cultures; for example, in Arab music theory there are over 100 meters called *mīzān*)

4. Maximum differentiation between the various musical components (as opposed to fixed connections that can be found in most modal traditions of non-Western cultures): scale, range, tessitura, the absolute area of occurrence, the dominant motifs and other pitch-related components, as well as a differentiation between components of duration, between components of pitch and duration, and between musical and extra-musical factors

5. As has been mathematically proven, the Western diatonic system of seven notes and the system of 12 notes ensure the maximum coherence of the system of intervals and allow for harmonic schemata as well as super-directionality with maximum super-complexity. In contrast, other systems, and especially the Arab system, allow for focusing on the moment with maximum momentary complexity.

9 Much like in Western music, most of these consist of seven notes. However, there are also smaller systems, mostly of five notes and sometimes even of three notes. In India, there are also systems of six notes.

Theory and Practice

THERE IS ALWAYS a certain gap between theory and practice and the nature of the gap can tell us much about the rules and characteristics of the music in question. Some theories offer a profusion of possibilities (such as scales and rhythmic patterns) which is beyond the scope of our ability to perceive and understand. Chinese theory of organizing scales exemplifies such profusion. On the other hand, there are musics that hardly have a theory, or that have theories that do not take into account some important aspects,[10] and it is up to researchers to uncover the relevant regularity.

The performance of Arab folk music serves as an interesting example of a gap between theory and practice. Measurements of the intonation of the singing of Arab singers indicated such a considerable gap between theory and practice, that many scholars (even Curt Sachs) claimed that in Arab music, there is no relation between the two. Indeed, Arab theoreticians have often asserted such a gap explicitly, and sometimes even disregarded practice. Nonetheless, careful examination of Arab folk music in Israel indicated that though the dispersion of the sizes of seconds is wide, and their average size is different in each song, there is still an interesting regularity. Each song has an "intonation skeleton," which represents the average of the sizes of the consecutive seconds of the scale, and when the intonation of two songs is considered equivalent (that is, the songs are in the same maqām), the consecutive seconds in the scale skeleton maintain a ratio of *bigger than . . .* (>), *smaller than . . .* (<), or *equal to . . .* (=) and not necessarily an accurate quantitative ratio. What is maintained, therefore, is an "intonation type," which allows for some freedom of performance, but still maintains a certain regular framework. Regularity was also detected in the degree of dispersion in the intonation skeleton. Some notes in the scale of the maqām were performed very consistently with a relatively small dispersion, while other notes were always performed with a large dispersion. In practice, therefore, the scale of a maqām is defined by the degree of the dispersion of its notes. In addition, it was discovered that there is a relation between the maqām and various types of texts, and other characteristics. This book introduces scales of maqāmāt as they are presented in theory.

In conclusion, in this foreword we tried to provide a background for the term *scale* and for its various manifestations in various musical cultures. This was done in order to study the scales of maqāmāt through a wide perspective of issues, both in terms of musical cognition and in terms of cultural activity (although without giving a detailed account of the significance of scales in terms of types of experiences).

In the present book, David Muallem has expounded the rich knowledge that he absorbed as a child growing up in a musical family in Baghdad and has updated it by using the theoretical literature available to him in Arabic, English and Hebrew. The result is a significant contribution to the appreciation of the world of maqāmāt, both for students of Arab music and for their teachers. Mr. Muallem draws an extensive background for the theory of maqāmāt and provides a collection of notated examples: 48 maqāmāt belonging to eight families, while presenting their scales' components and adding short explanations. This collection, which represents most maqāmāt used in practice, may also serve as a kind of a maqām lexicon, which can help students find their way in the complexities of maqāmāt and their scales.

Indeed, this book serves to fill a shortage of information that is increasingly felt as Arab music education becomes more widespread.

10 Western music theories barely refer to natural schemata.

INTRODUCTION

ABOUT THE BOOK

> THERE WAS a time, not too long ago, when a Westerner's initial encounter with Arab music hardly generated love at first hearing; exposure to this particular universe of sounds often reminded the uninitiated listener of a dog's howling. (Shiloah 1995: xiii)

This is how Amnon Shiloah describes the encounter between a Western ear and an Arab melody and tells of a French traveler who in 1648 witnessed a dervish ceremony and described it with horrible words. He also cites the famous European composer Hector Berlioz, who said about Oriental music: "They call music what we call *charivari* ['commotion,' 'a noisy procession']" (ibid).

Dalia Cohen is another music scholar who refers to this alienation between East and West:

> In the recent past, many Westerners had an ambivalent attitude towards any culture other than their own: on the one hand, scorn and contempt, and on the other, an admiration for the mysterious and the unknown. (Cohen 1986: 1)

And she adds:

> Today, when contact between the two worlds is tighter, and interest in acquiring direct, deep knowledge of other cultures has grown significantly, attitudes of Western superiority, as well as inferiority in relation to it, are not as common anymore. (ibid)

As an example of Western openness to Arab music, I would like to recount an anecdote concerning the famous violinist Yehudi Menuhin, who traveled the world in order to experience different musics and even played together with the famous *sitar* player Ravi Shankar. When, many years ago, Menuhin was visiting Israel and giving a series of lectures, he happened to hear the Iraqi *qānūn* player Abraham Salman. When Salman finished playing, the captivated Menuhin came to him, kissed his hand, and said, "Sir, please carry on with playing this heavenly music and never be tempted to change it. It is exquisite."

However, it seems that even after Westerners had started taking interest in the musics of the East and even researching them, they did not have the essential understanding that a certain culture could not be understood only by comparing it to another one, in this case, Western culture. Each culture should be studied, first and foremost, in relation to its own elements: its history, its traditions, and the conditions that formed it. There is no such thing as an inferior or a superior musical culture. It might be that even today, when they come to study the cultures of the East, Westerners have difficulties with getting rid of notions of Western superiority. Such perceptions hinder the discovery of the uniqueness of the studied culture, and many times, the result is misinterpretation. We should not, for example, evaluate the fact that in the history of the musics of the East, style changes occurred rarely, maybe once in a thousand years, and view this as a sign of stagnation since in European music, changes occurred often, once in every 50 years or so. We must research the reasons why changes take longer to happen in the East, because this phenomenon is an integral part of its culture. One of the reasons for that may be that the musics of the East tend to be strongly interconnected with emotional elements, and these do not change often. Another reason may be that owing to their richness in musical scales and modes, the musics of the East had no need for drastic changes, such as the development of atonal music in Europe, in order to achieve melodic variety.

The Islamic world, however, has some responsibility for the neglect of its heritage. Since the rise of Islam until the fourteenth century, many important Arab music theoreticians, such as Ibn Sīnā, (d. 1037), al-Urmawī (d. 1294), al-Kindī (d. 870), and al-Fārābī (d. 950), have left extensive literature of music scholarship and have laid the foundations for the science of music. After the awakening of Arab culture from its long period of stagnation which started at the end of the Middle Ages and ended at the end of the eighteenth century, Arabs remained entrapped in the beauty, sentiments, and charm of their musical culture and, to a large extent, forgot the science and theory so essential for the appreciation, understanding, and development of this music. As a result, many times, in concerts of Arab music, not enough attention is given to distributing knowledge concerning the Arab musical culture. While in any European music concert, there are handout concert programs that give details about the musical pieces to be played: their form, movements, scales, composers, and more. In an Arab music concert, there are no such programs, and the audience does not always know what piece is going to be played – surely, not in what *maqām* it is going to be. In Turkey, however, the situation is much better. I have to say that personally, I have always asked of various ensembles and managers to honor their audience's thirst for knowledge and to give some information about what is played in their concerts. I did not have much success, however. Many of them have retained the practice of the old days, when ensembles played for a small audience at private events and sometimes even determined their selections on the spot, according to the audience's requests, without ever seeing a need to present a piece or to explain anything about it. It must be noted that since the revival of Arab culture, most of the scholars of Arab music were actually non-Arabs. Few Arab scholars saw the necessity of researching their own culture, even though research done by a member of that culture would have given it a valuable personal dimension.

This state of affairs worried me and I decided to do something about it. In the end, I started a project called "Music between East and West," a series of lectures in which I explained the fundamentals of Arab musical culture and the differences between it and classical European music. The first lecture in the series was named "Why can Western ears not hear Eastern Music?" These lectures were much welcomed by audiences that were not knowledgeable about Arab music. I received many encouraging remarks, such as, "Why didn't they explain all of this to us before?" and "Maybe I still don't really like Eastern music, but now, I can understand it."

I spent more than five years among students of the Ethnic Music School at Bar Ilan University. There were no available books to help them understand the theory of the Arab musical system. The lectures at the school, though essential to their studies, did not answer their immediate desires for understanding the Arab system and revealing the mysteries of the *maqāmāt*. During that period, I decided to write a book that would spread the knowledge I had collected, which, together with the experience I gathered over the years with the students at Bar Ilan, was formed into a theory. I did it for the benefit of students and teachers of Arab music wherever they are.

This book is neither scholarly research nor a philosophy book. It is a theory book that explains the Arab musical system as it is today and enables quick reference to dozens of maqāmāt and scales that are used in this music. I worked on this book because I could not find an accessible theory book that methodically presents all the fundamentals of this musical system in a way that can be understood by everybody. Almost all of the Arab books and sources that I managed to get my hands on were limited, and only partially dealt with the fundamentals of the system; they gave no comprehensive, systematic explanation. No wonder that at the 1932 Cairo Congress of Arab Music, somebody said, out of ignorance we may presume, that "the Arab musical system is characterized by a lack of systematization."

The Cairo Congress of Arab Music, held in 1932, played a significant role in the development of the appreciation of Arab music. Many musicologists and musicians from all over the world were invited to this event, including some famous European music scholars. The purpose of the congress was to examine the state of contemporary Arab music and to find ways of advancing and improving it. In spite of the tremendous importance of the congress, it failed in reaching its goals when its participants, especially the "foreigners," found out that in Arab music, there are unbridgeable gaps between theory and practice. The congress was important mainly for two things: raising awareness of Arab music and its significance, and the large quantity of recorded and transcribed material that was gathered there.

I said above that a culture should be studied first by means of its own elements in the framework of the national and ethnic environment in which it developed: a culture should not be evaluated by comparing it to another culture. I also criticized the approach carried out by certain Western musicologists, of studying the musical cultures of the East only by comparing them to Western culture, an approach that was common until not so long ago and its traces can still be detected today. Nevertheless, I devoted the first part of this book to the analysis of some of the fundamentals of European classical music, which serves as a kind of introduction to the complexities of the Arab musical system. This approach is the result of the experience I gained during many years of lecturing and being in close contact with students and listeners. I came to understand that most students and music lovers of any background are usually more familiar with European music and with its system. Terms and concepts of Arab music that have parallels in European music are easier to explain and to understand. The fundamentals of European music that are relevant to our subject and the philosophy behind them are somewhat simpler than the fundamentals of Arab classical music (except for the subject of harmony, which is the pinnacle of European music but is almost irrelevant to Arab music). I learned that pedagogically, it is very helpful to give a relevant summary of the fundamentals of European music as an introduction to the lecture on Arab music, and that this allows for a better understanding of some of the intricate and complex elements of the Arab system.

The musical traditions of most of the cultures in the Islamic world, from its eastern end to its western, are founded on the same modal system, and many of the scales and scale names that appear in one have parallels in another. The quartertone octave forms the basis for their melodies, and various musical practices, such as improvisation and performing in small ensembles, are common to all of them. The modal system of these cultures is based, in all probability, on a single historical source. Evidently, people who study one of these traditions will find themselves learning much about the others. For producing a truly comprehensive work, it may have been proper to include all of these traditions in one book; this is what Cohen did in her book *East and West in Music* (1986). Nevertheless, there are various differences, sometimes many, between these musical cultures concerning the conception of maqām and its usage, its internal structure, and its function in musical creativity. Scales that are identical in two cultures might carry different names, and the perception of the relationships between maqāmāt may be different as well. Among these traditions, classical Arab music stands as an individual tradition. It is quite similar to the Turkish art music tradition; indeed, so similar are these two traditions that it can be said that whoever studies one will get to know the other one quite well. I decided to devote this book to the Arab tradition, the tradition to which I was exposed and from which I draw inspiration. Of all other related traditions, I refer mainly to the Turkish tradition, because of the similarities between the two; especially, since Arab music of the Middle East was greatly influenced by the Turkish musical tradition during the long years of Ottoman dominion in the area.

Before discussing the maqāmāt and their development, let us quickly survey a few other important elements of Arab music: its rhythmic patterns, musical instruments, Arab poetry, and the classical musical forms.

Rhythmic Patterns

TWO OF THE most important elements of music are melody (the element of *pitch*) and time (the element of *duration*). Melody is represented by musical scales and time is represented by rhythm.

In the music of the Islamic world, *meters* (the number of beats in a measure) range from the simple (those that consist of a small number of simple beats, such as $\frac{2}{4}$ and $\frac{3}{4}$) to very complex (such as $\frac{10}{8}$, $\frac{13}{8}$, and $\frac{32}{4}$). However, not only meters, but also their internal structures, which create various *rhythmic patterns* (also called *rhythmic modes*), are many and diverse. The meter of $\frac{10}{8}$, for example, features a variety of rhythmic patterns, each with its own usage.

Rhythm in Arab music, therefore, is not just an accompaniment to the played melody, but a model that determines the form and structure of the melody itself. The various rhythmic patterns carry distinctive names, and many classical forms are determined according to them. The important musical form called *samāʿī*, for example, is based on the meter of $\frac{10}{8}$, but also on the rhythmic pattern called *samāʿī thaqīl*, which gives this musical form its name, and is written like this:

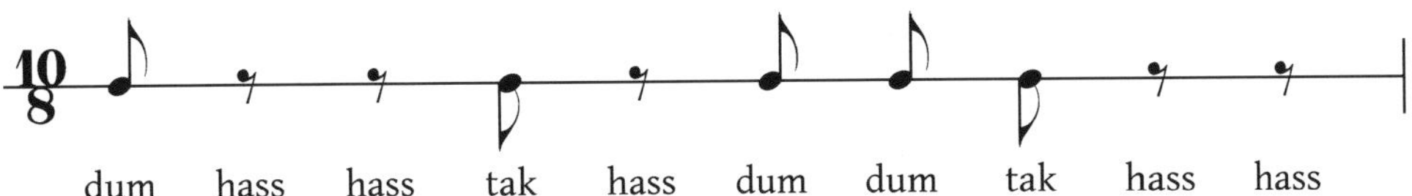

The sound *dum* represents a soft dampened stroke in the center of the drum; *tak* represents a sharp dry stroke near its frame; and *hass* represents a rest or silence; see also Shiloah 1995: 123.

However, sometimes another rhythmic pattern that is based on a $\frac{10}{8}$ meter is used for the samāʿī form; its name is *aksak samāʿī*, and it is written like this (see also al-Ḥilū 1972: 134 ff., 154, 182):

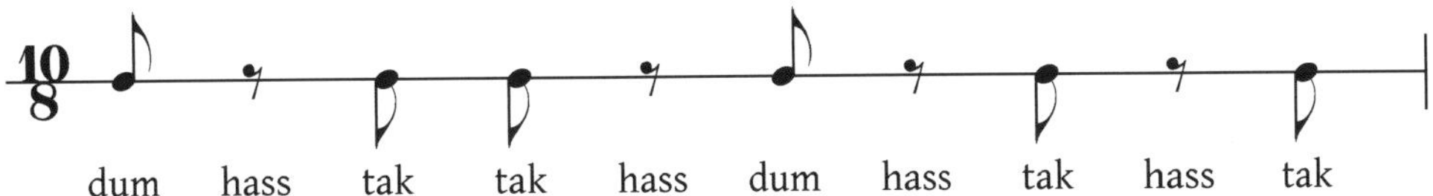

Today, in the Middle East and especially in Turkey, other rhythmic patterns of $\frac{10}{8}$ are used for the samāʿī form, such as the following two:

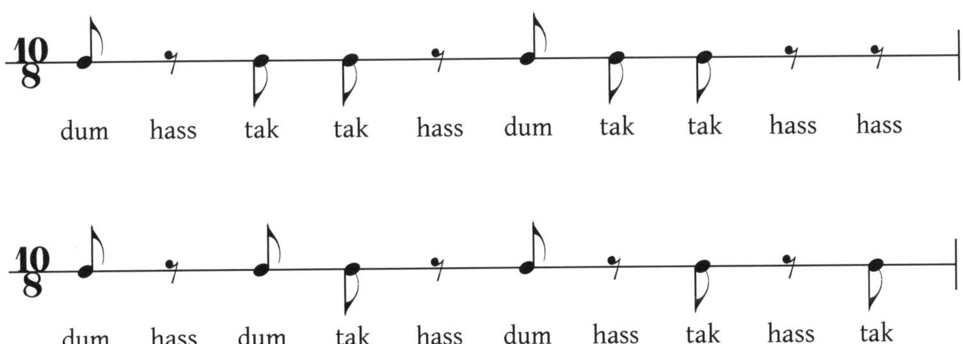

In fact, percussionists allow themselves the freedom to sometimes improvise and slightly alter the rhythms of 10/8 in order to adjust them to correspond to the melody of the performed samāʿī (Yinon Muallem).

The theoretical system of rhythmic patterns is called in Arabic (and in Turkish) *uṣūl*, which means "order," "tradition," or "manners" – meanings that signify the importance of rhythms in Arab music.

I could not find any Arab source that gives a clear and consistent terminology concerning the concepts related to meter and rhythm. In Arabic, there are two words that are quite similar to each other: one is *wazn* (plural: *awzān*) and the other *mīzān* (plural: *mawāzīn* or *miyāzīn*). The word *wazn* usually means "the weight of something," while *mīzān* usually refers to the instrument used for weighing.

The word usually used for meter is *mīzān*, which means "weight," and therefore, $\frac{10}{8}$ can be said to be representing the mīzān, or the meter of a certain piece. However, the same word is sometimes used to signify "a rhythmic pattern," which may also be called *ḍarb* ("a stroke") and *uṣūl* (al-Ḥilū 1972: 60, 134).

The inconsistency in the distinction between meters and rhythmic patterns in the Arabic language is apparent in the discourses of Arab musicologists. I prefer to distinguish between the two terms and to use the term *wazn* for "meter" and the term *mīzān* for "a rhythmic pattern." The term *uṣūl* will be used to represent the theoretical system of rhythmic patterns in general.

An Arab musician who wants to compose a musical piece, especially a vocal one, most often chooses first the appropriate rhythmic patterns, even before choosing the desired maqām. Not every rhythmic pattern is suitable for every melody.

Musical Instruments

EACH MUSICAL culture makes use of the musical instruments it has adopted and adapted. Musical instruments have a great influence on the formation of the characteristics of a certain musical tradition and its musical ideals, and should comply with its fundamental elements. The piano and the guitar are designed for a musical system based on the division of the octave into semitones and are therefore designed to comply with the characteristics of European diatonic scales; they cannot be used to play music that is based on a system of quartertones. Moreover, these two instruments cannot produce alterable or "flexible" notes, such as those produced by *glissando* and *vibrato*, which are the essence and soul of Middle-Eastern music. Therefore, Middle-Eastern instruments – primarily, the fretless string instruments – can produce microtonal notes (based on intervals smaller than the semitone) and allow the player to produce alterable notes.

It seems that the most ancient known instrument in Arab history is the *rabāba*, a one-stringed fiddle-like instrument which was held vertically on the player's lap, and which still is used by the Bedouin tribes of the Arab peninsula. After the rise of Islam and the formation of the Great Musical Tradition, the *ʿūd* has become one of the central and most important instruments of Arab music. The ʿūd is an ancient string instrument, which was used by the philosophers and music scholars of the turn of the first millennia (after the rise of Islam and its great conquests) to measure and determine the fundamentals of the science of music. The ʿūd is the ancestor of the European lute, and the first lutes were very similar to the Arab ʿūd – probably the result of Arab influence during the Golden Age of Islamic rule in Andalusia, Spain. The Arab *kamāndjah*, also a fiddle-like instrument held vertically on the player's lap, is similar to the *djūzah*, and is most likely the ancestor of the European violin. However, the Arab world has "readopted" the European violin and incorporated it into its musical practice, and today it is one of the most prominent instruments in Arab ensembles and orchestras.

We can find fretted instruments in the Islamic world, such as the Azeri *tar* and the Turkish *saz*. However, unlike the guitar, these instruments' frets are movable and their position can be adjusted according to the intervals of any desired scale. These instruments produce beautiful sounds, but are limited in terms of producing small, subtle changes in pitch as fretless instruments can. This limitation might be the reason why these instruments are not so common in those Arab countries where modulation (moving from one scale to another) is a very common musical practice.

Other common Arab instruments are the *nāy*, a type of flute that is played from the upper end of its tube, and the *qānūn*, a plucked zither-like instrument.

Certainly, it is difficult to determine what came first: the musical instruments that were adopted by the culture, and therefore dictated its melodic characteristics, or the melodies themselves, which required the development of instruments that could reproduce them. We can only determine that musical instruments are an inseparable part of any musical culture, its aesthetic ideals, its development, and its history; without understanding them, we cannot fully understand their musical tradition. In many cases, the structure of musical instruments fulfills the requirements of a certain musical system and the scales it employs. We can say, therefore, that musical instruments influence the formation of musical ideals, while alternatively, musical ideals and styles influence the development of musical instruments.

Arab Poetry

MOST OF ARAB POETRY is rhymed and is based on poetic meters, and therefore, it features rhythmic patterns and structures. The theory of meter and rhythm in Arab poetry is quite complex. When discussing the *qaṣīda*, a poetic genre,[1] Shiloah writes:

> The prevalent genre in this poetry – the *qaṣīda* – was based on a union of metre and rhyme, with the same rhythmical structure and rhymes repeated in each line (*bayt*) of the poem. The most distinctive unit in Arabic verse, the *bayt*, was divided into two equal half-lines, or hemistiches [called *ṣadr* and *ʿadjz*]. Every line consists of a certain number of feet. The metric system, which in essence is quantitative, is built on distinguishing clearly between the short and long syllables that comprise a word. (Shiloah 1995: 3)

And he adds:

---

1 The qaṣīda is a specific poetic genre, but regarding rhyming and rhythm, it is not much different from other forms of poetry.

> The defined rhythmic organization characterizing Arab quantitative metre tends to inspire rhythmic musical organization. (ibid: 4)

We can infer from the above that the qaṣīda, a poetical genre that was already quite developed during the pre-Islamic period (al- Djāhiliyya), required that musical rhythms be adapted to poetry, and therefore was the source of inspiration for the development of the system of musical rhythmic patterns. Such an assumption sounds quite plausible. Not every musical rhythm can be suitable for a certain poem, even if they both share the same meter, and the rhythmic pattern (i.e., the internal structure of the musical meter) applied to the melody of that poem should match the poetic rhythm of the poem itself.

Therefore, a composer who wants to write a melody to a certain poem checks firstly the poetic rhythm and meter of the song, then examines which musical rhythmic patterns are suitable for the poem, and only later decides about melodic aspects, such as maqām. This means that when composing poetry into a song, the decisions concerning rhythm precede those that concern melody. The composer may decide about a certain maqām in order to stress the emotional character of the song – happy, sad, emotional, or grave – but ultimately, poetry is more strongly connected with rhythm than with melody.

The Classical Musical Forms

WHEN I ONCE happened to mention to a group of well-educated friends who were music lovers but unacquainted with Arab music the term *classical Arab music*, they raised their eyebrows and asked me, "What does classical music have to do with Arab music? How is it possible that such a thing exists?" I view such a response as another indication of the rift between East and West.

"Classical music" is a concept strongly related to form and genre. A musical form is a composition that is based on a certain model that dictates to the composer the way the piece should be composed. The *rondo*, *concerto*, *variations*, and *sonata* are all classical European musical forms. Similarly, in Arab music we can find many classical musical forms, some of which are of ancient origins, such as the *bashraf* and *samāʿī*, which were adopted from Turkish music, the *muḥassabah*, and of course the *taqsīm*, which is the most important classical form in Arab music. Among Arab vocal forms, we can find the *mawwāl* and *layālī*, both of which are improvised vocal forms, and the *qaṣīda*, *ṭaqṭūqah*, *muwashshaḥ*, and *dawr*, which are composed vocal forms.

Undoubtedly, becoming familiar with musical forms is necessary for obtaining a comprehensive knowledge of a musical system. Sometimes the forms themselves are one of the factors that affect the development of the musical system.

***

SO WHY DID I not include the above subjects in the book, even though they are important? Mainly because of time limits. If I were to expand the book and include these important subjects (and others) in it, it would have taken much more time to publish it, and I thought it more pressing to present a comprehensive discussion of Arab scales and modes and of their system (i.e., the subjects related to pitch), because of the lack of comprehensive sources about them. In any case, I believe that in its present form, the book will be helpful to readers even without discussing in detail other subjects, which anyhow can be studied from other sources.

I suggest that readers study this book as a single unit – from its introduction to its end. Particularly, those who are unfamiliar with maqāmāt and their scales, should study the first two parts of the book and understand them, even if this requires receiving some help and guidance from teachers, tutors, or any other source. The core of my work is offered in Part III, which presents an analysis of the most common maqāmāt: this part forms a sort of a lexicon of the most common Arab scales and modes. Students are encouraged to continue studying and furthering their knowledge of the world of Arab maqāmāt, and to add any information they may obtain about each maqām in the section designated for it.

The book comes with an attached CD, which contains musical examples in the form of taqāsīm and exemplifies most of the maqāmāt that appear in Part III, so readers can experience by ear the real character of each of these maqāmāt. Recurrent hearing of a maqām's recording will undoubtedly help listeners to absorb its essence. Such a practice may lead to the stage in which maqāmāt can be easily recognized by ear. Readers who play an instrument are advised to try out the notations that appear in this book, especially the notations of the various scales. It must be remembered: in Arab music, listening comes before theory.

The theory of Arab music presented in this book is seemingly complex. Much of it is still unknown because it has not been thoroughly researched. Although this situation has changed in recent years, there are still many contradictions and disputes regarding many of the issues discussed here. In many books about Arab music, there are awkward mistakes. Furthermore, the Arab musical system allows for varied opinions that should not necessarily be considered as contradictions. In Arab music, especially in its performance practice, various conceptions and perceptions can be considered valid because they are culture-specific – in many cases, the particular culture of the musician. **For all of the above reasons, I will be thankful for any comments, additions, and corrections, which can be forwarded to me by mail, fax, email, or phone.**

BACKGROUND AND HISTORICAL REVIEW

THE ARAB WORLD stretches along the eastern and southern shores of the Mediterranean, and includes Syria, Lebanon, Iraq, and Jordan in the east and Egypt and the North-African countries in the south. On a broader scale, the Arab world forms part of the greater Islamic world, which includes Turkey, Iran, Uzbekistan, Tajikistan, Turkmenistan, Kyrgyzstan, Kazakhstan, Azerbaijan, Dagestan, Afghanistan, Singiang and Kashmir (Shiloah 1995: 100).

From the rise of Islam in the sixth century until the fall of Granada – the last Arab stronghold in Spain – in the year 1492, this large area has been subjected to many transformations. The big Arab conquests of the seventh century have led to the foundation of the Umayyad Caliphate, which started in the Fertile Crescent area and later expanded westward to Spain. The Abbasid caliphate, which was founded in Baghdad in 750, pushed the Ummayads out of the area. In the sixteenth century, the Ottomans started their large conquests of the Arab world, and they have ruled the area up to World War I. All these tremendous political forces have caused great changes in the Arab world. Obviously, the direct contact with the occupied people and with other conquerors has influenced, changed, and reshaped Islamic music.

Nevertheless, not all Islamic cultures were influenced and reshaped in an identical way. Though there are many similarities between the various musical systems developed in different Islamic countries, and most of these have developed out of the Great Tradition of Arab music, various regions have developed different styles and unique musical methods, which are easily identifiable.

In the music of the Arab world, we can distinguish two distinct styles: one is the style of the Arab east, which is called al-Mashriq and includes Lebanon, Syria, Iraq, Jordan, and Egypt; the other is that of the Arab west, which is called al-Maghrib and includes Algeria, Morocco, and Tunisia. The Arab east was influenced by Persian culture, and later by the Ottomans. The Arab countries of North Africa (al-Maghrib) were not as influenced by these cultures, and were influenced more by Andalusian music, which arrived there from Spain; these countries preserve this music to this day. The style of the countries of the Arab east is not completely homogenous; Iraq for example, has a distinctive music, which is different from the music of the rest of the Arab east. This book will focus on the music and the musical system of the Arab east.[1]

Arab music is modal. In the classical traditions of the Arab world, the musical scale is heptatonic (i.e. composed of seven notes), and the octave is divided into 24 quartertones, as opposed to the European scale where the octave is divided into 12 semitones. This division into 24 quartertones is the basis for all Arab scales, the great majority of which contain *microtonal intervals*. Microtonal intervals are intervals that are not necessarily made of semitones or of their multiplications. In Arab music, we can find microtonal intervals, such as the three-quartertone interval and the five-quartertone interval. These musical characteristics are the cause for the existence of so many scales in Arab music, and are most likely the source for the phenomenon of modulation, which is so common in this music.[2]

Arab music is monophonic and is largely improvisational. It is monophonic since there is hardly any harmony in this music, and it is improvisational since the performer is given a considerable amount of freedom to embellish the composed piece, as long as he or she does it within the framework of the musical tradition, and preserves the melodic

1 Since the Iraqi music that is known as *al-maqām al-'irāqī* is essentially different from the music of the rest of the Arab East, we will not discuss it in this book.

2 On modulation and the differences between its use in Arab music and in European music, see Chapter 3 and Chapter 10.

basis of the piece. These characteristics, of monophony and improvisation, may stem from the abundance of melody types, scales, and microtonal intervals, which makes it difficult to harmonize. They may also be related to the fact that for centuries, this music was mostly vocal, was not notated, and was orally transmitted; performers did not have a rigid framework for performance, and each performer performed according to his or her unique style. Therefore, this music was usually performed by a single performer, or by a choir singing in one voice, and was accompanied by a relatively small instrumental ensemble in which each type of instrument had only one representative. There is no doubt that the primary factor in the formation of the Arab style and musical ideals is the spontaneous and natural singing of the Arab people, which existed a long time before the formation of any musical system.

Arab music is very emotional and each *maqām* can be associated with a certain mood or emotion. Some scholars claim, for example, that the maqām Rāst is masculine and that the maqām Bayāt is feminine; maqām Sīkāh is related to the emotion of love, and Ṣabā is related to sadness (Karolyi 1998: 68). The profusion that is caused by the large number of scales and rhythms, on the one hand, and the complex emotional associations with music on the other, are in my opinion some of the main causes for the way Arab music has been preserved and for the lack of frequent changes in its styles.

The origins of Arab music are found in pre-Islamic times. In those times, known as the Djāhiliyya period, vocal and instrumental music flourished among the Bedouin tribes of the Arab peninsula, in the Arab kingdom of Ghassān, and in the kingdom of Lakhm, whose capital was al-Ḥīra (Shiloah 1995: 5–7). This music was performed mainly by slave-girl musicians called *qayna* (plural: *qaynāt* or *qiyān*). We do not know much about the music of this period, and there is little information concerning the musical system of these times, since there is scarcely any documentation of it left. The lack of documentation of the music itself is also true for the music of later times, which developed in the cultural centers of Baghdad and Andalusia after the rise of Islam and the conquests that followed it. Nevertheless, there are many sources written by scholars, philosophers, musicians, and musicologists who lived in the last centuries of the first millennium AD and the first centuries of the second one. These sources describe the rich musical life in the Arab peninsula, and especially those traditions that flourished after the rise of Islam. These sources, which are sometimes phenomenal in terms of depth and scope, describe in detail the musical systems and the *maqāmāt* of those times, but they do not supply enough detail to enable us to envision how this music actually sounded like.

The Koran, the Muslim sacred scripture, does not state clearly whether the enjoyment of music is allowed. As a result, various religious schools have developed different views on the subject. Some viewed listening to music with contempt, as a forbidden practice that diverts man from spiritual practices, while others saw it as a way to attain spiritual experiences and to get closer to God. This dispute is unsettled to this day, especially since today, music is available in so many contexts, both religious and secular ones.

After the Arab conquests in the Middle East and the rise of the Umayyad Caliphate in Syria (661 AD) and the Abbasid Caliphate (750–1258 AD), which established Baghdad as a political and cultural center, came the times of the flourishing of Arab culture, and Arab music in particular. From the foundation of Islam to the fall of Granada in Andalusia in 1492, a date that marks the regression into a time of cultural stagnation, these great caliphates produced the greatest musicians in Arab history – musicians who profoundly influenced the formation of Arab music. These musicians founded and formed what is called the Great Arab Musical Tradition, which forms to this day the basis of Arab music and its system.[3]

One of the most significant artists of the Abbasid period was Ziryāb (c. 789—857), a non-Arab who was a prominent musician in Baghdad, but later had to flee the city because of his colleagues' jealousy. After fleeing, he first arrived in North Africa and then moved to Granada in Andalusia, where the Umayyads ruled after moving their sovereignty from the east to the west. In Granada, Ziryāb established the Andalusian school of Arab music; he made a tremendous influence on the musical system and instruments, and left a unique musical culture, which later, after the fall of Granada, moved to North Africa.

Three prominent musicians from the Arab east, whose contribution to the formation of the Great Musical Tradition is immense, should be mentioned. These are Ibrāhīm al-Mawṣilī (d. 804), his son Isḥāq al-Mawṣilī (d. 850), and his

3 The Great Musical Tradition also formed the cultural basis for other musical cultures, such as the Ottoman one.

son-in-law Zalzal (d. 791). All these musicians were active in the court of the famous Abbasid Caliph Hārūn al-Rashīd (786–809) (Shiloah 1995: 26–30).

The music of the Arab east was subjected to many diverse influences by various musical cultures, and especially by the Persians, the Byzantines, and the Ottomans. As early as the pre-Islamic period (al-Djāhiliyya), Persia was a great cultural power and had a considerable influence over the Arab peninsula, from which later the Arabs started out for their conquest, and over the greater area. The influence of Persia on Arab musical culture and on the formation of the Great Musical Tradition can be a subject for a separate study. Signs of Persian influence can be detected in Arab music even today. For example, it is probable that the origins of the unique musical genre *al-maqām al-'irāqī* are Persian, since such a genre, the like of which cannot be found in other Arab countries, is similar to some Persian genres of music. Furthermore, most of the names of the Arab musical scales are of Persian origin. Nevertheless, the Arabs preserved the distinct characteristics of their own music, and today it stands as a separate tradition which is worthy of the name "the Arab Tradition."

The Ottoman-Turkish Muslim Empire ruled a large area of the Middle East and Europe for over 400 years until its fall in World War I. The Ottomans, who were also influenced by the Persian culture and the Arab musical tradition, attained in their music a new level of artistic quality; they developed the maqām modal system, and created new musical forms and genres. The Ottomans developed many instrumental genres, while the Arab world preferred vocal genres. As Shiloah writes:

> In the capital and other major centres of the Ottoman empire, an art music flourished that was essentially rooted in the basic concepts of the Great Musical Tradition. However, in the course of time, it developed characteristics of its own that had their source in the Turkish temperament, the specific nature of their folk musical traditions and centuries of acculturation with subjected countries. In time, the distinctive style exerted influence on the entire region dominated by the Ottomans, while the separate folk traditions survived and continued to flourish, occasionally interacting with art music. (Shiloah 1995: 90)

Turkish tribes roamed central Asia many years before the foundation of the Ottoman Empire; with time, they absorbed many Persian, and later, Arab influences. The influence of the Ottomans on the regions of their conquests was tremendous; the Ottomans brought with them an enhanced musical culture – one that had absorbed many influences.

After the fall of Granada, the Arabs entered a time of stagnation in all cultural and political areas, which continued to the nineteenth century. At the end of the eighteenth century, great changes in the balance of power had occurred; many areas that were under Islamic rule were conquered by European colonial armies. Very quickly, nationalistic movements emerged in Arab countries, which wanted to break free from the bonds of stagnation and return to the splendor of the past in all cultural areas, including music. Arab Music, which was still rooted in the Great Tradition, and was already influenced by Ottoman and Persian culture, now acquired new influences from the encounter with European culture. The new terms *qadīm* (old) and *djadīd* (new) were formed in order to distinguish between traditional styles and modern styles of music. Nevertheless, these new influences did not cause the neglect of old traditions; there was an effort to preserve these traditions, and for the most part, Arab music did not lose its unique characteristics which were rooted in the Great Tradition. On the other hand, a new style of "light" music developed which was based on simpler rhythms and was freer from the strict rules of old classical music.

At the end of the 1920s, new currents that wished to imitate the big European orchestras started to form, first in Egypt and later in other countries. These imitations caused stylistic changes that were foreign to traditional Arab music. Arab music adopted foreign instruments, such as the accordion and the guitar, and a new popular-classical style was formed, which was often a mixture of Eastern and Western styles.[4] After World War II and towards the end of the twentieth century, these developments led to the formation of styles that combine Eastern and Western influences – styles that later acquired names such as Ethnic Music and World Music.

I think that the tradition of Arab music should be preserved in its most essential form. This will help us preserve a beautiful and interesting music – a music that can be enjoyed even without submitting it to extreme modifications. On

4 See Chapter 10.

the other hand, learning the foundations of this musical culture can contribute to musical innovations, which tend to be based on the combination of styles, and therefore may lead to the formation of a new style.

PART I

THE FUNDAMENTALS OF THE EUROPEAN SYSTEM OF SCALES

A CULTURE is studied, first and foremost, according to its foundations and within the framework of the national and ethnic environment in which it developed. A culture should never be evaluated by comparing it to another culture.

Nevertheless, Part I will be devoted to the examination of some of the basic principles of European classical music. This will be done not in order to form an evaluation or a comparison, but in order to develop a kind of a "journey" from the relatively known area of European music to the unfamiliar regions of Arab music. I have used this method because I see it as a better didactic method in light of the experience I have acquired while lecturing and teaching Arab music.

In Part I, we will learn general terms and concepts that are common to both cultures, the Arab and the European. We will explore the significance of *scales* and *intervals*, the European *system of scales*, the *hierarchy of notes* in a scale, and such terms as *mode, diatonic system, note alteration, reposition,* and *transposition*.

CHAPTER 1

SOUND AND MUSIC

MUSIC IS THE ART of combining notes into melodies. The raw material of music is sound, and therefore its essential influence is on the sense of hearing. In her foreword to this book, Dalia Cohen writes, "Generally speaking, we can say that music is manifested in experiences that are derived from the organization of sounds."

Usually, music utilizes sounds with definite frequencies and intensity; these sounds are produced by vibrating objects that create air vibrations. These vibrations move in the air, they cause the air molecules to come closer and this causes a rise in the barometric pressure (i.e. air pressure). The rate of this rise establishes the resulting wavelength, and therefore its frequency, and this sets the pitch. The shorter the wavelength, the higher the frequency and pitch; the longer the wavelength, the lower the frequency and pitch. The amplitude of the sound wave sets its intensity.

Nevertheless, not every sound is a musical sound and defining a musical sound is an aesthetical issue that is dependent on the musical culture. Sometimes, even what we call "noise" can be used for music, and indeed, in modern European music noise is sometimes used for music. In cultures whose music is based on melodies and especially in those musical systems that utilize modal systems and musical scales, such as Arab music and European music, most of the melodic raw material consists of *musical sounds*, which are usually called *tones* or *notes*. In this book, our discussion will concentrate mostly on these musical sounds.

It must be noted that nature did not provide man with music; there is no music in nature. Nature only furnished man with sounds, and man organized these into music. In light of this view, we must examine the differences among various ways in which cultures formed their music. Every culture organizes its sounds according to its own aesthetical ideals, although there is no doubt that cultures are influenced by one another in the formation of their music and its system.[1]

A sound can be considered a *musical sound* if it emanates from a flexible and vibrating source and it has a regular frequency at any given time. Regular sound waves create a musical sound with a distinct pitch.

Musical Sounds, Tones, and Notes

BEFORE CONTINUING, let us clarify the meaning of several terms that are sometimes used in a confusing and unclear way.

The Latin word *tone* is used in various meanings and contexts, two of which are relevant to the present discussion. The term *tone* can be used to represent a single *musical sound* (as in "the *tone* is high" or "the *tone* is low"). The term *tone* also means the *interval* between two musical sounds that equals a sixth of the octave (therefore, there are six *tones*, or twelve *semitones* [half-tones] in an octave; these terms will be explained below). Some dictionaries do not make the

1 The phenomena of *tonic* and *octave* do exist in nature and were used in the formation of the tonal-modal system that was adopted by many musical cultures. This will be discussed below.

distinction between these two uses, and therefore in order to prevent any misunderstandings, I would like to establish the definitions of these terms, and the related term *note*, at least as they are used within the context of this book:

Tone (a musical sound): a name given to musical sounds that have a distinct and definite pitch. The string of the guitar, for example, produces a *tone* when it is plucked.

Tone (a musical interval): An interval that is a sixth of the octave. We can say for example, that there are six *tones*, or twelve *semitones*, in an octave.

Note: a musical sound as it appears graphically, as on the European staff for example. Therefore, we can speak of the *note* D, which is placed under the lowest line of the staff, and the *note* G, which is placed on the second line of the staff. Only when we define the placement of a scale on the staff, that is, its *tessitura*,[2] can we refer to its notes by name. In English, the term *note* is often used for the musical sound itself; in this sense, the meaning is identical to the meaning of a *tone* (*musical sound*) as it appears above.

In spite of attempts to define these three terms clearly and definitely, they are sometime confused, and this may be the case for the reader of this book. The reader is advised to pay close attention to the context in which these terms appear in order to get a clear understanding of the text.

Pitch and Loudness

IN THE FOLLOWING chapters, I will use the string of a stringed instrument as an example of a source of musical sounds, though of course many other kinds of instruments can produce musical sounds. In my experience, examples relating to strings are the easiest to understand and comprehend.

Any specific definite *frequency* (the number of cycles in a given time) of a source of sound produces a note in a certain pitch that does not change. This note is perceived by our ear as being at the same pitch even if it is produced by any other source with the same frequency. Let us take a guitar string for example. The pitch of a vibrating string is determined by the number of cycles in a given time that were caused by an initial action, such as plucking or hitting. If we suppose that it vibrates at a rate of 400 cycles a second for example (this is its *frequency*), then it would produce a note of a certain pitch corresponding to this frequency.

It does not matter how much force we use, how fiercely or gently we pluck the string, it always vibrates at the same frequency and produces the same pitch, from the moment of plucking to the time the sound dies away. If we pluck a string fiercely, it produces a stronger, louder, sound, and its loudness decreases until the sound is too faint for the human ear to perceive; however, the pitch of the sound does not change and stays the same from the moment of plucking to when the sound disappears. Plucking strongly does not affect the length of the sound wave but only its *amplitude*. When the amplitude decreases, the sound becomes fainter and fainter.

The human ear cannot perceive sounds in any possible frequency. Scientists have found that the range of audio waves that can be perceived by humans lies between 16 and 16,000–20,000 cycles per second. Vibrations in frequencies that are lower or higher than these frequencies cannot be perceived by the human ear. Dogs on the other hand, can perceive sounds of much higher frequencies than we humans can; dog whistles produce sounds in very high frequencies, which can drive dogs crazy but which we cannot perceive.

In European music, an international standardization system has been developed in order to set the absolute tuning of various instruments and establish their diapason (range). According to today's standards, the note A of the middle octave (a') is tuned to the frequency of about 444 Hz (cycles per second), and has become a sort of a "tuning reference note." There are minor differences between various musical systems concerning the frequency of the reference note. Some cultures do not have any reference note; others do not give any importance to its absolute pitch. Today, since pitch is standardized, any musician in any culture can use this standard for tuning. Arab ʿūd players for example, can tune their ʿūds so they are in tune with other instruments, even European instruments; in fact, today most Arab musicians tune their instruments according to the piano.

In this book, the terms *high* and *low* will be used to describe notes according to their pitch and their placement on the scale of notes; for example, we may say that D is *higher* than C but is *lower* than E. The terms *loud* and *soft* will be used only in the context of the loudness of the sound.

2 For an explanation of the term *tessitura* see the foreword by Dalia Cohen.

CHAPTER 2

THE MUSICAL SCALE

A *MUSICAL SCALE* is a sequence of notes in the range of an octave that are arranged according to pitch and have certain definite intervals between them.

In order to illustrate the material of the following chapters, we will use the guitar and its frets as an example. Let us take one string and assume it is tuned to the note C, and the frequency of this note is equal to 500 cycles per second. If we place a finger exactly in its middle, that is, we divide it in half, and then we pluck the remaining half, we produce a note that sounds similar to C but is much higher and sharper. The frequency of half of a string is double that of its full length; in our example, it is 1000 cycles per second. Therefore, if we double the frequency of a certain note, we receive the same note but it sounds higher. If we reduce the frequency to a half, we receive the same note but much lower. The higher note of this pair is called the *octave* of the lower note. An octave note of an open string, therefore, is situated in its middle.

Why is the higher note of this pair called the *octave* of the lower one? In Greek, the word *octa* means eight. The heptatonic scale, which is the type of scale most common in Arab and European musical cultures, consists of seven notes. The first note of the scale is called the *tonic* of the scale. When the same note of the tonic, but with a higher pitch, is placed at the end of the scale it becomes the eighth note of the scale, therefore it is called the *octave*. However, the *interval* between any note and its octave note is also called an *octave*, and therefore we can say that a scale exists in the range of an octave and consists of eight notes. It is important to pay attention to the differences between these two usages of the term *octave* and to understand their use in the text according to the context.

In Arab music, the tonic is called *qarār*, or *qarār al-maqām*, the tonic's octave is called *jawāb* or *jawāb al-maqām*, and the octave as the interval between the tonic and its octave (that is, the interval between the *qarār* and the *jawāb*) is called *dīwān*.

Intervals

AN *INTERVAL* is the distance between any two notes on the musical scale. In European music, intervals are named according to the number of notes that they span. The interval between two consecutive notes is called a *second*; the distance between C and D, for example, is a *second*. The interval between a note and the third note from it is called a *third*; the distance between C and E, for example, is a *third*. Two very important intervals that are discussed in this book are the *fourth* and the *fifth*. Scales are often constructed by combining these two intervals, the *fourth* and the *fifth*, and in this book, we will use these intervals extensively. The word for interval in Arabic is *buʿd*, and its plural is *abʿād*.

Intervals between two notes can have various sizes when we measure them in semitones; therefore, there are several sizes of seconds, several sizes of thirds, etc. The name *minor second* for example, stands for an interval of a semitone; the name *major second* stands for an interval of one tone. Usually, when I use the term *interval* in this book, I use it with the meaning of a *second* – that is, the interval between two consecutive notes – unless it is stated otherwise.

Following is a list of the names and the sizes of intervals that are used in European music.

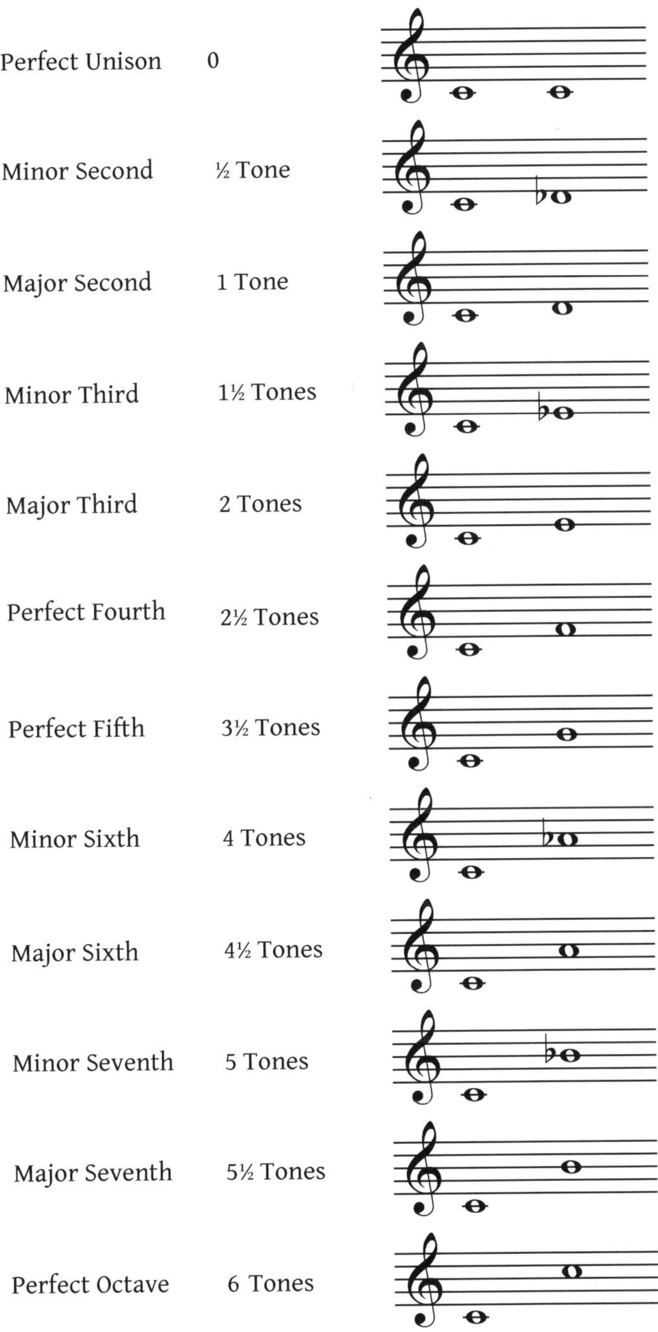

Figure 2.1 List of intervals

Any interval can be *augmented* or *diminished.* The interval between E♭ to F♯, for example, which is equal to 1½ tones, is called an *augmented second*. The distance between F and B, which is equal to three tones, is called an *augmented fourth.*

In Arab music, the octave is divided into 24 quartertones. Therefore, there are Arab scales that use intervals that are different from the ones used in European music. In Arab music, we can find intervals such as a second of three quartertones or 1¼ tones. We can also find a fourth that consists of only two tones. These intervals will be discussed in Part II.

There are seven intervals or seconds that comprise a heptatonic scale; these are the intervals between the seven notes together with the concluding octave note. However, we cannot just combine any seven intervals, in whatever sequence, in order to create a musical scale. Every culture has developed its music based on certain defined combinations of notes; this kind of development produces different systems in each culture. A certain musical scale may sound pleasant to the ears of one culture, but might be rejected by another, because it is not enjoyable to its listeners. Therefore, we should examine the way each culture selects the interval combinations it prefers, and how it constructs its musical scales.

A scale is constructed by combining intervals in the framework of an octave. Therefore, a musical scale can be illustrated or identified both by its constituting notes (C–D–E, etc.) and by the sequence of its intervals. The C major scale, for example, is comprised of the notes C–D–E–F–G–A–B–C (Do–Re–Mi–Fa–Sol–La–Si–Do) and its intervals, measured in tones, are 1–1–½–1–1–1–½ ("1" stands for a whole tone, while "½" stands for a semitone).

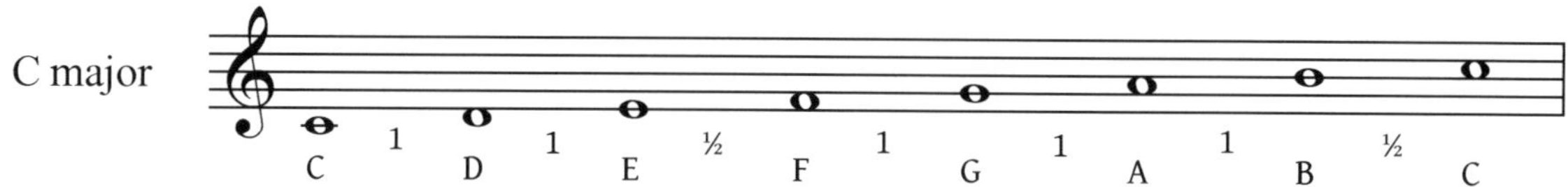

Fig. 2.2 The C major scale and its intervals

We will see later that studying a scale by its intervals (its seconds) is sometimes more important than studying the names of its notes. Major scales are always built from the same intervals as in figure 2.2, no matter on which tonic we position the scale. I have learned from experience that it is much easier to study a scale by memorizing its intervals, which stay the same, than by studying the names of its notes, which change when the fundamental note of the scale (its tonic) changes. If we remember that a major scale is comprised of the intervals 1–1–½–1–1–1–½ (tones), it is easy to play it on any tonic, without having to remember what notes should be played. Studying a scale by its intervals is especially relevant when we want to study Arab scales; without applying this method, it would be almost impossible to do it. There are three reasons for this:

1. In Arab music, there are many types of scales. In European music, on the other hand, there are only two types of scales – the *major* and the *minor*.

2. In Arab music there are many types of intervals (seconds); this is caused by the use of intervals which include quartertones (microtones).

3. Each maqām in Arab music always has a conventional tonic for its scale. For example, the conventional tonic of maqām Nahawand is the middle C and the conventional tonic of maqām Ḥidjāz is middle D.[1]

Some musicologists prefer using the term *mode*, instead of *scale*. It is true that according to European definitions, any scale is a mode, and therefore the musical systems of both European and Arab music are referred to as *modal systems*. Nevertheless, it is important to differentiate between a maqām and the group of notes from which it is composed.[2] In order to emphasize this differentiation it is preferable to term the group of notes that forms a maqām – a *scale*. This terminology is common in Arab countries.

1 On the subject of *conventional tonics* and the conventional position of the maqām, see Chapter 9.

2 This differentiation will be discussed extensively in Part II.

Scales and the Scalar System (The Octave of Twelve Semitones)

Scales

AS WE SAID, intervals in the musical cultures that are discussed here are the primary basis for the creation of melodies. These melodies can only manifest themselves in the framework of the *musical scale*, which is produced by the combination of these intervals. The scale is the basis for the presentation of the essence and content of the musical culture in which it developed.

As Dalia Cohen puts it:

> Pitch is the most distinguished representative of musical style. The collection of pitches that take part in musical structures and the way they are organized may supply the most factual representation of stylistic ideals and tendencies. Indeed, various musical theories focus mainly on the many elements that are derived from pitch: intervals, scales, chords, and the like. (1986: 71)

Scales are the most significant expression of the way pitches and intervals are organized by a musical culture; they are the most distinctive representations of the pitch parameter. Scales are produced by extracting and sorting the many *musical sounds*, or *notes*, that form the musical system of a culture. In other words, scales are produced by selecting a group of notes from a larger *system of notes*.

Systems of Notes

A SINGLE NOTE has no value in creating a musical ideal unless it is perceived with reference to another note. Therefore, each culture selects its own system of notes as a "raw material" from which it produces intervals and scales.

In European music, the system of notes is based on the division of the octave into 12 equal semitones. In this way, a system of notes called the *chromatic scale* was produced; it has 13 notes to an octave (the 13th note is the octave of the first note). *Chromatic* means "colorful" – the notes that are left outside of the selected scale are used to decorate and "color" the scale itself.

From this system of notes, European music has selected a scale called the *diatonic scale*, which is based on the division of the octave into five whole tones and two semitones, as in the arrangement of 1–1–½–1–1–1–½ (tones) in the major scale. The diatonic scale is made of seven notes and its tonic can be established on each of the 12 notes of the chromatic scale.

In Arab music, the octave is divided into 24 equal quartertones, and therefore, it can use for the construction of its scales not only the semitone and its multiplications (such as one tone or 1½ tones), but also intervals of three quartertones or five quartertones. This is the main reason for the profusion of types of scales in Arab musical culture.

I would like to express my reservations for the expressions "12 equal semitones" and "24 equal quartertones." Semitones were not always of equal size in European music. Only in the eighteenth century, equal temperament became the standard tuning system of European music, and the octave was divided into 12 equal semitones.

In Arab music, the subject of the equal division of the octave is much more problematic. To this day, there is a big gap between theory and practice in this matter. Theoreticians have tried, and are still trying, to establish that quartertones are equal, and this attempt goes back to similar endeavors in the famous Cairo Congress of Arab Music, which was held in 1932. These attempts, however, have never succeeded in practice. Intonation in the practice of Arab music is a complex issue, and musicians carried on performing Arab music according to tradition.

Equal division of the octave is good for theoretical and didactic purposes, but we must remember that in practice things are different. These issues will be discussed more extensively below.

The Internal Structure of Diatonic Scales

IN EUROPEAN music, as was said, the octave is divided into 12 semitones, and therefore the octave contains six whole tones. A heptatonic scale is constructed from seven intervals, and therefore it cannot be built from these six tones. In a system of semitones, when the available intervals are semitones and whole tones, a scale constructed of seven intervals can be made by dividing one of the six whole tones into two semitones. The resulting scale, which is called a *diatonic scale*, is constructed from five whole tones and two semitones. The question, therefore, is how and where the two semitones should be placed amid the five whole tones. This question has three possible answers:[3]

1. By dividing the five whole tones into two groups of one and four, and placing the two semitones at the edges of these groups, as in figure 2.3.

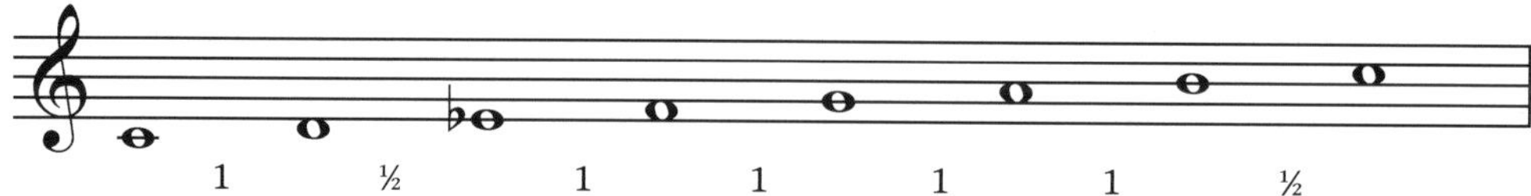

Figure 2.3 First option for the construction of a diatonic scale

2. By placing the two semitones next to each other, as in figure 2.4.

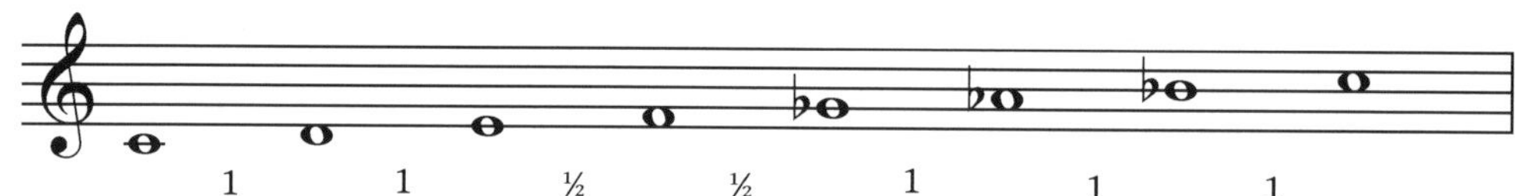

Figure 2.4 Second option for the construction of a diatonic scale

3. By dividing the five whole tones into two groups of two and three, and placing the two semitones at the edges of these groups, as in figure 2.5.

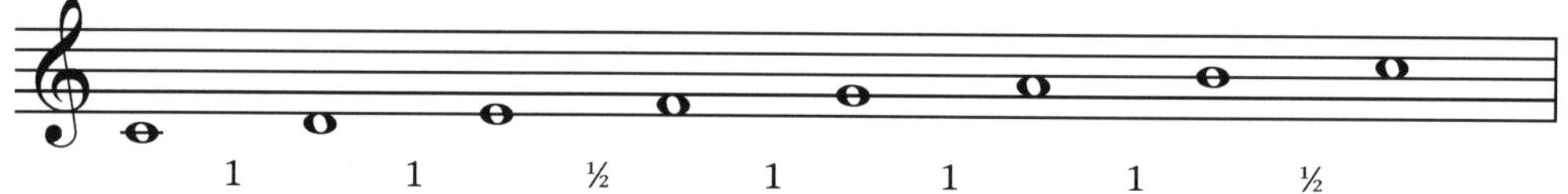

Figure 2.5 Third option for the construction of a diatonic scale

The scale in figure 2.5 is the C major scale, which will be discussed below.

These options for the construction of diatonic scales are not merely theoretical. In Indian music, for example, these three options are used for the construction of various scales. In European music, diatonic scales are constructed only according to the last option presented here (figure 2.5). When we speak about a *diatonic scale* or a *diatonic system* in this book, we mean the European diatonic structure as it appears in figure 2.5.

In Part II, we will see that in the Arab musical system, there are many examples of diatonic scales of the type adopted in European music, but most of the other scales in the Arab system are built according to other methods of dividing the octave into seven intervals. This is because the Arab system has many microtonal intervals, and because it frequently uses the augmented second (an interval of 1½ tones).

3 I thank Dalia Cohen for introducing these concepts to me.

The Diatonic System as a Scalar System

THE DIATONIC scale adopted in European music is cyclical; that is, it repeats itself in all the octaves in which the human voice or a musical instrument can produce a sound. In order to illustrate this, let us take a C major scale and place it on two consecutive octaves:

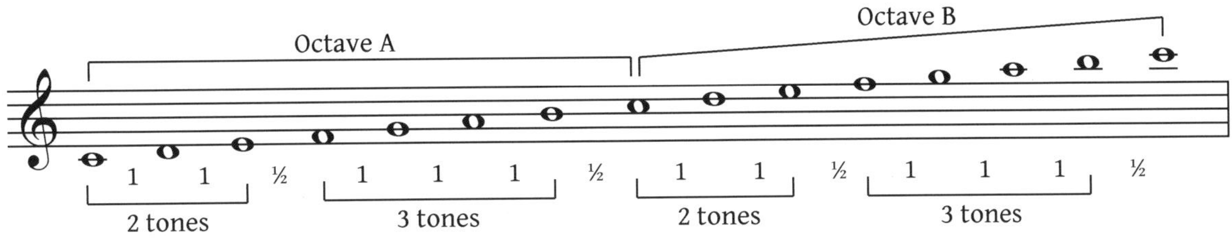

Figure 2.6 The C major scale on two consecutive octaves

If we look at the resulting sequence of notes, we can better understand the significance of the grouping, or distribution, of the diatonic scale's five whole tones into groups of two and three.

On the sequence of notes, which is made of semitones, there is a cyclical diatonic system from which we selected, as in the example above, a major scale. The major scale is constructed from the intervals 1–1–½–1–1–1–½ (tones). Nonetheless, any scale we select out of the above *diatonic system* would be considered a *diatonic scale*. If we move the tonic to the note D on the above system, we would get another diatonic scale – from the lower D to the higher D.

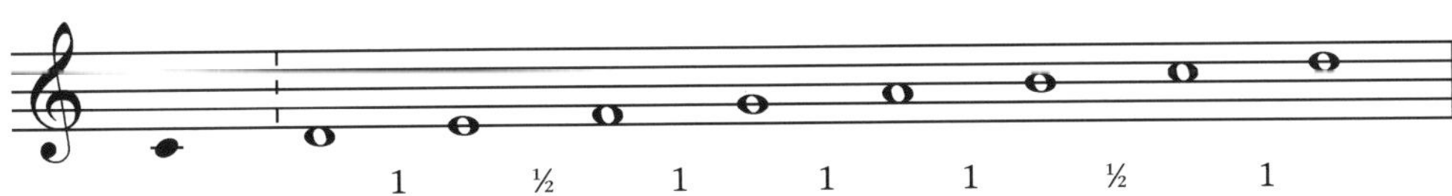

Figure 2.7 A diatonic scale starting on D

In order to illustrate it better, we can imagine that the notes of the scale are placed on a circle. We can then observe that the first whole tone (between D and E) and the last whole tone (between C and D) are joined into the same group of two whole tones of the diatonic scale.

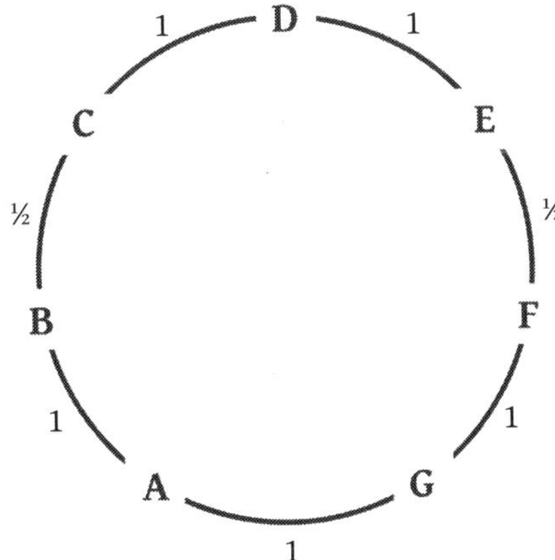

Figure 2.8 A diatonic system as a closed circle

It is difficult to make a clear distinction between the two terms – a *diatonic system* and a *scalar system*; both of these terms are used in theoretical literature. From the European diatonic system, we can create seven different diatonic scales by positioning the tonic on various notes of the diatonic system; therefore, it is called a *diatonic scalar system*. The scales that result from the positioning the tonic on various notes are called *modes*.

In European music, therefore, there is one scalar system, the diatonic scalar system, which is placed on the sequence of 12 semitones. In Arab music, there is more than one scalar system. Furthermore, some Arab scales do not create a scalar system, and therefore they cannot be considered cyclical. Since the diapason (the range of notes) in Arab music is limited to only two octaves, the subject of scalar systems in Arab music is a complex one, and I do not know about any extensive research on this subject.[4]

Modes and Tetrachords in the European Scalar System

IN THE PREVIOUS section, I mentioned the European medieval modes. In this section, I will discuss the subject of modes and their inner division into tetrachords; this subject is closely connected to the study of Arab music.

As was shown above, when we take the diatonic scale (the scale of five whole tones and two semitones) as it is represented by the C major scale, and we position the tonic on the other six notes of this scale, we get six more scales – all together seven scales. These scales are different from one another in their structure, i.e. the way the intervals are organized and ordered. Each one of these scales is a separate melodic framework, and the melodies that are formed from each of these scales are typical of that specific scale.

In her book *East and West in Music*, Dalia Cohen defines *mode* in this way:

> A general term for a modal framework and for a particular group in a modal framework. In dictionaries, this term is usually defined as a scale or a melody type; that is, as a certain type of melodies with typical motifs and similar characteristics. (1986: 337)

It is hard to understand this issue just by that definition alone, but before continuing I would like to stress again that surveying and summarizing this subject will help us later with the understanding of similar concepts in Arab music. The subject that we will learn in this chapter has many parallel aspects in Arab music theory.

Figure 2.9 presents the seven modes that are generated by positioning the primary note of a scale (its tonic) on the diatonic system. The figure shows all the scales that are produced in this way, from the note C to the note B. The notes of the actual mode appear in white while the notes that precede it on the staff, from the note C upwards, appear in black. The interval values are written below each mode; the names of the modes appear to the left of each respective staff. If we look at the intervals of each mode, and at their succession along the scale, we will notice that there are no two identical scales. Each scale (or mode) that is presented in this figure is divided into two sections of notes: the first four notes of the scale, and the last four notes of it. Between these two sections, there is one interval, which can be a whole tone or a semitone. These two sections, the lower and the upper sections of the scale, are called *tetrachords.* Their name is derived from the Greek words *tetra*, which means "four," and *chord*, which means "a string." In this book, we will use the terms *first tetrachord* for the lower tetrachord and *second tetrachord* for the upper one.

Some dictionaries define a *tetrachord* as a scale of four notes that takes up half of the octave. In my opinion, this definition is not accurate. First, a tetrachord is not a scale but only a fragment of a scale.[5] Secondly, a tetrachord is not always half of the octave, as can be seen in the modes in figure 2.9.

When we examine all the tetrachords of all the modes, we find that they can be classified into four species of tetrachords, based on their succession of intervals:

a. **Tetrachord 1–1–½ (tones)** – both tetrachords of the Ionian mode; the second tetrachord of the Lydian mode; the first tetrachord of the Mixolydian mode.

b. **Tetrachord 1–½–1 (tones)** – both tetrachords of the Dorian mode; the second tetrachord of the Mixolydian mode; the first tetrachord of the Aeolian mode.

c. **Tetrachord ½–1–1 (tones)** – both tetrachords of the Phrygian mode; the second tetrachord of the Aeolian mode; the first tetrachord of the Locrian mode.

d. **Tetrachord 1–1–1 (tones)** – the first tetrachord of the Lydian mode and the second tetrachord of the Locrian mode.

4 For more discussion about this issue, see Chapter 7.

5 In the past, such scales of one tetrachord were used, but in this book, we will not discuss this subject.

We can see that each of the seven modes is constructed by combining two of the four species of tetrachords or by joining two identical ones.

Figure 2.9 The Modes of European Music and Their Intervals

The species of tetrachords are:

a. The tetrachord **1–1–½** is named **major** or **Ionian.**

b. The tetrachord **1–½–1** is named **Dorian.**

c. The tetrachord **½–1–1** is named **Phrygian.**

d. The tetrachord **1–1–1** is named **Lydian.**

The tetrachords that appear above have the same names as the modes, but we should make a distinction between modes and tetrachords. Some modes have the same name as their first tetrachord, as in the case of the Ionian, Dorian, Phrygian, and Lydian modes. Other modes, however, carry a different name than their first tetrachord, and their names are actually different from any tetrachord name. The Mixolydian mode begins with an Ionian tetrachord, the Aeolian mode starts with a Dorian tetrachord, and the Locrian mode starts with a Phrygian tetrachord.

The division of the musical scale into tetrachords is a form of internal organization across the scale's sequence of notes. This organization is important to the understanding of many musical processes such as *reposition*, *transposition*, and *modulation*. As we will find out later, understanding the division of the scale and its organization into sections is even more important when studying the Arab musical system. We will use the subjects learned in this chapter when we discuss Arab music and the organization of its scales.

In Arab music theory, a section of the scale is termed *djins*, and its plural is *adjnās*. A *djins* is sometimes, but not always, constructed from four notes – a tetrachord; however, it can also be constructed from three or five notes.

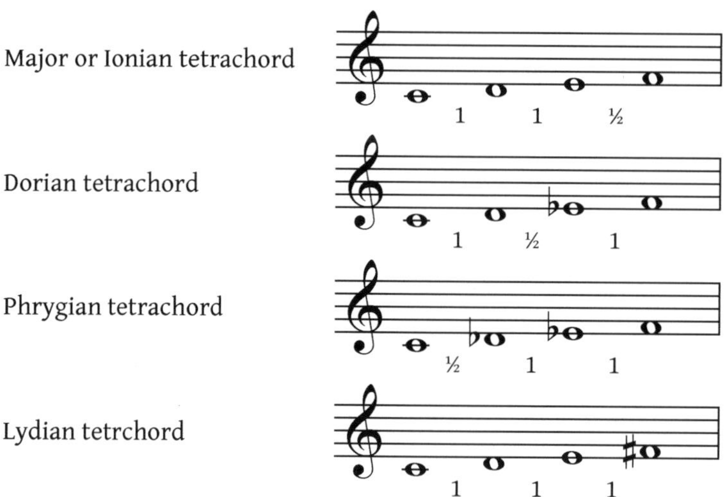

Figure 2.10 The tetrachords of European music and their intervals

The Hierarchy of Notes in a Scale

EVERY SCALE HAS an inner hierarchy of notes, which determines the levels of importance within the scale's structure. Following, are some of the more important notes of the scale:

1. **The Tonic:** This is the most important note of the scale; by defining the first note of a scale, we are actually defining many of its qualities. In a modal system, you cannot define a scale, nor set its framework, without determining the tonic. The tonic is the final note of the melody, and the melody should always conclude with this note. The tonic has a "gravitational force": the listener is expecting this note even from the very beginning of the performance; when the melody concludes with this note, the tension built up by this expectation is released. In Arabic, the tonic is called *qarār*, which means "a base" or "a conclusion," or *qarār al-maqām*, which means the "the base of the maqām" or "the conclusion of the maqām."

2. **The Dominant:** This is the second most important note in the scale. In the prevailing European diatonic system, this is always the fifth note of the scale. Its position within the scale is important for the division of the scale into two tetrachords since the second tetrachord is always positioned on the dominant. It is a stable and central note in the scale, and takes on an important role in establishing the main harmonic degree. The dominant is called in Arabic *ghammāz* or *ghammāz al-maqām*. *Ghamza* means in Arabic "winking with the eye." The *ghammāz* in Arab music has a special and complex role, as will be shown below. In Arab music, the *ghammāz* is not always the fifth note of the scale – sometimes it is the third or the fourth note.

3. **The Leading Note:** This is the note that comes below the tonic or the octave of the scale. It pulls and "leads" towards these notes and helps to strengthen them. In Arabic, the term for this note is *ẓahīr* or *ẓahīr al-maqām*; the word *ẓahīr* means "assisting," "supporting."

4. **The Octave Note:** This note is as important as the tonic. Like the tonic, the octave can conclude the scale, melodic phrases, or the whole piece. In Arabic, the octave is called *djawāb* or *djawāb al-maqām*, which means "an answer" or "a response." As we will see below, the *djawāb* in Arab music has much more significance than the octave of European music, because sometimes it establishes a tonal center that determines the *maqām*.

The meanings and the functions of these notes are not identical in the two musical systems, the Arab and the European. Some of the differences were pointed out above; in Part II, we will learn more about the role of these notes in Arab music.

As was said above, the division of the scale into two sections can also be found in Arab music in a similar way to the division into tetrachords in European music. A section of the scale is called in Arabic *djins*, and its plural is *adjnās*. Nevertheless, similar to the way the dominant in Arab music (the *ghammāz*) can be the third, fourth, or fifth note of the scale – depending on the *maqām* in question – the *djins* may also be a *trichord* (three notes) or a *penatchord* (five notes).

Summary

THE INTERVALS that are used in European musical scales can only be multiplications of semitones. European music is based on the system of 12 semitones in the octave, from which one type of a diatonic scale was selected. The diatonic scale is a scale that is constructed of five whole tones and two semitones. Out of the seven scales, or modes, that constitute this diatonic system, European music has selected only the Ionian and Aeolian modes and named them the *major* and *minor* scales; all other scales were almost completely neglected.

CHAPTER 3

NOTE ALTERATION, TRANSPOSITION, REPOSITION, AND MODULATION

NOTE ALTERATION is the raising or lowering, or in musical terms, the *sharpening* or *flattening*, of a note. A figure of the neck of the guitar with its frets will help illustrate what alteration is.

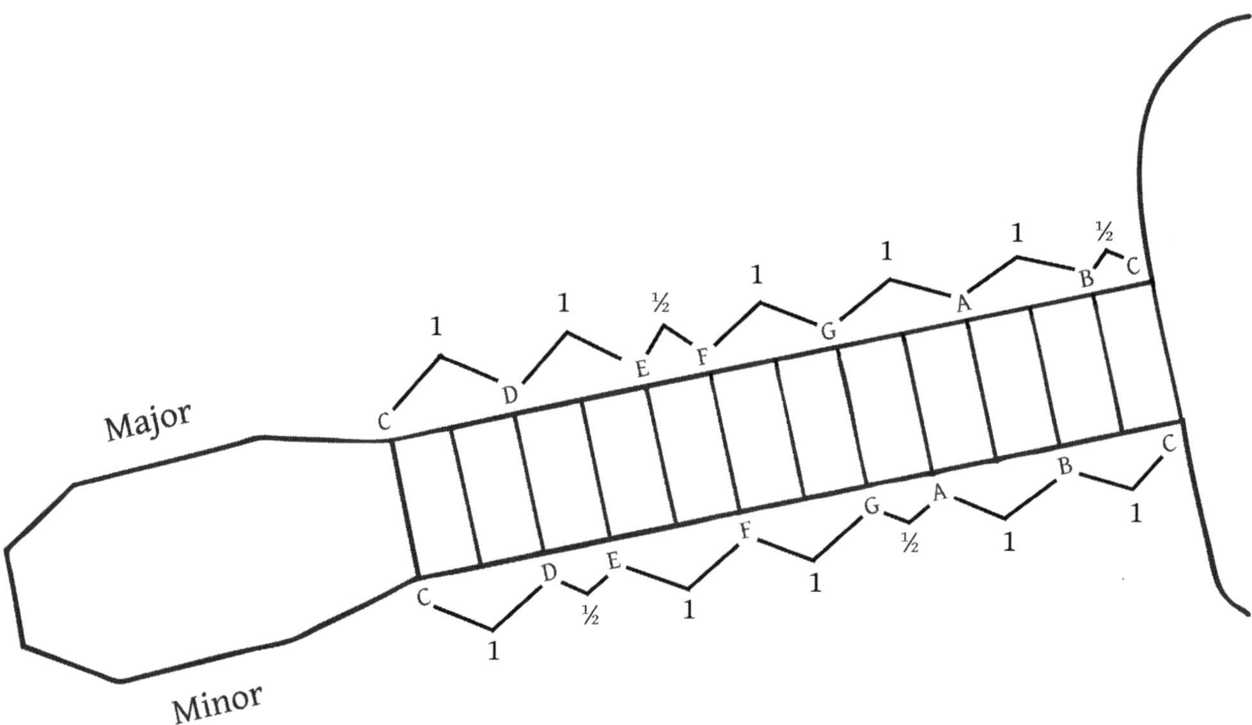

Figure 3.1 The notes and intervals of the C major and C minor scales placed on the frets of a guitar string

Figure 3.1 shows a range of one octave on a string stretched over a guitar. As we learned, the octave in European music is divided into twelve semitones; the frets of the guitar represent this division. They determine the places where the various notes are placed.

The intervals appearing on the top, above the guitar's neck, are the intervals of a major scale. Since the open string is a C string, and scales in European music are named after their tonic note, these intervals form the C major scale. On the bottom, I wrote the intervals of a minor scale, and therefore they form the C minor scale. Obviously, the notes of these two scales, C major and C minor, do not fall on the same frets. The note E in the C minor scale, for example, is a semitone lower than the note E of the C major scale. The same is true for the notes A and B.

The European musical system uses the seven letters C, D, E, F, G, A, and B (or the names Do, Re. Mi, Fa, Sol, La, and Si) as note names. These notes, the notes of the C major scale, are termed *natural notes*, because they are not altered. However, sometimes a note needs to be *sharpened* (raised) or *flattened* (lowered). How would we name those notes that were altered – shifted from their natural place – in order to form a new scale or to change their position in the scale? For that, we use special alteration signs; these signs are usually called *accidentals*.

Accidentals

WHEN ACCIDENTALS appear next to a note, they indicate that it should be shifted up or down to create a new note. This altered note will still have the name of the natural note, but it will carry the accidental as a suffix indicating in what way it was altered, for example: "C sharp" or "E flat." The accidentals of the European notation system are:

♯	*sharp*	–	indicates the raising of a note by one semitone
𝄪	*double sharp*	–	indicates the raising of a note by one tone
♭	*flat*	–	indicates the lowering of a note by one semitone
𝄫	*double flat*	–	indicates the lowering of a note by one tone
♮	*natural*	–	cancels any accidentals previously applied to the note

Let us go back to the guitar neck:

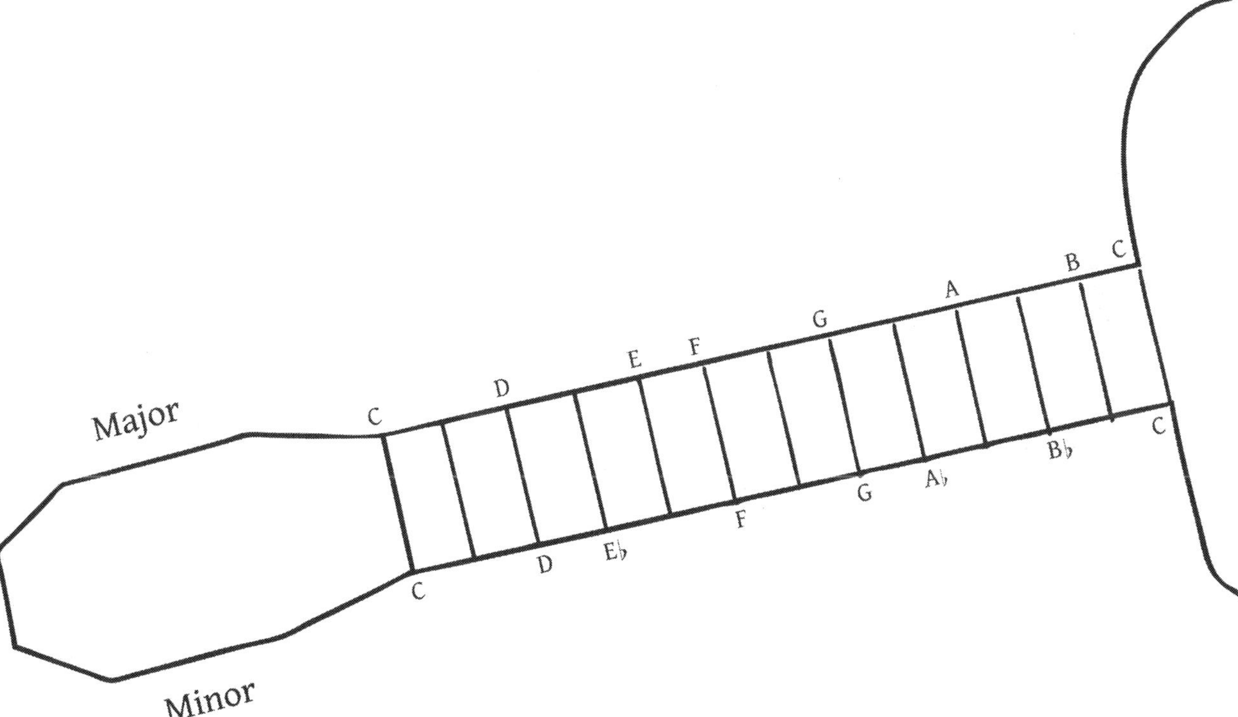

Figure 3.2 The C minor scale, with its accidentals, placed on the frets of a guitar string

What did we do in order to construct the C minor scale from the C major scale? We lowered the notes E, A, and B of the C major scale by one semitone each. To each of these notes we assign the accidental *flat* (♭), which indicates the lowering – the *flattening* – of the note by one semitone.

In order to conclude this discussion and to illustrate it, let us write down the C major and C minor scales on the staff:

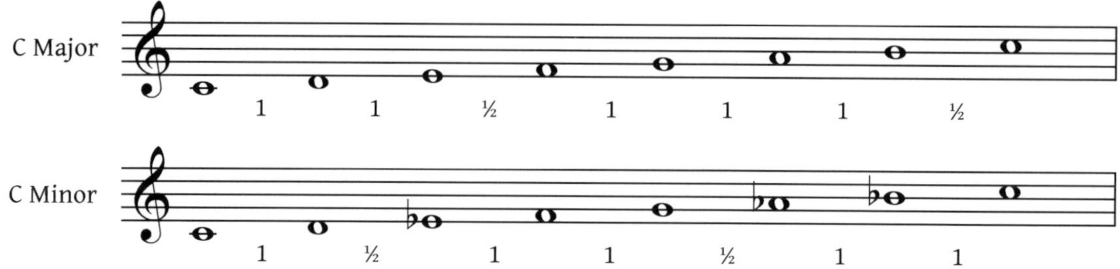

Figure 3.3 The C major and C minor scales as they are written on the staff

If we memorize the consecutive intervals of a scale, it would be easy to find which notes construct this scale, on any tonic.

Let us do an exercise: we will write down the notes of the D major scale.

First, we write down the notes from D to D on the staff.

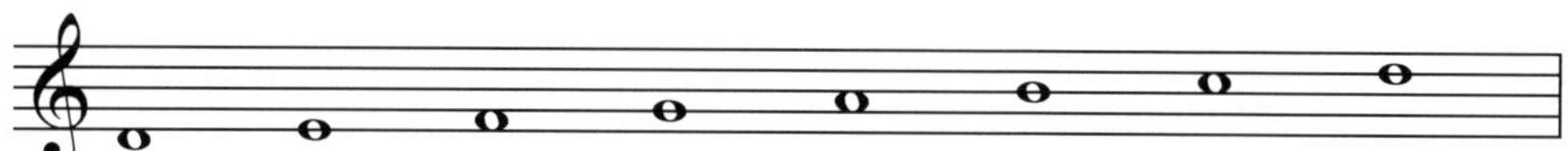

Figure 3.4 The notes from D to D

Next, we write down the consecutive intervals of the major scale: 1–1–½–1–1–1–½ (tones) – between the notes.

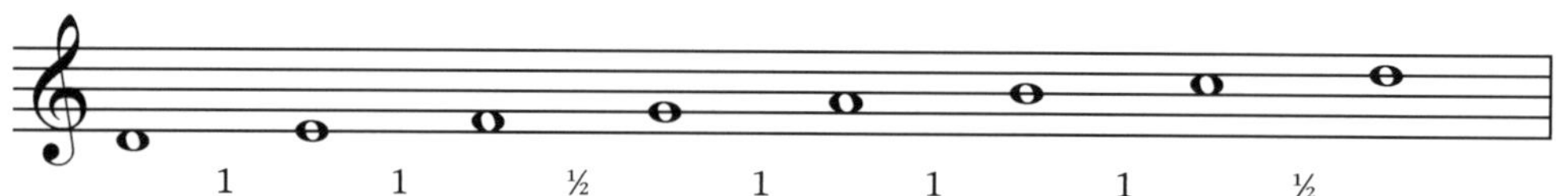

Figure 3.5 The notes from D to D and the intervals of the major scale

Now it will be easy to see which notes should be altered, or shifted, in order to build a major scale on the tonic D:

1	From D to E:	This is the right interval
1	From E to F:	This interval is a semitone; we need it to be a whole tone. Therefore, we will raise it by using the accidental *sharp* (♯)
½	From F♯ to G:	Now that the F is sharpened, this is the right interval
1	From G to A:	This is the right interval
1	From A to B:	This is the right interval
1	From B to C:	This interval is a semitone; we need it to be a whole tone. Therefore, we will raise it using the accidental *sharp* (♯)
½	From C♯ to D:	Now that the C is sharpened this is the right interval

We can see that the D major scale contains two notes with accidentals – F♯ and C♯.

Now, we can write the scale with the altered notes:

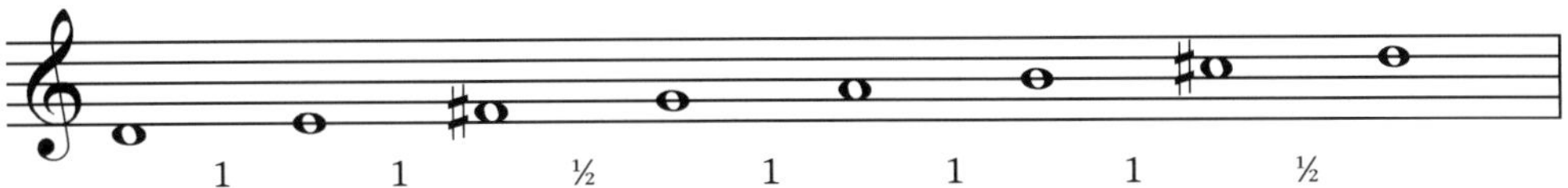

Figure 3.6 The D major scale with its accidentals

Getting used to thinking about the structure of scales in terms of their consecutive intervals is very important, and practicing it makes it easy to perform them and to write them down; this is especially true concerning Arab music.

Sometimes two different names represent the same note, or in other words, the same note is "spelled" differently. For example, when we look on the frets of the guitar we can see that G♯ and A♭ are placed on the same fret, and therefore they sound the same. The same is true for E and F♭. These kinds of "spellings" are called *enharmonic* spellings.

Before the eighteenth century, the 12 semitones of the octave were not equal. Only in the eighteenth century did the tuning system that is called *equal temperament* become the prevailing and standard tuning system. According to this system, the octave is divided into 12 equal semitones, and so each semitone equals a 12th of the octave.

In the 1932 Cairo Congress of Arab Music, it was decided that, in a similar way to the European octave, the octave of Arab music be divided into 24 equal quartertones. This equal division survived only in theory; in practice, musicians continued to perform Arab music in the traditional way, without equalizing the notes of Arab scales.[1]

Changing and Moving Scales

IN THE FIRST part of this chapter, we discussed the alteration, or the shifting, of notes within a given scale. In the following sections, we will discuss moving and changing complete scales – by moving the whole scale to a different tonic or by moving the tonic within the scale itself. These kinds of changes to scales are done by using the methods of transposition and reposition. *Transposition* is the method of changing the tonic of a given scale while keeping its intervals. *Reposition* is the method of changing the tonic within a given scale, thus forming a new scale with different intervals.

Transposition

AS WE LEARNED, the musical scale is constructed by using specific intervals within the framework of an octave. Since a scale is comprised of eight notes (the eighth note being the octave of the tonic note), the scale has seven consecutive intervals. The major scale, for example, comprises the following intervals: 1–1–½–1–1–1–½ (tones). The conventional position for a major scale – the tonic on which all its notes are natural – is the tonic C. However, we can construct a major scale on any other tonic, as long as the intervals we play are the intervals of a major scale.

Suppose we want to play a D major scale – that is a major scale with the tonic D (We constructed a D major scale in the beginning of this chapter when we learned how to alter notes by using accidentals). By sharpening the natural notes F and C by a semitone, we have constructed a major scale with two sharps:

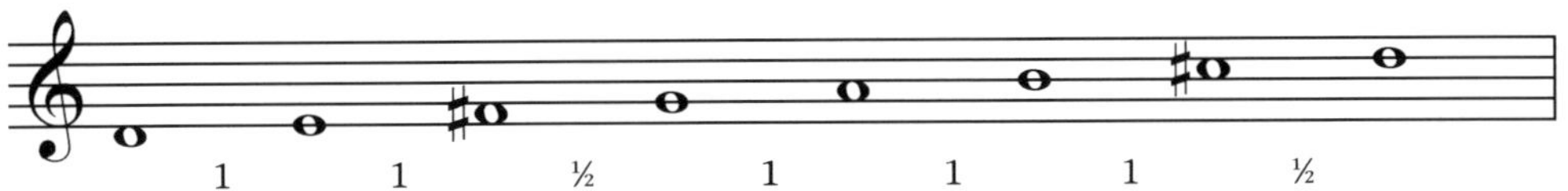

Figure 3.7 The D major scale

What we did was to *transpose* the major scale to a different note – in this case, to the tonic D. We can transpose any musical scale to any other tonic by changing its placement on the sequence of semitones while keeping its structure of intervals.

1 For a discussion about the complex subject of intonation in Arab music, see Chapter 6.

Transposition is therefore the shifting and reconstruction of a musical scale from one tonic to another on the sequence of notes that a particular musical system uses. Transposition is of great importance to the internal organization of music. In Arab music, transposition plays a significant role in determining the structure, functions, and characteristics of the maqām. Transposition is also one of the means for performing a *modulation.*

The use of transposition in Arab music is slightly different from its use in European music. In European music, transposition is used mostly in the meaning of transposing melodies, for example, transposing a song from C major to E major. In this book, we discuss transposition mostly in the meaning of moving a scale, and not a melody, from one place to another. As we will see, maqām scales in the Arab musical system are assigned to conventional tonics, and they are usually played on these. Therefore, transposing the scale of a maqām in Arab music means moving it from its conventional tonic, and this causes changes in its characteristics. These changes are sometimes so significant that the transposed scale establishes a new maqām – an independent and distinct maqām with its own name.

Reposition

THE CONCEPT OF *reposition* is discussed in Dalia Cohen's book *East and West in Music.*[2] *Reposition* is the method of creating a new scale by moving the tonic to another note within the scale without altering its notes. In Chapter 2, we discussed the diatonic scalar system and the modes. We learned that various modes are produced by *repositioning*, or moving, the tonic to another note within the diatonic European scale. Unlike transposition, repositioning a scale produces a scale that has different intervals than the original one.

Let us look at an example. Figure 3.8 shows the C major scale with some of its notes that are below the tonic and above the octave note. The notes from the tonic C to its octave note form a C major scale with the intervals 1–1–½–1–1–1–½ (tones). If we move the tonic to D and use the same notes, the notes from D to its octave note form a different scale with different consecutive intervals: 1–½–1–1–1–½–1 (tones).

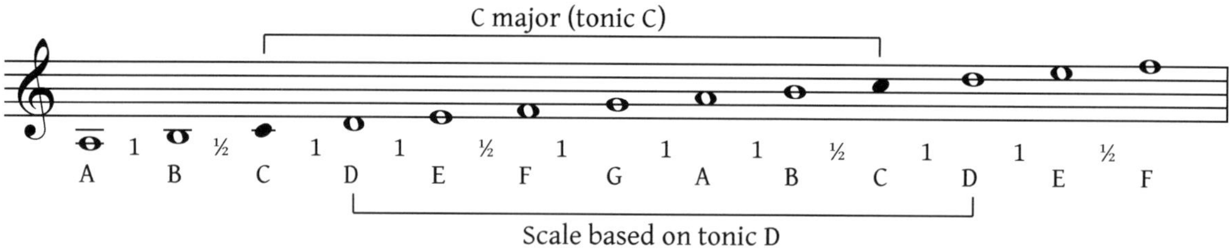

Figure 3.8 Reposition of the tonic from C to D within the C major scale

Therefore, in a scalar system that is based on the C major scale, we can produce seven different scales (including C major) by moving the tonic between the seven notes of the scale. Since the C major scale is a diatonic scale, which is built out of five whole tones and two semitones, all the scales that are produced by repositioning the tonic within it are diatonic. These scales are the seven modes, which we studied in Chapter 2.

Not all the scales that are produced from repositioning within the major scale are used in European music. Out of the seven medieval modes, five were neglected, and later European music was based, almost entirely, on the Ionian mode (the major scale) and the Aeolian mode (the minor scale).

Going back to figure 3.8, if we reposition the tonic to A, we produce a scale with the intervals 1–½–1–1–½–1–1 (tones). These intervals form the *natural minor scale.* The A minor and C major scales are *relative scales*, because they are composed of the same notes. We can say that A minor is a reposition of C major, or that C major is a reposition of A minor – it all depends on which scale we started with.

2 I chose the term *reposition*, because as far as I know, there is no widespread musicological term for this phenomenon or practice. It is sometimes termed *scalar transposition, diatonic transposition*, or *tonic shifting*. – Trans.

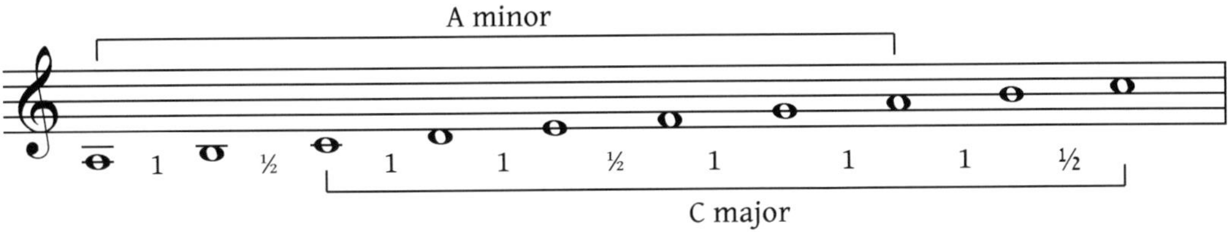

Figure 3.9 The C major and A minor scales

In this book, I name repositions according to the number of steps along the scale we take in order to reach the new tonic note. For example, a reposition to D on the C major scale is named *the first reposition on the C major scale*. A reposition to E is named *the second reposition* and so forth.

We can reposition tonics in both directions of course. For example, if we want to reposition to A minor on the C major scale, we can reposition five steps up or two steps down.

Reposition is a very important feature of Arab music and other Middle-Eastern musical cultures that use modulation extensively. Assimilating the knowledge of the various possible repositions of scales is important for both composers and performers.

In classical European music only two types of scales are used – the major and the minor. Therefore, reposition has significance only in the context of switching between these two scales. In Arab music, on the other hand, which has such an abundance of scales and different types of scales, various repositions even within one scale produce many other scales that form a part of the musical system.[3] Therefore, reposition in Arab music acquires a special role, and its importance to the formation of the Arab maqām system is immense.

Modulation

THE TERM *modulation* means moving from one scale to another in the course of a musical piece. For example, in European music, a piece may start in a major scale and then move to a minor scale. Alternately, a piece may start on one major scale (such as a C major scale) and then move to a different major scale (a G major scale for example) – in this case the piece *modulated* by transposing the scale.

There are various ways to perform a modulation, four of the main ones are:

1. **By keeping the tonic of the original scale while changing its intervals.** Let us take a C major scale for example:

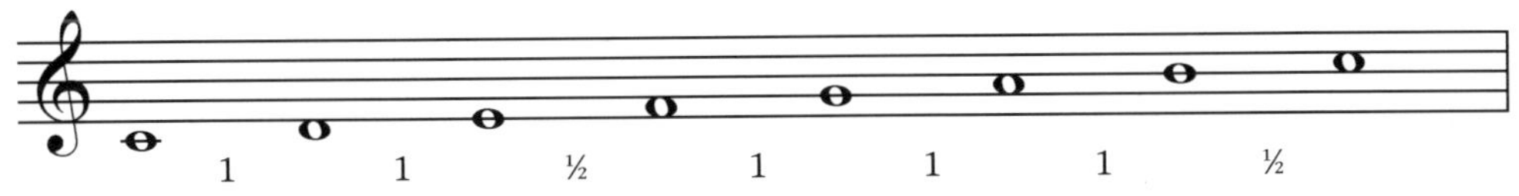

Figure 3.10 The C major scale

Now we want to move, to *modulate*, to a minor scale on the same tonic – to the C minor scale. The intervals that form the minor scale are 1–½–1–1–½–1–1 (tones). In order to get this sequence of intervals on the tonic C we have to alter certain notes of the C major scale by sharpening (raising) or flattening (lowering) them by a semitone.

We place the intervals of the minor scale between the notes of the C major scale.

3 See for example the analysis of the Rāst scale in Chapter 17.

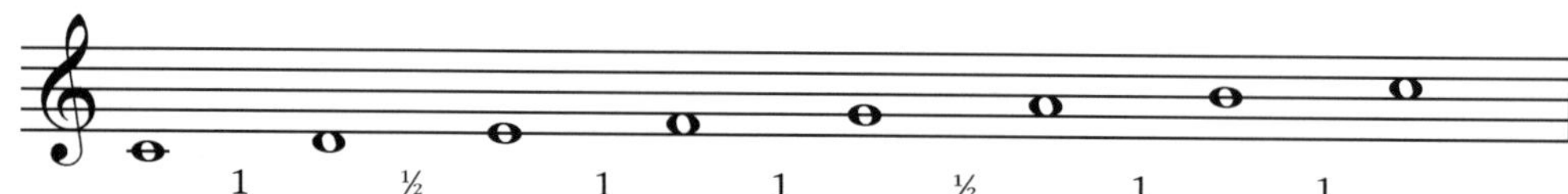

Figure 3.11 The intervals of the minor scale placed on the C major scale

Now we alter the notes by using accidentals to get a C minor scale.

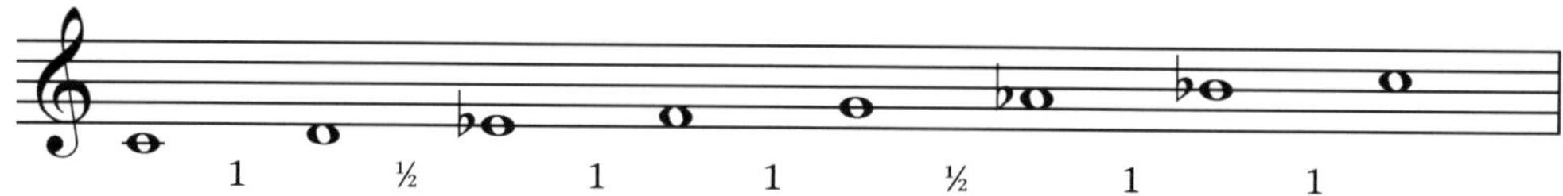

Figure 3.12 Modulating to the C minor scale

We can say that by flattening B, E, and A we modulated to the C minor scale. We changed the intervals while keeping the tonic.

2. **By changing the tonic of the original scale while keeping its notes.** This kind of modulation is done by the method of *reposition*, which we learned in the previous section. The best example in European music for this kind of modulation is the move from one scale to its relative scale, such as the move from C major to A minor, or vice versa, which was demonstrated in figure 3.9 above.

3. The third way is a combination of the two previous ones: **Changing both the tonic of the original scale and its notes, while keeping its intervals.** This kind of modulation is actually identical with the method of *transposition*. As we learned above, transposition is one of the methods for modulation.

Let us take the C major scale:

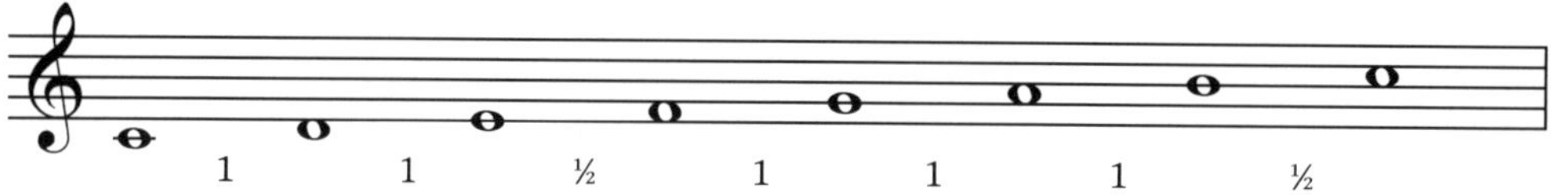

Figure 3.13 The C major scale

If we want to modulate to the G major scale, we have to change the tonic to G. We also have to change one of the notes – we have to sharpen the note F by a semitone – in order to get the sequence of intervals that forms the major scale.

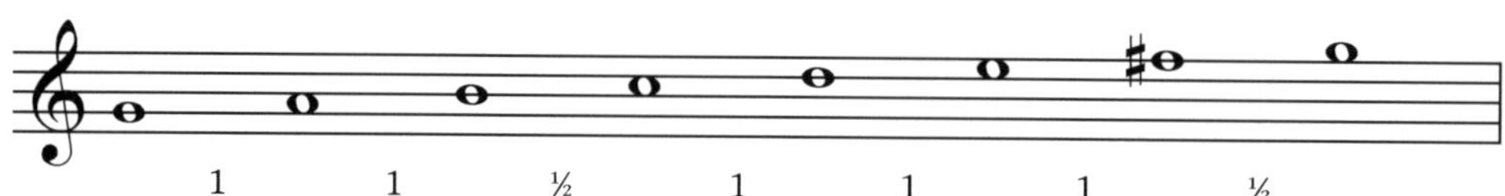

Figure 3.14 The G major scale

When we look at figure 3.15, we can see the relation between these scales and their intervals.

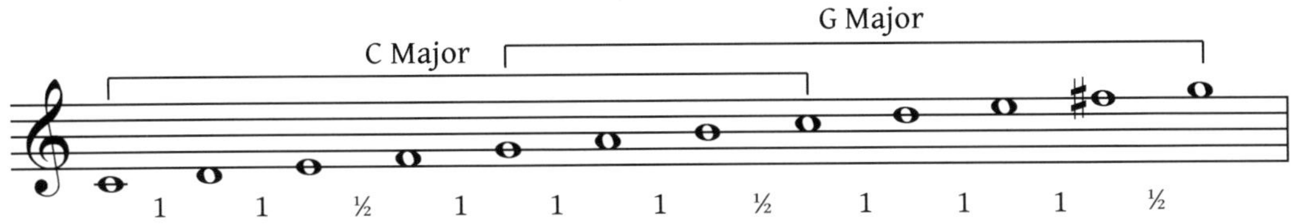

Figure 3.15 The C major and G major scales

4. **By changing the tonic of the original scale and its intervals.** This kind of modulation produces a scale that has very little in common with the original scale. Let us perform a modulation from C major to D minor for example:

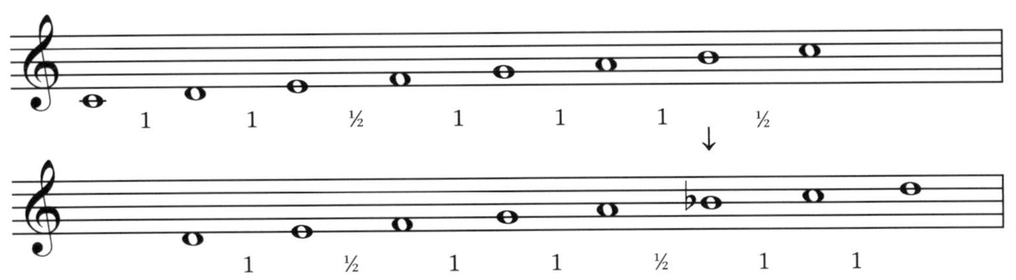

Figure 3.16 The C major and D minor scales

If we compare the two scales in figure 3.16, we see that in order to modulate from C major to D minor we have to move the tonic from C to D, and we have to flatten B by a semitone in order to get the sequence of intervals that forms a minor scale.

As we will see in Part III, Arab music has developed an abundance of scales and types of scales. This, and the fact that Arab music is monophonic and improvisational, caused the extensive development of the practice of modulation. This practice became a part of its musical system and one of its most important characteristics.

It must be noted that the subject of modulation in Arab music is a very intricate and complicated one. It cannot be explained and understood simply by using the explanations above and the four methods of modulation we discussed. In the complex system of the Arab maqāmāt, modulation does not simply mean moving from one scale to another. There are various rules of how to modulate, what to change, and how to perform it in order to produce music that is acceptable to the listeners of this culture. Modulation is one of the most complicated and complex subjects in Arab music, and this book, which presents basic understanding of the Arab musical system, cannot attempt to explain it fully.

Furthermore, no written theoretical explanation can teach all the meanings and implications of modulation in Arab music. The student who is interested in fully understanding this practice must listen to this music extensively and learn its performance from an experienced teacher. A student must assimilate this music in order to combine experience in listening and performance with the theoretical knowledge that he or she learned. In Part III, when we will learn the Arab maqāmāt and their scales one by one, we will learn some practices of modulation. These will be shown only as examples, and they will not cover the subject completely.

CHAPTER 4

FROM THE KNOWN WEST TO KNOWING THE EAST

The European and Arab musical systems share many common characteristics. Both of these systems are based on *modal musical scales*. The scales of these systems are *heptatonic* – they are constructed from seven notes and contain seven intervals in the framework of an octave. Both systems are *tonal systems* – in each scale, there is one note, the *tonic*, which is the most important one. Both the European and the Arab musical systems utilize more than one octave, and both employ the methods of note alteration, transposition, reposition, and modulation.

Nevertheless, there are many differences between these two systems. These differences stem from various factors and reasons, among them are:

- While in European music, the octave is divided into 12 semitones, in Arab music it is divided into 24 quartertones.
- Because of this division, European music utilizes only intervals that are multiplications of semitones. In Arab music, on the other hand, we can find intervals that are multiplications of quartertones, such as the three-quartertone interval and five-quartertone interval.
- Because it uses so many types of intervals, Arab music has an abundance of scales as well as many different types of scales; these scales are derived from a number of scalar systems. This characteristic of Arab music stands in contrast to the limited use of only two scales in European music, the major and the minor, which are derived from one scalar system, the diatonic system.
- European music has developed harmony into an intricate and complicated art. Harmony has become one of the key characteristics of this music. In Arab music, harmony is seldom used, and this music is performed in one part.
- Because European music is polyphonic (from the Greek *polyphōnos*, "many-voiced") and harmonic, improvisation does not form an extensive part of its performance practice; when many people perform different parts at the same time they cannot improvise too much. Arab music, on the other hand, is monophonic and essentially improvisational. These are its two main characteristics, and they affect its performance, its theory, and its philosophy.
- Other differences between these two musical cultures can be explained by the use of different musical instruments and the differences in their rhythmic systems and in the relation between rhythm and melody.

Sometimes it may seem that these two musical cultures are very different and the gap between them cannot be bridged. This book intends to introduce the Arab musical system to students who have little musical background as well as to people who are familiar with European music. As such, it tries to bridge the gap between these two musical cultures. This kind of integration is gradually becoming more common; we can hear it in the contemporary musical style that is referred to as Ethnic Music or World Music.

In the next part of the book, we will learn each of these factors thoroughly, focusing this time on the Arab musical system.

PART II

SCALES AND MAQĀMĀT IN ARAB MUSIC

IN THIS PART, we will analyze the Arab musical system. We will learn the features that it shares with European music, which we studied in Part I, while exploring the features that are unique to Arab music. In our discussion, we will expand on some of the special characteristics of Arab music, such as:

- The concept of maqām
- The system of 24 quartertones
- Its special notation and the names of its notes
- The profusion of maqāmāt,[1] scales, and scalar systems
- The meaning of djins – the equivalent to the European tetrachord in Arab music
- The monophonic texture and the improvisational nature of Arab music
- The use of modulation
- The cultural aspects – including extra-musical aspects
- The performance of the *taqsīm* – the most important musical genre in Arab music

I hope that by understanding the differences and similarities between the European and the Arab musical cultures, the reader will find it easier to understand and comprehend the Arab musical system.

1 *Maqāmāt* is the plural form of *maqām*.

CHAPTER 5

MAQĀM

The Term *Maqām* and its Meaning

THE MEANING of the word *maqām* in Arabic is "a place" or "a stand"; it can also mean "a level." The word *maqām* has obtained a number of meanings in various Asian musical systems. We must distinguish between the following meanings of the word *maqām*:

1. **The complete scalar and modal system of a certain culture:** The scalar system of some Central Asian countries, such as Uzbekistan, Tajikistan, Azerbaijan, and Khwarizm, for example, is composed of a basic system of six *maqāmāt* and is called *shashmaqom* (that is, "six *maqāmāt*"). This system is the basis of the Central Asian classical style (Shiloah 1995: 131–132). In the Arab-Turkish musical culture, the scalar system is called *maqām*. Persian classical music is organized into 12 scalar systems that are called *dastgāh*.

2. **A classical musical form:** In Iraq, there is a very complex musical form that is called *al-maqām al-'irāqī*, which will not be discussed extensively in this book. Nevertheless, the reader must note this meaning of the word, since this usage is particularly common in the Iraqi tradition.[1]

3. **The scale of a particular mode**: In my opinion, this common usage of the term *maqām* is incorrect. People that use the term *maqām* for a scale, actually refer to the group of notes in the framework of an octave and their tonic, which are used for a particular maqām. This usage does not include a discussion of how these notes are used to produce the special characteristics of the maqām. The scale of a maqām is only the raw material used for presenting its progression.

   For example, the scale of maqām 'Adjam, which is similar to the major scale, is written like this:

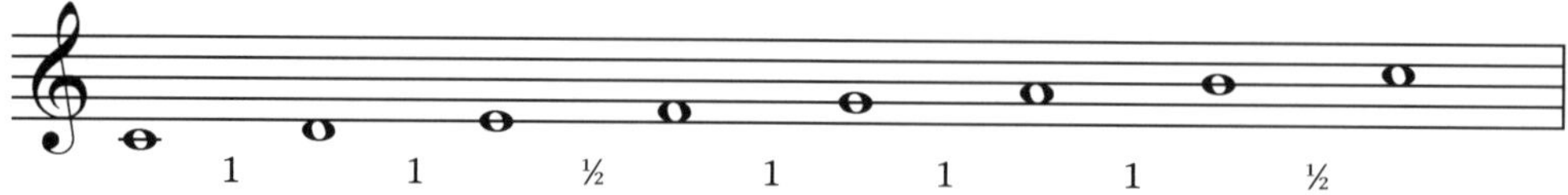

Figure 5.1 The scale of maqām 'Adjam

This is the group of notes used for maqām 'Adjam on its conventional tonic – C. However, when it comes to performing maqām 'Adjam, we cannot simply play its notes randomly. Each maqām has its own unique approach and rules on how to organize the notes of its scale for its performance. Each maqām has its own nature and

1 For a discussion of *al-maqām al-'irāqī* see Kojaman 2001 and 'Ubadyā 1999.

characteristics. The use of the word *maqām* to represent a group of notes is confusing, as it does not refer to the way these notes are organized in the performance of this maqām.

4. **The way of organizing the notes of a maqām's scale in order to present this particular maqām and its progression:** Each maqām has many musical characteristics and rules for organizing its notes, which we call the *melodic progression* of the maqām. These rules of organization determine the way a maqām is presented or performed, or as some say, "treated." They determine, for example, whether a performance of the maqām should start from its tonic and then go up to its octave, or the opposite – start from the octave and then go down. They establish which notes of the maqām are important and dominant, on which notes it is common to stop, and which notes should be turned into temporary tonal centers. These and many other rules are difficult to define, and musicologists find it hard to explain them in written form. These special features of Arab music are learned mostly by continuous and careful listening.

   The melodic progression that defines the organization of the musical material for the performance and presentation of the maqām is called in Arabic *sayr al-maqām*. In Arabic, *Sayr* means "a move," "a way," or "behavior."

In this book we will make a distinction between a scale of a maqām (that is, its group of notes), and the organization and use of its notes and musical material – what we call the *progression* of the maqām or *sayr al-maqām*. This distinction is common in theory books of Arab music. The group of notes that forms the maqām is called *sullam al-maqām*, which means the scale of the maqām, and it must be distinguished from the maqām itself. We will use the term *scale* to represent a group of notes, and the term *maqām* to represent their use and organization.

The first note of a scale, its *tonic*, is called in Arabic *qarār*. *Qarār* means, in this context, "an ending" (*qarār* is also a legal term that means verdict). The melodic progression of a *maqām* usually concludes on the tonic (*qarār*) in accordance with its rules of organization. This is the reason why many musicologists prefer using the term *finalis*, "final," instead of the term *tonic*. In this book, we will use the term *tonic* in our discussion about both scales and maqāmāt.

The differences between Arab scales and European scales

AS WE HAVE noted before, there are a basic similarities between Arab scales and European scales. In both of these systems, the tonic (*qarār*) and the octave (*djawāb al-maqām*) are important notes. Both scales are heptatonic – they are constructed of seven notes as a series of seconds. Like the European scale, the Arab scale contains a dominant note, called in Arabic *ghammāz*, and it can be divided into two tetrachords that are called *adjnās* (singular: *djins*). The above characteristics are common to both the Arab and the European scales; they distinguish them from other musical systems that use other types of scales, such as pentatonic scales (scales that are composed of five notes), and from systems that do not use scales at all.

Nevertheless, there are many differences between these two musical systems. In this part and the next one, we will discuss the Arab system. We will analyze it and explain it on its own – as opposed to comparing it to the European system. From time to time, however, we will discuss the differences and similarities between the two.

CHAPTER 6

SCALES AND MAQĀMĀT

AS WE HAVE said, in European music the octave is divided into 12 equal semitones. In Arab music, on the other hand, the octave is divided into 24 equal quartertones; as will be shown in this chapter, this division is not as simple as it seems.

According to Shiloah, the 24-note system is attributed to the Syrian-Lebanese theoretician Mīkhā'īl Mashāqah (1800–1889). However, this division was actually set by Mashāqah's teacher, the Syrian theoretician and mathematician Muḥammad Ibn Ḥusayn ʿAṭṭārzade (1764–1828) (Shiloah 1995: 116–117).

Arab theoreticians who wrote between the tenth and the fourteenth century dealt extensively with the structure and division of the octave. The most important of these theoreticians was Ṣafī al-Dīn al-Urmawī (d. 1294), who divided the octave into seventeen consecutive intervals by using intervals of two sizes.[1]

The Quartertone Octave

THE ARAB quartertone system enables the use of intervals other than semitones and therefore expands and enriches the number of notes and intervals that are available in Arab Music. The three-quartertone interval, for example, is a very important interval in Arab music, and many other intervals are formed by using quartertones.

As an example of a three-quartertone, let us look at the trichord D–E–F:

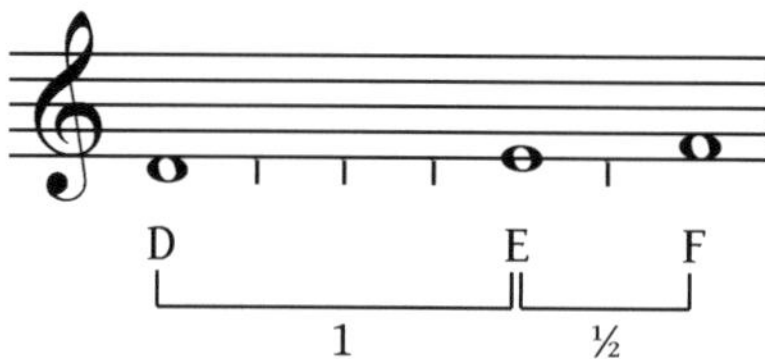

Figure 6.1 The trichord D–E–F

Between these notes, we can see two intervals: a whole tone and a semitone. The tone is divided into four quartertones and the semitone is divided into two quartertones; these subdivisions are marked by small lines. The whole trichord, therefore, contains six quartertones. If we flatten E by a quartertone we get two intervals of three quartertones each – one between D and the flattened E and one between the flattened E and F.

1 See the foreword to this book by Dalia Cohen as well as Shiloah 1995: 112–113.

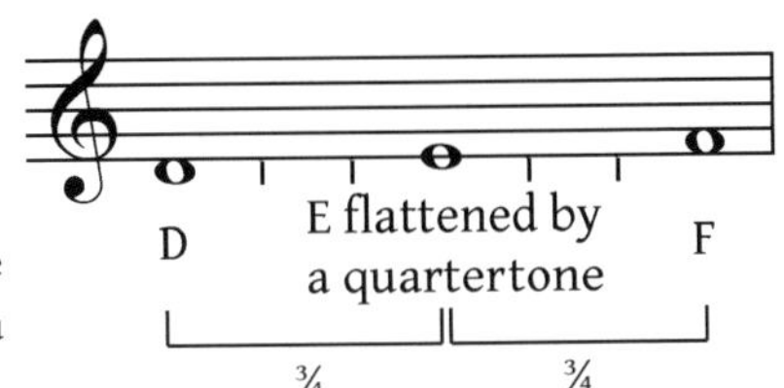

Figure 6.2 Forming a three-quartertone interval by flattening the note E by a quartertone

Those intervals that are not based on the 12-semitone system are termed by musicologists *microtonal intervals*. This term is a little misleading when used in the context of Arab music. In Arab music theory, there is no real use of the quartertone as an integral interval of a scale – only its multiplications are used. The smallest interval that is used in Arab scales is the semitone. The three-quartertone interval, which is the next smallest interval after the semitone, is of course larger than a semitone.

Therefore, we cannot apply the term *microtonal* to the intervals of the Arab scale; yet we must note that in musicological literature, the use of this term is quite common. In this book we will use the terms *quartertonal intervals* and *quartertonal notes* to indicate intervals (such as the three-quartertone) and notes (such as B𝄳) that are produced by using quartertones.[2]

The Two-Octave Scale

IN EUROPEAN MUSIC, we find that the scale is based on one octave. Of course, that does not mean that European music uses only eight notes. What it does mean however, is that the scale is defined and determined within the framework of one octave; that is, for defining scales, we do not need to use notes from several consecutive octaves.

On the other hand, the Arab scale consists of two octaves, called the *first octave* and the *second octave*. In Arab music, it is not always sufficient to use only eight notes in order to define the scale of a maqām. It is not possible to perform or present a maqām without using notes from other octaves; sometimes the use of notes from below the tonic, between the tonic and the octave, and above the octave is needed. There are maqāmāt in which the intervals of the second octave are different from those of the first octave. Furthermore, the case is the same even regarding cyclical scales, in which the intervals of both octaves are identical. Therefore, we cannot define a maqām by using only one octave.

For example, the first octave of the scale of maqām Ḥidjāz-Kār is constructed from the following intervals: ½–1½–½–1–½–1½–½ (tones). It is written like this:

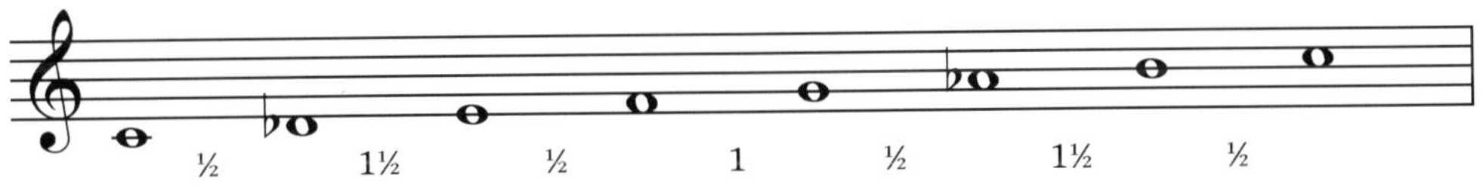

Figure 6.3 The first octave of maqām Ḥidjāz-Kār

However, the intervals of the first tetrachord of the second octave are 1–½–1 (tones); and the whole scale should be written as below:

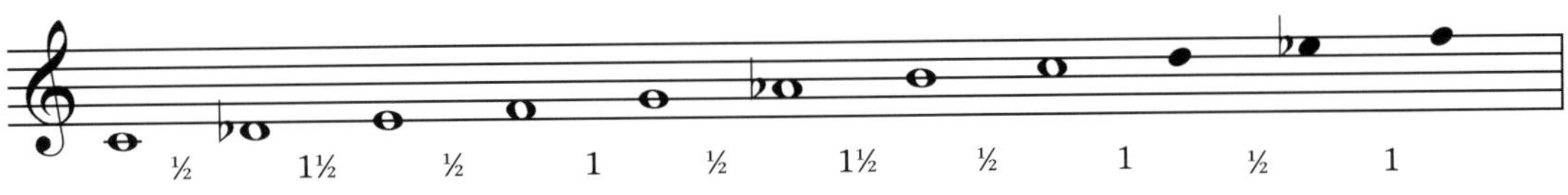

Figure 6.4 The scale of maqām Ḥidjāz-Kār with its second octave

This third tetrachord is essential for the definition and characterization of maqām Ḥidjāz-Kār; it should be considered as part of its scale.

---

2 These terms are not so common in musicological writings, but are offered here as an alternative to the use of the term *microtonal* when discussing Arab music theory.

Some scholars present the scale of a maqām in a one-octave framework, and include the changes of the second octave only as written explanations. Others write all the notes of the maqām as a continuous scale, as with the scale of Ḥidjāz-Kār in figure 6.4.

Diapason in Arab Music

THE TERM *diapason* means the *range of notes* in which the music is performed. Arab music, whether vocal or instrumental, is usually performed in the diapason, that is, in the range, of only two octaves. Theoretically, any instrument capable of producing notes in this range can be used for the performance of any scale and maqām, and therefore any musical piece. For matters of convenience of tuning, the absolute pitch of this diapason has been determined and standardized.

There are several reasons why the diapason of Arab music is limited to no more than two octaves. In the past, Arab music was primarily a vocal music, and musical instruments were used mostly for accompanying the singer. In olden times, these were either very simple melodic instruments, sometimes having only one or two strings, or percussion instruments. The diapason of scales and their absolute pitch were probably set and determined by the constraints and requirements of the human voice.

The two octaves that form the diapason of Arab music – as it is written today – stretch from the low G to the middle G and up to the high G:

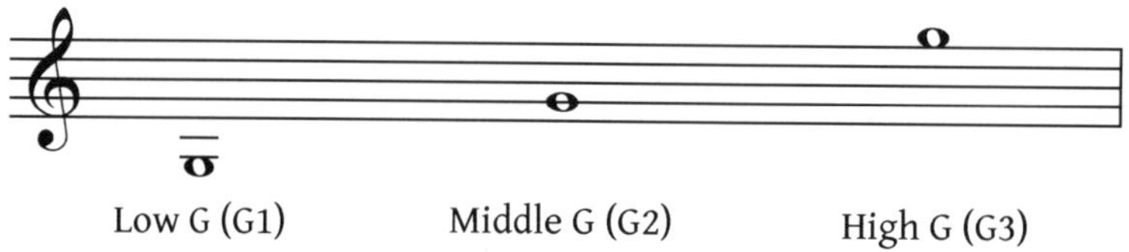

Figure 6.5 The diapason of Arab music

When we look at the two-octave scale of Arab music as it is written in modern staff notation, we can see that every note repeats twice, except for G, which repeats three times. In this book, especially in Part III where we analyze maqāmāt and their scales, we will use numbers to indicate the note place in the two-octave scale. G1 is the lowest G, G2 is the middle G, and G3 is the highest G.

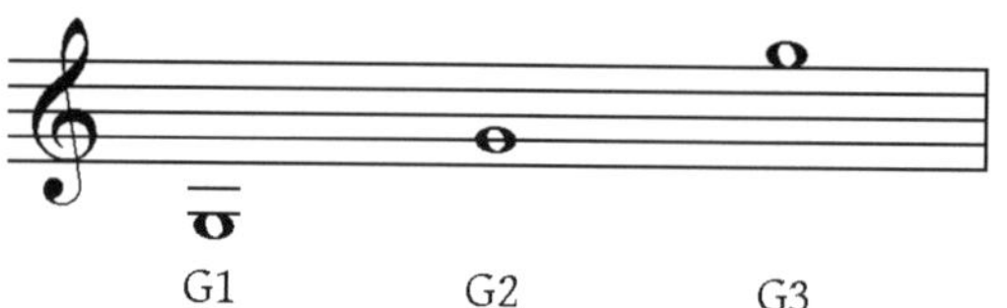

Figure 6.6 Indicating the place of notes in the Arab two-octave scale

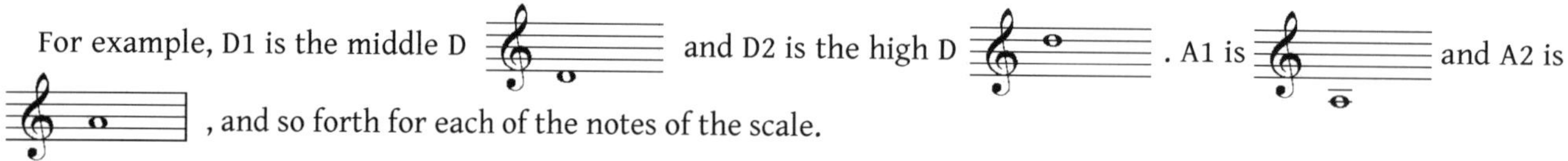

For example, D1 is the middle D and D2 is the high D . A1 is and A2 is , and so forth for each of the notes of the scale.

Notation and Names of Notes in Arab Music

Notation

AS IN EUROPEAN music, Arab scales are composed of seven notes. For the last hundred years or so, Arab musicians and composers have been using European staff notation for writing down their music. Today, most of the composed music is written using standard European staff notation, in the G clef, and naming notes is done according to the European solmization system, that is, they are named Do, Re, Mi, and so forth.

As in European notation, Arab modern notation also uses accidentals in order to flatten or sharpen notes. However, the European accidental signs, the sharp (♯) and the flat (♭), can only sharpen and flatten notes by semitones and their multiplications. In order to represent notes that cannot be represented by standard European notation, namely quartertonal notes, Arab notation uses special accidentals. These can indicate the flattening or sharpening of a note by a quartertone or by a multiplication of quartertones, for example, by three quartertones. In figure 6.7 we can see the list of all accidentals used in Arab music; some of these are common to both Arab and European music, and some are unique to Arab music.

Accidental Sign	Name	Meaning
𝄳	Half flat	Flattens a note by a quartertone
♭	Flat	Flattens a note by a semitone
𝄳♭	Flat and a half	Flattens a note by three quartertones
𝄫	Double flat	Flattens a note by a whole tone
𝄲	Half sharp	Sharpens a note by a quartertone
♯	Sharp	Sharpens a note by a semitone
𝄰	Sharp and a half	Sharpens a note by three quartertones
𝄪	Double sharp	Sharpens a note by a whole tone
♮	Natural	Cancels any accidentals that were applied to the note

Figure 6.7 Accidentals used in the modern Arab notational system

The use of these accidentals and their placement, either at the beginning of the staff, in order to indicate the scale, or before a note, in order to indicate its alteration, is done in the same way as in European music. It must be noted that some Middle-Eastern notational systems use accidentals for microtonal intervals that are different from the ones presented in figure 6.7.

The Names of the Notes

FOR THE LAST century or so, Arab music has been notated using the European staff notation system, and today notes in Arab music are named using European note names. However, traditionally, each note in the two-octave system of Arab music has a distinct name. For example, the middle C, which is placed on the staff like this 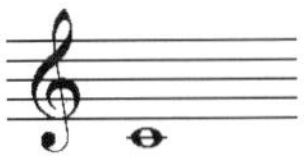 , is called Rāst in Arabic, but the octave note of Rāst, 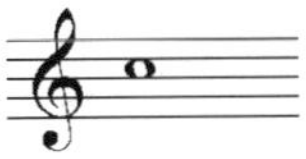 , is not called Rāst but rather Kardān. Some Arab musicians and scholars, even those who learned classical European music at conservatories, still use these traditional note names, but this practice is slowly disappearing. Note names are used sometimes to indicate strings of instruments. For example, the strings of the violin, when tuned the Arab way, are referred to by their Arab note names:

The lowest string, called Yakāh, is tuned to the low G  ;

The second string, called Dūkāh, is tuned to the middle D  ;

The third string, called Nawā, is tuned to the middle G  ;

The fourth string, called Muḥayyar, is tuned to the high D  .

The names of the notes are especially relevant when examining the position of various scales. The conventional position of the scale of maqām Sīkāh, for example, is the tonic Sīkāh, that is, E𝄳 (E half-flat), in the middle octave: the name of the scale is obviously derived from the name of its tonic. The scale of Rāst is played on the middle C – the note Rāst; this is its conventional tonic.[3] Some maqāmāt, however, are named after the name of the octave note of their tonic. For example, a maqām that starts on the octave note of the note Rāst, i.e. the note Kardān (C2), and then descends to the note Rāst is called maqām Kardān, after the name of the octave note. As we will learn later, many maqāmāt are named after important notes of their scales, either their tonic, their octave note, or another important note.

Below is a table with the traditional names of the notes used in Arab music and their corresponding notes in the modern notational system; the table is based on the one given by Shiloah (1995: 116) with several additions and revisions. It must be noted that there are a several variations for some of the names, and throughout history, some of these names have changed.[4] Even today not all scholars and musicians completely agree about all of these names. In this book, we will use the modern names of notes as they appear in contemporary theoretical works and as they are usually pronounced today. It is important to know the traditional names since they are related to the names of maqāmāt and because they are sometimes used by musicians to indicate a specific tonic of a scale.

G1	**Yakāh**	G2	**Nawā** (Djawāb Yakāh)
G𝄲1	Qarār Nīm Ḥiṣār	G𝄲2	Nīm Ḥiṣār
A♭1	Qarār Ḥiṣār	A♭2	Ḥiṣār (Shūrī)
A𝄳1	Qarār Tīk Ḥiṣār	A𝄳2	Tīk Ḥiṣār
A1	**ʿUshayrān**	A2	**Ḥusaynī**
A𝄲1	Qarār Nīm ʿAdjam	A𝄲2	Nīm ʿAdjam
B♭1	Qarār ʿAdjam	B♭2	ʿAdjam (Nirāz)
B𝄳1	**ʿIrāq**	B𝄳2	**Awdj**
B1	Kawasht	B2	Nuhuft
B𝄲1	Tīk Kawasht	B𝄲2	Tīk Nuhuft
C1	**Rāst**	C2	**Māhūr** *or* **Kardān**
C𝄲1	Nīm Zarkula	C𝄲2	Nīm Shāhnaz (Kināz)
D♭1	Zarkula	D♭2	Shāhnaz
D𝄳1	Tīk Zarkula	D𝄳2	Tīk Shāhnaz
D1	**Dūkāh**	D2	**Muḥayyar**
D𝄲1	Nīm Kurdī	D𝄲2	Nīm Sunbulah (Nīm Zual)
E♭1	Kurdī	E♭2	Sunbulah (Zual)
E𝄳1	**Sīkāh**	E𝄳2	**Buzurk**
E1	Būsalīk	E2	Djawāb Būsalīk (Ḥusaynī Shadd)
E𝄲1	Tīk Būsalīk	E𝄲2	Djawāb Tīk Būsalīk (Tīk Ḥusaynī Shadd)
F1	**Djahārkāh**	F2	**Māhurān**
F𝄲1	Nīm Ḥidjāz	F𝄲2	Djawāb Nīm Ḥidjāz
F♯1	Ḥidjāz	F♯2	Djawāb Ḥidjāz
G𝄳2	Tīk Ḥidjāz	G𝄳3	Djawāb Tīk Ḥidjāz
		G3	**Ramal Tūtī**

Figure 6.8 The names of notes in Arab music

The prefixes *nīm* and *tīk*, which appear frequently at the beginning of some of the note names, represent the alteration of a note by a quartertone. *Nīm* means lowering the note by a quartertone, while *tīk* means raising it by a quartertone (Shiloah 1995: 117). For example, the note A♭2 is called Ḥiṣār. Nīm Ḥiṣār is this note lowered by a quartertone (G𝄲2), and Tīk Ḥiṣār is this note raised by a quartertone (A𝄳2).

3 See Chapter 9 for a discussion about conventional tonics.

4 See Marcus 1989: 810–817 for a list of alternative names and spellings.

The notes that appear in bold in the table are the notes of the primary scale of Arab music – the scale of Rāst. This scale is the most important scale in the Arab musical system; figure 6.9 shows the classical names of its notes alongside their modern notation on the staff.

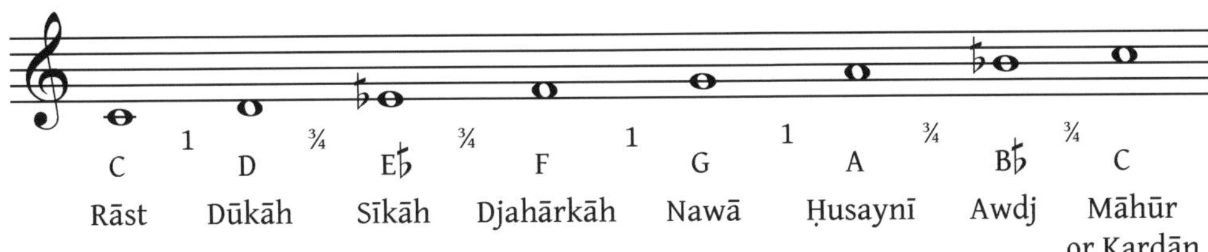

Figure 6.9 The notes of the scale of Rāst

In the past, the notes of the primary scale of Rāst were given names that corresponded to the names of the numbers 1 to 8 in Persian: *yāk*, *dū*, *sī*, *djahār*, *bandj*, *shash*, *haft*, and *hasht*. The suffix *kāh*, from the Persian *gāh*, which means "a position," was added to these numbers. Therefore, these old note names represent "positions" in the sequence of notes of the scale – the first position, the second position, and so forth (Marcus 1989: 74).

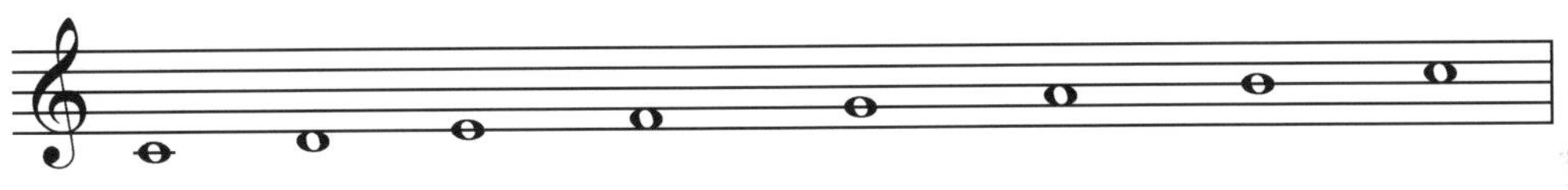

Figure 6.10 The old names, derived from Persian, for the notes of the primary scale

If we look at the table in figure 6.8, we can see that some of the older names have been changed. The first note of the scale, Yakāh, has been changed to Rāst; the name Yakāh is used today for the lowest note of the two-octave scale of Arab music – G1. The fifth note (Bandjkāh) has changed to Nawā, The sixth (Shashkāh) to Ḥusaynī, and the seventh (Haftkāh) to Awdj. Only the second (Dūkāh), Third (Sīkāh), and fourth (Djahārkāh) notes have preserved their original names. The names of notes in Arab music gave their name to a number of maqāmāt, such as maqām Sīkāh, maqām Djahārkāh, and maqām Bandjkāh

Intonation in Arab Music

THE TERM *intonation* refers to determining pitches of sounds, especially when referring to very subtle, microtonal, differences. When a person is out of tune, we can say that "his intonation is inaccurate." In European music, the problem of intonation was solved by applying the system of equal-temperament tuning (Cohen 1986: 75). In European equal temperament, the semitones are made equal by dividing the octave into 12 identical intervals. In the 1932 Cairo Congress of Arab Music, similar attempts were made to divide the octave of Arab music into 24 equal quartertones. This attempt did not succeed and Arab musicians continue to use the same intonation as they had used before. We can represent microtonal differences of intonation by using one of the systems used to measure very small intervals, such as the comma measuring system and the cent measuring system.

Commas and Cents

ONE OF THE ways to refer to intervals that are smaller than a semitone is by the division of the tone into nine equal intervals called *commas*. This measuring system, which originates in ancient Greek music theory, forms the basis for modern Turkish music theory; it is also used by some Arab music scholars to measure accurate intonation in Arab music practice. Figure 6.11 shows the way the comma system is used in modern Turkish theory and the accidentals that are used to indicate the various intervals that are produced by such a division:

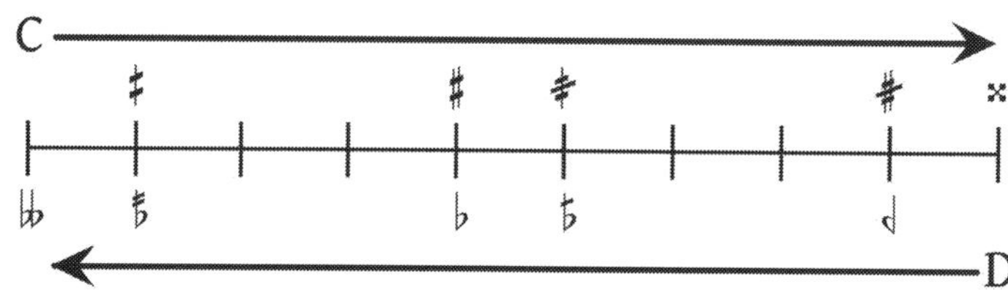

Figure 6.11 The division of the tone into nine commas and the accidentals used in Turkish music

If we look at figure 6.11, we can see that Turkish music theory does not use quartertones. Instead, this division produces "small" and "large" semitones (of four and five commas) and "small" and "large" tones (of eight and nine commas). These intervals form the basis of measurement in Turkish music theory. As is the case with the division into quartertones in Arab music, this division is purely theoretical. In performance practice, Turkish musicians use many different sizes of intervals.

When musicologists want to measure intervals very accurately and precisely, they use the cent measuring system, which was developed by Alexander J. Ellis. This system divides the equally-tempered semitone into 100 equal parts called *cents*. A whole tone, therefore, is equal to 200 cents and the octave is equal to 1200 cents. We should not conclude though, that a quartertone in Arab music measures exactly 50 cents. As was said before, Arab quartertones are not equal in practice.

If we listen to musicians from different musical cultures, such as a Turk and an Arab, we can notice differences in intonation, even when they play the same maqām. This is one of the main factors in distinguishing the styles of these musical traditions. An experienced listener, however, would be able to recognize which style of playing belongs to which tradition.

Some notes and intervals may sound different in various contexts even within the same musical tradition. Sometimes certain notes may sound higher in one maqām and lower in another. The intonation of some notes changes even within the same maqām. Ḥabīb Ẓahir Al-ʿAbbas explores the subject of intonation in Arab music by using the division of the tone into nine commas. By dividing the octave into 53 commas and measuring their distribution among the seven intervals of the octave, he determines the accurate intervals used in Arab musical scales. Al-ʿAbbas notes how the note Sīkāh (E𝄳1) is played lower in the context of the scale of maqām Bayāt and higher in the scales of Huzām, Sīkāh, and Rāst (Al-ʿAbbas 1986: 98). Following is a translation of the introduction to a section in his book that is dealing with these issues, which may highlight some important points concerning intonation in Arab music:

> The comma is the unit of sound on which the measurement of Arab and other Eastern scales is based. The comma is a ninth (1/9) of a tone, and therefore each group of nine commas forms the interval of a tone. On these scales, we first apply the science of music and then our subtle perception, because performing the intervals that form musical scales by using accidentals alone cannot represent the real intervals accurately; it can only represent them approximately. For example, we see that the note Kurd appears in notation as the note E♭ in both the scales of Ḥidjāz and Nahawand. However, in reality the note Kurd in the scale of Ḥidjāz is played higher than in the scale of maqām Nahawand. The note Sīkāh, which is written in both Rāst and Bayāt scales as E𝄳, is actually played higher in the scale of maqām Rāst than in the scale of maqām Bayāt [...] and so forth. Therefore, we must regard the [division into] quartertones and the use of accidentals as inaccurate, and there is no alternative other than establishing the accurate measurement of intervals by using commas. (al-ʿAbbas 1986: 90)

Al-ʿAbbas provides a complete chart with the accurate measurements of intervals in commas as they are performed in practice (1986: 90 ff.). For example, the interval between D1 and E𝄳1 in the scale of Rāst is seven commas, while in Bayāt it is six commas. Below are the accurate measurements in commas of the intervals of two scales, Rāst and Ḥidjāz, as they appear in al-ʿAbbas's book. In the bottom line, between parentheses, I put the theoretical measurements of these intervals in tones.

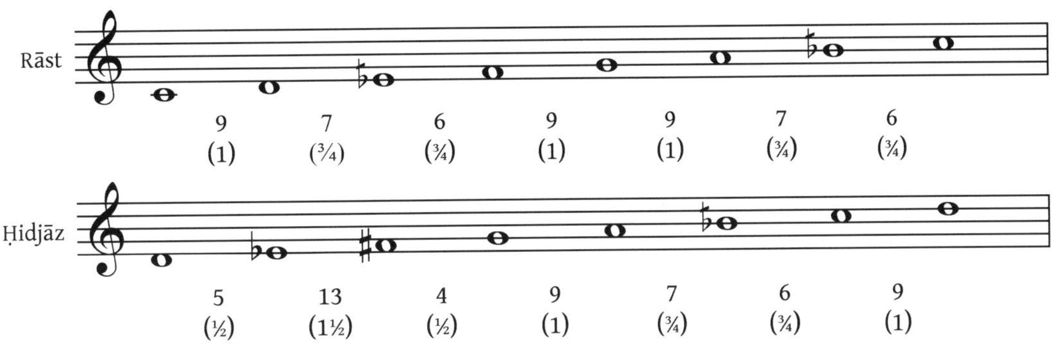

Figure 6.12 Accurate measurements in commas of the intervals of the Rāst and Ḥidjāz scales.

There is no need for beginner students, who make their first steps in understanding Arab music theory, to fully understand these complex divisions of scales into the accurate intervals that are performed in practice. This kind of information will be relevant after students become advanced in comprehending this music by listening to it and performing it. Trying to analyze Arab scales and to determine their accurate intonation by using commas and cents is, after all, purely theoretical. Accidentals and the division into commas and cents cannot help us perform Arab music with precise intonation. These theoretical attempts try to represent as closely as possible the practical performance of music. Arab music, however, is performed by musicians who are deeply acquainted with it, have absorbed it from a young age, and have learned how to produce it accurately, whether vocally or instrumentally. The use of theory alone can never replace practice in fully presenting and explaining a musical system.

CHAPTER 7

SCALAR SYSTEMS

THE EUROPEAN scalar system is based on one diatonic system that was selected out of the sequence of 12 semitones. Out of all possible scales that could be derived from the diatonic system, only two scales (or modes) have remained in use in European music – the major (the Ionian mode) and the minor (the Aeolian mode). This scalar system is cyclical – the sequence of intervals repeats itself in all octaves. In Arab music, the situation is quite different; as Dalia Cohen writes:

> [...] In most of the styles of various musical cultures, there are a number of scalar systems, and in each system, there are a number of scales. A good example would be the wealth of scalar systems in the *maqāmāt* of Arab music and in the *ragas* of Indian music. The Western system is unique in that it is only one – the diatonic system, from which the church modes are derived. (Cohen 1986: 73)

Unlike the situation in European music, it is difficult to indicate a common scalar system for **all** the scales of Arab music. Some of the reasons for this are:

1. Though there are diatonic scales in Arab music, such as ʿAdjam, Nahawand, Kurd, and Lāmī, the structure of these scales does not repeat in all octaves; that is, they are not necessarily cyclical.
2. There are many scales that are based on the 12-semitone sequence but are not diatonic, such as the scale of maqām Nawā-Athar. This scale contains four semitones, one whole tone, and two intervals of 1½ tones:

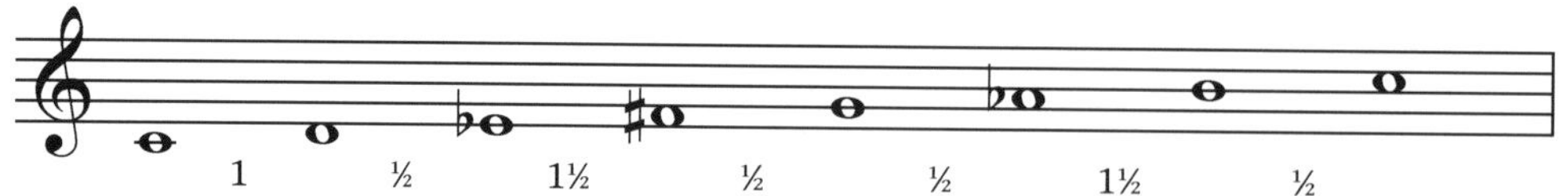

Figure 7.1 The scale of maqām Nawā-Athar

Another example is the scale of maqām Ḥidjāz-Humayūn. This scale consists of three semitones, three whole tones, and one interval of 1½ tones:

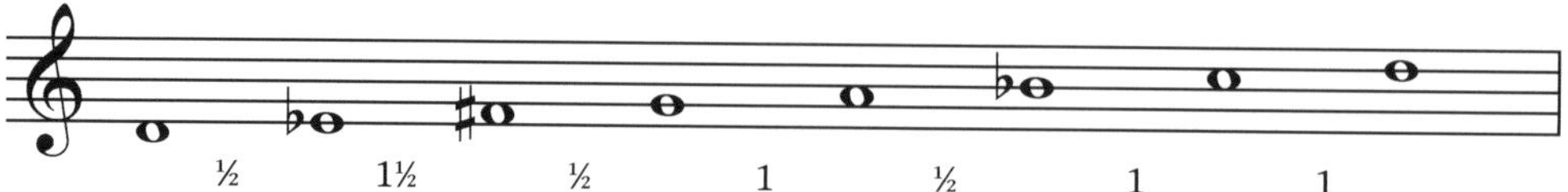

Figure 7.2 The scale of maqām Ḥidjāz-Humayūn

3. In many maqāmāt the notes change when we move to the second, upper, octave of the scale. Here is the scale of maqām Ḥidjāz-Kār for example:

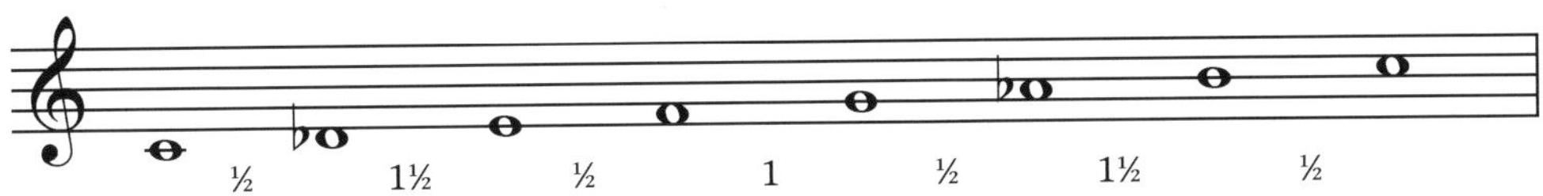

Figure 7.3 The first octave of the scale of maqām Ḥidjāz-Kār

The second octave of this scale, however, is not identical; it consists of the intervals 1–½–1 (tones); these intervals construct the djins (tetrachord) Nahawand:

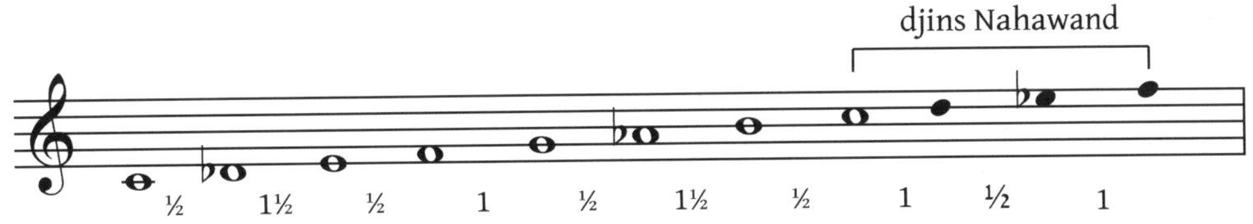

Figure 7.4 The scale of maqām Ḥidjāz-Kār with part of its second octave

On the other hand, the second octave of maqām Shadd-ʿArabān (a transposition of maqām Ḥidjāz-Kār) is a cyclical repetition of the first octave – it repeats the djins Ḥidjāz:

Figure 7.5 The scale of maqām Shadd-ʿArabān with part of its second octave

4. Some maqāmāt have certain notes that are altered (that is, flattened or sharpened) even within the same octave. For example, the scale of Ḥusaynī is written like this:

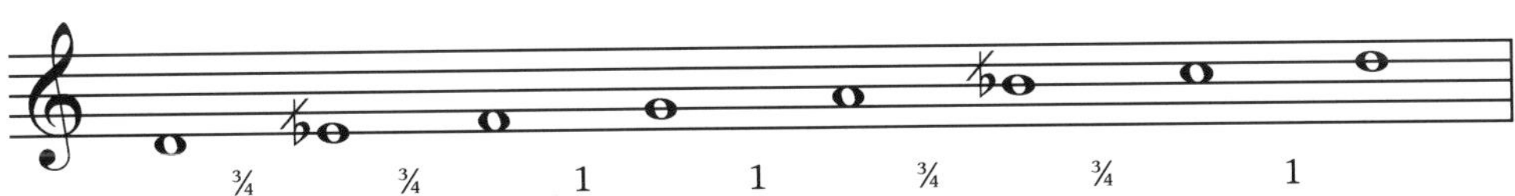

Figure 7.6 The scale of maqām Ḥusaynī

However, the note B𝄳2 changes to B♭2 when the progression of the scale descends. This alteration forms a part of the structure of the maqām. The alteration between B𝄳2 and B♭2 is typical of many other maqāmāt in Arab music, such as Rāst.

5. Some maqāmāt have specific characterization concerning the direction of their performance – that is, whether they are ascending or descending in nature. These maqāmāt, therefore, can only be fully presented and performed within the context of a two-octave scale. Even if a maqām has a cyclical scale, which repeats exactly in all octaves, performing just one of these octaves would not be sufficient for its presentation. The scale of Muḥayyar, for example, is written as follows:

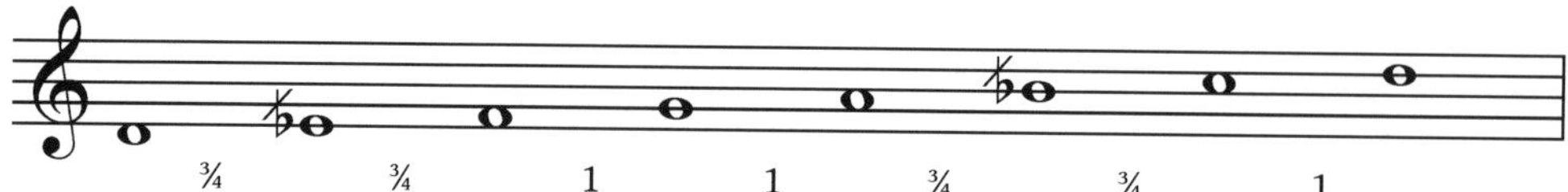

Figure 7.7 The scale of maqām Muḥayyar

The scale of this maqām is identical with the scale of Ḥusaynī, which appears in figure 7.6. However, contrary to Ḥusaynī, maqām Muḥayyar is performed by starting from its octave note (D2), playing a few notes above it, in the second octave, and then descending to its first octave. This kind of pogression is an integral part of maqām Muḥayyar's characterization.

Another example is the alteration of the note below the tonic in maqām Nahawand. The note B♭1 in Nahawand is sometimes changed into B♮1 (that is, it is raised by a semitone) in order to create a "stronger" leading note; this helps in establishing the tonic.[1] This alteration of a note that belongs to the lowest octave forms a part of maqām Nahawand and is essential to its characterization.

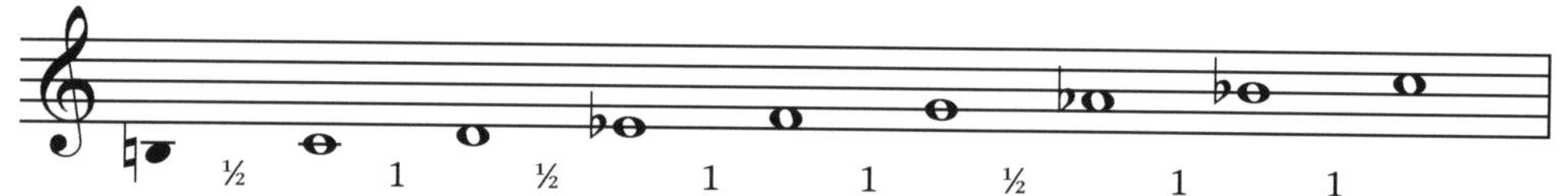

Figure 7.8 The scale of maqām Nahawand and the leading note below its tonic

6. The scales that are represented in a framework that is wider than an octave can therefore be considered as scales of 11, 12, 13, or 14 notes. It is hard to see how such a scale can be incorporated into a scalar system – a system from which many other scales can be created by repositioning the tonic.

7. Many maqāmāt in Arab music are *compound maqāmāt*. They are more recent maqāmāt that were formed by compounding old ones. Maqām Bastah-Nikār, for example, is a compound of Sīkāh and Ṣabā:

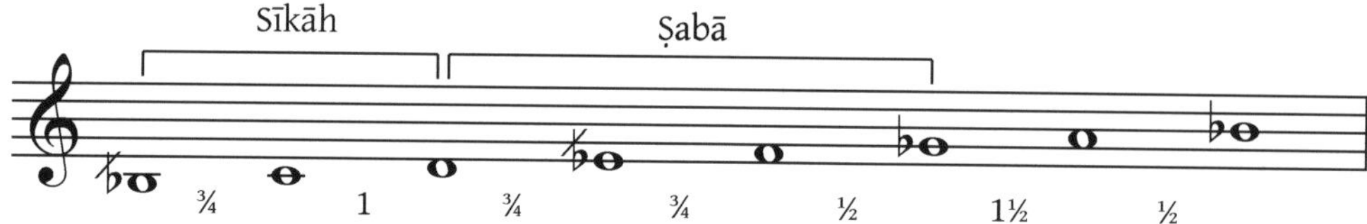

Figure 7.9 The scale of maqām Bastah-Nikār

Another example is Maqām Sūznāk, which is a compound of Rāst and Ḥidjāz:

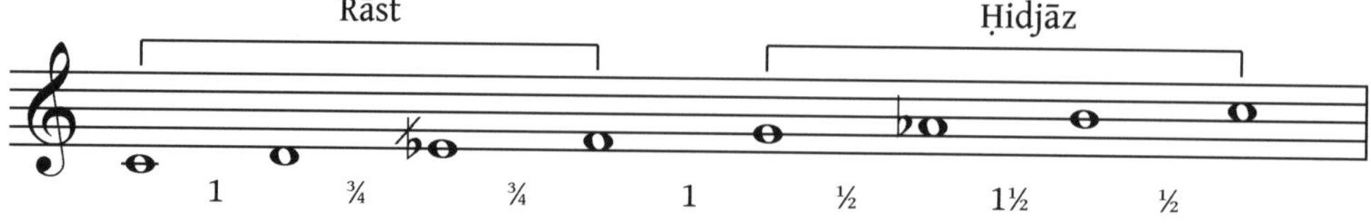

Figure 7.10 The scale of maqām Sūznāk

There are many scales of this kind, and it is hard to establish a scalar system for them. However, some scholars think that there is no problem with attaching such scales to a scalar system (Bar-Yosef).

1 See Chapter 2 for an explanation of leading notes.

Because of the above-mentioned factors, there is no one single scalar system from which **all** Arab scales can be said to be derived. Furthermore, many scales cannot be attributed to **any** certain scalar system. It is impossible, for example, to establish a scalar system for non-cyclical scales (scales thatv their notes do not repeat in the adjacent octaves).

One Arab music theory book, presents 52 Arab musical scales (Al-Mahdī 19??: 134). These are the most commonly known and used scales. The medieval theoretician Ṣafī al-Dīn al-Urmawī found that by combining various *adjnās* (such as tetrachords and pentachords) 84 octave scales can be formed (Shiloah 1995: 113). The great theoretician al-Fārābī (d. 950) produced more than 1400 scales by combining notes and intervals (al-Ḥilou 1972: 72). This discussion is of course quite theoretical, because it seems rather unlikely that a musical culture would use so many musical scales. In my opinion, the subject of scalar systems in Arab music needs to be studied further.

In this book, I use a different approach to the subject. I show how sorting and classifying scales into groups that share common characteristics makes it easier to understand the Arab musical system. It also allows for a clearer discussion of the subject of scalar systems in Arab music.

The Method of Combining Intervals

THE MOST common theoretical solution to the problem of establishing a scalar system for Arab music is the method of combining intervals. A musical culture creates its various musical scales by combining consecutive intervals (seconds). Obviously, not all such combinations can produce an "acceptable" or a "playable" musical scale. The produced scale must be made into an aesthetic mode that is accepted by the musical culture. Many scales and modes that were constructed by theoreticians and that appear in various theoretical books are purely theoretical and they were never used in practice. However, using the method of combining intervals can help us understand many of the characteristics of those Arab scales that cannot be attributed to a scalar system.

The system of Arab music has six kinds of consecutive intervals, or seconds, that can be used for the construction of scales:

1 quartertone (¼ tone)
2 quartertones (1 semitone)
3 quartertones (¾ tones)
4 quartertones (1 tone)
5 quartertones (5/4 tones)
6 quartertones (1½ tones)

Scales are produced by combining these intervals in various ways.

Another method of creating scales is by combining adjnās – the trichords, tetrachords, and pentachords of Arab music.[2] Shiloah discusses this concept:

> Such derivations [of modes] are potentially inherent in one of the basic principles of the entire system, wherein a whole range or scale is conceived as the sum of several smaller elements; this also permits mobility and permutation of these elements within the framework of the resulting extended range. The process, then, is a kind of mosaic composed of multiple combinations derived from relatively minimal elements. (Shiloah 1995: 115)

It is possible that, practically speaking, the method of combining intervals is first used to create types of adjnās, and these are later combined to create scales (see Chapter 8). Therefore, we will not resign to only using the method of combining intervals, but we will look for various common characteristics of scales. Such an analysis can help us understand the structure of the various scales and become proficient in recognizing them. Let us look at some types of scales that can be found in Arab music.

2 This method will be discussed in Chapter 8.

Diatonic Scales in Arab Music

THOUGH DIATONIC scales are usually associated with European music, there are some diatonic scales in Arab music as well. The scale of maqām ʿAdjam, for example, is identical to the major scale and its intervals are 1–1–½–1–1–1–½ (tones). The scale of Nahawand is identical to the natural minor scale with the intervals of 1–½–1–1–½–1–1 (tones).

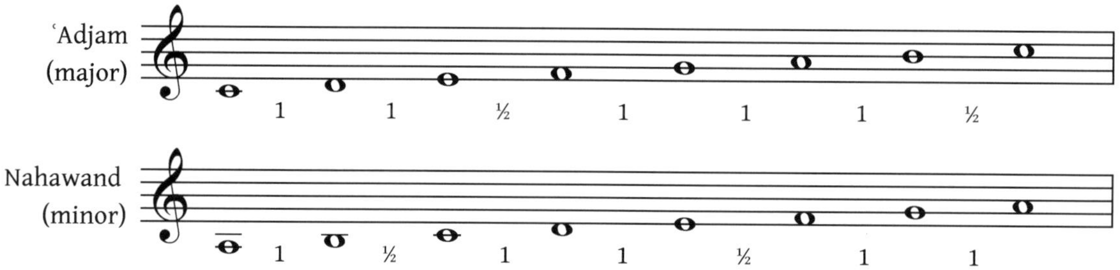

Figure 7.11 The scales of maqām ʿAdjam (major) and maqām Nahawand (minor)

In Arab music, we can also find many scales that correspond to the ancient modes of European music, which were abandoned in favor of the major-minor system. One example is the Phrygian mode, with the intervals of ½–1–1–1–½–1–1 (tones); its equivalent in Arab music is the scale of maqām Kurd. Another is the Locrian mode, with the intervals of ½–1–1–½–1–1–1 (tones); in Arab music, this is the scale of maqām Lāmī, which originated in Iraq but has spread to other Arab countries, such as Egypt.

Another diatonic scale is the scale of maqām Nahawand Kabīr, which is parallel to the Dorian mode: 1–½–1–1–1–½–1 (tones); this scale is not widely used.

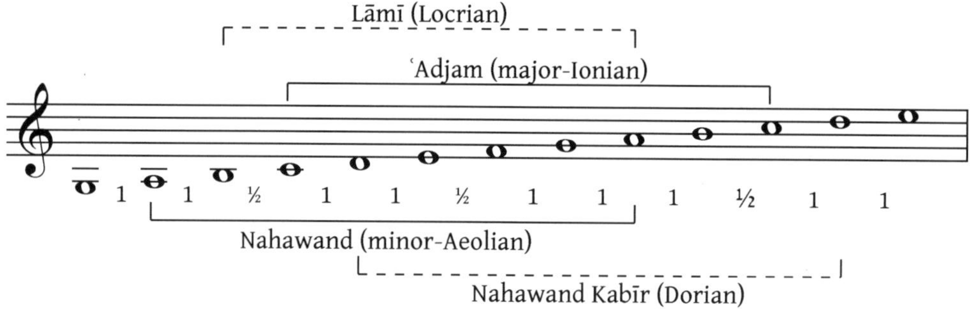

Figure 7.12 The diatonic scales in Arab music

Other scales from the European diatonic system may be used by Arab musicians, who always introduce new scales and other innovations. Furthermore, with time, Arab music introduces new scales by altering existing ones.

Other Scales on the Sequence of Semitones that Are Not Diatonic

AS WE HAVE said, in European music, all intervals are based on the division of the octave into 12 semitones, but only certain kinds of scales that can be constructed using these 12 semitones are used; these are the diatonic scales. In Arab music, we can find scales that are based on the chromatic sequence of notes (the sequence of semitones) but are not diatonic. An example of such a scale is the scale of Ḥidjāz-Kār. It is written as follows:

Figure 7.13 The scale of maqām Ḥidjāz-Kār

This scale is composed of two intervals of a semitone, one whole tone, and two intervals of 1½ tones. As we learned from figures 7.4 and 7.5, this scale is not cyclical – it changes according to the octave. Therefore, we cannot say that it belongs to a cyclical scalar system. There are many other scales that are constructed by using the 12 semitone division, such as Nawā-Athar, Ṭarz Nawīn, Nakrīz, and Zandjarān; in Part III all these scales are discussed.

Scales Containing Quartertonal (Microtonal) Intervals

THE DIVISION of the octave into 24 quartertones is one of the main characteristics that distinguish Arab music from European music. This division extends the possibilities for constructing scales since it allows the use of intervals that are not available in the European system. Many of the scales that contain quartertonal intervals are related to one another and have certain relationships between them. It is important to listen attentively to Arab music, with its unique intonation and its use of quartertone notes, in order to understand its theoretical system and comprehend it completely. Only by repeatedly listening and experiencing it can a musician obtain the tools that allow him or her to understand, perform, and compose Arab music.

The Scale of Maqām Rāst as an Example of a Scale Containing Quartertonal Intervals

IN ORDER TO start becoming familiar with scales that contain quartertonal (i.e., microtonal) intervals we will look at the scale of Rāst. This scale is one of the most important scales of Arab music and many other scales are derived from it. A significant amount of musical repertoire is based on maqām Rāst and the scales that are related to it. When discussing the modal systems of various Asian musical cultures, Shiloah writes:

> [...] everyone [i.e., theoreticians] gives absolute primacy to the *rast* and it is designated as the first, central, most complete source of all *maqāmāt*. (Shiloah 1995: 115-116)

Rāst is not just one of many scales that contain quartertonal intervals (we will call these "quartertonal scales"), but it is the scale from which many quartertonal scales are derived. By repositioning the tonic on the various notes of the scale of Rāst we can construct some of the main maqāmāt of Arab music. Other scales that use quartertonal intervals seem to be further elaborations of the scales derived from Rāst. Many compound maqāmāt, which are constructed by combining adjnās from various scales, contain elements that are related to the scale of Rāst. The scale of Rāst is constructed from the following intervals: 1–¾–¾–1–1–¾–¾ (tones); its conventional tonic is the note Rāst (C1) and it is written as follows:

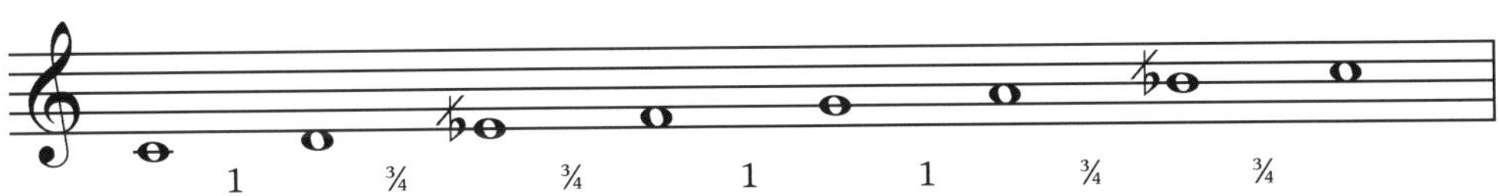

Figure 7.14 The scale of maqām Rāst

When we look closely at the scale's structure, we can see that it resembles the major scale, but its third and seventh notes are flattened by a quartertone. In the major scale, these two notes, E and B, and the notes that follow them, F and C, are separated by a semitone. In the scale of Rāst, they are separated by a three-quartertone interval. They are therefore called E half-flat (E𝄳) and B half-flat (B𝄳).

In Chapter 9, we will learn how various repositions of the tonic within the scale of Rāst produce six other independent scales. These are some of the most important scales of Arab music.

CHAPTER 8

ANALYZING MUSICAL SCALES

IN CHAPTER 2, we learned about the scales of the seven European modes that are derived from the diatonic scalar system. Each of these scales is constructed differently, but since they are all diatonic, each one of them contains five whole tones and two semitones. Each scale is divided into two *tetrachords* (a tetrachord is a unit of the scale constructed out of four notes, that is, three consecutive intervals). These two tetrachords form the two sections of the scale – the lower section (the *first tetrachord*) and the upper section (the *second tetrachord*); separating these sections is an interval of either a whole tone or a semitone. By analyzing the various European diatonic scales, we concluded that there are only four different tetrachords – the Ionian, Dorian, Phrygian, and Lydian (see figure 2.10). Out of the seven European modes, four are named according to their first tetrachord: the Ionian, Dorian, Phrygian, and Lydian. The other three are named differently: the Mixolydian, Aeolian, and Locrian. Some scales, therefore, are named according to their first tetrachord, while others are named differently; but none are named according to their second tetrachord.

If we want to classify these modes, we can sort them into "families" according to their first tetrachord. We can say that the Ionian and Mixolydian scales belong to the Ionian family, since the first tetrachord of these two scales is the Ionian tetrachord. In a similar way, the Dorian and Aeolian belong to the Dorian family, the Phrygian and the Locrian to the Phrygian family. The Lydian mode forms a family of its own, since there is only one scale that starts with this tetrachord.

The Meaning and Significance of the Adjnās

In Arab music theory, in order to analyze and to categorize scales, we use principles that are very similar to the ones presented above. As is the case with European modes, Arab scales contain two main sections. Each of these sections is named *djins* (plural: *adjnās*). This Arabic word comes from the Greek *genus*, which means "a species," or, "a type." In ancient Greek music theory, this term was used for classifying various types of tetrachords. Every main octave of an Arab scale contains two adjnās: the lower djins, and the upper djins. We will call these the *first djins* and the *second djins* respectively. There are scales in Arab music that are named after their first djins. The scale of maqām Ḥidjāz, for example, starts with djins Ḥidjāz; the scale of Rāst starts with djins Rāst (Figure 8.1).

Not always is a maqām named after its first djins, or even its second one. In Maqām Sūznāk, for example, the first djins is Rāst, and the second one is Ḥidjāz (Figure 8.2).

There is one big difference between the concept of tetrachords in European music and the concept of adjnās in Arab music. A djins is not necessarily constructed from four notes. A djins can also be constructed from five notes (a *pentachord*) or three notes (a *trichord*).

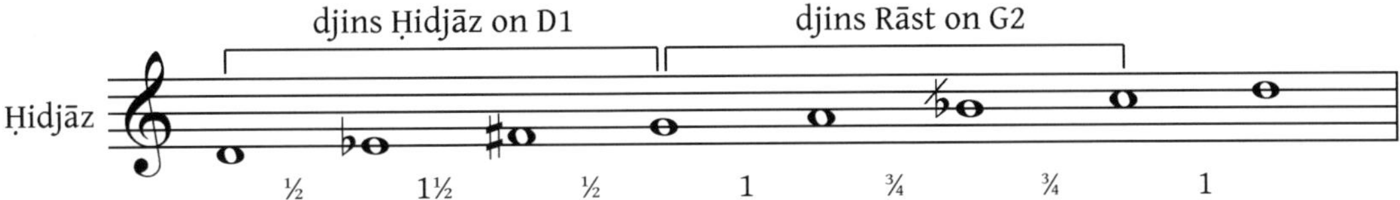

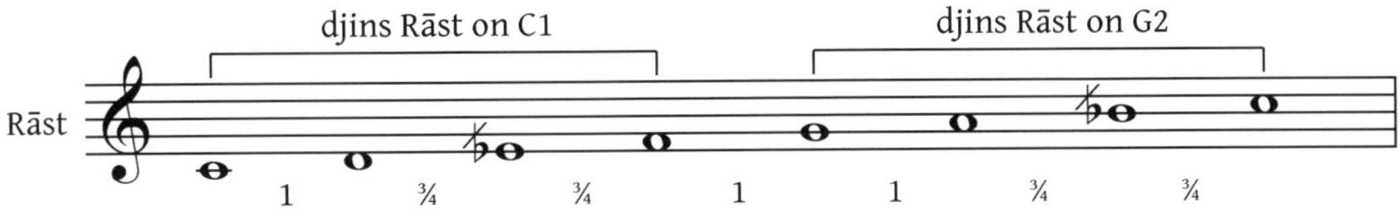

Figure 8.1 The scales of maqām Ḥidjāz and maqām Rāst and their adjnās

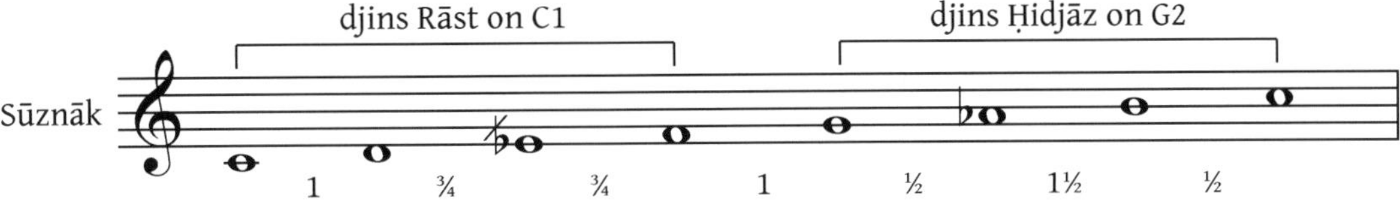

Figure 8.2 The scale of maqām Sūznāk and its adjnās

Arab music scholars do not agree upon the sizes of the various adjnās. The djins of maqām Sīkāh, for example, is sometimes presented as having three notes, that is, as a trichord:

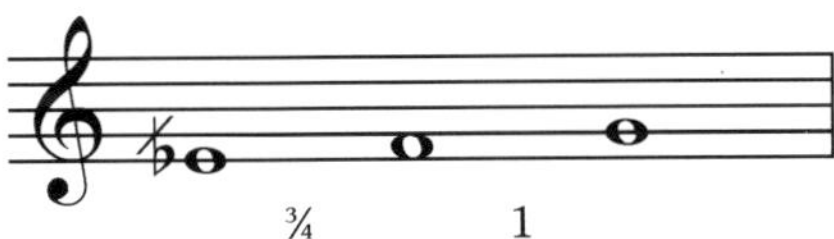

Figure 8.3 Djins Sīkāh as a trichord

In other sources, we can find it as having four notes – a tetrachord:

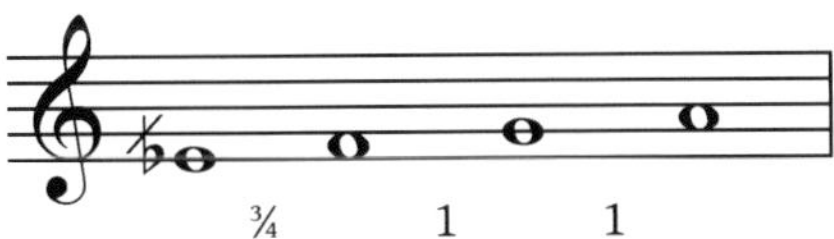

Figure 8.4 Djins Sīkāh as a tetrachord

Another example is the djins ʿAdjam, which is sometimes presented as a tetrachord:

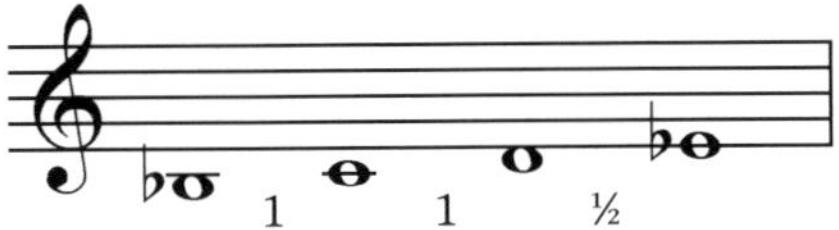

Figure 8.5 Djins ʿAdjam as a tetrachord

While other scholars argue that it is a trichord:

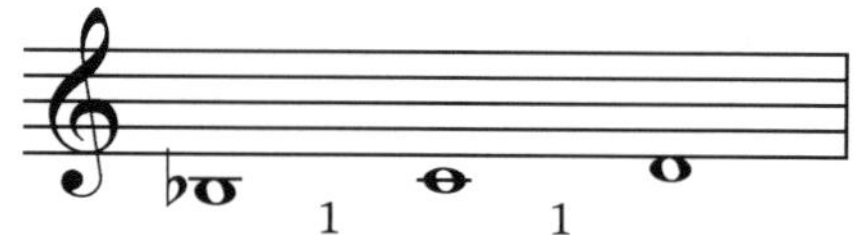

Figure 8.6 Djins ʿAdjam as a trichord

According to the classification and analysis system that is used in this book, I establish that djins Sīkāh has three notes and djins ʿAdjam has four. Let us look at the reasons for these conclusions because they touch on some important issues concerning the analysis of Arab scales:

Djins is not a mere technical term, an arithmetic tool for "organizing" the scale. A djins can be thought of as a melodic unit, or a modal entity, having its own musical characteristics and distinctiveness. The melodic structure of the djins gives it its unique *color* or *shade*.

In order to illustrate this, let us look at djins Ḥidjāz:

Figure 8.7 Djins Ḥidjāz

An experienced listener of Arab music would recognize immediately these mere four notes as the djins of Ḥidjāz. Performing fewer notes than these four notes, that is, fewer intervals than the three intervals of ½–1½–½ (tones), would not be sufficient to establish the djins as Ḥidjāz. On the other hand, there is no need to perform more than these four notes in order to establish the djins of Ḥidjāz. Neighboring notes to these four notes either function in the context of other adjnās or form a connection with them. Therefore, we can say that the number of notes in a djins is defined as the smallest number of notes that are needed in order to represent the djins's melodic characteristics – to give it its "color" or "shade."

When performing a djins of three notes (a trichord) with the intervals of 1–¾ (tones) it is immediately perceived as djins Sīkāh, with its characteristic melodic structure. Therefore, we can conclude that djins Sīkāh has only three notes.

An example to where at least five notes (a pentachord) are needed to represent a djins can be found in the djins of Nawā-Athar – the first djins of a maqām with the same name. This djins contains five notes with the intervals of 1–½–1½–½ (tones):

Figure 8.8 Djins Nawā-Athar

In this case, if we do not perform all the five notes of this djins, but only four notes, for example, we cannot represent the djins; a listener would not perceive its characteristic color.

Another important reason for this variety in sizes of adjnās is the various positions of the dominant note, the *ghammāz*, in the scales of Arab music. As we learned in Chapter 2, in the European diatonic musical system, the dominant is always the fifth note of the scale. In a similar way, in Arab scales, the ghammāz is most of the time the fifth note. The scales are usually divided into two adjnās of four notes: the second djins is usually positioned on the fifth note, and there is an interval of a whole tone between the two adjnās. Nevertheless, this is not always the case. In many maqāmāt, the ghammāz is the third, fourth, or even the sixth note of the scale.

The ghammāz is the second most important note in the scale after the tonic, because the second djins of the maqām is always placed on it, that is, it functions as the tonic of the second djins of the maqām. It is played repeatedly and used as a departure point for modulations. The position of the ghammāz, and therefore the position of the second djins of the scale, varies according to its structural functions within the scale of the maqām.

If we compare the two scales in figure 8.1, we can see that while the second djins of maqām Rāst is placed on the fifth note of the scale, the second djins of maqām Ḥidjāz is placed on the fourth note. Another example can be found in the scale of maqām Bayāt:

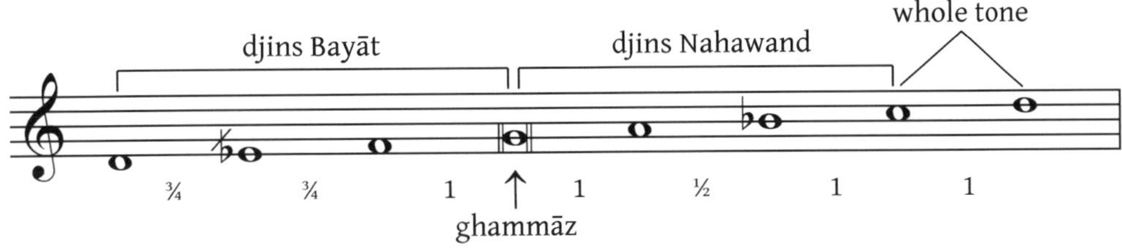

Figure 8.9 The scale of Maqām Bayāt and its constituent adjnās

In maqām Bayāt, the second djins is placed on the fourth note of the first djins. Therefore, the ghammāz of Bayāt is its fourth note – G2. The case is the same with many other scales that start with djins Bayāt.[1]

If we look at figure 8.10, we can see that the second djins of maqām Sīkāh is placed on the third note – G2. In fact, in all the scales that belong to the Sīkāh family (scales in which the first djins is Sīkāh), the second djins is placed on the third note of the scale. This is because the third note of maqām Sīkāh is its ghammāz.[2]

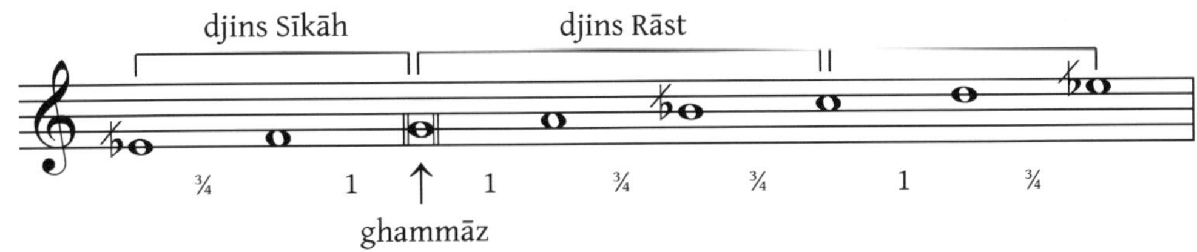

Figure 8.10 The scale of Maqām Sīkāh and its constituent adjnās

The Most Commonly Used Adjnās

BELOW (figure 8.11) are the most commonly used adjnās in Arab music. This list includes all the adjnās that are used for analyzing the maqāmāt in Part III. As you can see, all the adjnās are notated on the tonic C1. They are presented like this for an important reason:

The identity of a djins is determined by its structure of consecutive intervals. Djins Rāst, for example, is formed from the intervals of 1-¾-¾ (tones). When this combination of intervals appears somewhere in a scale, we can call it djins Rāst. Though the conventional tonic of **maqām** Rāst is C1, it makes no difference on which note we place these consecutive intervals – they would always form the **djins** Rāst. Many scholars, when notating adjnās, tend to present a djins on the conventional tonic of the maqām that bears its name. Therefore, they always notate djins Rāst on the tonic C1, djins Kurd on D1 (the conventional tonic of maqām Kurd) and djins Sīkāh on E𝄳, to give just a few examples.

I find this method of presenting adjnās confusing. A djins can be placed on any note and within many types of scales; therefore, it is confusing to depict it as having a conventional tonic. The best way to study adjnās is by referring to their intervallic structure. The following figure presents all the adjnās on one tonic – C1, as well as on the conventional tonic of their corresponding maqāmāt.

---

1 See the chapter on the Bayāt family in part III.

2 See the chapter on the Sīkāh family in Part III

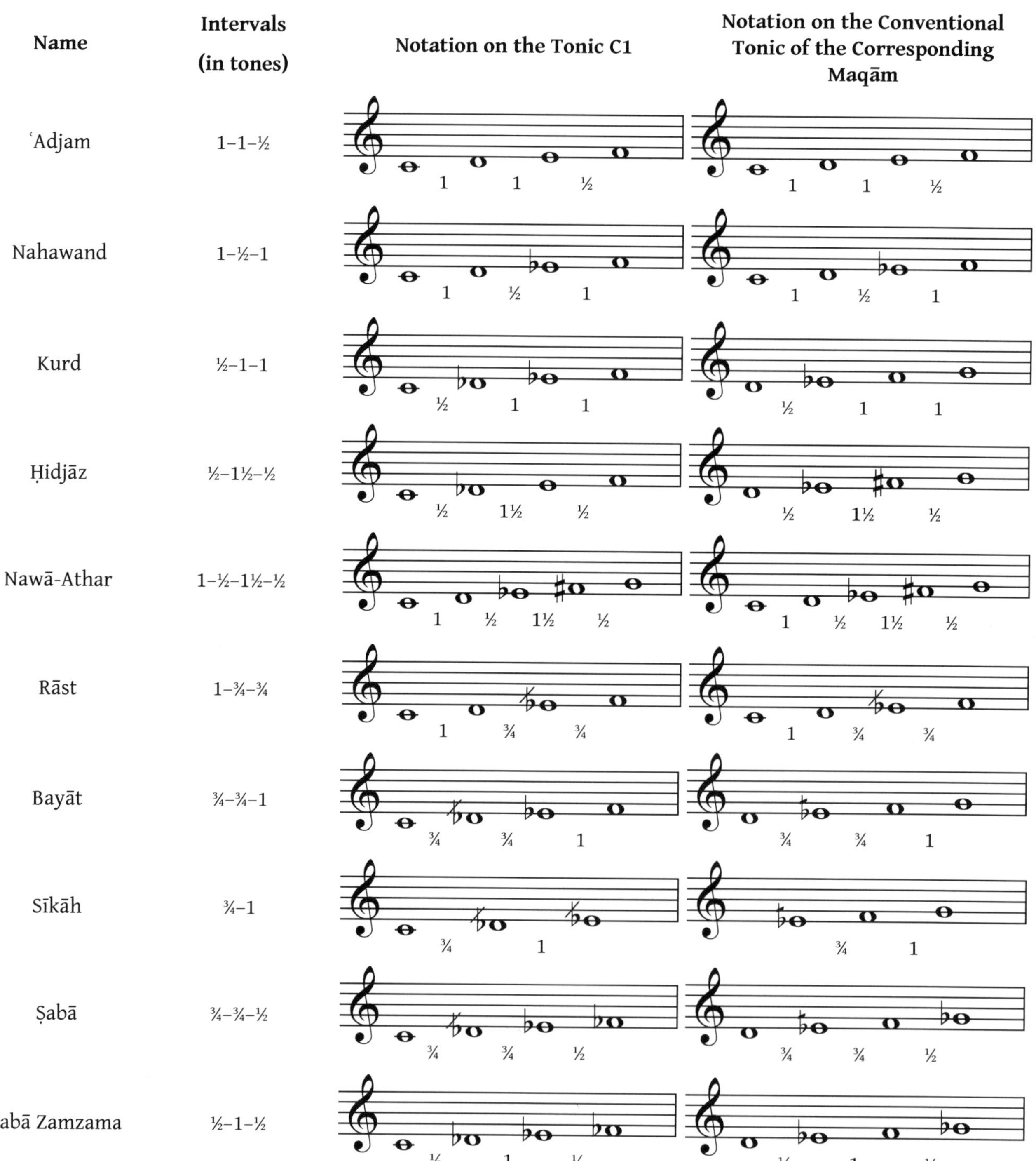

Name	Intervals (in tones)	Notation on the Tonic C1	Notation on the Conventional Tonic of the Corresponding Maqām
ʿAdjam	1–1–½	1 1 ½	1 1 ½
Nahawand	1–½–1	1 ½ 1	1 ½ 1
Kurd	½–1–1	½ 1 1	½ 1 1
Ḥidjāz	½–1½–½	½ 1½ ½	½ 1½ ½
Nawā-Athar	1–½–1½–½	1 ½ 1½ ½	1 ½ 1½ ½
Rāst	1–¾–¾	1 ¾ ¾	1 ¾ ¾
Bayāt	¾–¾–1	¾ ¾ 1	¾ ¾ 1
Sīkāh	¾–1	¾ 1	¾ 1
Ṣabā	¾–¾–½	¾ ¾ ½	¾ ¾ ½
Ṣabā Zamzama	½–1–½	½ 1 ½	½ 1 ½

Figure 8.11 The most commonly used adjnās in Arab music

Disjunct Adjnās, Conjunct Adjnās, and Overlapping Adjnās

Disjunct Adjnās (Adjnās Munfarida)

AS WE SAW above in Chapter 2, the scales of the European diatonic system are always constructed from two tetrachords. These tetrachords are positioned in the lower and upper sections of the scale and are named the *first tetrachord* and the *second tetrachord* respectively. Each tetrachord is constructed from three intervals (four notes), so two tetrachords give us six intervals. To complete a scale of seven intervals, a seventh interval of a whole tone or a semitone appears between the two tetrachords (see figure 2.9). The seven European modes are constructed, therefore, from combining the four species of tetrachords in this fashion.

Many scales of Arab maqāmāt are constructed in a similar way. The scale of ʿAdjam, for example, is constructed from two adjnās of ʿAdjam, which are separated by a whole tone. Since these adjnās are separated by an interval, they are named *disjunct adjnās* (Arabic: *adjnās munfarida*).

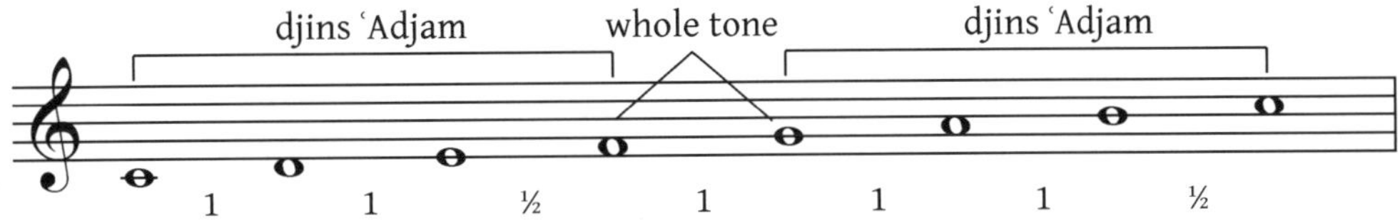

Figure 8.12 The scale of maqām ʿAdjam and its constituent adjnās

Another example of disjunct adjnās: If the second djins of the scale of ʿAdjam is changed to djins Ḥidjāz, the resulting scale is the scale of Shawq-Afzā, which belongs to the ʿAdjam family because its first djins is ʿAdjam.

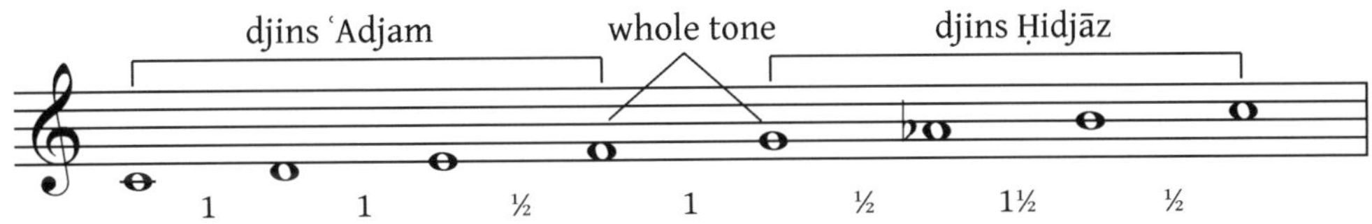

Figure 8.13 The scale of maqām Shawq-Afzā and its constituent adjnās

The ghammāz of both of these scales is their fifth note, and therefore the second djins is placed on this note.

Conjunct Adjnās (Adjnās Muttaṣila)

IN ADDITION TO scales in which an interval separates the two adjnās, many scales in Arab music are constructed from two adjnās that are connected to one another. This means that the last note of the first djins is the first note of the second one. This kind of structure is called *conjunct adjnās* (Arabic: *adjnās muttaṣila*). The second djins is always placed on the ghammāz of the scale, so when the ghammāz is the third or fourth note of the scale, the two adjnās are connected. Since there is no separating interval between the two adjnās, any "extra" interval that is needed in order to complete a scale of seven intervals appears after the second djins. As an example, let us take the scale of maqām Bayāt:

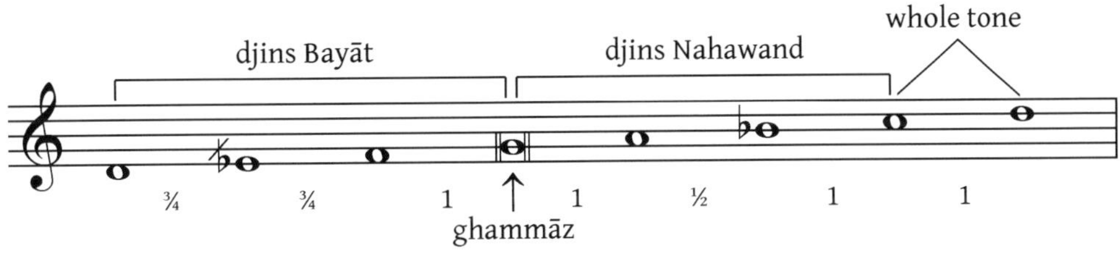

Figure 8.14 The scale of maqām Bayāt

The first djins of maqām Bayāt is djins Bayāt (¾–¾–1 tones). Its second djins is djins Nahawand (1–½–1 tones), which is placed on the fourth note of the scale – the last note of the first djins and the ghammāz of Bayāt. In this case, the interval that is left appears at the end of the scale.

Another example can be found in the scale of maqām Huzām, which belongs to the Sīkāh family. The first djins of this maqām is djins Sīkāh, which has three notes. The second djins of this maqām is Ḥidjāz. It is placed on the third note of the scale because this is the ghammāz of the scale. The two intervals that are needed in order to complete seven intervals appear at the end of the scale.

Figure 8.15 The scale of maqām Huzām

Overlapping Adjnās (Adjnās Mutadākhila)

ACCORDING TO some scholars, some adjnās are combined in a form that is termed *overlapping adjnās*. This means that in some scales the adjnās are not separated by an interval (disjunct) nor connected by the same note (conjunct), but overlap one another. Let us take for example the scale of maqām Huzām, which we have already discussed. Al-Ḥilū suggests that the adjnās in this scale are overlapping; he analyzes the scale of Huzām in this way (1972: 132):

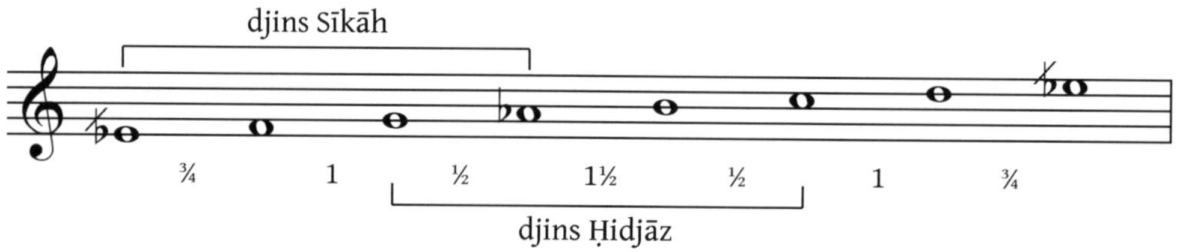

Figure 8.16 The scale of Huzām and its overlapping adjnās according to al-Ḥilū

Al-Ḥilū, as other scholars, places the second djins on the third note of the scale, because this note is the ghammāz of the scale, but he claims that djins Sīkāh consists of four notes. In his list of adjnās, Al-Ḥilū indeed presents djins Sīkāh as consisting of four notes, but he notates it in this way:

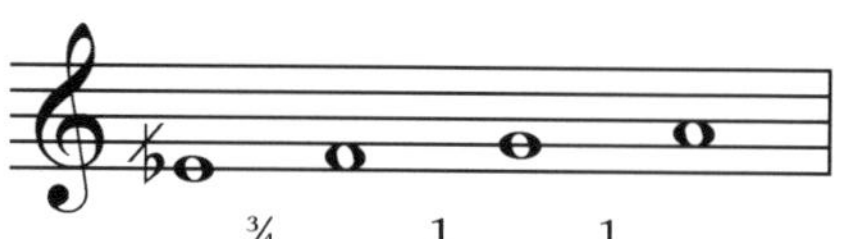

Figure 8.17 Djins Sīkāh according to al-Ḥilū

We can see that there is an inconsistency between these two figures: In the scale of Huzām (figure 8.16), al-Ḥilū notates the fourth note of djins Sīkāh as A♭2, creating the intervals ¾–1–½ (tones). However, when he presents the djins itself (figure 8.17), the fourth note of the djins is A♮2, and the intervals are ¾–1–1 (tones). Mashʿal also presents djins Sīkāh as consisting of four notes (1959: 67). Other scholars, such as al-Mahdī (1990: 39) and al-ʿAbbas (1986: 43) hold the opinion that djins Sīkāh consists of three notes (or two intervals).

I agree with the approach that claims that djins Sīkāh consists of three notes. Therefore, in this book, we will not use the analysis method of overlapping adjnās. However, in Part III, we will sometimes examine this approach with regard to some specific scales.

Secondary Adjnās

IN MOST SCALES, we can identify some adjnās that are "hidden" between the notes of the scale and are not one of the scale's primary adjnās. We call these adjnās *secondary adjnās*. Let us examine the scale of maqām ʿAdjam for example:

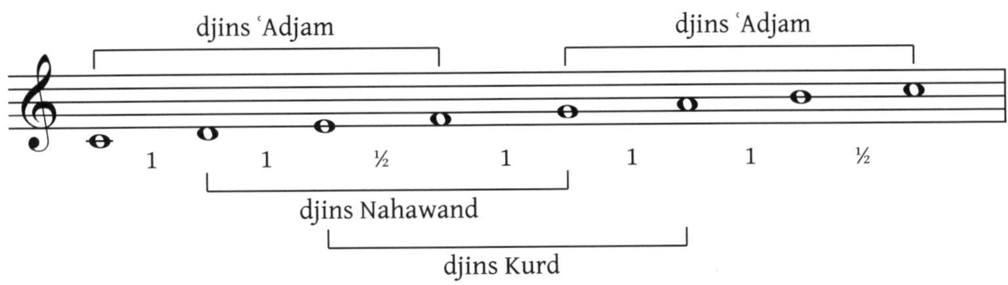

Figure 8.18 The scale of maqām ʿAdjam and its secondary adjnās

We can see that the scale of ʿAdjam is composed of two adjnās of ʿAdjam; the first is placed on the note C, and the second on the note G. These are the scale's *primary adjnās*. However, if we look closely, we can see that there are some other species of adjnās, placed on other notes of the scale. For example, a djins Nahawand can be found on the note D, and a djins Kurd on the note E. These are the scale's *secondary adjnās*.

Developing the skill of analyzing the secondary adjnās of scales is very important. It enables us to understand the internal structure of scales and maqāmāt; it explains the scale's relation to other scales and simplifies issues regarding reposition and transposition. With some maqāmāt, emphasizing the secondary adjnās of the maqām's scale is an integral part of its characteristic melodic progression. Therefore, it is very important to analyze and learn the secondary adjnas of each scale. In Part III, we will analyze the secondary adjnās of each of the maqāmāt that we will learn.

The Turkish Conception of Adjnās

IT IS IMPORTANT that we examine the way Turkish music theory views the subject of the division of the scale into adjnās:

> By this point, it should be obvious that our Turkish theoreticians were not exactly unfamiliar with ancient Greek theory.[3] [...] It is no surprise then, that a cornerstone of their analysis of the makam system is the idea of tetrachords. They recognize a number of "basic" (basit) tetrachords and pentachords. Arel [an important and influential Turkish music theoretician from the beginning of the twentieth century] [...] determined that there were six basic tetrachords: ÇARGÂH, PUSELIK, KÜRDI, RAST, UŞŞAK, and HICAZ. Each is named for a known makam and the tetrachord delineates the most characteristic part of the makam scale [...]. Extending each tetrachord upwards by a large whole tone [...] produces the pentachords of the same name. (Signell 1997: 31)

Adjnās in Turkish music, therefore, can be composed of four or five notes, and each djins can appear either as a tetrachord or a pentachord. The musical scale, which contains eight notes, is always composed of one tetrachord and one pentachord, and these will necessarily be connected (conjunct). In the Turkish system, there are no intervals between the adjnās or at the top end of the scale – the adjnās are always combined as conjunct adjnās.

Let us take the scale of Rāst as an example.[4] In Arab music theory, the scale of Rāst is divided into two adjnās of Rāst, each containing four notes. Between these two adjnās there is an interval of a whole tone:

---

3 It should be noted that the Arabs were aware of Greek music theory much before the formation of the Ottoman Empire and based their own music theory on Greek concepts. Later Turkish theoreticians continued to develop the concepts that they received from the Arabs (D.M.).

4 Turkish music theory uses a different notation system than that of Arab music theory. Names of maqāmāt and adjnās also sometimes differ between these two systems. In this section, I adapted the notation of scales to the Arab system. Arab names appear in parentheses next to the Turkish ones.

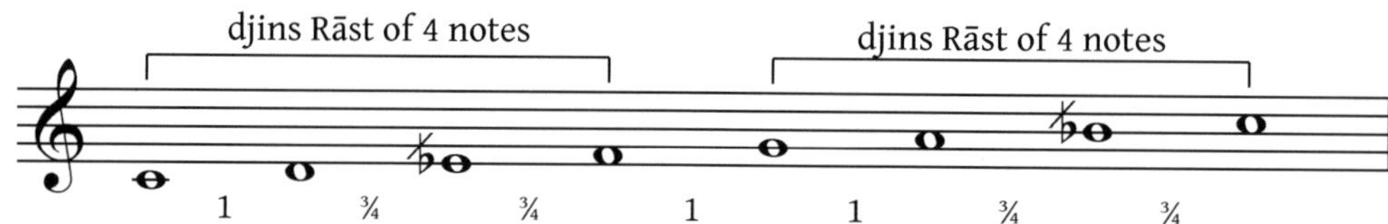

Figure 8.19 The scale of Rāst, and its constituent adjnās, as it is notated in the Arab system

In the Turkish system, the scale is also divided into two adjnās of Rast, but here one of these contains five notes while the other contains four notes. These two adjnās connect on the note G2.

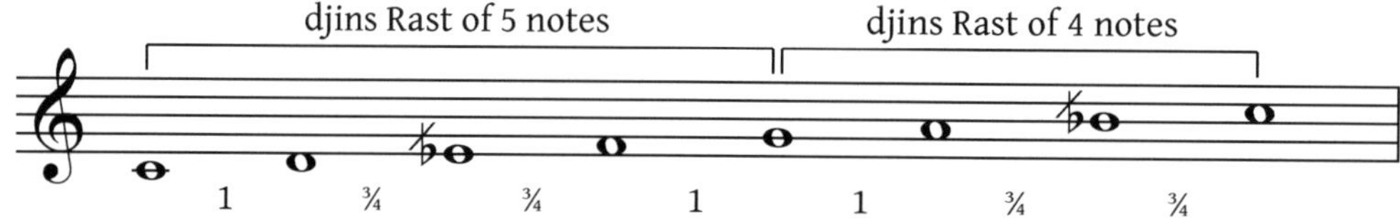

Figure 8.20 The scale of Rast, and its constituent adjnās, as it is notated in the Turkish system

When we examine Turkish scales, we can notice that the two adjnās always connect on the dominant of the scale. We can see it clearly when we examine the scales of Hüseynî and Nevâ (in Arabic: Ḥusaynī and Nawā) as they are notated in Turkish music theory. In both of these scales, the first djins is djins Uşşak (the Turkish equivalent to the Arab djins Bayāt).

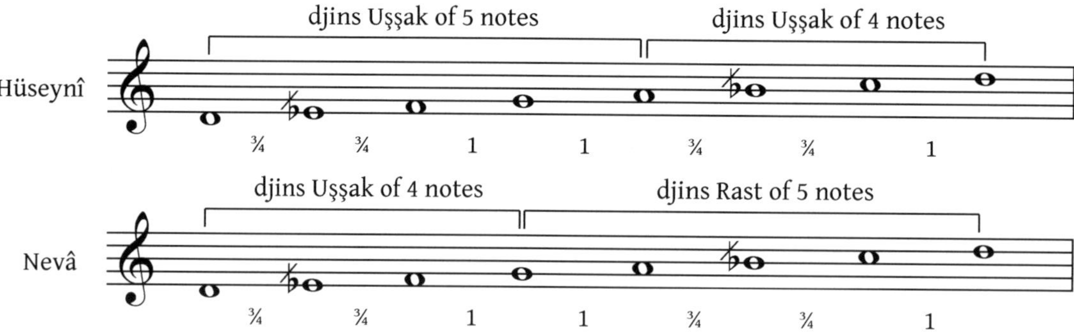

Figure 8.21 The scales of Hüseynî and Nevâ (Ḥusaynī and Nawā) as they are notated in the Turkish system

The two scales in figure 8.21 are identical in terms of their notes and intervals. However, the dominant in the scale of Hüseynî is its fifth note (A2) while the dominant in Nevâ is its fourth note (G2). Therefore, in Turkish theory, the first djins Uşşak (Bayāt) of Hüseynî appears as a pentachord while in Neva it appears as a tetrachord. The remaining notes of the scale change accordingly: In Hüseynî there is a djins Uşşak of four notes placed on the dominant, while in Nevâ, there is a djinns Rast of five notes placed on the dominant.

As we can see from the example above, the system of combining conjunct tetrachords and pentachords to create full eight-note scales is applicable only as long as the dominant of the scale is its fourth or fifth note.

According to Karl Signell (1977: 31-36), Arel distinguished between two kinds of adjnās: (1) "basic" tetrachords and pentachords; and (2) "non-basic," or "other," tetrachords and pentachords.

Basic (Turkish: *basit*) tetrachords and pentachords: These are adjnās in which the fourth note forms a perfect fourth (2½ tones) with the first note of the djins, and the dominant is the fourth or the fifth note. There are six such "basic" tetrachords/pentachords:

1. Çargâh (In Arab music: ʿAdjam on F)
2. Puselik (Nahawand on D)
3. Kürdi (Kurd)
4. Rast
5. Uşşak (Bayāt)
6. Hicaz (Ḥidjāz)

Non-basic, or "other" tetrachords and pentachords: These are adjnās in which the fourth note does not form a perfect fourth with the first note of the djins or the dominant is neither the fourth nor the fifth note. Following are six such non-basic tetrachords/pentachords (their notation adapted to the Arab system):

1. Sabâ (Ṣabā)	Its fourth equals two tones and its dominant is its third note	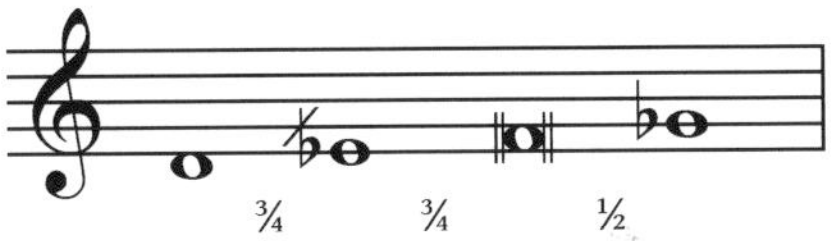 ¾ ¾ ½
2. Segâh (Sīkāh)	Its fourth equals 2¾ tones and its dominant is its third note	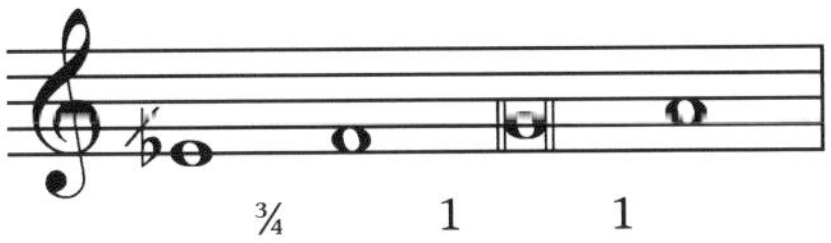 ¾ 1 1
3. Hüzzâm (Huzām)	Its fourth equals 2¼ tones and its dominant is its third note	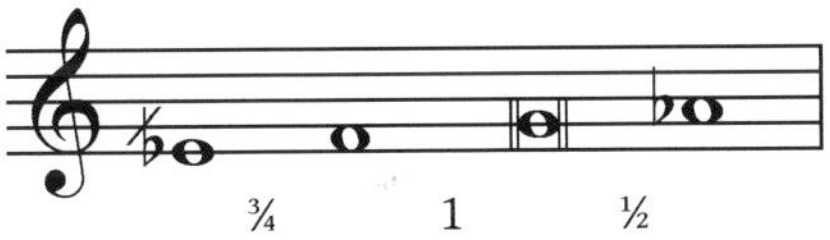 ¾ 1 ½
4. Nikriz (Nakrīz or Nawā-Athar)	Its fourth equals three tones	 1 ½ 1½
5. Pencgâh (Bandjkāh)	Its fourth equals 2¾ tones	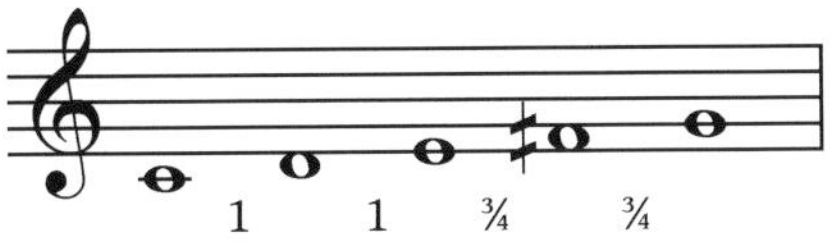 1 1 ¾ ¾
6. Ferahnâk	Its fourth equals 2¾ tones	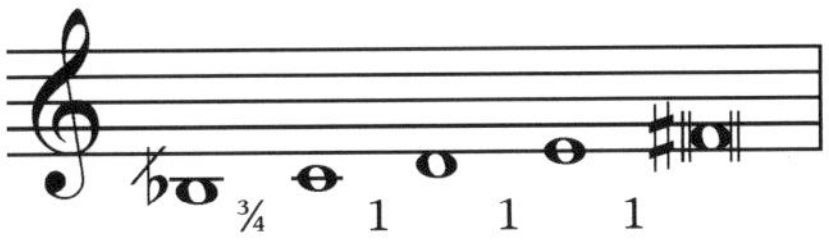 ¾ 1 1 1

Following this classification of adjnās into basic and non-basic, Arel also defined "basic scales" as those scales that are composed of basic tetrachords and pentachords only. According to Arel there are 13 such basic scales, and since they are all presented in the framework of one octave, each one contains one tetrachord and one pentachord. Sometimes the first djins is a tetrachord and the second djins is a pentachord, and sometimes vice versa. "Non-basic scales" are all those scales that contain some non-basic tetrachord or pentachord.

The Arab and the Turkish Conception of Adjnās

I DISCUSSED in detail the Turkish conception of adjnās and their classification and usage according to it, because this is one of the most important subjects of Turkish and Arab music theory. We can use the same kind of analysis for Arab scales as well. Conceptualizing the structure of a scale as a "tetrachord + pentachord" (or vice versa) is an interesting analysis method – it is easier to perceive, both intellectually and visually, and it disposes of the use of intervals between adjnās or at the top end of the octave scale when the adjnās are conjunct. Even the classification into basic and non-basic scales has something that makes it easier to understand the essence of some scales.

Nevertheless, we will stick to the Arab conception of this subject. The Arab conception of adjnās and scale structure is rooted in literature and established by tradition among theoreticians, and it is beyond the endeavor of this book to contradict it, change it, or even deviate from it.

Summary

SOME READERS might wonder why we spend so much time dealing with this headache called *adjnās*. "Why can't we sing and play just using scales. What do we care about the internal structure of the scale?" they might ask. Nevertheless, it is important to be familiar with the adjnās and their functioning in order to fully understand the theory of Arab music, its performance, and the maqām phenomenon in Arab musical culture. There are various reasons for this:

1. The adjnās constituting a scale of a maqām are an integral part of its essence – its nature or "feeling." Most often, when performing a maqām, some of its adjnās are emphasized more than others in the beginning, middle, or end of the performance. In maqām Huzām, for example, djins Ḥidjāz must be emphasized in the beginning; in maqām Faraḥ-Fazā, djins ʿAdjam (a secondary djins of this scale) must be emphasized in the beginning. Knowing the structure of a scale and its adjnās is necessary for proper performance and composition of Arab music.

2. The djins is the most basic organization of intervals in Arab music; it serves as a connecting link between the scale and its constituent intervals.

3. Analyzing scales, knowing their constituent adjnās, and understanding their internal structure makes it easier for the musician to perform maqāmāt, much like assimilating the intervals of scales can help with transposing them.

4. Studying adjnās helps distinguish between scales and become familiar with the differences between them.

5. Studying adjnās helps the musician to better recognize the important notes of the scales. During improvisation, such notes can be turned into temporary tonics.

6. Studying adjnās helps with understanding the classification of maqāmāt into families.

7. Studying adjnās and the internal structure of scales helps with developing proficiency with modulation – a skill that is very important for performing improvisations in Arab music.

CHAPTER 9

REPOSITIONS AND TRANSPOSITIONS IN ARAB MUSIC

Repositions

REPOSITION IS THE method of creating a new scale by moving the tonic to another note within the scale, without altering its notes. Reposition does not change the notes or the intervals between them; therefore, by repositioning the tonic we create a new scale that uses the same notes as the original scale.[1]

By repositioning the tonic to each of the seven notes of the diatonic scalar system, we can produce seven various scales; these are the seven European medieval modes presented in Chapter 2. Repositioning the tonic of a major scale to its sixth note produces its relative minor scale. Out of the seven modes, these two relative scales, the major (Ionian mode) and the minor (Aeolian mode), are the only ones that remained in use in European music. In Arab music, the situation is the opposite. There are many scales, and in the course of history the number of scales did not diminish, but on the contrary – more and more scales were introduced.

Some of the scales used in Arab music are indeed diatonic and correspond to the European modes. In figure 9.1, we can see the various diatonic scales that are used in Arab music. Two of these correspond to the major and minor scales – ʿAdjam corresponds to the major scale (Ionian mode), while Nahawand corresponds to the minor scale (Aeolian mode). There are three other scales that correspond to European modes. Kurd, which corresponds to the Phrygian mode, Lāmī, which corresponds to the Locrian mode, and Nahawand Kabīr, which corresponds to the Dorian mode.

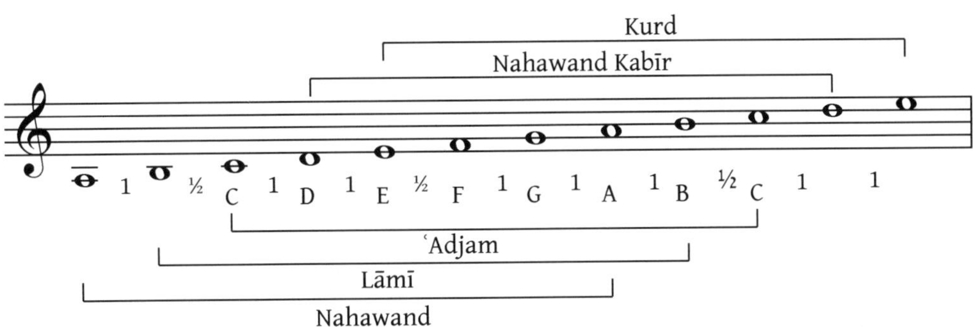

Figure 9.1 Diatonic scales used in Arab music

1 See also Chapter 3.

Another example of scales that are produced by repositioning the tonic is given below in figure 9.2. If we reposition the tonic of the scale of Rāst to its second note, D1, we get one of the most common scales in Arab music – Ḥusaynī. We can say that Ḥusaynī is the *first reposition* of Rāst.

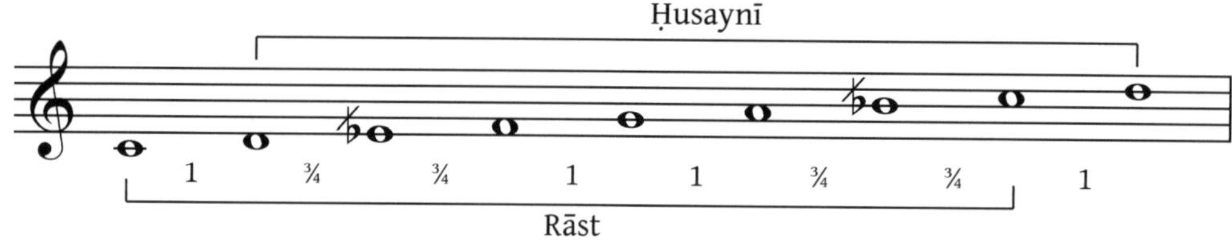

Figure 9.2 The first reposition of Rāst – the scale of maqām Ḥusaynī

When the tonic is moved to the third note of the scale of Rāst (the second reposition), E𝄳1, the resulting scale is composed of the intervals ¾–1–1–¾–¾–1–¾ (tones). This is the scale of Sīkāh – one of the most majestic scales in Arab music.

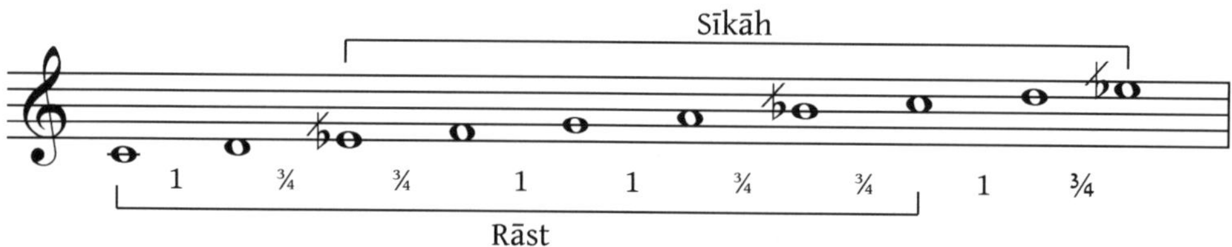

Figure 9.3 The second reposition of Rāst – the scale of maqām Sīkāh

The fact that the scales of Ḥusaynī and Sīkāh are repositions of Rāst does not mean that they belong to the family of Rāst. As we will learn, families of maqāmāt are usually established according to the first djins of the scale. The scale of maqām Ḥusaynī, in which the first djins is djins Bayāt, belongs to the Bayāt family; the scale of Sīkāh belongs to the Sīkāh family, while the scale of Rāst belongs to the Rāst family.

The above scales are only a few examples of how scales in Arab music are formed by reposition. The technique of reposition is one of the reasons why Arab music came to acquire such a profusion of scales – a profusion that is one of its main characteristics. Learning and memorizing the various scalar systems of Arab music and the scales that are produced by their repositions helps composers, performers, and listeners to understand the Arab maqām system, to better analyze the structure of scales, and to recognize maqāmāt easily. If a performer knows how to perform the scale of Rāst, for example, it is easy for him or her to move the tonic one note up, from C1 to D1, and consequently to move to the scale of Ḥusaynī. This technique, which is a form of modulation, is especially important for the Arab musical improvisation – the *taqsīm*.[2] Some of the most common and important scales in Arab music are repositions of the scale of Rāst and of other scales in the system; in Part III, we will analyze these repositions thoroughly.

The Conventional Positions of Scales and Transpositions

The Conventional Positions of Scales

EACH MAQĀM, and its scale, has its own *conventional position* – its "natural" or "traditional" tonic. The system of conventional positions for scales is connected with the structure of musical instruments and is the result of the tradition of musical practice. Arab music theory has adopted these conventions, and each maqām is assigned a tonic on which it is typically presented. On the other hand, the development of musical instruments and the formation of conventional

2 On the taqsīm, see Chapter 10.

positions and absolute pitches for the various scales were affected by the range of the human voice, since Arab music was essentially vocal, and instruments were used mostly for accompaniment.

The conventional position of the scale of Rāst, for example, is the note C1; this note is also called Rāst, and the scale is probably named after its tonic. The scales of Ḥidjāz and Ṣabā, on the other hand, are conventionally positioned on the tonic D1. Some scholars find the issue of conventional tonics to be so important that they classify maqāmāt according to their conventional tonics. In some theory books, all the scales that are conventionally positioned on C1 appear in one section, while all the scales that are positioned on D1 appear in the next section. In Part III, I give a list of maqāmāt classified according to their conventional position or tonic.

We can say that the tradition of music theory and practice has determined that each maqām has its ideal position – the tonic on which it sounds best and on which its unique musical characteristics can be presented in their most essential form. At any rate, it is quite apparent that a maqām sounds a bit different when it is played in a different musical range. This does not mean that each maqām has to be performed on its conventional tonic. Each maqām scale is constructed by combining intervals of various sizes, and as long as these are retained, any scale can be transposed and performed on any other tonic. The scale of Rāst played on the tonic D1, for example, is still the scale of Rāst – as long as its unique combination of intervals is retained. However, when we want to transpose the scale of a certain maqām to a different tonic, we have to consider several factors:

1. **The difficulty of performing the maqām on a tonic that is different from its conventional one.** This usually depends on the musical instruments on which the maqām is performed. Usually, the structure of Arab musical instruments makes it easier to play a maqām on its conventional tonic than on other tonics. In the case of a vocal performance, the range of the singer's voice must be considered; when a musical piece is performed within the singer's range, the singer's voice sounds at its best. In case the conventional position of the scale does not suit the singer's voice range, the tonic should be either raised or lowered.

2. **The absolute pitch that suits the musical piece.** This factor is usually more relevant for vocal music, but it sometimes applies to instrumental music as well. Whether a musical piece is played at a low or at a high range changes the emotional effect it has on listeners. The type of music being performed, whether it be religious, classical, or folk and the emotion it conveys, whether it be happiness, sadness, or love should determine the absolute range in which a piece is performed.

   As we will see later, some scales acquire a new name when they are transposed to a new tonic. The scale of Ḥidjāz-Kār Kurd, for example, is considered a transposition of the scale of Kurd from the tonic D1 to the tonic C1.

3. **The possibilities of performing modulations on the new tonic.** Modulation – the move from one scale to another – is one of the most important characteristics of Arab music and one of its stylistics ideals. Since there are so many scales in Arab music, there are many possibilities for performing modulations within a musical piece. It seems that the practice of modulation became more widely spread at the beginning of the twentieth century. At that time, many songs were still composed in one maqām only; even the first songs of Riyāḍ al-Sunbāṭī (1907–1985), one of the greatest Arab composers of the twentieth century, were composed in this fashion. With time, a new style of composition became fashionable. According to this new style, each verse was composed in another maqām. The pioneer of this style of composition was the composer Zakariyyā Aḥmad (1896–1961).

   Modulation is one of the hardest and most complex crafts in Arab music. It is not a mere move from one scale to another – it is part of the aesthetic tradition of Arab music. There are various intangible rules for modulation, and each maqām carries with it its own possibilities for modulation and the rules of how to perform them. When modulating from the primary scale of a maqām to a new scale, several things have to be considered: which scales can be modulated to, which notes of the primary scale can serve as tonics for the new scales, and how to modulate from a new scale back to the primary scale.

The above issues must be taken into account when we consider transposing a scale. Musicians must ask themselves: "Can this scale be performed with the same ease on a new tonic, in a different range?" It often happens that it is nearly impossible to perform a particular scale on a certain tonic. Sometimes when transposing a scale not all modulations are easy to perform as when the scale is performed on its conventional tonic. On the other hand, other modulations may become easier to perform when the scale is transposed. The answers and solutions to these questions and issues can only be realized by learning and experience.

The Names of Transposed Scales (Taṣwīr)

THE ACT OF transposing a scale to a tonic other than its conventional tonic is called *taṣwīr* in Arabic, which means "copying" or "imitating."[3]

Many times, especially when referring to transposed scales, musicians and scholars would state the note of the tonic next to the name of the scale. For example, when transposing the scale of Rāst to the tonic D1, they say that they are playing "Rāst on D." However, some transposed scales have acquired their own unique names, and they function as independent scales, with their own unique characteristics. The conventional tonic of Nahawand, for example, is C1, and so the scale of Faraḥ-Fazā is said to be a transposition of Nahawand to the tonic G1. In a similar way, the scale of Shadd-ʿArabān is considered as a transposition of Ḥidjāz-Kār from C1 to G1.

These transposed scales cannot be considered as just mere transpositions of other scales. They have their own distinct names and they are considered to be scales of independent maqāmāt. Not every transposition of a scale acquires its own name. The scale of Nahawand when transposed to E, for example, does not have its own unique name; it is simply called "Nahawand on E." Moreover, if we take a musical piece in Nahawand and play it on the tonic G1 instead of on the tonic C1, we cannot then say that it is now played in Faraḥ-Fazā.

We can conclude, therefore, that those transposed scales that acquired their own name have also certain unique characteristics that distinguish them from their original scales.[4] Maqām Faraḥ-Fazā, for example, is treated and performed differently than Nahawand, and therefore the progressions of these two maqāmāt differ. As is illustrated in figure 9.4, a piece in Faraḥ-Fazā, starts usually from the note B♭2 and its surroundings, and explores the scale of ʿAdjam on B♭1. Furthermore, since the performance of Faraḥ-Fazā starts from its second octave, its melody usually descends. Indeed, some Arab musicians would define Faraḥ-Fazā as "a descending Nahawand," but this kind of definition is still insufficient, since this is not the only characteristic that distinguishes it from Nahawand.[5]

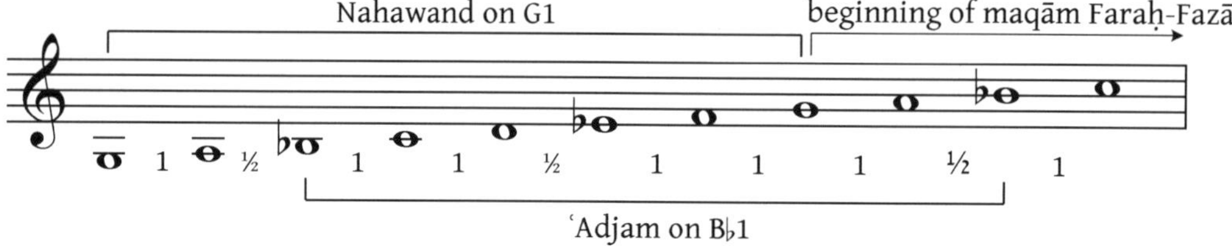

Figure 9.4 The scale of Faraḥ-Fazā and its characteristic performance

Similarly, the scale of Shadd-ʿArabān is performed differently than Ḥidjāz-Kār, though it is considered its transposition. The first djins of Ḥidjāz-Kār is djins Ḥidjāz on C1. However, the first djins of its second octave is djins Nahawand (on C2).

Figure 9.5 The scale of Ḥidjāz-Kār

3 In Turkey, the term used for transposition is *shed* (spelled in Turkish *şed*).

4 In Part III, I discuss the unique characteristics of transposed scales that became independent scales.

5 See also the section on Maqām Faraḥ-Fazā in Part III.

In Shadd-ʿArabān, on the other hand, djins Ḥidjāz appears also in the second octave (on G2).

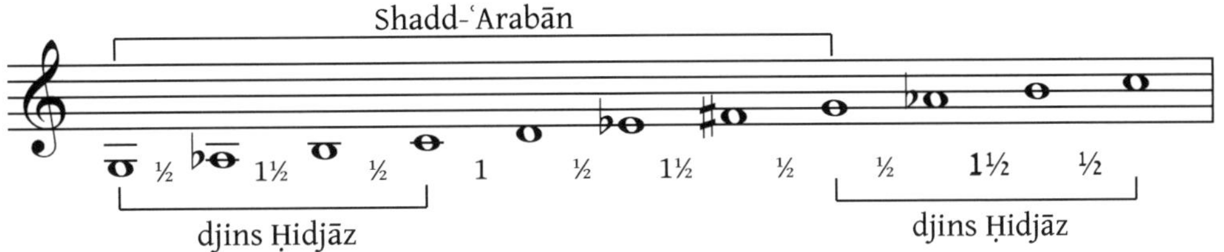

Figure 9.6 The scale of Shadd-ʿArabān

Scales That Require Note Alterations

THE PERFORMANCE of some maqāmāt requires that certain notes in their scales be altered – sharpened or flattened – according to whether the melody ascends or descends. Let us look at the scales of Ḥusaynī and Bayāt for example. These scales are almost identical, but the ghammāz of Ḥusaynī is A2, while the ghammāz of Bayāt is G2, and the sixth note of Bayāt is B♭2, while in Ḥusaynī the sixth note is B𝄳2. The performance of Ḥusaynī requires that the melody start from the area of the note A2 – its ghammāz; it should then explore the notes above A2 – A2, B𝄳2, C2, and D2 – before descending to the tonic D1. When the melody descends, the note B𝄳2 is altered to the note B♭2 – as though it was the scale of Bayāt. In a similar way, in the performance of Bayāt, the note B♭2 is altered to the note B𝄳2 when the melody ascends above the note A – as in the scale of Ḥusaynī. These *note alterations* are some of maqām Ḥusaynī's and maqām Bayāt's most distinctive characteristics – they are essential for presenting the progression of these maqāmāt.[6]

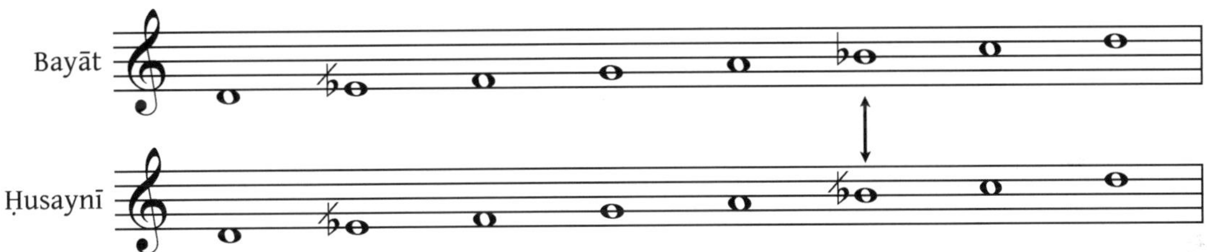

Figure 9.7 The scales of Bayāt and Ḥusaynī

Three methods are commonly used in theory books to demonstrate note alterations when writing down scales. In the first one, the alternative accidental is put in parentheses, as in figure 9.8:

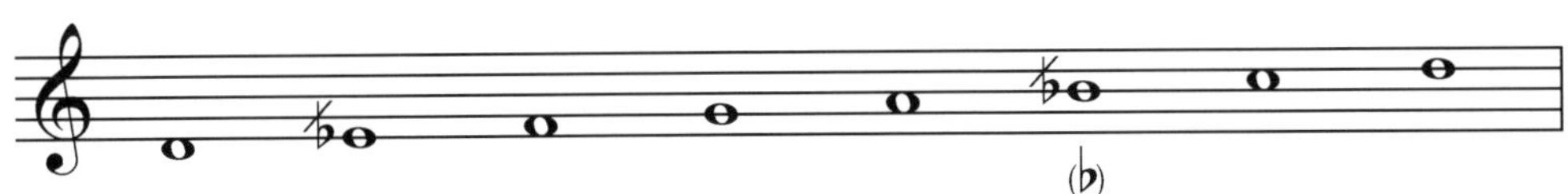

Figure 9.8 The scale of Ḥusaynī with its alternative accidental

Another common way of representing note alterations in the scale is writing the scale in both its ascending and descending forms, as is illustrated in figure 9.9.

Figure 9.9 The scale of Ḥusaynī in both its ascending and descending forms

6 For more about note alterations, see Chapter 3.

Sometimes, the two forms of the scale – the ascending and the descending – are presented in two separate figures; this is usually done for technical reasons and because of the need to analyze the structure of the scale and its constituent adjnās.

Note Alterations as Embellishments

IN ARAB MUSIC, notes are often altered not because it is one of the maqām's characteristics or because of modulation, but as an embellishment to the melody. These note alterations serve as temporary ornaments, their unanticipated appearance adding beauty and "sentiment" to the melody.

In the performance of maqām Nahawand, for example, the fifth note – G2 – is often flattened by a semitone to G♭2 when descending towards the tonic C, as shown in figure 9.10

Figure 9.10 Note alteration as an embellishment in the scale of Nahawand

The same note alteration is also very common in the performance of maqām Ḥidjāz-Kār.

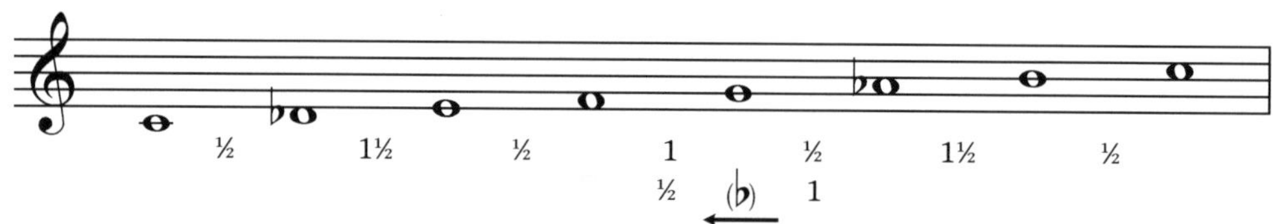

Figure 9.11 Note alteration as an embellishment in the scale of Ḥidjāz-Kār

It must be noted that not every possible note alteration is suitable for every maqām. Each maqām has its own characteristic alterations and those that can be used for its embellishment. Composers and performers keep introducing new types of embellishments and experiment with various kinds of note alterations and modulations. Nevertheless, each of these innovations must be evaluated and aesthetically accepted by experienced listeners of Arab music.

The Profusion of Maqāmāt and Their Various Names

The Names of Maqāmāt

FREQUENTLY, NAMES OF maqāmāt are derived from Turkish and Persian names and words. During the spread of Islam, after the time of the prophet Muhammad, Arabs came into close contact with Persian culture, which at the time was at its peak. Later, a new empire had risen in the Middle East – the Turkish Ottoman Empire. Ottoman music had a tremendous influence on Arab music, which can be seen in the close resemblance between these two musical systems and in the similarities between their scales and scale names, musical genres, and various other features. In Iraq, on the other hand, a distinct musical style had evolved, with its own unique terminology and maqāmāt. The musical system of the Iraqi maqām (*al-maqām al-ʿirāqī*) is quite different from the Syrian-Egyptian musical style that is prevalent in the Middle East and in most of the Arab world. Many of the names of Iraqi scales, even those that are similar to other Arab scales, are derived from Arabic.

The Profusion of Maqāmāt

AS WE LEARNED in this chapter, the profusion of maqāmāt and their scales in Arab music is not only the result of combining the many intervals and notes made available by its system. This profusion is also the result of the tendency of Arab-Turkish musical culture to consider each variation in the way a maqām is performed as a "transformation" of the maqām, which creates a new and distinct maqām. We can conclude that a given maqām may be transformed into a new maqām, with its own distinctive scale and a new and unique name, when one or more of the following happens:

1. The maqām is transposed to another tonic that is not its conventional one.
2. There is a change in the direction of the performance of the maqām or in the area of the scale from which its performance begins. For example, instead of starting the performance from its tonic, the new maqām may start from the ghammāz of the scale.
3. The new maqām emphasizes a certain note that was not emphasized in the original scale.
4. Some notes of the maqām's scale are altered during its performance.

The development of new maqāmāt as a result of introducing various changes to the scales of existing ones is a phenomenon that has often been strongly criticized. Al-Ḥilū, for example, complains about the abundance of names, which burdens the student with unnecessary information, although most maqāmāt are derived from several basic scales. Furthermore, he notes that in many cases, the same identical scale acquired different names in various countries. In Iraq, for example, maqām Bayāt is named ʿArab-ʿUraybūn, and in Turkey, maqām Bayāt Shūrī is named Karciğar (Qārdjighār) (al-Ḥilū 1972: 72). He also claims that there are no differences between the maqāmāt Nahawand, Būsalīk, Faraḥ-Fazā, and Sulṭānī-Yakāh. For him, the scales of all these maqāmāt are just mere transpositions of the scale of Nahawand to various tonics. Similarly, according to him, the maqāmāt Ḥidjāz-Kār and Shadd-ʿArabān are identical (ibid.).

Seemingly, there is much truth in what al-Ḥilū says, and it seems a shame that no standardization of Arab terminology and maqāmāt names was ever established. Not only do the names of maqāmāt vary from place to place in the Arab world, but also do the names of adjnās, notation systems, accidentals, and various other terms. On the other hand, al-Ḥilū's claim that such maqāmāt as Nahawand and Faraḥ-Fazā are just two different names for the exact same maqām is too generalized. Though the group of notes used for any two maqāmāt may be similar or even identical, each maqām has its own distinctive melodic movements and various other unique characteristics, which distinguish it from similar maqāmāt.

The pedagogic solution to this problem is to limit, at least in the first stages, the number of maqāmāt that are being taught. In the beginning of their studies, students should not be overburdened with all available scales and their transpositions; they should only study the most known, common, and important maqāmāt. With time, they will become familiar with other, less known, maqāmāt.

CHAPTER 10

OTHER CHARACTERISTICS OF THE ARAB MUSICAL CULTURE: MODULATION, MONOPHONY, IMPROVISATION, AND THE TAQSĪM

IN PREVIOUS CHAPTERS, we talked about the system of Arab music; we talked about regular and systematic rules and conventions that can be analyzed by using the art and science of music. However, a musical culture cannot be characterized only by its systematic parameters. For example, we cannot characterize Arab music just by its use of microtonal notes or its use of modulation. When we study a musical culture, we must study its tradition of performance and its unique characteristics, and understand the fundamental concepts that have influenced its development.

Music reflects the characteristics of the culture that produced it. Cultural changes, whether caused by contact with other cultures, a change in religious belief, or any other factor, affect music considerably. Nevertheless, cultural changes do not affect music as quickly as they affect other cultural aspects: "Changes in musical culture are, most often, a part of more general cultural changes. Of all the types of changes that take place in a cultural exchange [. . .] music is one of the elements that are most preserved" (Cohen 1986: 31).

The following sections expand on four characteristics of Arab music: modulation, monophony, improvisation, and the taqsīm. The final section of this chapter summarizes the characteristics of Arab music.

Modulation

WE ALREADY DISCUSSED modulation in Chapter 3. *Modulation* is the method of moving from the scale of one maqām to another within a musical piece. *Transposition* – moving a scale from one tonic to another while keeping the structure of the scale and its intervals – is also considered a type of modulation.

Modulation is performed by using notes that are "borrowed" from the scale to which we modulate. Let us take for example the scale of maqām ʿAdjam on the tonic C1 with several notes from its second octave:

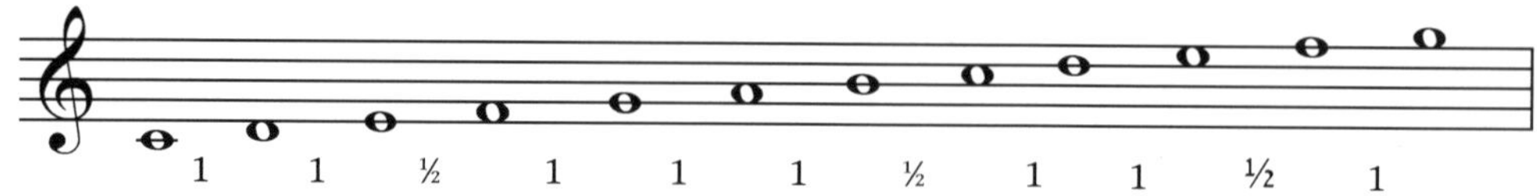

Figure 10.1 The scale of ʿAdjam on C1 with several notes from its second octave

In order to modulate from ʿAdjam on C1 to the scale of Nahawand on G2 (figure 10.2), we need to "borrow" the notes B♭2 and E♭2, which do not appear in the primary scale.

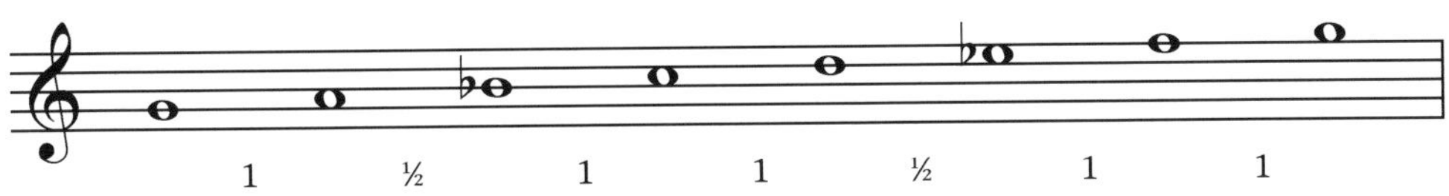

Figure 10.2 The scale of Nahawand on G2

The above example shows us how to modulate from one scale to another by borrowing notes. However, we can borrow a single note, a short musical motif, or a complete musical phrase from another scale and still stay in the framework of the same scale.

Borrowing a Single Note

AS AN EXAMPLE of borrowing a single note, let us look at the scales of Bayāt and Ḥusaynī. In the scale of Bayāt, the sixth note is B♭2, and the scale is written like this:

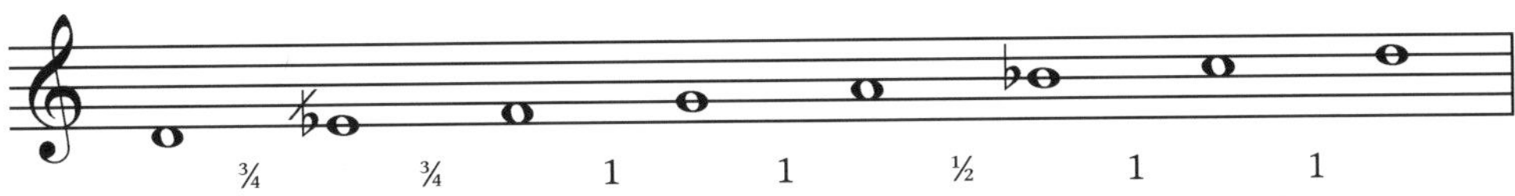

Figure 10.3 The scale of Bayāt

In the scale of Ḥusaynī, the sixth note is B𝄳2, and the scale is written thus:

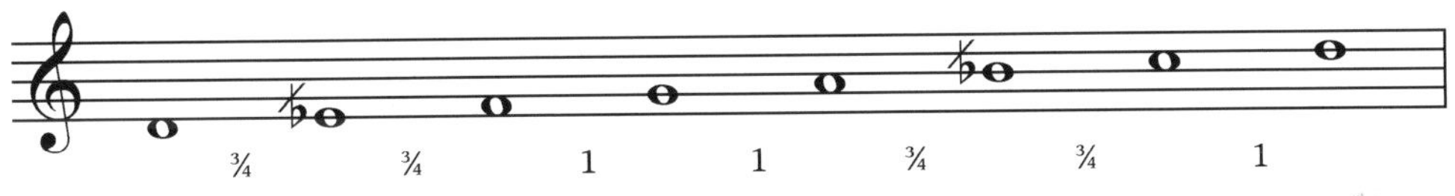

Figure 10.4 The scale of Ḥusaynī

By borrowing, or changing, the sixth note of one of these scales we can modulate between the two.[1]

Not all note alterations can be considered a borrowing of a single note from another scale and, consequently, a modulation. Notes are sometimes altered in the context of a specific scale, either for embellishment or for when there is a need to use a leading note.

For example, in maqām Nahawand, many times the note that is below the tonic is sharpened by a semitone in order to form a leading note to the tonic; for instance, in Nahawand on C1, B♭1 is sharpened to B♮1. Altering this single note to form a leading note is needed in order to emphasize maqām Nahawand's unique melodic characteristics.

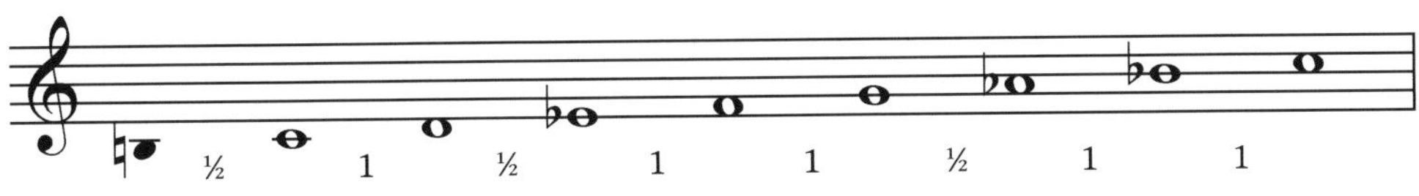

Figure 10.5 The scale of Nahawand with its leading note, B♮1

In the progression of maqām Rāst, the note below the dominant is sometimes sharpened by a semitone in order to form a leading note to it. In the scale of Rāst on C1, for instance, the note F1 is sometimes sharpened to F♯1 when the dominant G2 is emphasized.[2]

1 Other characteristics can be used to distinguish between these scales. See the chapter on the Bayāt family of maqāmāt in Part III.

2 In Turkish music there is a maqām called Pesendide, which employs such a progression.

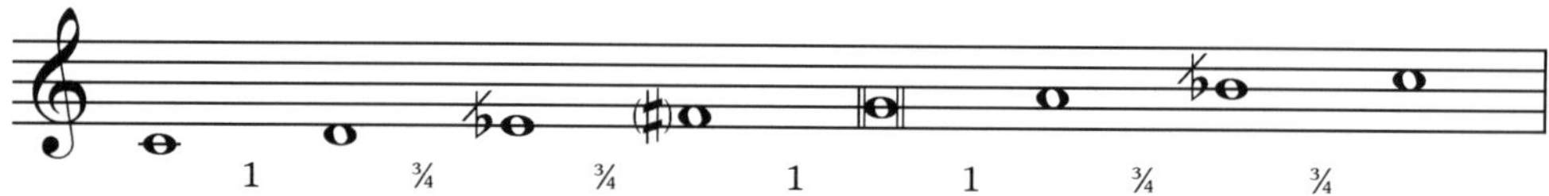

Figure 10.6 The scale of Rāst with F♯1 as the leading note to the dominant G2

These two examples of borrowing a single note show us that when we encounter an alteration of a single note, we have to carefully examine whether this is a move to another scale, that is, a modulation, or it is a mere alteration of a single note in the framework of a particular maqām.

Borrowing a Short Musical Motif

AS AN EXAMPLE of modulation by borrowing a short musical motif, let us look at the scale of Bayāt on the tonic D1:

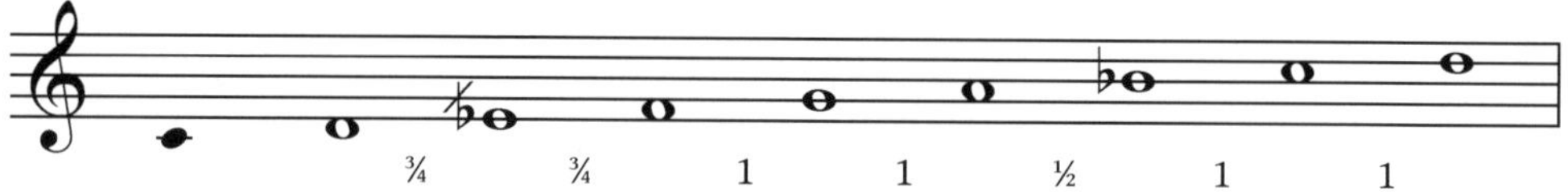

Figure 10.7 The scale of Bayāt

The dominant of maqām Bayāt is G2. If we start the melodic progression on G2, descend to the tonic D1, or even to the note C1, and then ascend back while altering G2 to G♭2, we perform a temporary modulation to maqām Ṣabā, because we form djins Ṣabā on the tonic D1:

Figure 10.8 Djins Ṣabā on D1

However, if we do not stay long on djins Ṣabā and further develop its progression, but return to the scale of Bayāt by descending again to the tonic D1 and ascending back to the note G♮2, then we can say that in the context of performing maqām Bayāt, we "borrowed" a motif from maqām Ṣabā. We did not establish it as a new maqām, nor develop it. This progression can be notated like this:

Figure 10.9 Borrowing djins Ṣabā in the framework of maqām Bayāt

Should borrowing a motif from another maqām for a short time be considered a modulation to this other maqām, or should it be perceived as an embellishment that uses notes from another maqām? In my opinion, it all depends on the extent of borrowing. Not all cases of borrowing notes can be considered a modulation. We must take into account how long we employ the other maqām compared with the total time of the progression in which we employed the borrowed motif. We must examine whether we develop the motif long enough and in a way that establishes the other maqām as the new prevailing maqām, or whether we simply use it as a short diversion, in order to embellish the progression or to create suspense.

We can find examples of borrowing notes and note alterations in many musical pieces, especially in taqāsīm. Sometimes these alterations sound like they direct the melody towards a different maqām than the one that is being played, but these alterations turn back to the primary scale so quickly, it would be difficult to label them as real modulations.

Borrowing a Complete Musical Phrase

WHEN IN THE course of a musical piece in a certain maqām, complete musical phrases are being borrowed from another maqām, then we can say that the music moved, or modulated to another maqām. The musical piece is now based on this other maqām until the next modulation – whether to a third maqām or back to the primary one. This type of modulation is the one discussed in this book.

Modulation is one of the most important musical elements that characterize Arab music. Because Arab music has such a profusion of scales, which are related to one another and are connected to each other, and since Arab music is essentially improvisational, Arab musicians and composers have developed a tradition of moving from one scale to another in the context of a single musical piece. Today, it is hard to find a composed or improvised piece, whether vocal or instrumental, that is based on only one maqām and that does not employ any modulation to other maqāmāt.

The art of modulation has evolved from the unique characteristics of Arab music and has become a cornerstone of Arab musical culture. It is considered one of the most complex aspects of Arab music composition and improvisation because it requires an extensive knowledge of the structure of maqāmāt, their scales, their melodic characteristics, their important notes and melodic progressions, and the relations between them and other maqāmāt.

As an example of modulation, let us take maqām Huzām. The scale of this maqām is composed of two adjnās – djins Sīkāh on B♮1 and djins Ḥidjāz on G2:

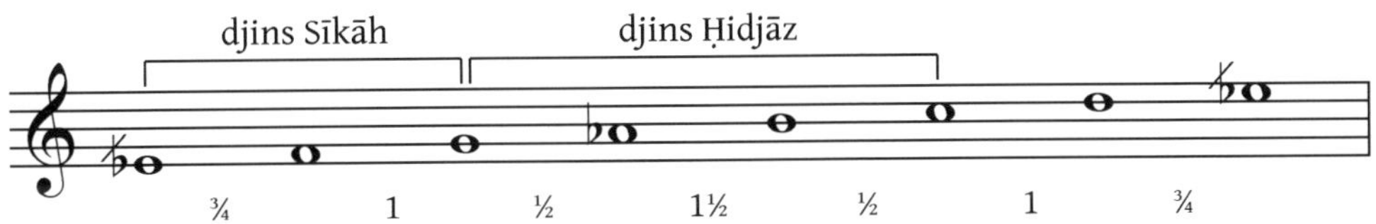

Figure 10.10 The scale of maqām Huzām and its adjnās

The first djins of maqām Ḥidjāz is djins Ḥidjāz. If we want to modulate from the scale of Huzām on B♮1 to Ḥidjāz on G2, we need to emphasize the note G2, make it the new tonic of the new scale and djins Ḥidjāz its first djins, and then ascend with the notes of the scale of Ḥidjāz.

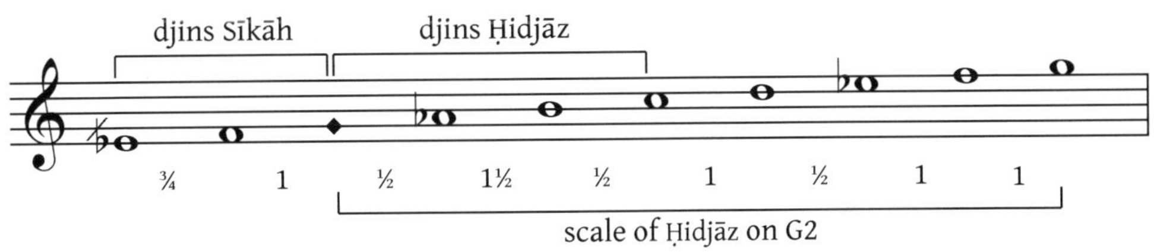

Figure 10.11 Modulating from Huzām on B♮1 to Ḥidjāz on G2

Another possible modulating progression from maqām Huzām is to maqām Ḥidjāz-Kār on C1. By giving emphasis to djins Ḥidjāz on G2, which is common to both scales, we can use it as a point from which to descend to djins Ḥidjāz on the tonic C1:

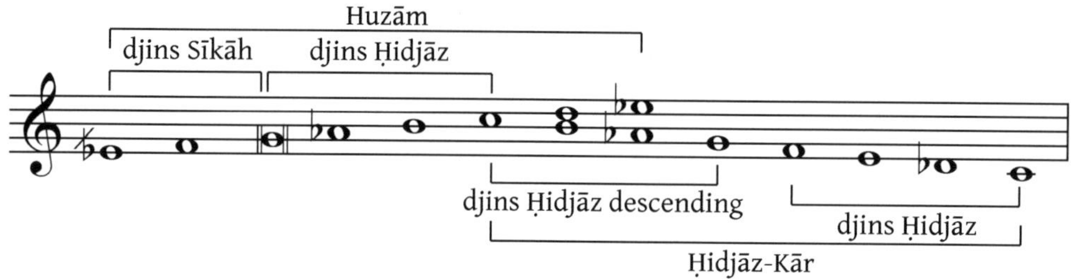

Figure 10.12 Modulating from Huzām on B𝄳1 to Ḥidjāz-Kār on C1

By analyzing the structure of the scale of Huzām and the adjnās from which it is composed, we learned how to perform proper and simple modulations to other scales, such as Ḥidjāz and Ḥidjāz-Kār.

These are examples of how to perform modulations by changing both the tonic and some of the intervals of the scale. Let us look at some examples of how to perform modulations by maintaining the tonic and changing the intervals. The scale of maqām Sūznāk belongs to the Rāst family of maqāmāt and is composed of djins Rāst on C1 and djins Ḥidjāz on G2 in disjunct sequence:

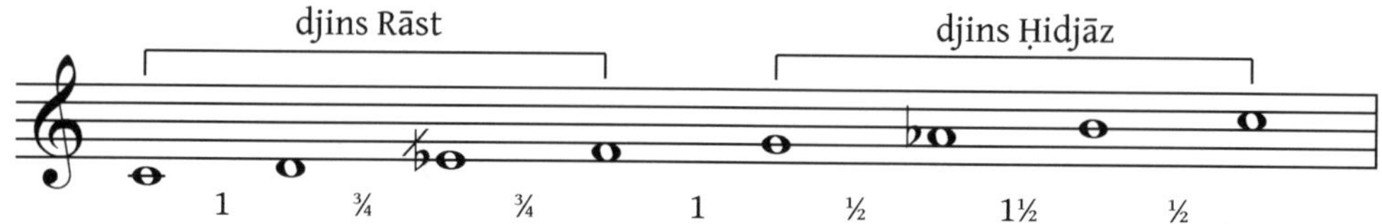

Figure 10.13 The scale of maqām Sūznāk

We can modulate from the scale of Sūznāk to the scale of Ḥidjāz-Kār by ascending to the octave note of Sūznāk, C2, and then descending back to the tonic C1 through the scale of Ḥidjāz-Kār, which is composed of djins Ḥidjāz on C1 and djins Ḥidjāz on G2 in disjunct sequences:

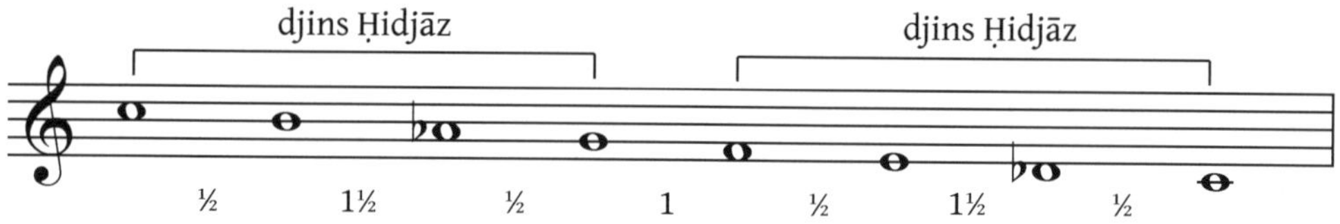

Figure 10.14 Modulating to Ḥidjāz-Kār by descending from the octave note

In this form of modulation, we maintain the tonic of the scale while changing its intervals. Modulation can also be performed by changing the tonic while maintaining the intervallic structure. This type of modulation is actually employing the technique of reposition. Transposing a scale from one tonic to another while maintaining its intervals is also considered a type of modulation.[3]

It is almost impossible to give a complete explanation of the art of modulation in writing. In Part III, we will analyze all maqāmāt and their scales one by one, and I will try to give a few "tips" concerning modulations as much as possible. Nevertheless, even tens and hundreds of written examples cannot teach the student of Arab music the art of modulation, because the theory that underlies these examples is the result of practice. Only listening continually and frequently to this music, while trying to follow it closely, can help the student of Arab music develop the ability to recognize the various Arab scales and their progressions and modulations.

3 See Chapter 3 and Chapter 9 for discussions about the techniques of reposition and transposition.

Monophony

ARAB MUSIC is monophonic, that is, it has only one melodic line. Harmony, or music that employs several voices or parts, is almost completely absent in Arab music, and the use of choirs that sing in several voices is uncommon.

Arab musical pieces employ only one melodic line. Today, Arab music is notated in European staff notation. A composer of Arab music writes only one score, and this score is the same for all players in the ensemble – the violin, the qānūn, and the ʿūd – all play the same score.

This does not mean that all instruments play the exact same melody. Sometimes, the instruments of the ensemble play alternately, or one of the instruments plays solo while the others accompany it in the background and keep rhythm. Later, the melody may be played by another instrument.

A dialogue between the various instruments of the ensemble is very common in Arab music performances – some musical forms, such as the *taḥmīlah*, are based on this kind of musical dialogue. Sometimes one of the instruments is playing solo while the other instruments maintain one continuous note, usually one of the primary notes of the scale, such as the tonic or the dominant.

Even when all the instruments of the ensemble play the same melody together, it is easy to identify each of them and distinguish between them. This is not only because the instruments of an Arab music ensemble produce very distinctive sounds and tones, but mostly because Arab music is essentially improvisational and is played in small ensembles.

Improvisation

IMPROVISATION is one of the unique features of Arab music and it distinguishes it from European music. In Arab music, improvisation does not only mean performing an improvised musical piece, as in the performance of a taqsīm. Improvisation in Arab music is also the freedom given to the performer to add to the basic composed melody various embellishments and slight changes, according to his or her taste and skills. The performer does not have to strictly perform the score written by the composer. The composed piece forms a "skeleton," an outline, which provides the basic melodic content of the piece. The performer performs this outline while adding embellishments and trills, some extra notes, triplets, or glissandos. He or she may slightly change the rhythmic division of notes, the dynamics, or the tempo – all in keeping with the framework dictated by the composed piece.

The text of a composed piece, for example, may contain the motif  . The composer does not usually indicate embellishments, such as trills and glissandos, or the dynamics, like whether it should be played loudly or quietly. It is all in the hands of the performer. The performer may play this motif like this:  , or like this:  , or like this:  . Performers of Arab music have a large variety of embellishments at their disposal, but these must be used in accordance with the tradition and conventions of their musical culture.

Therefore, we can say that the performance style of Arab music is not *syllabic*, but *melismatic*. In a *syllabic style*, each syllable of the text receives one note. In a *melismatic style*, each syllable receives a group of notes called a *melisma*. In Arab music, the notes of the melisma are usually not set by the composer but are added by the performer as a type of embellishment to the core of the melody. This type of melismatic style distinguishes the performance style of Arab music from that of European music.

Each style of improvisation has its unique characteristics, and these can indicate the geographic origin, much like intonation. By identifying the style, an experienced listener can distinguish between an Iraqi, a Turkish, and an Egyptian performance of the same musical piece.

The Taqsīm

IN THE INTRODUCTION to this book, it was said that this book does not discuss any of the Arab musical forms. Nevertheless, I feel it is important to discuss, if only shortly, one musical form, the taqsīm, because it is related to the study of maqāmāt and their scales. The taqsīm, like modulation, is an integral part of Arab musical culture, and therefore I decided to include it in this chapter.

The meaning of the word *taqsīm* (plural: *taqāsīm*) is "division," or "partition." The taqsīm is an improvised instrumental musical form in Arab music. The taqsīm is the most commonly performed and the most important instrumental form in Arab music; it is also the most complicated and difficult form. It offers a unique way to present the maqām and the system of scales related to it.

Similar to the practice of improvisation in Jazz, the taqsīm is a non-composed, unwritten, musical piece, which is improvised by the player at the time of performance. Therefore, the taqsīm is usually played solo, by only one instrument. In the course of the performance, taqāsīm are usually referred to by the instrument that performs them, i.e., "taqsīm ʿūd," "taqsīm kamān (violin)," or "taqsīm qānūn."

A performer can perform a taqsīm as part of a musical program or concert, or as an independent musical piece. The taqsīm is a prominent part of any musical program, such as a strictly instrumental concert or a vocal concert, which includes songs or other vocal forms. Usually, any musical program begins with a taqsīm. A taqsīm can also be performed between one part of the program and another, as well as between musical pieces. For example, if the ensemble plays an introduction to a song, such as a *bashraf*, a taqsīm can be inserted after the bashraf and before the singer starts to sing. Many times the taqsīm serves as a presentation for the following piece. Sometimes it can even be played in the middle of a song or an instrumental piece. It can also serve as an intermission between one song and another, so the singer may rest.

A taqsīm starts in a certain maqām and it is often named after it, i.e., "taqsīm ʿAdjam," or "taqsīm Ḥidjāz." However, the taqsīm is a form that usually presents modulations to other maqāmāt, and modulation is one of the most important aspects of the art of taqsīm. After presenting various modulations, the taqsīm usually concludes on the initial, primary, maqām. The performer is not obliged to conclude the taqsīm in the initial maqām, and many beautiful taqāsīm end in a different maqām than the one they started with. However, it is customary to conclude the taqsīm in the initial maqām.

As was said, the taqsīm is usually played as an introduction to a musical piece, instrumental or vocal. As is the case with the taqsīm, composed Arab musical pieces are also based on a primary maqām, and until the twentieth century, it was customary to name pieces after their primary maqām, i.e., "bashraf (in) Rāst," "samāʿī (in) Nahawand," or "a song in ʿAdjam." In modern times, when composers started diverging from the traditional forms of composition, they stopped naming pieces after maqāmāt and started giving them poetic names, for example, *Rawḍat al-Jamāl* ("The Garden of Beauty") by Farīd al-Aṭrash, and *Bint al-Balad* ("Village Girl") and *ʿAzīza* ("Dear One") by Muḥammad ʿAbd al-Wahhāb. These new pieces were called *qiṭʿah mūsīqiyyah*. Nevertheless, even in these modern pieces, an attentive listener can distinguish a primary maqām, which is the most prevalent one; this maqām is usually the one in which the musical piece starts or ends.

An artist performing a taqsīm must take into account the maqām of the piece that will be performed after it; the taqsīm must be in this maqām and conclude in it. Moreover, the performer of a taqsīm must know the piece that follows it and should refer to its structure and include motifs taken from it. Not all musical pieces in the same maqām share the exact same structure and motifs. They may even differ in the way they make use of the melodic progression of the maqām (sayr al-maqām). The differences in structure, motifs, and progression may change the character of the maqām and the piece. The performer of the introductory taqsīm must take all these considerations into account.

Why must an artist that performs a taqsīm take into account the musical piece that follows it? To answer this question, we must understand the concept of *salṭanā*. The meaning of the term *salṭanā* is "control," or "dominion," and is related to the word Sultan, which means "sovereign." Because of the large number of maqāmāt and scales in Arab music, and because each maqām has its own unique structure, intervals, and emotional connotations and nuances, it is sometimes difficult for singers to move from one maqām to another – from one sentiment to another – without preparation. A singer might also lose his or her intonation and go out of tune when moving from one scale to another.

The instrumental accompaniment is intended to help the singer overcome these potential obstacles, to regain the proper intonation, and to achieve salṭanā, that is, full control, over the maqām that is being performed. The taqsīm that precedes a song has, among other things, a role in helping the singer achieve this salṭanā, and therefore, it should be in the same maqām as the song it precedes and, very importantly, relate to this song.

What is the structure of the taqsīm? The taqsīm is an improvised piece composed of musical phrases. Many scholars think that since the word *taqsīm* means "division," the name of this form refers to the way it is divided into fragments, or phrases, by short pauses. The pauses between the phrases are very short, a few seconds or even shorter, and are used to indicate that one phrase is finished and another one is about to begin.[4] Most often, the taqsīm starts with short, simple, and slow phrases, which are used to convey to the listener the basic structure of the maqām. The taqsīm then continues to develop and to expose the maqām slowly and gradually, phrase by phrase. It starts to employ longer phrases and more complex modulations, and then finally returns to the primary maqām and concludes in it.

As the taqsīm develops, two things happen. Firstly, with each phrase, the melody goes higher and is gradually focused around higher notes. Secondly, the phrases are becoming denser, faster, and more complex and virtuosic.

By stressing these contradicting elements – slow and fast tempo, low and high notes, simple and complex phrases – the performer builds up tension. At the end of the taqsīm, the performer returns to the primary maqām, descends back to the tonic, and concludes on it, usually by using a short concluding phrase called *qaflah*, as well as by slowing down and reducing density. When the taqsīm concludes on the tonic of the primary maqām, the tension accumulated in its development is released.

The taqsīm is unrestricted by meter, that is, its rhythm is not based on a regular beat. The length and density of notes and the tempo of performance are at the artist's hand, and can be changed at will during performance. In some forms of taqsīm, the solo instrument is accompanied by another melodic or percussion instrument that provides a background rhythm; this kind of taqsīm is called *taqsīm ʿalā al-waḥdah*, that is, "rhythmic taqsīm." The rhythmic accompaniment affects the taqsīm and gives it a special quality, but even in a rhythmic taqsīm, the performer is not constricted by any rhythmic formula or meter.

Despite the fact that the taqsīm is not restricted by rhythm or meter, the performer must organize its time structure in a comprehensive way. He must decide about the length of the phrases – where to use short phrases and where to use longer ones. He must decide on the length of the whole taqsīm as well as on the length of the pauses between phrases and between sections; sometimes a very short pause is required, so the following phrase sounds like a continuation of the previous one, while in other times, longer pauses are required in order to distinguish clearly between phrases. According to the tradition of improvising taqāsīm, the tempo of performance changes also with each phrase of the taqsīm. The abstractness of the rhythm of the taqsīm is what makes the performance of a taqsīm such a difficult and complex art.

According to Taiseer Elias, who dealt extensively with the research of the taqsīm in Arab musical culture, the taqsīm has a "hidden" or "concealed" underlying rhythm, which can be discerned by careful listening. According to Elias's conclusions, since any musical piece is related to time, it must have a rhythm. Although the taqsīm does not have an obvious rhythmic framework, the various rhythmic motifs that change during the course of the taqsīm's performance and the time structure of the taqsīm outline this concealed, imperceptible, rhythm (Elias 2007).

Although the taqsīm is an improvisational form, the performer cannot just play whatever notes he or she wants and disregard all aesthetic rules. In Arab music, there are strict rules regarding improvisation. Without adhering to these rules, the musician cannot produce a taqsīm that has a high artistic value. These rules are learned and acquired primarily by constant and frequent listening to taqāsīm, and also by trying to follow the progressions of these taqāsīm and by imitating them. In the next stage after imitating other artists, the student starts combining these learned progressions, phrases, and motifs with original ideas of his or her own.

The opening and closing motifs and progressions in each phrase or section of the taqsīm are very important. Some progressions are considered traditional while others were composed by artists, and with time, have become a part of the repertoire of the motifs used in the taqsīm. These progressions and motifs must be learned and taken into

4 See also Arnon 2008.

consideration when performing a taqsīm. A bad concluding phrase might "kill" a taqsīm, even if it was superb all along up to the end.

Although the performer of a taqsīm has a lot freedom in choosing which modulations to perform, there are aesthetic rules that govern which modulations are acceptable and appropriate. They determine to which maqāmāt the taqsīm should modulate, which scales should be emphasized and which ones should only be hinted, and through which scale the taqsīm should modulate back to its primary maqām – the one that concludes the phrase, the section, or the whole taqsīm. There are also rules that establish which are the important notes of the scale, which notes should be emphasized, and which should be used as new tonics for modulations.

These are only some of the significant characteristics of the taqsīm, and this chapter is far from covering the whole subject. The taqsīm form is the ideal form for representing a maqām, and usually, whenever a musician wants to illustrate a maqām, its scale, and its melodic progression he or she uses a taqsīm; therefore, the audio examples that are included on the attached CD are all in the form of taqāsīm. This is why it is important to explain this important musical form.

Summary of the Characteristics of Arab Musical Culture

THE WIDE USE of modulation and improvisation in Arab-Turkish music and its monophonic texture have formed various characteristics that are summarized in the following sections:

- **Vocal Music:** The origin of Arab music, as with almost all other musical cultures of the world, lies primarily in the human voice. Arab music was a music of singing. Instrumental accompaniment was of secondary importance and was used only to back up the singer, who was the center of the performance; it was simple and usually consisted of only one melodic or percussion instrument. Such a conception was held in Arab countries up to modern times, when instrumental music started to become more prominent and widespread.

- **Small Ensembles:** Even when instrumental accompaniment became widespread, the accompanying ensemble was, until recently, a small one, and included only one representative of each instrument. The Iraqi ensemble known as the *djālghī baghdād* consisted of only two melodic instruments – the *sanṭūr* and the *djūzah* – and two percussion instruments – the *darbūkah* and the *riqq* (a small frame drum). The Egyptian *takht* ensemble consisted of a violin, an *ʿūd*, a *qānūn*, a *nāy* flute, and percussion instruments. Two players, one playing a melodic instrument and another playing a percussion instrument, can form an ensemble that can play Arab instrumental music or serve as an accompaniment for a singer.

- **Improvisation and Small Ensembles:** Because Arab music is improvisational, it is usually performed in small ensembles that consist of only a few instruments; naturally, many instruments cannot improvise all together without causing confusion. It is hard to know what came first – whether improvisation is a consequence of the performance in small ensembles, or its cause. Today we know that these two characteristics of Arab music are interrelated.

- **Musical Instruments:** The structure of musical instruments and their characteristics have a close relation with the musical culture in which they are used. Again, it is hard to know whether the fact that Arab music was vocal is what caused the development of the instruments that are used to perform it, or whether these instruments were adopted from other cultures and influenced the development of this music. At any rate, there are interrelations between the two.

- **The Performing Artist as a Composer:** Because of the improvisational nature of Arab music, and specifically the taqsīm form, in which the artist "composes" at the time of performance, the performer of Arab music is also a "composer in real-time." He or she interprets the melodic material of the musical piece and the maqām in a unique individual way.+

- **Improvisation is Obligatory:** In Arab music, improvisation is obligatory – it is not an option. Performing the music only according to the score that is in front of the performer is unacceptable in Arab musical culture. Listeners expect that songs that they know be performed in a new way and include improvisation as a way of varying the performance and creating new and surprising elements.

- **Interaction between the Audience and the Performer:** Because in Arab music the artists are actually composing music at the time of performance, an interesting interaction has developed between the audience and the performers. The audience listens to the music, and when they enjoy it, they may reach the state of *ṭarab*, which may be translated as "ecstasy," or "elation." When such a thing happens, the audience feels that they need to express their satisfaction and joy, to thank and cheer the artists, so they continue or even repeat the melodic progression or development that was just performed. Therefore, the audience may interfere with the course of the performance, applaud, shout, interject, or even give money to the performers. Arab musicians expect such reactions – an indifferent audience, which is not participating in the concert by cheering, would not cause the performers to elevate and give their best, and the performance might therefore be a dull one.

- **The Participation of the Audience in the Performance:** Because of the interaction between the audience and the performers, it is not uncommon that the audience "takes part" in the performance by singing along or humming the music. In the past, ensembles did not usually perform in big concert halls or before a large inhomogeneous crowd, but in private houses and small places, such as cafés, and in front of a small audience. The ensemble and the listeners were practically sitting together and at the same eye level. Even a smile or a wink could act as a message directed at the musician, and an expression of emotions was not a rare thing.

- **The Introduction of Large Orchestras and Westernization:** In the second third of the twentieth century, many large orchestras with many instruments were established, mostly in Egypt, based on the model of European symphonic orchestras. At the same time, European musical instruments that were not used before, such as the guitar and the accordion, were introduced. These orchestras played on stages in large concert halls. The audience no longer sat around tables, eating and drinking, but on numbered chairs organized in parallel rows. The musicians could no longer improvise freely as before; a group of eight or ten violinists, for example, now needed to play the same part, exactly like in a philharmonic orchestra. Solo instrumental parts, which were intended to display the musicians' improvisation skills, were now restricted to short, in-between, sections. The interaction between the audience and the performers was damaged, and improvisation lost its high status and was used more scarcely. Music has lost some of its power and its essence. Some interaction between singers and the audience remained when the concert evolved around one star singer, with an orchestra accompanying him or her. Then, the singer still had some freedom to improvise. Overall, however, Arab instrumental orchestras have become somewhat detached from the music that gave rise to them.

This development, which is highly criticized by many Arab musicologists and musicians, is, of course, inevitable. The effects of westernization on Arab countries have become stronger the more the latter were exposed to modern developments in the fields of transportation and communication. One of the first effects of westernization took place at the end of the nineteenth century, when the European violin has become the prominent bowed instrument of Arab music, and the traditional *kamān* and *kamāndjah* were neglected.

Muḥammad ʿAbd al-Wahhāb (1907–1991), the famous Egyptian singer and composer, was one of the greatest Arab composers of the twentieth century. He was a remarkable innovator and introduced many elements of European music in his compositions and orchestrations. In his pieces, both vocal and instrumental, ʿAbd al-Wahhāb managed to do so without losing the essential characteristics of Arab music. However, not all composers have managed to maintain such a perfect balance, and many of us might say that it is regretful.

PART III

ARAB MAQĀMĀT AND THEIR SCALES

THIS PART OF the book presents in detail 48 of the most common and important maqāmāt of Arab music.

I divided the maqāmāt into "families." The "family name" of a maqām is determined by its first djins; all the maqāmāt that have the same first djins are assembled under one family name. For instance, the family of Rāst includes maqām Rāst, obviously, as well as other maqāmāt that have djins Rāst as their first djins, such as Sūznāk, Māhūr, and Yakāh.

Each chapter of Part III deals with one family of maqāmāt. The introduction to each chapter supplies general information concerning the family it deals with. The first maqām that appears in each of the chapters is the maqām that carries the family name. The chapter on the ʿAdjam family, for example, starts with maqām ʿAdjam, and the chapter on the Nahawand family presents maqām Nahawand first. This part of the book serves as a kind of index to the most commonly used maqāmāt in Arab music.

Attached to this book is an audio CD containing musical examples, performed as taqāsīm, which illustrate almost all the maqāmāt that appear in this part. These musical pieces are performed by the qānūn master Abraham Salman, one of the greatest qānūn players in the Middle East. I thank him for his contribution.

CHAPTER 11

CLASSIFYING ARAB MAQĀMĀT AND THEIR SCALES

IN PREVIOUS chapters, we discussed Arab maqāmāt, explored their general structure, and learned various terms and general concepts related to Arab music. In the following chapters, we will devote our discussion to the analysis of maqāmāt and their scales. Each maqām will be discussed individually.

There are various methods for classifying Arab maqāmāt. Let us look at the three most common methods of classification: according to tonic, according to intervals, and according to family.

Classification according to the Conventional Position (the Tonic) of the Scale

ACCORDING TO this method, maqāmāt are classified according to their conventional position, or tonic. The listing of maqāmāt starts with all those maqāmāt that are positioned on the tonic G1 (Yakāh), then with all those positioned on the tonic A1 (ʿUshayrān), and so forth. The maqāmāt, Rāst, Ḥidjāz-Kār, and Nahawand, for example, are all listed under the tonic C1 (named Rāst), because this is their conventional tonic. Bayāt, Ḥidjāz, and Ṣabā are all listed together, because their conventional tonic is D1 (Dūkāh). This method of classification is employed by al-ʿAbbas (1986) and by al-Ḥilū, who gives a complete list of scales classified according to this method (1972: 88ff.). Following is a list of all the scales that appear in Part III of this book classified according to their tonic. The names that appear in parentheses are the Arabic names of these tonics.[1]

1. **G1 (Yakāh)**
   Faraḥ-Fazā, Sulṭānī-Yakāh, Shadd-ʿArabān , Yakāh

2. **A1 (ʿUshayrān)**
   Ḥusaynī ʿUshayrān, Nuhuft, Sūzdāl

3. **B♭1 (ʿAdjam or Qarār ʿAdjam)**
   Adjam-ʿUshayrān, Shawq-Afzā

4. **B𝄳1 (ʿIrāq)**
   ʿIrāq, Rāḥat al-Arwāḥ, Bastah-Nikār, Awdj

5. **C1 (Rāst)**
   ʿAdjam, Sūzdalāra, Nahawand, Nahawand Muraṣṣaʿ, Ḥidjāz-Kār-Kurd, Ṭarz Nawīn, Nawā-Athar, Nakrīz, Ḥidjāz-Kār, Zandjarān, Rāst, Sūznāk, Māhūr, Nayrūz, Dalanshīn.

1 For names of notes, see Chapter 6.

6. **D1 (Dūkāh)**
   ʿUshshāq Miṣrī, Būsalīk, Kurd, Lāmī, Ḥiṣār, Ḥidjāz, Shāhnaz, Nishābūrk, Bayāt, Bayāt Shūrī, Ḥusaynī, Ṣabā, Ṣabā Zamzama, Muḥayyar.

7. **E𝄳1 (Sīkāh)**
   Sīkāh, Huzām, Awshār, Mustaʿār, Mukhālaf

8. **F1 (Djahārkāh)**
   Djahārkāh

The list above shows that many scales are positioned on the tonics C1 (Rāst) and D1 (Dūkāh). This indicates the structural importance of these two notes, which is probably due to their position in the middle of Arab music's range of notes.

Classification according to the Types of Seconds from which the Scale Is Formed:

IN HER BOOK *East and West in Music*, Cohen presents an attempt to classify Arab scales according to the types of seconds from which they are formed (1986: 111-112).

With her kind permission, I reproduce here one way of classification, taken from her book.

Adjnās that include microtonal seconds

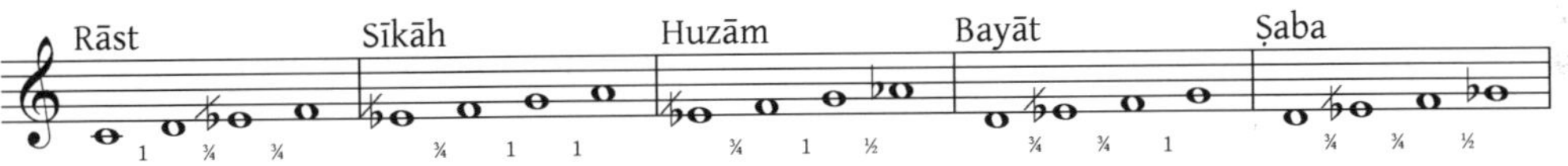

Adjnās that do not include microtonal seconds

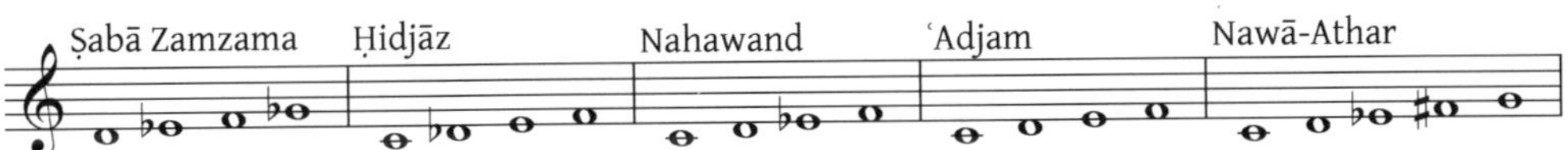

Māqām scales that include adjnās with microtonal seconds

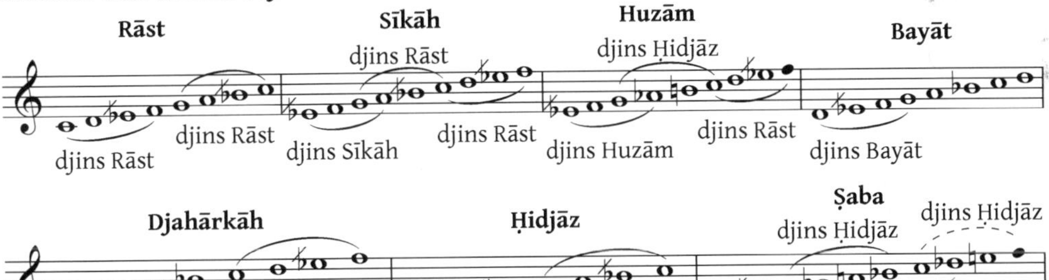

Māqām scales that do not include adjnās with microtonal seconds

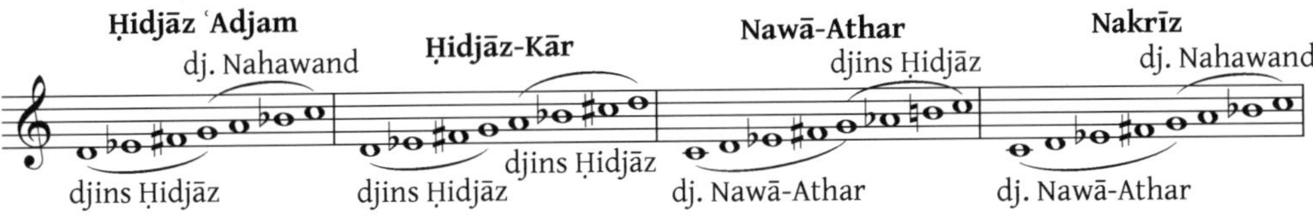

Figure 11.1 Classification of adjnās and maqām scales according to the types of seconds they include (Cohen 1986: 111-112)

Figure 11.1 is an example of a classification of adjnās and scales of maqāmāt into two main groups: those that include microtonal seconds (i.e., three-quartertones, five-quartertones) and those that include only seconds that are either semitones or their multiplications (i.e., semitones, whole tones, augmented seconds). In fact, it is a classification into two groups: scales that cannot be performed on equal-tempered instruments, such as the guitar and the piano, and those that can be performed on such instruments.

Classification according to Families of Maqāmāt

IN THE SYSTEM of Arab music theory, a maqām's family is determined by the first djins of its scale, and is named accordingly. The first djins of the scale Ḥidjāz, for example, is Ḥidjāz, and its conventional tonic is D1. The first djins of Shadd-ʿArabān is also Ḥidjāz, and its conventional tonic is G1. Though these two scales do not share the same tonic, they belong to the same family – the Ḥidjāz family – because they both have djins Ḥidjāz as the first djins of their scales.

The melodic characteristics of a maqām are determined largely by its first djins, because the first djins is the one that leads to the conclusion of the progression of the maqām on its tonic. Scales of the same family may sound similar and their close relation may be recognized by ear. By passing through the first djins of a family of maqāmāt, it is easy to modulate to other maqāmāt from the same family.

In this part of the book, I use the method of classifying maqāmāt into families. I think that this method is preferable to the method of classification according to the tonic. Classifying maqāmāt into families makes it easier to understand their structure and their proper performance. In all maqāmāt of the same family, the first djins is identical, and it is easier to explore various possible modulations when they are grouped together.

In order to make it easier for readers with a background in European music theory, I first present those families of maqāmāt that are formed of intervals that are semitones or their multiplications, such as ʿAdjam, Nahawand, Kurd and Nawā-Athar. Next, I present the family of Ḥidjāz, which is based essentially on semitones, but sometimes introduces quartertonal (microtonal) intervals. The final chapters present scales that are based mainly on quartertonal intervals, such as Rāst, Bayāt, Sīkāh, and Ṣabā.

Each section about a maqām is divided into several categories, which give detailed explanations concerning various aspects of the maqām:

The Scale

THE SCALE OF each maqām is presented within the framework of one octave. The scale represents the "group of notes" that is used for the exposition of the maqām's progression. Presenting the scale within one octave only does not always give all the notes that are used by the maqām. Such additional notes, either taken from adjacent octaves, borrowed from other scales, or just used as embellishments, are usually discussed in the section devoted to the analysis of the scale.

When necessary, I give both the ascending and descending scales of the maqām. If the scale is presented only in its ascending form, it means that the descending scale is composed of exactly the same notes as the ascending one, unless it is noted otherwise.

Analysis of the Scale

THE ANALYSIS starts by presenting the various adjnās that constitute the maqām and its scale, giving the primary and secondary adjnās separately. I then explain the structure of the scale and, when necessary, I mention some of the additional notes that are used by the maqām. Wherever I found in literature some contradicting opinions and views concerning the analysis, I tried to present and explain them.

The Name of the Maqām

HERE I GIVE information concerning the name of the maqām, its origin and its meaning, and its relation to names of notes and to other maqāmāt in the Arab system.

The Conventional Position (Tonic)

THIS SECTION gives the note that is conventionally used as the tonic of the scale in the Arab musical system.

Repositions

HERE I LIST the various scales that can be formed by repositioning the tonic to another note within the scale of the maqām.

Transpositions

IF THERE ARE any transpositions of the scale that form new maqāmāt, with their own names and unique characteristics, they are discussed in this section.

Modulations

IT IS ALMOST impossible to teach and explain modulation in writing. Yet, suggesting several modulation progressions can still prove beneficial. These can form a methodological basis for students, so they can later expand their knowledge of this subject in practice. I usually give the simplest and most basic modulations that are typical for each maqām.

The Progression of the Maqām

THE SCALE OF a maqām can only give us the notes that are employed by it; the scale does not give information concerning the way – or **how** – these notes are to be used in its performance. Each Arab maqām has its own melodic characteristics and a unique way in which the notes of its scale are combined for its exposition that is termed the *melodic progression* of the maqām, and in Arabic, *sayr al-maqām*. This section gives a detailed account of how the maqām is typically exposed, or "treated." It relates to issues such as the direction of the progression, that is, whether it is ascending or descending, the notes that should be emphasized or embellished, and the way the tonic is approached in the conclusion.

Musical Examples

THE CD attached to this book contains musical examples, in the form of taqāsīm, to most of the maqāmāt discussed here. Listening to these examples can teach students and help them remember the progressions of these maqāmāt better than any written explanation. The number of the CD track of the performance of the maqām appears in each section next to the name of the maqām, inside a CD icon; it looks like this:

CHAPTER 12

THE ʿADJAM FAMILY OF MAQĀMĀT

1. **Maqām ʿAdjam**
2. **Maqām ʿAdjam ʿUshayrān**
3. **Maqām Djahārkāh**
4. **Maqām Shawq-Afzā**
5. **Maqām Sūzdalāra**

MAQĀM ʿADJAM, which corresponds to the major scale (the Ionian mode) of European music, is one of the most popular and favorite maqāmāt. It combines nicely with maqām Ṣabā, maqām Bayāt and maqām Shawq-Afzā.

Together with Nahawand, Kurd, Lāmī, and Nahawand Kabīr, maqām ʿAdjam is one of the Arab scales that are diatonic. All the scales in the ʿAdjam family start with djins ʿAdjam (1–1–½ tones) and return to the tonic through the same djins. Therefore, we list them as belonging to one family.

1. Maqām ʿAdjam

The Scale

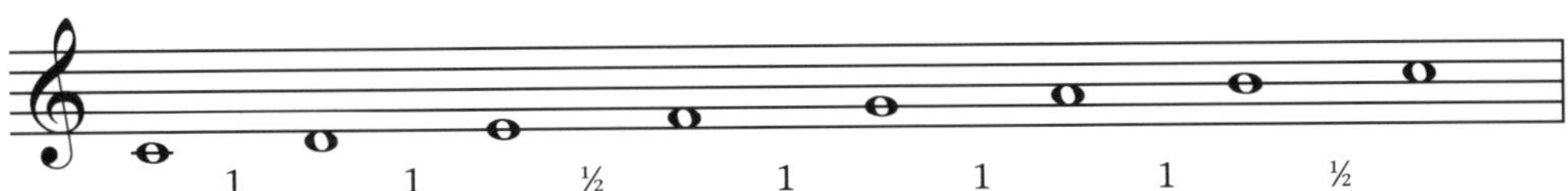

Intervals: 1–1–½–1–1–1–½ (tones)

Analysis of the Scale

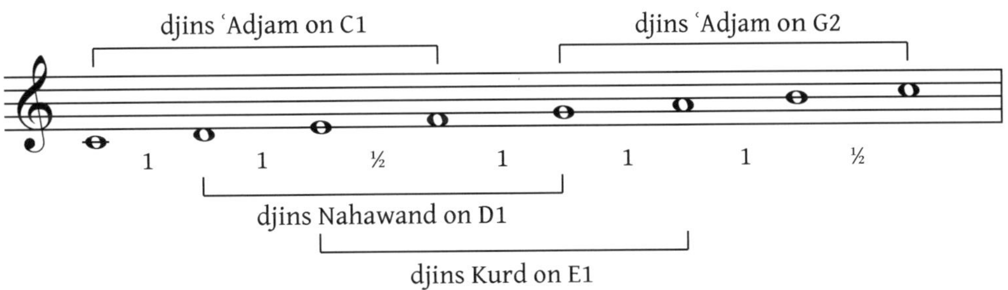

Adjnās

Primary adjnās:	djins ʿAdjam on C1 djins ʿAdjam on G2 (disjunct adjnās)
Secondary adjnās:	djins Nahawand on D1 djins Kurd on E1

The Name

THE TERM *ʿadjam* or *ʿadjamī* was used by the Arabs to refer to anything that is non-Arab, including people and nations. The name "Bilād al ʿAdjam" ("The Land of the Strangers") was particularly used when referring to Persia. Therefore, some scholars assume that maqām ʿAdjam was borrowed from another musical culture and it entered the Arab system at a later stage than other maqāmāt. However, al-Mahdī notes that this scale was already mentioned in the tenth century by the theoretician al-Iṣfahānī (d. 967) in his book *Kitāb al-Aghāni* (19??: 43).

As we will see below, there are many contradictions between available sources as to the use of the name and the conventional position of the scale. Some sources list other scales, such as Māhūr, Djahārkāh, and ʿAdjam ʿUshayrān, under the title of ʿAdjam. These scales are indeed related to the ʿAdjam scale, and may be derived from its transpositions, yet, as maqāmāt, we must consider them separately.

The Conventional Position

SOME SCHOLARS position maqām ʿAdjam on the tonic C1 (Rāst), as it is written above. This is the way Mashʿal notates it (1952: 18), though he calls it also Māhūr. Other sources do not mention ʿAdjam at all but only ʿAdjam ʿUshayrān, which is positioned on B♭1 (al-Ḥilū 1972: 100; al-Mahdī 1990: 43).

In practice, positioning ʿAdjam on C1 fits the generally accepted Arab scalar system. This way, it is positioned on a central note, in a position that is convenient for its performance. ʿAdjam is related to maqām Rāst, which is also positioned on C1, and it is easy to modulate between these two maqāmāt. Al-Nur maintains that C1 is the conventional position of ʿAdjam. He suggests that ʿAdjam ʿUshayrān was invented or developed by the Turks because it combines nicely with maqām Bayāt on D1 – one of the most common and popular scales in Arab and Turkish music.

Repositions

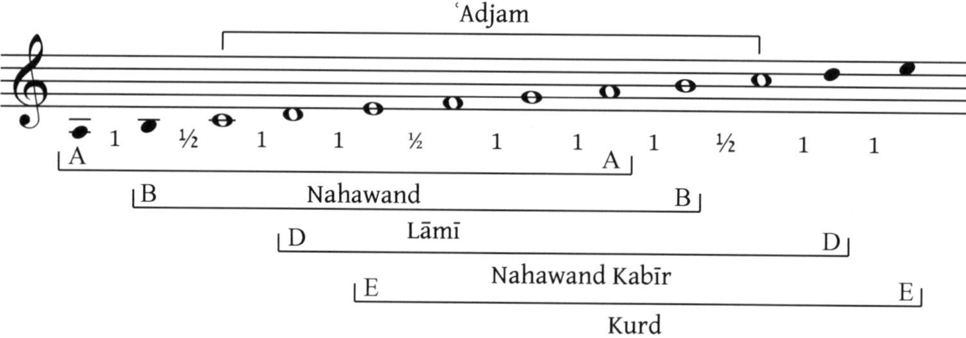

THE FIFTH reposition up, or the second reposition down, of ʿAdjam forms the scale of Nahawand. In ʿAdjam on C, this is a reposition to A.
The sixth reposition up, or the first down, forms the scale of Lāmī. In ʿAdjam on C, this is a reposition to B.
The second reposition up forms the scale of Kurd. In ʿAdjam on C, this is a reposition to E.
The first reposition up – to D1 – forms the not-so-common scale of Nahawand Kabīr.

Transpositions

AS WE HAVE noted above, when the scale of ʿAdjam is played on the note B♭1, it is named ʿAdjam ʿUshayrān. Sometimes, when ʿAdjam is played on C1, it is called Māhūr, though many writers point to small differences in intervals between Māhūr and ʿAdjam.

Modulations

Modulating by reposition: This is the easiest way to modulate in maqām ʿAdjam. When performing ʿAdjam on C1, we can move to E1, make it the tonic, and modulate to Kurd. We can then return to C1 (the conventional tonic of ʿAdjam) and reestablish ʿAdjam effortlessly.
Similarly, we can modulate to Lāmī on B1 if we establish B1 as a temporary tonic.

When we want to return to the tonic C1, we can return from B1 to C1 like this: 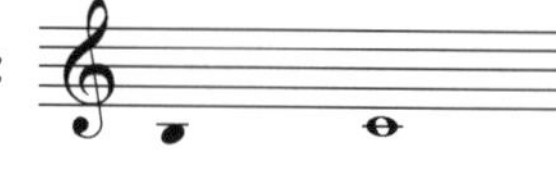

We can also go up an octave to C2, like this: 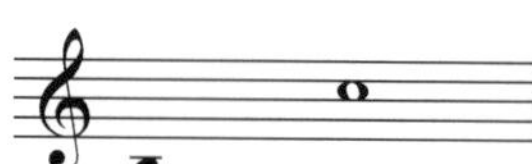

Another possibility is to ascend stepwise like this: 

Modulating by retaining the tonic and changing the intervals: Another way to modulate is by retaining the tonic of the primary scale and changing the intervals to form a new scale.

If we ascend on the scale of ʿAdjam from C1 to C2, we can descend through the scale of Rāst by altering the notes B2 and E1 to B𝄳2 and E𝄳1:

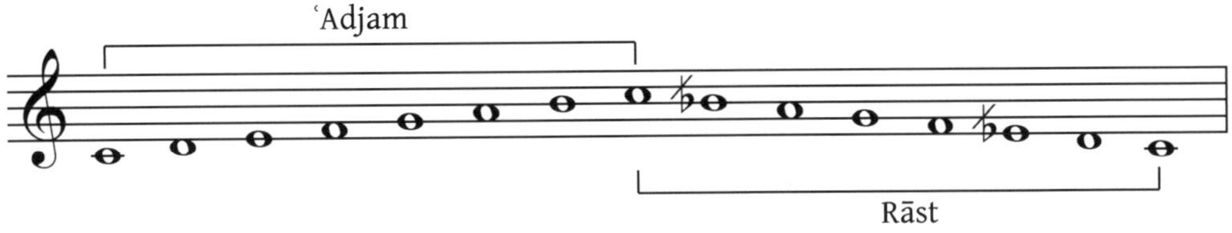

Even by descending in ʿAdjam we can modulate to Rāst by descending below C1 to A1 and G1 while altering B♭1 to B𝄳 :

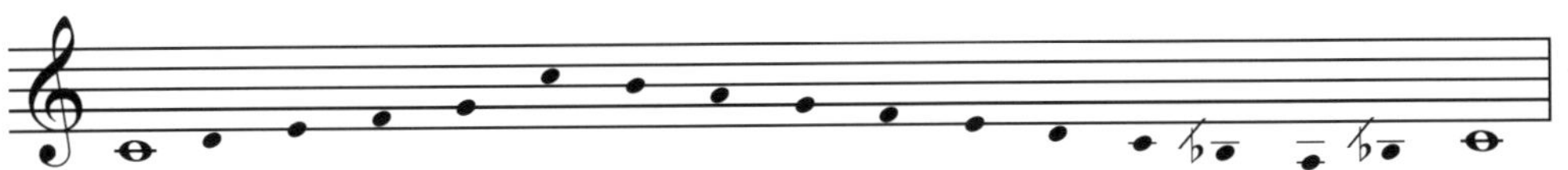

In a similar way, we can modulate from ʿAdjam to Ḥidjāz-Kār or to Nawā-Athar.

If we ascend in ʿAdjam to C2, and while descending, flatten A2 to A♭2, we get djins Ḥidjāz on G. If we continue descending through djins ʿAdjam to C1, we get the scale of Shawq-Afzā on C1:

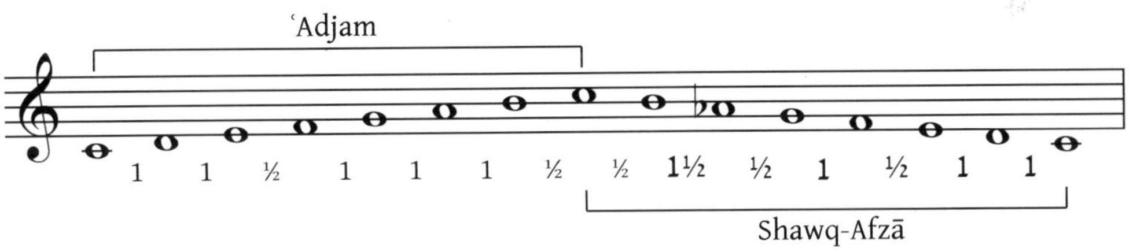

Modulating by changing the tonic and altering the intervals: This is a more difficult type of modulation that requires a thorough knowledge of maqāmāt in general, and of the primary maqām specifically. It is almost impossible to learn the secrets of modulation just by reading written explanations. Nevertheless, the reader may refer to the examples below as exercises.

For example, it is possible to modulate from ʿAdjam on C1 to Nahawand on G2. After ascending to C2 (the octave of the tonic), we can descend to G2 by way of B♭2 and modulate to djins Nahawand on G. However, in this case, it is important to use F♯1 as a leading note, in order to establish G2 as the tonic and stress the characteristics of Nahawand:

It is common to modulate from ʿAdjam on C1 to Ṣabā on A1 or on E1. We make a cadence in ʿAdjam on the tonic and then move to E1 in order to position djins Ṣabā on it:

It is also possible to make a cadence in ʿAdjam on C1 and then modulate to Ṣabā on A1. However, in this case, moving straight from C1 to A1 in order to establish djins Ṣabā on A1 would not sound appropriate. It is better to move to Ṣabā by first using D♭1 and then descending to A:

Another possibility is to ascend in ʿAdjam to C2 and then descend in djins Bayāt to G2:

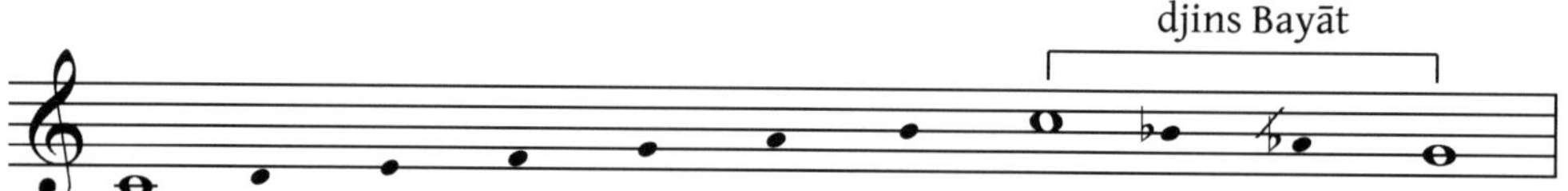

The Progression of the Maqām

IT IS CUSTOMARY to start ʿAdjam by emphasizing its fifth and eighth notes (in ʿAdjam on C1 these are G2 and C2). The exposition of the maqām starts from its second djins by entering from the fifth note (G2), ascending to C2, and then descending to the tonic (C1). The melody should then ascend again to the octave area and descend again to the tonic.

2. Maqām ʿAdjam ʿUshayrān

The Scale

Intervals: 1–1–½–1–1–1–½ (tones)

Analysis of the Scale

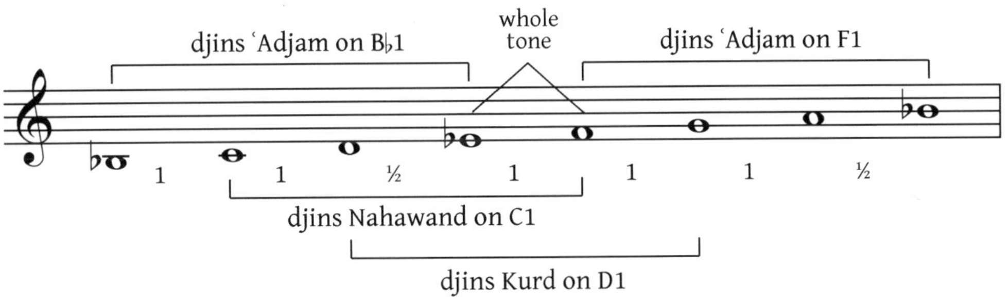

Adjnās

Primary adjnās:	djins ʿAdjam on B♭1 djins ʿAdjam on F1 (disjunct adjnās)
Secondary adjnās:	djins Nahawand on C1 djins Kurd on D1

The Name

THE STRUCTURE of the scale of ʿAdjam ʿUshayrān is identical to that of ʿAdjam, but it is played on the tonic B♭1, which gives this maqām its name. This note is also named ʿAdjam,[1] and on the ʿūd, it is played on the string ʿUshayrān (A1).

The Conventional Position

B♭1 (Qarār ʿAdjam)

1 Sometimes it is called Qarār ʿAdjam because it is an octave lower than the note ʿAdjam.

Repositions

THE TYPICAL repositions of ʿAdjam ʿUshayrān are the same as with ʿAdjam, but we must notice that since ʿAdjam ʿUshayrān is positioned a tone lower than ʿAdjam, all its repositions are also a tone lower.

A typical reposition of ʿAdjam ʿUshayrān is to Nahawand on G – the second reposition down to G1 or the fifth reposition up to G2. This move is typical of maqām Faraḥ-Fazā, which is a transposition of Nahawand to G1. However, in order to preserve the special characteristics of maqām Faraḥ-Fazā, the tonic G1 should be approached by descending from its octave note – G2.

Transpositions

ʿAdjam and ʿAdjam ʿUshayrān can be considered as transpositions of the same scale.

Modulations

Three common modulations of ʿAdjam ʿUshayrān are:

1. To Faraḥ-Fazā on G1 by reposition
2. To Djahārkāh on F1 by reposition
3. To Bayāt on its conventional tonic, D1:

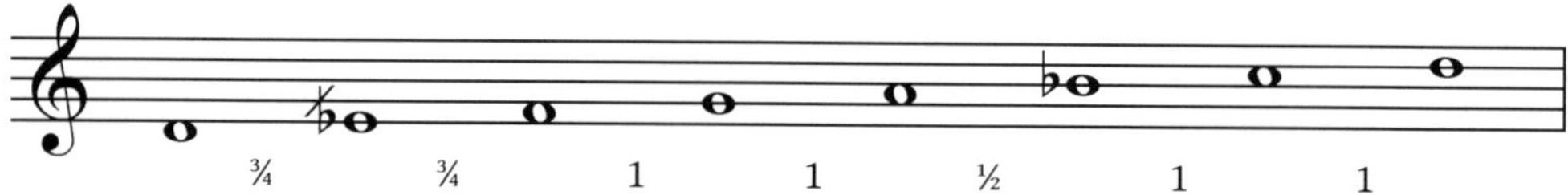

In order to return to ʿAdjam ʿUshayrān we should emphasize B♭ make it the tonic, and return to our primary scale.

The Progression of the Maqām

In order to convey the unique melodic characteristics of ʿAdjam ʿUshayrān, the notes F and B♭ should be emphasized. It is customary to start the exposition of the maqām from its second djins, starting from F1, and then descend to its first djins before concluding on the tonic.

3. Maqām Djahārkāh

The Scale

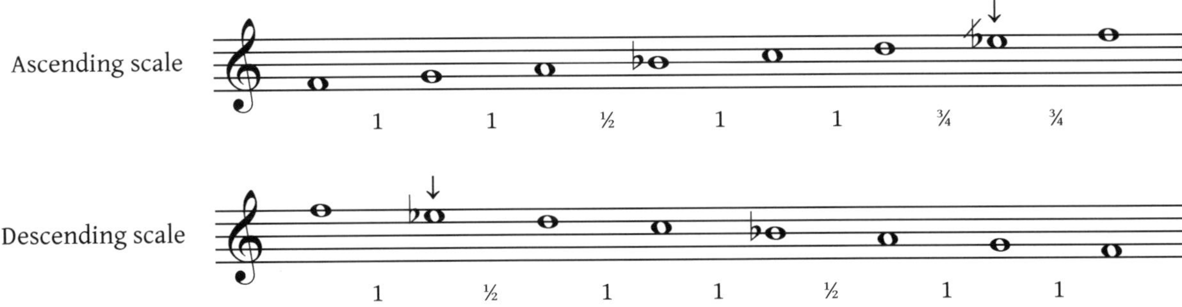

Intervals: ascending scale 1–1–½–1–1–¾–¾ (tones)
descending scale 1–1–½–1–1–½–1 (tones)
(when descending, E𝄳 is altered to E♭)

Analysis of the Scale

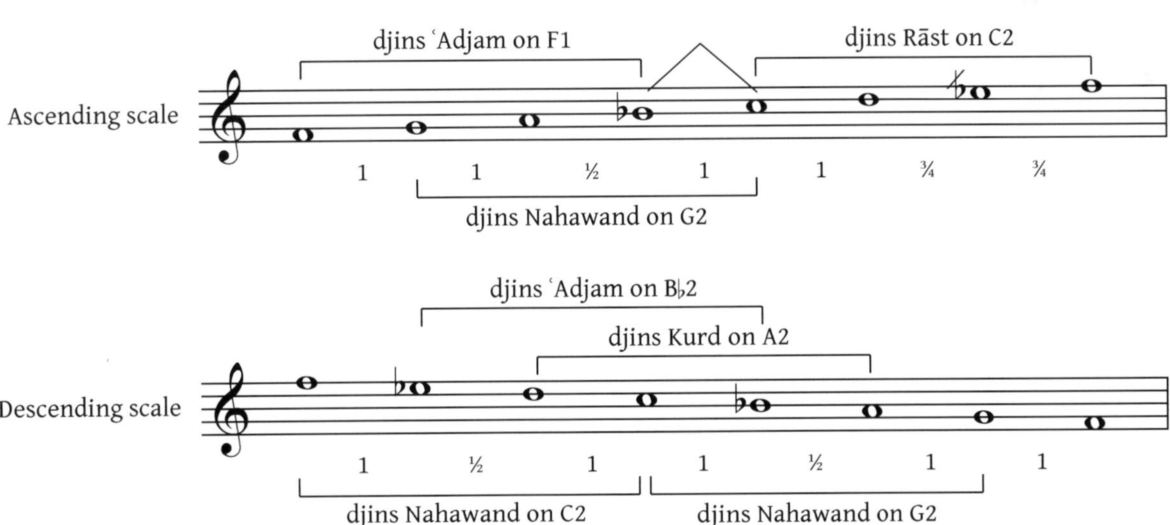

Adjnās

Primary adjnās: djins ʿAdjam on F1
djins Rāst on C2
(disjunct adjnās)

Secondary adjnās:

In the ascending scale: djins Nahawand on G2

In the descending scale: djins Nahawand on C2
djins ʿAdjam on B♭2
djins Kurd on A2
djins Nahawand on G2

It must be noted that some scholars analyze the structure of maqām Djahārkāh differently. Al-Mahdī, a Tunisian theoretician, divides this scale into djins Djahārkāh, consisting of five notes, and djins Rāst; these are connected as conjunct adjnās (1990: 42):

Both Al-Mahdī and Mashʿal (1959: 63) do not refer to the alteration of E𝄳 to E♭. On the other hand, al-Mahdī stresses that an important characteristic of maqām Djahārkāh is a descent to djins Rāst below the tonic before concluding on the tonic F1. These differences in analysis may be the result of cultural differences.

The Name

IN PERSIAN, the word *djahār* means "four" or "fourth" and *kāh* (pronounced *gāh* in Persian) means "a place," "a position." Djahārkāh, therefore, means the "fourth position," which is the name of the note F1 – the fourth note in the scale of Rāst. Maqām Djahārkāh, therefore, is named after its tonic. In Persian music, there is a scale called Chargah. However, this scale is similar to the Arab scale of Ḥidjāz-Kār and not to the scale of Djahārkāh.

The Conventional Position

F1 (Djahārkāh)

Repositions

SINCE THE SCALE of Djahārkāh contains the notes E𝄳 and B♭, it can be considered the second reposition up of Bayāt. Hence, the scale of Bayāt is the second reposition down or the fifth up of Djahārkāh. These two scales are therefore closely related:

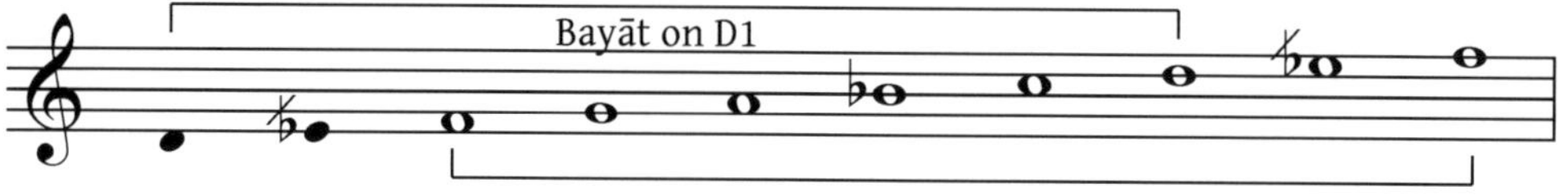

A third reposition down will give us a scale that is very similar to the scale of Rāst but has the note B♭2 instead of the note B𝄳2, which is usually the seventh note in Rāst. Al-Nur claims that such a scale is a variant of the scale of Rāst.[1]

In his song *Habīb al-Qalb* ("Lover of My Heart") the Egyptian composer Muḥammad ʿAbd al-Wahhāb uses such a scale in the context of a larger scale, which can be written like this:

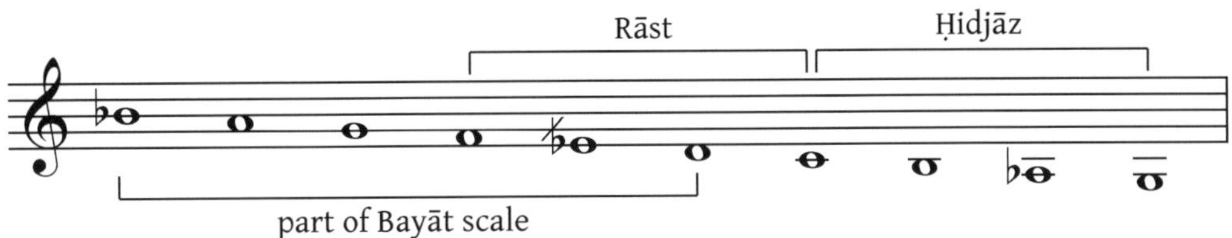

The above scale may be explained as the scale of Ḥidjāz on G1 with its second djins being Rāst on C1, while the ascent to A2 and B♭2 is used as an embellished variance.

Transpositions

AL-ʿABBAS (1986: 76) lists the scale of Sūzdalāra as a transposition of Djahārkāh. In his analysis, Sūzdalāra's adjnās are identical to those of Djahārkāh, but only in its ascending scale. In its descending scale, according to him, Sūzdalāra employs E𝄳 instead of E. This descending scale employs djins Rāst on C1, and the scale of Sūzdalāra, according to al-ʿAbbas, should be written as follows:

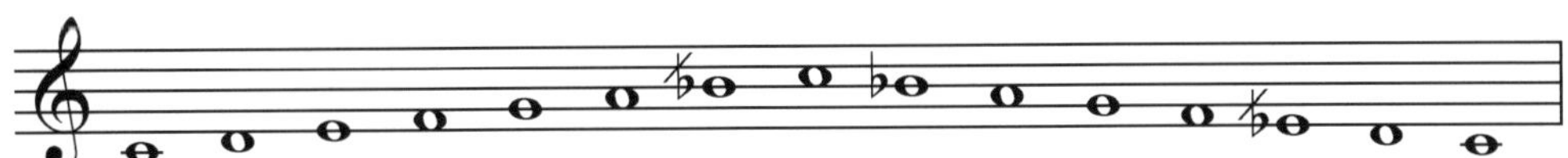

Therefore, saying that Sūzdalāra is a transposition of Djahārkāh is not quite accurate. Al-Ḥilū, on the other hand, classifies Sūzdalāra as belonging to the Rāst family (1972: 109). This classification is more plausible since the scale descends to the tonic through djins Rāst.

Modulations

SOME SCHOLARS claim that the scale of Djahārkāh is in fact a transposition of ʿAdjam (or ʿAdjam ʿUshayrān) to F1 (al-Ḥilū 1972: 133 fn. 1). If this is the case, then the alteration of E to E𝄳 can be considered an embellishment. At any rate, maqām Djahārkāh is very similar to ʿAdjam, and all modulations available in ʿAdjam can be performed in this scale as well.

A descent to Bayāt on D1 or to Rāst on C1 by employing E𝄳1 can sound very natural. Shifting to Ṣabā on D1, possibly by way of djins Bayāt on D1, is also a common modulation.

The Progression of the Maqām

THE MAIN MELODIC characteristic of this maqām is the emphasis of djins ʿAdjam on B♭2. The maqām should be entered from F1 or B♭2. Then the melody should ascend to the second djins while alternating between djins ʿAdjam on B♭2 and djins Rāst on C2 by altering E♭2 to E𝄳2. Finally, the melody should conclude with djins ʿAdjam on F1. As was noted, some scholars claim that before concluding on the tonic, the melody should descend to djins Rāst on C1.

1 Indeed, descending melodies in the scale of Rāst often employ the note B♭1 instead of the note B𝄳1.

4. Maqām Shawq-Afzā

The scale

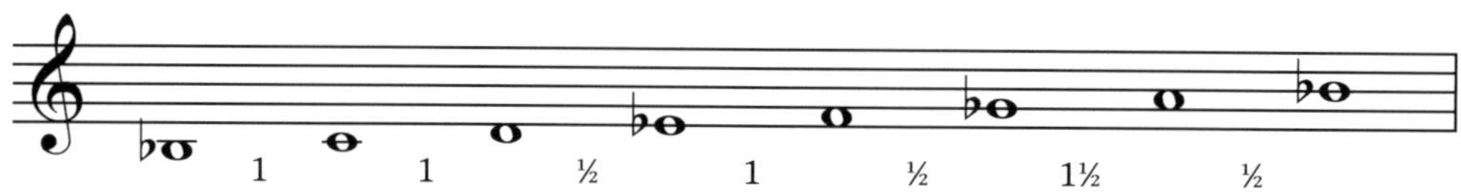

Intervals: 1–1–½–1–½–1½–½ (tones)

Analysis of the Scale

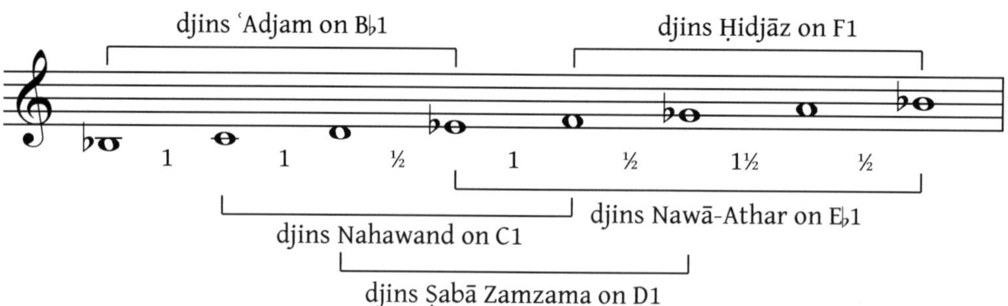

Adjnās

Primary adjnās: djins ʿAdjam on B♭1
djins Ḥidjāz on F1

Secondary adjnās: djins Nahawand on C1
djins Ṣabā Zamzama on D1
djins Nawā-Athar on E♭1

Some scholars analyze the structure of this scale differently and claim that its primary adjnās are ʿAdjam on B♭1 and Nawā-Athar on E♭1 in a conjunct sequence (al-Ḥilū 1972: 101):

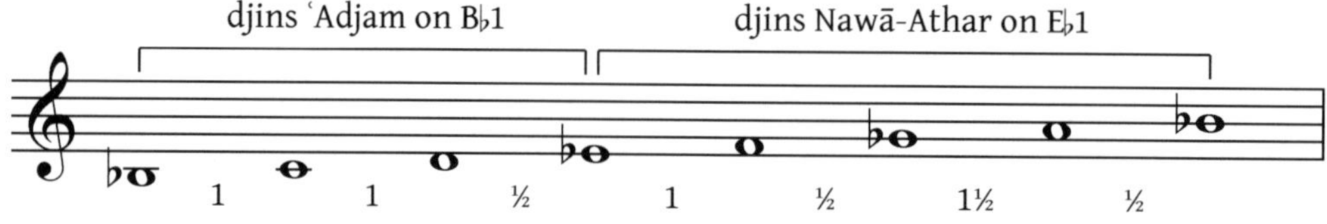

Al-ʿAbbas analyzes the scale in a similar way, but in the verbal explanation that follows, he analyzes the scale as consisting of djins ʿAdjam and djins Ḥidjāz in a disjunct sequence (1986: 78).

Al-Ḥilū claims that in the second octave of the scale, the order of the adjnās switches – Nawā-Athar is the first djins and ʿAdjam is the second:

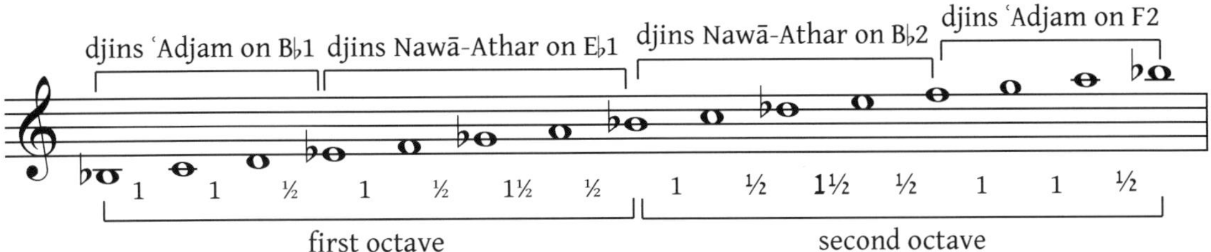

I prefer the division of the scale into djins ʿAdjam and djins Ḥidjāz. This kind of division implies a similarity between the scale of maqām Shawq-Afzā and the scale of Sūznāk. In the scale of maqām Sūznāk, the first djins is Rāst and the second is Ḥidjāz.

According to al-ʿAbbas, maqām Shawq-Afzā is not widely used (ibid.). This fact may explain the differences in the analyses of various scholars, which can be the result of listening to different musical pieces.

The Name

THE NAME Shawq-Afzā means "abundance of longings" in Persian. When referring to the scale of ʿAdjam ʿUshayrān, al-Ḥilū states that in that scale, the second djins may be changed into djins Ḥidjāz (1972: 100). He does not give this new scale a different name, but in fact, by that, he suggests that the scale of Shawq-Afzā is a variant of ʿAdjam ʿUshayrān.

Al-Nur stresses that such a scale, comprised of djins ʿAdjam and djins Ḥidjāz in a disjunct sequence, is called Sūznāl. I could not find a maqām with such a name in any of the sources I used, nor could I find this scale under a different name.

The famous Egyptian composer Zakariyyā Aḥmad (1896–1961) used this scale in his song *ʿAnil ʿUshshāq Saʾalūnī* ("They Asked Me about the Lovers") which was sung by the great diva Umm Kulthūm in the film *Salāma*. Unfortunately, this wonderful song is not included in the compilation of the songs of Umm Kulthūm (1896–1975) in my possession, and therefore, I cannot know how this maqām is named in Egypt. It may be that al-Nur uses the name Sūznāl because he learned it from Egyptian musicians.

We can assume that the name Sūznāl is assigned to the transposition of Shawq-Afzā to the tonic C1. As we learned in the section on maqām ʿAdjam, in some Arab countries, the conventional tonic of ʿAdjam is C1, and therefore, playing Shawq-Afzā on this tonic is another option.

The Conventional Position

BOTH AL-ʿABBAS and al-Ḥilū place Shawq-Afzā on B♭1 (the note ʿAdjam or Qarār ʿAdjam) as its conventional position. However, as suggested in the previous section, this maqām can also be played on the tonic C1, and then it may be called Sūznāl.

Repositions

ACCORDING TO al-Ḥilū's analysis, the scale of Shawq-Afzā is not cyclical, and in this case, no repositioning is possible. However, if we consider al-ʿAbbas's view that this scale is cyclical, then the following repositions are possible:

The first reposition up produces the scale of Nahawand Muraṣṣaʿ on C1, consisting of the intervals 1–½–1–½–1½–½–1 (tones).

The second reposition up produces the scale of Ṣabā Zamzama on D1, consisting of the intervals ½–1–½–1½–½–1–1 (tones).

The fourth reposition up produces the scale of Zandjarān on F1, consisting of the intervals ½–1½–½–1–1–½–1 (tones):

The structure of the scale of Zandjarān is an inversion of the structure of Shawq-Afzā – that is, its first djins is Ḥidjāz and its second is ʿAdjam:

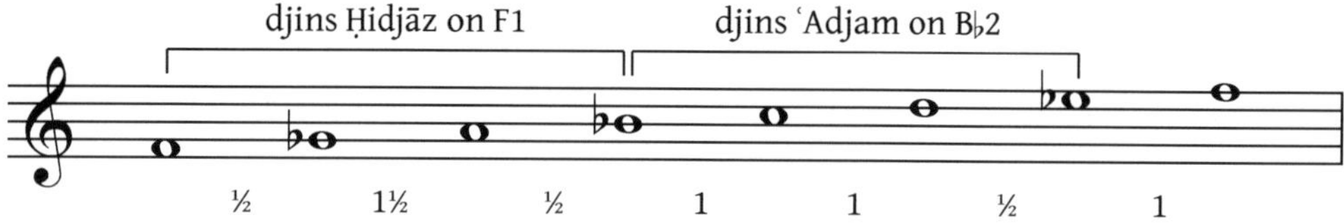

Transpositions

TRANSPOSING THE scale of Shawq-Afzā does not produce any well-known maqāmāt. However, as was noted in the section about the name of this maqām, it can easily be transposed to C1, a tonic often used for the scale of ʿAdjam. When the scale of Shawq-Afzā is transposed to C1, djins Ḥidjāz is positioned on G2:

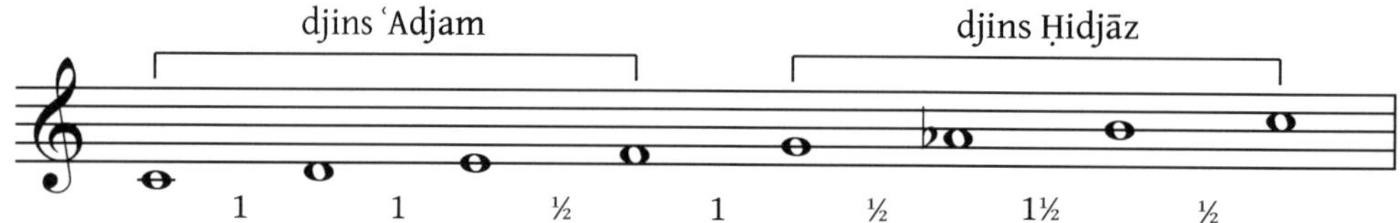

Modulations

MODULATING TO ʿAdjam ʿUshayrān (or in the case of Shawq-Afzā on the tonic C1, to ʿAdjam) can be done very easily. All modulations that are applicable for maqām ʿAdjam ʿUshayrān (or ʿAdjam) can be applied to this maqām as well.

By using djins Ḥidjāz as a point of departure, many other modulations can be performed. In the case of Shawq-Afzā on C1, we can easily modulate to Ḥidjāz-Kār on C1 or to Huzām on E𝄳1. Following is the outline of a modulation from Shawq-Afzā on C1 to Huzām on E𝄳1:

We start by ascending to the octave note, C2. We then descend to djins Ḥidjāz on G2 and then alter the note E1 to E𝄳 and establish it as a new tonic:

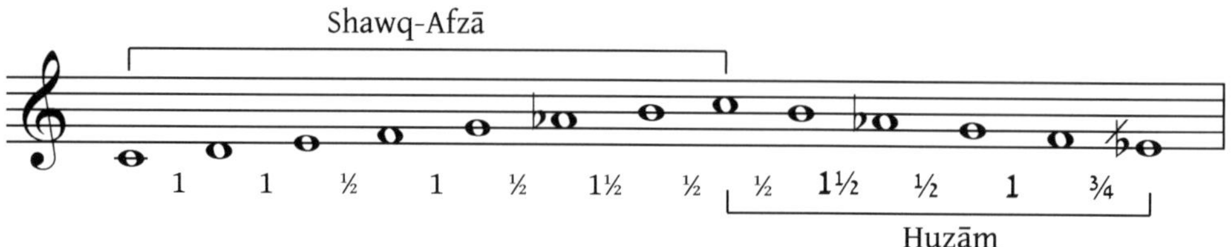

The complete scale of maqām Huzām is written like this:

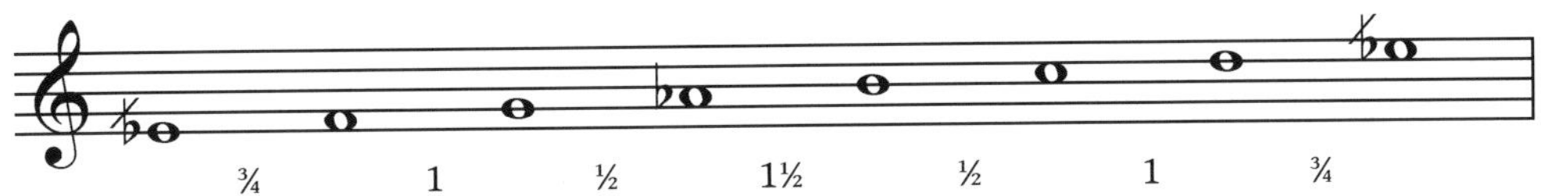

After modulating to Huzām, it is easy to move to Rāst on C1, modulate to ʿAdjam on C1, and then move back to Shawq-Afzā on C1.

The Progression of the Maqām

IN ORDER TO emphasize the unique melodic characteristics of Shawq-Afzā, its exposition should start from its second djins (either Ḥidjāz or Nawā-Athar). The melody should then descend to the first djins – djins ʿAdjam on the tonic of the scale. When descending, it is customary to use G♮2 instead of G♭2; the descent to the tonic may then be G♮2–F1–E♭1–D1–C1–B♭1.

5. Maqām Sūzdalāra

MAQĀM SŪZDALĀRA will only be mentioned here, but not analyzed. Both al-ʿAbbas and al-Ḥilū mention it, but they do not agree on its analysis. Al-ʿAbbas classifies it as belonging to the ʿAdjam family, while al-Ḥilū classifies it as belonging to the Rāst family (al-ʿAbbas 1986: 76; al-Ḥilū 1972: 109).

As far as I know, this maqām is not widely used. It is demonstrated in the accompanying CD.

CHAPTER 13

THE NAHAWAND FAMILY OF MAQĀMĀT

1. Maqām Nahawand
2. Maqām Faraḥ-Fazā
3. Maqām ʿUshshāq Miṣrī
4. Maqām Būsalīk
5. Maqām Nahawand Muraṣṣaʿ
6. Maqām Sulṭānī-Yakāh

NAHAWAND IS A name of a city in Iran. It is a very common scale in both Arab and Turkish music. In Turkey, it corresponds to the scales of Būsalīk and Sulṭānī-Yakāh. The scale of maqām Nahawand corresponds to the minor scale (the Aeolian mode) of European music, and it has three variants that are similar to the variants of the minor scale – the natural minor, the melodic minor, and the harmonic minor. In this chapter, we will explore several more variants of this scale that can be found in Arab music, all of which start with djins Nahawand (1–½–1 tones), and are therefore classified as belonging to the Nahawand family.

1. Maqām Nahawand

The Scale

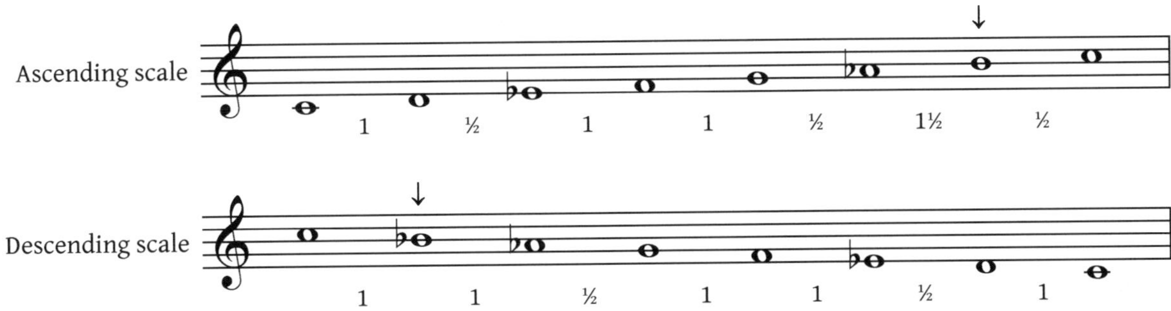

Intervals: ascending scale: 1–½–1–1–½–1½–½ (tones)
descending scale: 1–½–1–1–½–1–1 (tones)
(ascending with B♮2; descending with B♭2)

Analysis of the Scale

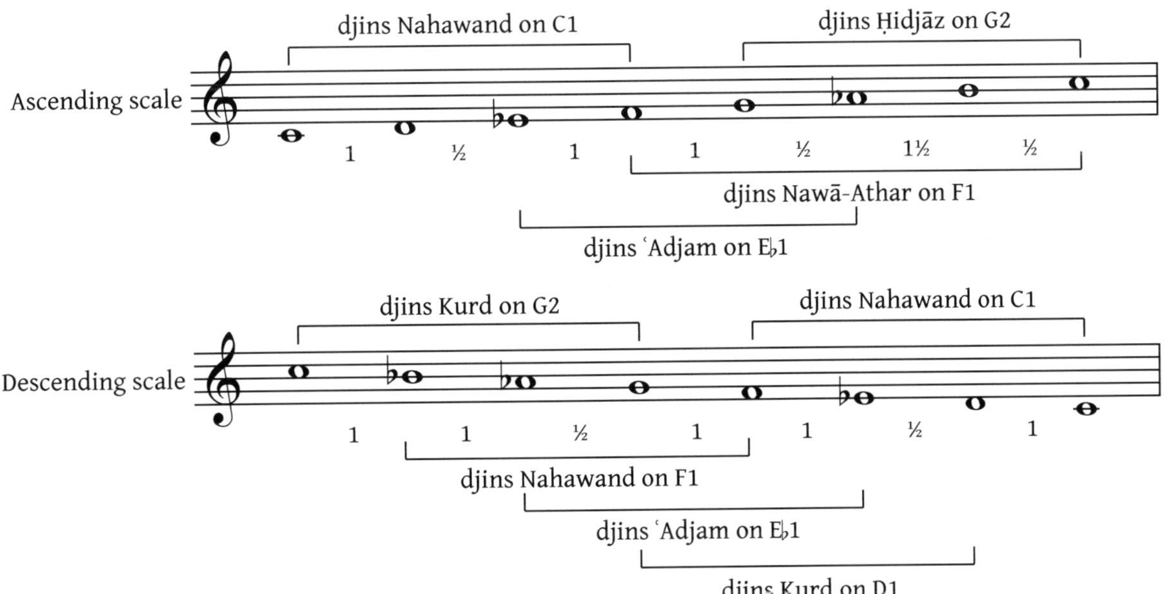

Adjnās

Primary adjnās:

In the ascending scale:	djins Nahawand on C1 djins Ḥidjāz on G2 (disjunct adjnās)
In the descending scale:	djins Nahawand on C1 djins Kurd on G2 (disjunct adjnās)
Secondary adjnās:	djins ʿAdjam on E♭1 djins Kurd on D1 djins Nawā-Athar on F1 (when ascending) djins Nahawand on F1 (when descending)

The above analysis conforms to al-ʿAbbas's approach (1986: 55). Al-Mahdī also follows this analysis (1990: 29). Al-Ḥilū presents a contradicting analysis, in which the ascending scale has B♭2, as in the descending scale of al-ʿAbbas (1972: 113). Furthermore, he stresses that the progression of the maqām requires B♮2 to be used when **descending**, in order to emphasize djins Ḥidjāz on G2 or djins Nawā-Athar on F1. Mashʿal mentions only B♭2 and does not mention djins Ḥidjāz on G at all, neither when ascending nor when descending.

The scale of maqām Nahawand has the same structure as the minor scale (the Aeolian mode) of European music. It is the fifth reposition up, or the second down, of the scale of ʿAdjam, which corresponds to the European major scale (the Ionian mode):

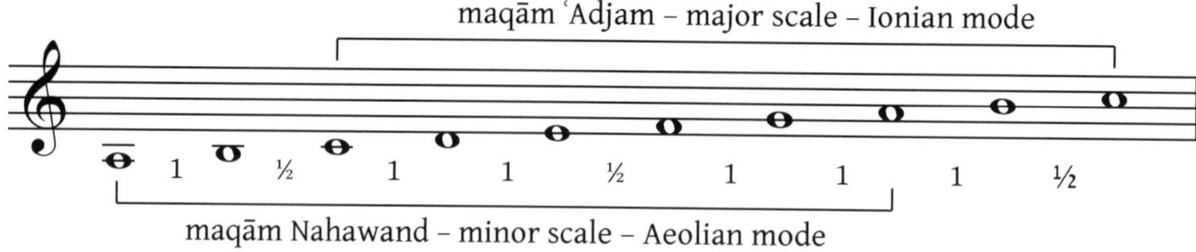

There are several variants, or species, of the scale of Nahawand, and some of them resemble the variants of the minor scale – the natural minor, the harmonic minor, and the melodic minor scales:

1. First Species:

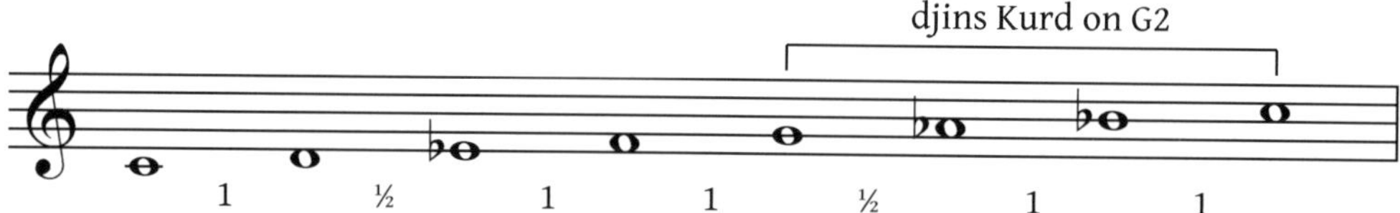

   This scale ascends and descends with the same notes. It corresponds to the natural minor scale. It is sometimes called Nahawand Kurdī.

2. Second Species:

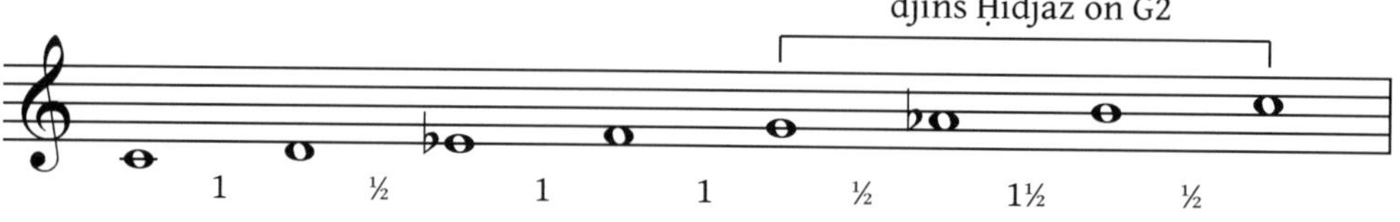

This scale ascends and descends with the same notes. It corresponds to the harmonic minor scale. When transposed to G1, it is used as the scale of Sulṭānī-Yakāh.

3. Third Species:

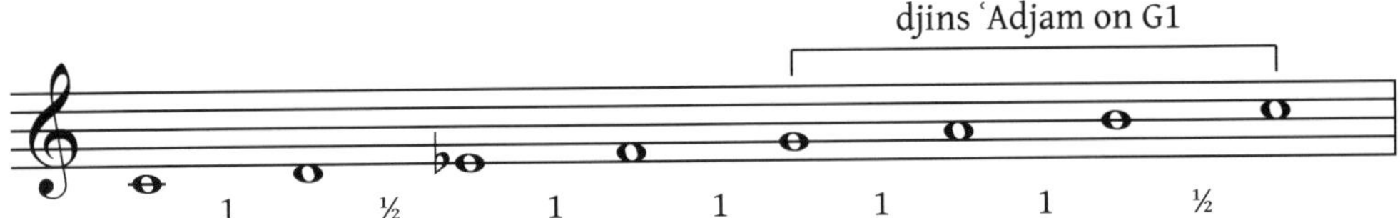

This scale ascends and descends with the same notes.

4. Fourth Species:

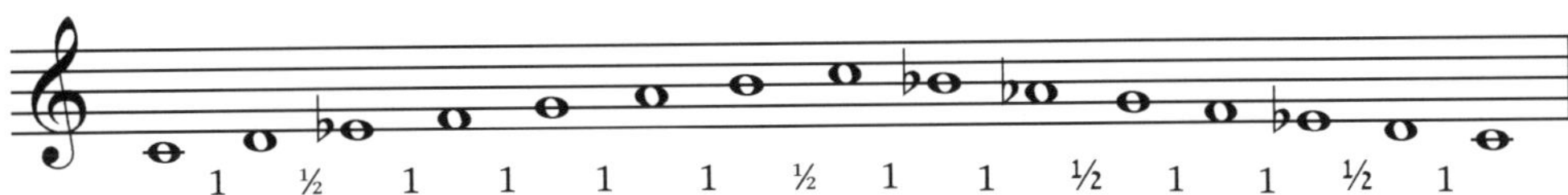

This scale ascends as the third species and descends as the first one. It corresponds to the melodic minor scale.

5. Fifth species;

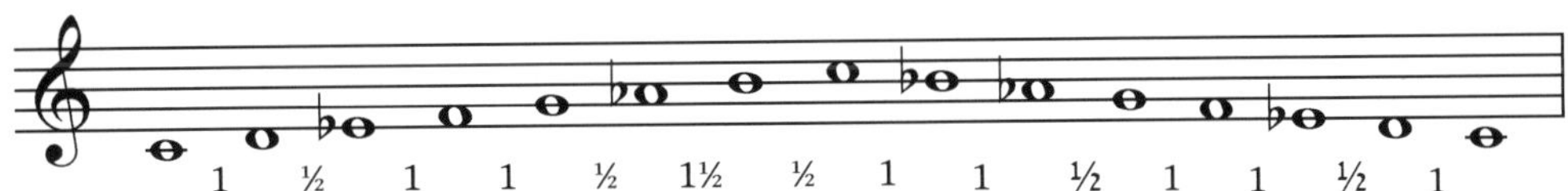

This scale ascends as the second species and descends as the first one.

From the various analyses of maqām Nahawand in the many sources available, it is not clear whether these various species should be considered as distinct maqāmāt or as variants of the scale of Nahawand. The differences between the various scales offered by maqām Nahawand seem to confuse musicologists, who do not agree on the exact analysis of this maqām and its scale. At any rate, the analysis presented above provides information regarding the various ways in which this maqām can be interpreted and the various approaches to the structure of its melodic progression. Each of the above variants has its own unique "shade," and composers sometimes choose to compose pieces in maqām Nahawand while emphasizing one of these variants.

Al-Ḥilū, for example, writes the scale of Nahawand like this:

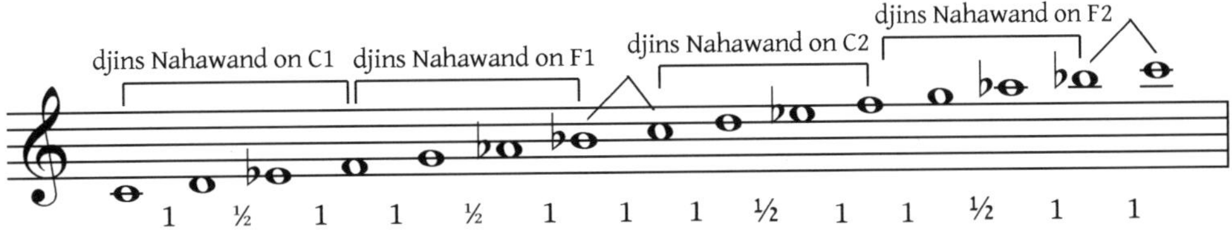

Al-Ḥilū, therefore, claims that the ascending and descending scales are the same, and he analyzes its structure as two adjnās of Nahawand in conjunct sequence. However, in his written explanations, he acknowledges the frequent appearance of djins Ḥidjāz on G in the performance of Nahawand, and so he adds that the second djins of Nahawand can be either "Nahawand on F or Ḥidjāz on G" (1972: 113).

In my opinion, the various variants of the scale of Nahawand presented here did not develop as separate and distinct scales. This opinion is supported by the fact that most of these variants did not acquire distinctive names of their own. Musicologists do not agree on one form of analysis for the scale of Nahawand because there are many ways to perform this maqām, and each musician performs and interprets it slightly differently.

The Name

Nahawand is a name of a city in Iran. According to al-Mahdī, in Algeria, this scale is called Rāhawī or Sāhilī, in Tunisia, Muḥayyar Sīkāh, in Turkey, Būsalīk, Sulṭānī-Yakāh, or Faraḥ-Fazā, and in Persia, Iṣfahān (1990: 29). I do not agree with al-Mahdī's opinion that all these names are just different names of maqām Nahawand. Many of these scales differ from Nahawand not only in the position of their conventional tonic, but also in their characteristic progression. Most of these maqāmāt have developed distinct characteristics that can be recognized by careful listening and analysis.

The Conventional Position

C1 (Rāst)

Repositions

1. First species of Nahawand (djins Nahawand on C1 + djins Kurd on G2)

   The first reposition up of this species, which corresponds to the natural minor scale, forms the scale of Lāmī on D1. The second reposition up forms the scale of ʿAdjam on E♭1, the third reposition up, the scale of Nahawand Kabīr on F1, and the fourth reposition up, the scale of Kurd on G2.

2. Second species of Nahawand (djins Nahawand on C1 + djins Ḥidjāz on G2)

   The first reposition up of this species, which corresponds to the harmonic minor scale, forms the scale of Ṭarz Nawīn, from the family of Kurd, on D1:

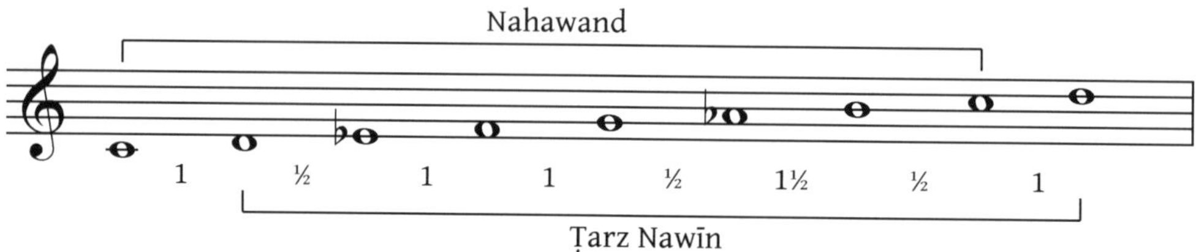

The second reposition up, to E♭1, forms the scale of Ṭarz Djadīd, which is a new scale, invented by the Egyptian musician Dāʾūd Ḥusnī (1870–1937):

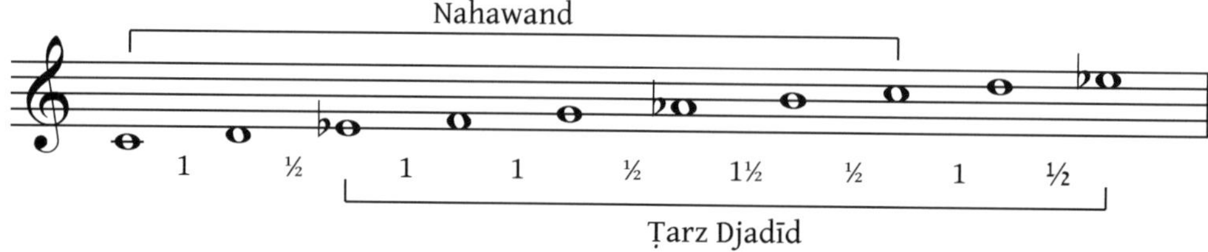

The third reposition forms the scale of Nakrīz on F1:

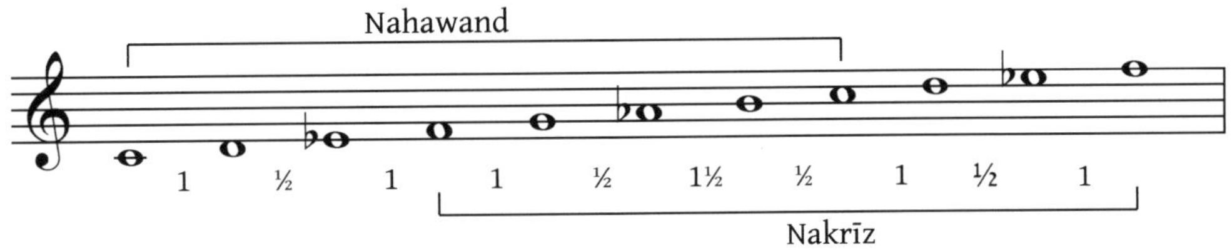

The fourth reposition forms the scale of Ḥidjāz-Humayūn on G2:

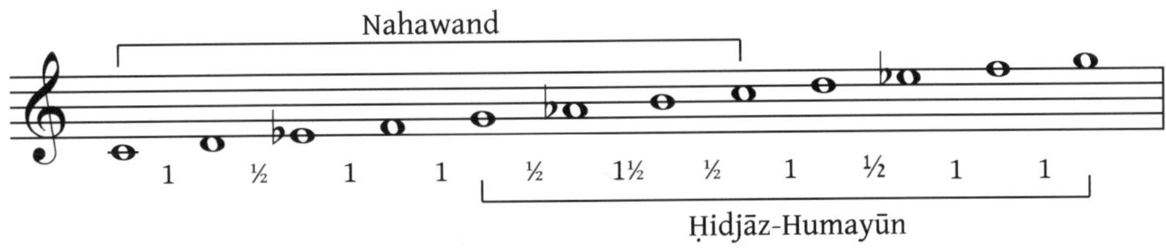

Transpositions

TWO TRANSPOSITIONS of Nahawand to G1 are called Faraḥ-Fazā and Sulṭānī-Yakāh. The transposition of Nahawand to D1 is often called Būsalīk by Turkish musicians; in fact, the Turks view Nahawand as a transposition of Būsalīk and not vice versa.

The distinct characteristics of these three maqāmāt are discussed in the sections devoted for them.

Modulations

NAHAWAND CAN BE considered a reposition of ʿAdjam, and therefore, modulating from Nahawand to ʿAdjam, Lāmī, or Kurd can be done very easily and naturally.

The second djins of Nahawand is positioned on its fifth note; in the case of Nahawand on C1, this note is G2. Modulating to Bayāt on this note is very common. Another common modulation is to Ṣabā on G2.

By using djins Ḥidjāz on G2, we can perform many modulations to scales that employ this djins. For example, we can modulate to Huzām on E𝄳1, to Ḥidjāz-Kār on C1, to Shadd-ʿArabān on G1, to Shawq-Afzā on C1, or to Nawā-Athar or Nakrīz on C1. If we combine djins Ḥidjāz on G2 with djins ʿAdjam on C2, we can modulate to the scale of Zandjarān on G2.

A good way to remember various possible modulations is to memorize similar scales as a group. We can, for example, memorize the structure of Nahawand, Kurd, and Bayāt very easily because their scales differ only in one note – the second note – which can be altered in order to produce each one of these scales. The example below places these three scales on the tonic D1:

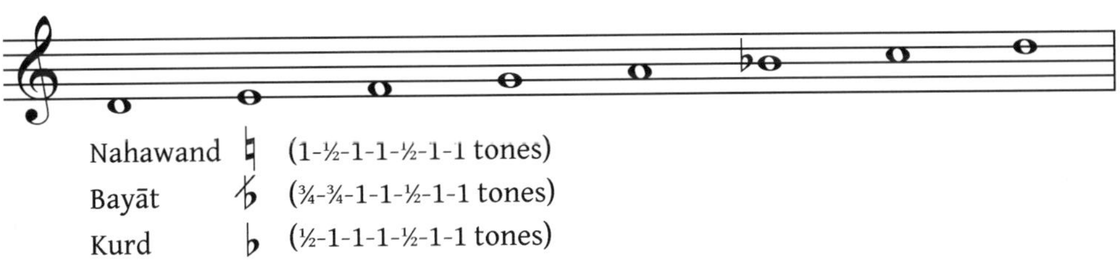

The Progression of the Maqām

THE TYPICAL progression of maqām Nahawand starts by ascending from the tonic and the first djins on C1 to the second djins on G2. To establish the tonic of the maqām firmly, it is necessary to use the note B1, which is a semitone below the tonic. This note, which helps to confirm the tonic, is termed in European music the *leading note* of the scale and in Arabic *ẓahīr*.[1]

2. Maqām Faraḥ-Fazā 

The Scale

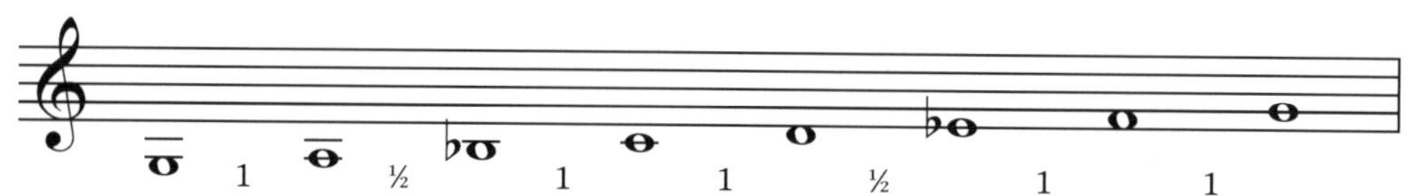

Intervals: 1–½–1–1–½–1–1 (tones)

Analysis of the Scale

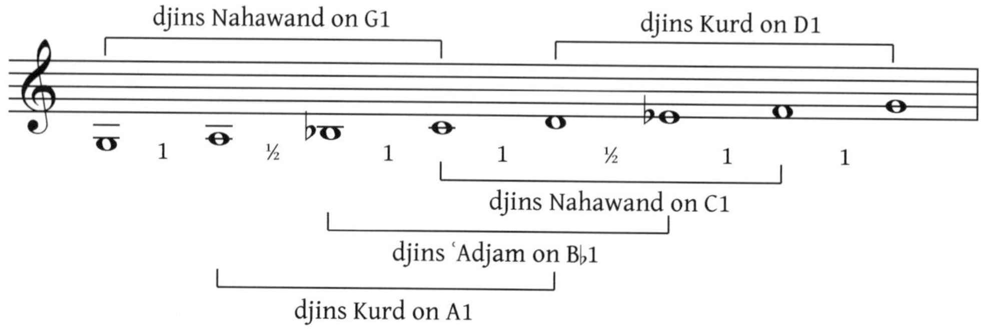

Adjnās

Primary adjnās:	djins Nahawand on G1 djins Kurd on D1 (disjunct adjnās)
Secondary adjnās:	djins Kurd on A1 djins ʿAdjam on B♭1 djins Nahawand on C1

1 See Chapter 2.

The scale of Faraḥ-Fazā is a transposition of the first species of Nahawand to the tonic G1. However, its unique melodic progression makes it a distinct maqām. Some scholars find it sufficient to explain that Faraḥ-Fazā is a descending Nahawand on G1, that is, its progression starts from its second or third djins and then descend to the tonic G1. This is only a partial definition; this maqām has many more characteristics that will be explained below.

The Name

The name Faraḥ-Fazā comes from Persian and means "overjoyed."

The Conventional Position

G1 (Yakāh)

Repositions

ALL THE REPOSITIONS that were discussed concerning Nahawand are applicable to Faraḥ-Fazā. Nevertheless, it should be remembered that the tonic of this scale is the lowest note in the Arab two-octave range of notes. On the Arab violin, for example, there is no lower note than this tonic. This fact means that all repositions must be done up.

Transpositions

Faraḥ-Fazā is a transposition of the scale of Nahawand from C1 to G1.

Modulations

THE SAME modulations that can be applied to Nahawand are applicable to Faraḥ-Fazā. However, the range should be taken into account.

The Progression of the Maqām

THE TYPICAL progression of maqām Faraḥ-Fazā starts by emphasizing the notes B♭2 and F1. Such an emphasis suggests the descending scale of ʿAdjam ʿUshayrān. The progression starts, therefore, from the third djins of the scale (Nahawand on G2). When descending, E♮1 can be used temporarily as the leading note to F1. Before descending to the tonic, djins Kurd on D1 can be emphasized for a while.

3. Maqām ʿUshshāq Miṣrī 8

The Scale

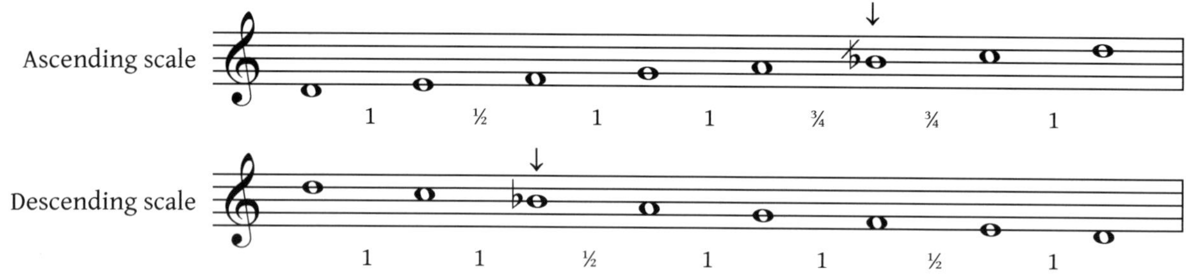

Intervals

Ascending: 1-½-1-1-¾-¾-1 (tones)
Descending: 1-½-1-1-½-1-1 (tones)

Analysis of the scale

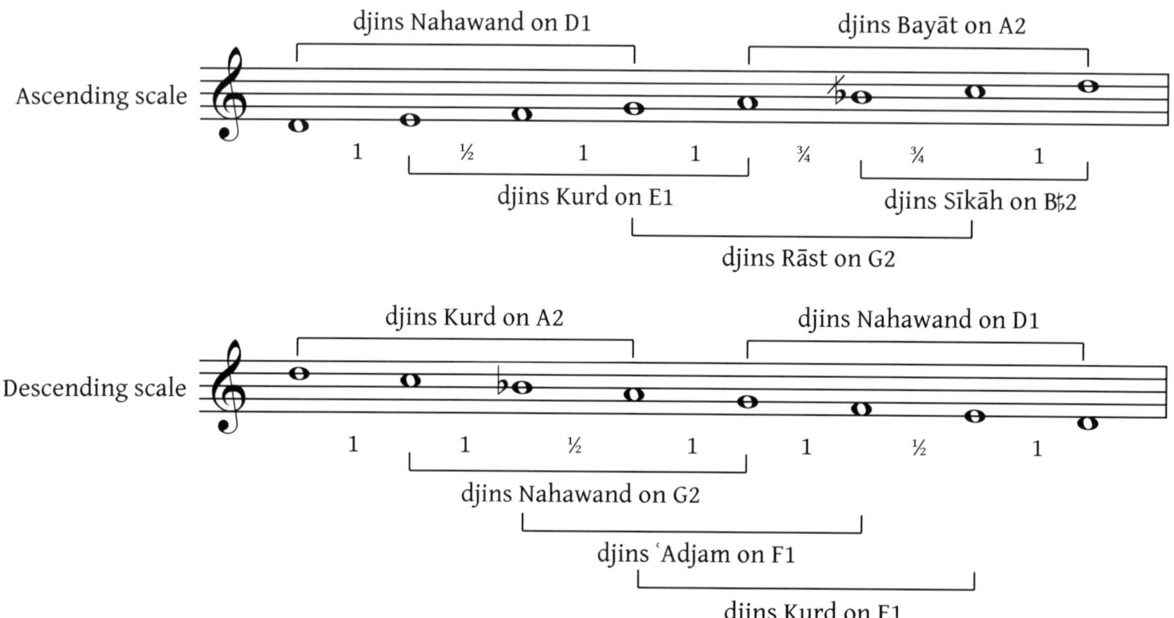

Adjnās

Primary adjnās

Ascending:	djins Nahawand on D1
	djins Bayāt on A2
Descending:	djins Nahawand on D1
	djins Kurd on A2

Secondary adjnās

Ascending:	djins Kurd on E1
	djins Sīkāh on B𝄳2
	djins Rāst on G2
Descending:	djins Kurd on E1
	djins ʿAdjam on F1
	djins Nahawand on G2

The Name

THE WORD *miṣrī* means "Egyptian" in Arabic. This scale originated in Egypt, and therefore its name distinguishes it from the Turkish maqām ʿUshshāq. Al-Mahdī says that the Egyptian representatives to the Cairo Congress of Arab Music in 1932 performed this maqām in front of the congress (al-Mahdī 19??: 47).

The Conventional position

D1 (Dūkāh)

Repositions

Not known

Transpositions

Not known

Modulations

TYPICAL MODULATIONS of this maqām are to the primary and secondary adjnās that appear in the analysis above, such as to Bayāt on A2, Rāst on G2, and Nahawand on G2. The scale of ʿUshshāq Miṣrī is similar to the scales of Bayāt and Muḥayyar, and so modulating to these scales by descending through djins Bayāt on D1 instead of Nahawand can be done easily. Other possible modulations are to Kurd on D1, to Ṣabā on D1 or Ṣabā on A2, and to ʿAdjam or Djahārkāh on F1.

The Progression of the Maqām

TYPICALLY, THE MELODY starts with the second djins – djins Bayāt on A2. From there, it is possible to perform short modulations to Rāst on G2 and to Nahawand on G2, which is a secondary djins of the descending scale. The melody then ascends to djins Nahawand on D2, which is the third djins of the scale, and descends to the tonic through djins Nahawand on G2 and djins Nahawand on D1.

The scale of ʿUshshāq Miṣrī employs three more notes from the second octave, in order to make djins Nahawand on D2 (D2–E2–F2–G2).

Al-Ḥilū suggests that the intonation of the various progressions of ʿUshshāq Miṣrī may vary. However, an old recording of the song *Lā Taḥsabū ʾAnna Maylī Baynakum Taraba* ("Do Not Think that I Move among You with Joy"), sung by the singer al-Manyalāwī, confirms the analysis above. This song is written in maqām ʿUshshāq Miṣrī, and it can be heard clearly that it starts with djins Bayāt on A2 and then descends to djins Nahawand on D1.

4. Maqām Būsalīk

The Scale

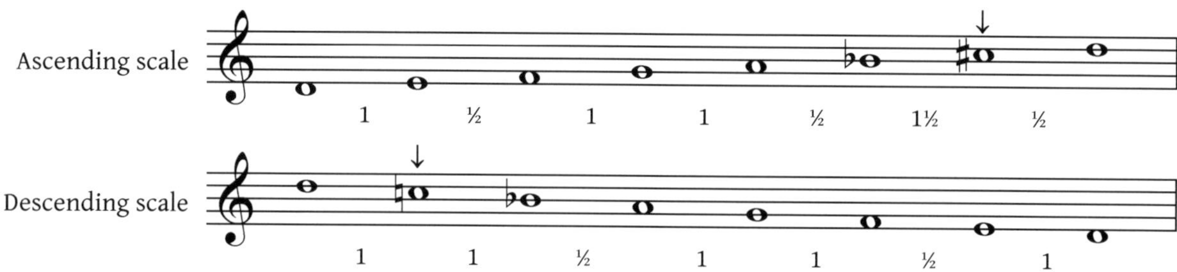

Intervals

Ascending: 1–½–1–1–½–1½–½ (tones)

Descending: 1–½–1–1–½–1–1 (tones)

Analysis of the Scale

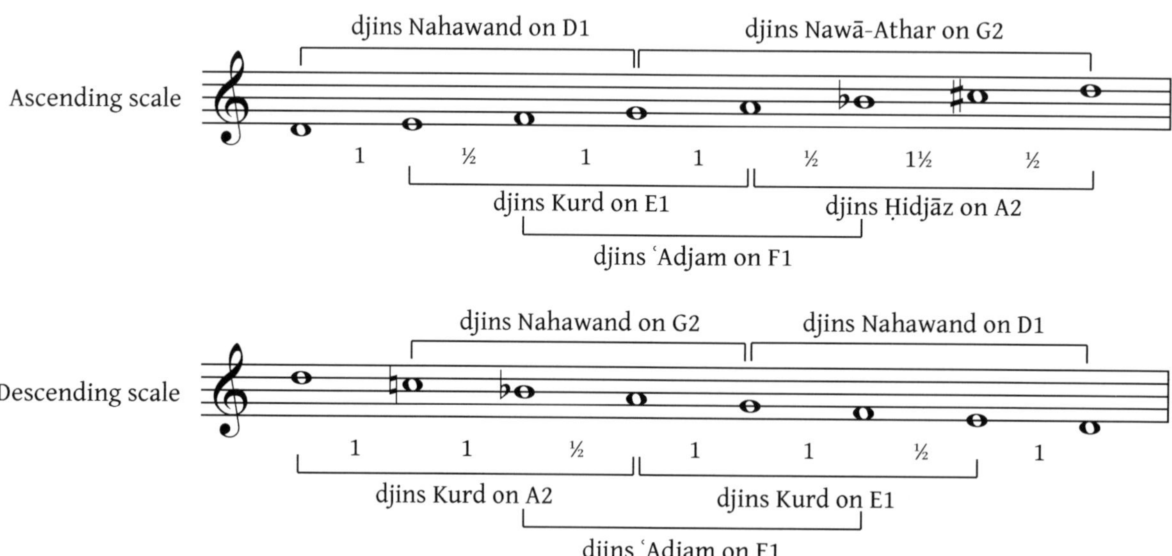

Adjnās

Primary adjnās

Ascending:	djins Nahawand on D1 djins Nawā-Athar on G2 (conjunct adjnās)
Descending:	djins Nahawand on D1 djins Nahawand on G2 (conjunct adjnās)

Secondary adjnās

Ascending:	djins Kurd on E1 djins ʿAdjam on F1 djins Ḥidjāz on A2
Descending:	djins Kurd on E1 djins ʿAdjam on F1 djins Kurd on A2

The above analysis is given by al-ʿAbbas (1986: 80).

Maqām Būsalīk comes from Turkey. As we can see, its ascending scale has the structure of the second species of Nahawand, which corresponds to the harmonic minor scale. Its descending scale has the structure of the first species of Nahawand, which corresponds to the natural minor scale, and it is sometimes called Nahawand Kurdī in Arabic. This ascending-descending progression corresponds to the fifth species of Nahawand.[1]

There is an essential structural difference, however, between the scale of Būsalīk and the scale of Nahawand. The ghammāz (dominant) of Nahawand is its fifth note, therefore the second djins of Nahawand is always positioned on its fifth note, and the two adjnās are connected in disjunct sequence. In Būsalīk, on the other hand, the ghammāz is the fourth note of the scale, and therefore its second djins is always positioned on its fourth note, forming a disjunct sequence. The main difference between these two scales, therefore, is that the second djins of the ascending Nahawand is djins Ḥidjāz on its fifth note, while in the ascending Būsalīk, the second djins is Nawā-Athar on its fourth note.

We must note, however, that some Arab scholars give different analyses of the scale of maqām Būsalīk. According to al-Ḥilū, for example, the second djins of the ascending scale of Būsalīk is djins Nahawand on G2 in conjunct sequence. Only when ascending to the second octave, the second djins of the second octave is changed into djins Ḥidjāz on A3 and the adjnās are in disjunct sequence. When descending, the second octave stays the same as the ascending one, but in the first octave, the second djins (which was Nahawand on G2) becomes djins Ḥidjāz on A2. Al-Ḥilū adds that when descending, the progression may feature occasional variations, such as djins Bayāt on A2, djins Rāst on G2, and djins Kurd on A2 (al-Ḥilū 1972: 128).

As we can see in the analysis above, according to al-ʿAbbas, the second djins of the scale of Būsalīk is djins Nawā-Athar. The ghammāz al-maqām (dominant) is the fourth note of the scale (G2), and therefore, the adjnās are in conjunct sequence. However, he too gives the variation of djins Ḥidjāz on the fifth note (A2) as a secondary djins. It seems that there are inconsistencies between the analyses of various Arab scholars concerning this maqām, but if we examine the two analyses carefully, we will see that they are essentially the same, and the differences between them are minor.

Maqām Būsalīk is a Turkish maqām, and in Turkish music, it is also positioned on the note D1 (Dūkāh). However, according to the Turkish analysis, its ghammāz is the fifth note of the scale (A2) in both the ascending and the descending scale, and its second djins in the ascending scale is Ḥidjāz on A2.

Since maqām Būsalīk is a Turkish maqām, and it is almost certain that the Arabs adopted it from the Turks, I tended at first to adopt the Turkish analysis as a basis for the analysis presented here. But after much consideration, I decided to stick with the analyses given by Arab scholars. Even if the approach of the Arab scholars might change the original conception of the maqām, it still seems that their analysis is the one common in the Arab world, and since this book deals with Arab musical culture, I decided to present it here.

1 For the various species of Nahawand, see the section on Nahawand above.

The Name

THE NAME BŪSALĪK is the name of the note E2 in the Arab system. As Elias suggests, some scales are named after one of the notes of their scales. I think this maqām is named so because of the structural importance of the note Būsalīk for its scale: In the section on maqām Nahawand, I explained how there are three scales that are almost identical in their intervals, but vary in their second note. These are the scales of Kurd, Bayāt, and Nahawand. When we place these three scales on the tonic D1, we can see that the second note is E♭1 (Kurd) in Kurd, E𝄳1 (Sīkāh) in Bayāt, and E♮1 (Būsalīk) in Nahawand. It makes sense that the scale of Būsalīk, which is essentially the scale of Nahawand on D1, is named so after its second note, which distinguishes it from those other similar scales.

The Conventional Position

D1 (Dūkāh)

Repositions

All the repositions discussed in the section on maqām Nahawand are applicable for maqām Būsalīk.

Transpositions

Būsalīk is a transposition of Nahawand to the tonic D1.

Modulations

All the modulations discussed in the section on maqām Nahawand are applicable to maqām Būsalīk.

The Progression of the Maqām

MEHMET EMIN BITMEZ, a Turkish ʿūd player, taught me that the progression of Būsalīk starts from the tonic, or even below it, and then goes up quickly to the ghammāz.

5. Maqām Nahawand Muraṣṣaʿ

The Scale

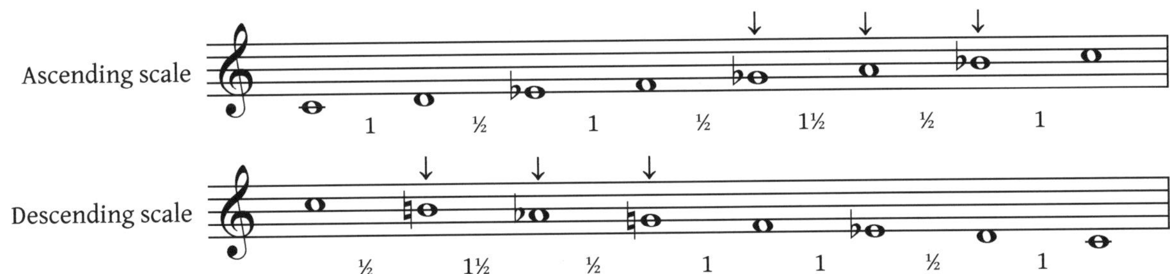

Intervals

Ascending: 1–½–1– ½–1½–½–1 (tones)

Descending: 1–½–1–1–½–1½–½ (tones)

Analysis of the scale

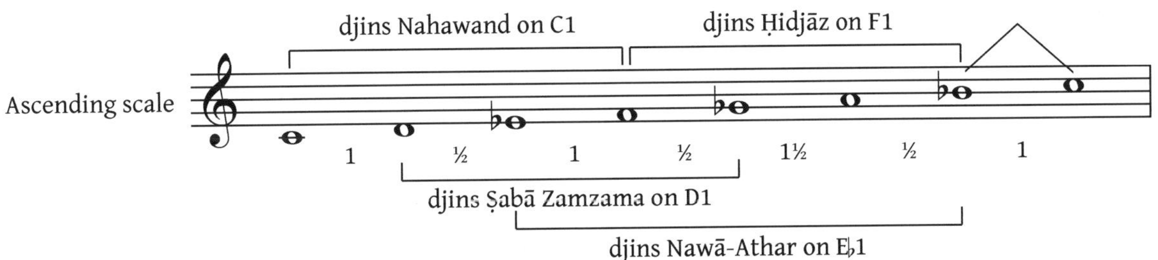

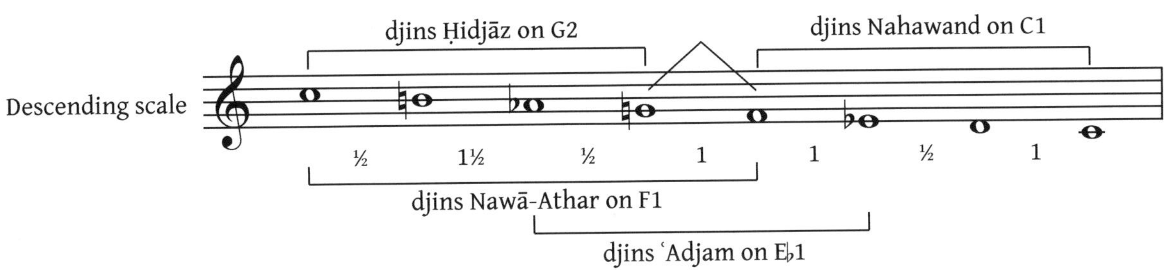

Adjnās

Primary adjnās

Ascending:	djins Nahawand on C1 djins Ḥidjāz on F1 (conjunct adjnās)
Descending:	djins Nahawand on C1 djins Ḥidjāz on G2 (disjunct adjnās)

Secondary adjnās

Ascending:	djins Ṣabā Zamzama on D1 djins Nawā-Athar on E♭1
Descending:	djins Nawā-Athar on F1 djins ʿAdjam on E♭1

The above analysis is according to al-ʿAbbas (1986: 74), while al-Ḥilū and Mashʿal do not refer to this maqām. Al-Mahdī (19??: 70) analyses it differently: according to him, the descending scale is also composed of djins Nahawand on C1 and djins Ḥidjāz on F1 in conjunct sequence, but he adds djins Ḥidjāz on C2, in the second octave:

The descending scale in al-ʿAbbas's analysis, in which there is djins Ḥidjāz on G2, emphasizes the melodic characteristics of Nahawand. Al-Mahdī's version has its own unique characteristics, and does not necessarily emphasize progressions that are typical of Nahawand.

As was mentioned above, in the section on maqām Nahawand, there is a resemblance between the scales of Kurd, Bayāt, and Nahawand. Al-Nur suggests that because of this resemblance, there is an analogy between the scale of maqām Bayāt Shūrī, which is composed of djins Bayāt on D1 and djins Ḥidjāz on G2, and the scale of Nahawand Muraṣṣaʿ. He names the latter "Nahawand Shūrī," since its structure is similar to Bayāt Shūrī: it has djins Nahawand on the tonic and djins Ḥidjāz on the fourth note of the scale. In a similar way, he names a scale that is composed of djins Kurd and djins Ḥidjāz on the fourth note "Kurd Shūrī." This kind of scale resembles the scale of maqām Ṭarz Nawīn. I could not find the names that he suggests in theoretical literature.

I could not find an explanation of the origin of the name Nahawand Muraṣṣaʿ in theoretical literature. The word *muraṣṣaʿ* means "embellished," or "decorated," in Arabic. It may be that the "embellishment" is the placement of djins Ḥidjāz in an unconventional position – on the fourth note, instead of the fifth note, of the scale of Nahawand. Some musicians believe that this maqām originated in Egypt (Elias).

The Conventional Position

Both al-ʿAbbas and al-Mahdī agree that the conventional position of Nahawand Muraṣṣaʿ is on C1 (Rāst).

Repositions

The third reposition up forms the scale of Zandjarān on F1. The first reposition up forms the scale of Ṣabā Zamzama on D1:

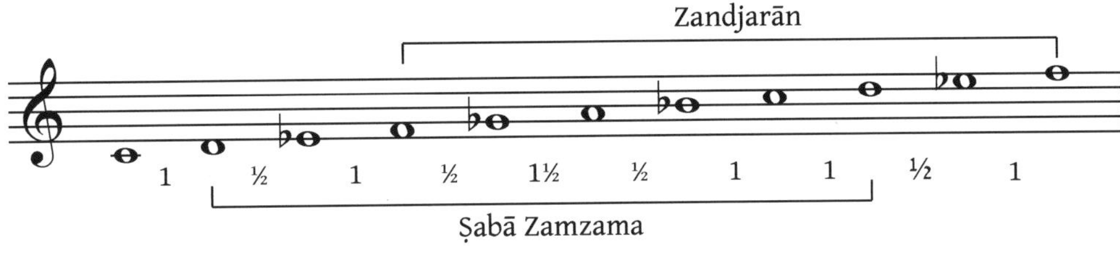

Transpositions

Not known.

Modulations

SINCE NAHAWAND MURAṢṢAʿ belongs to the Nahawand family, it is very easy to modulate to Nahawand. Any of the modulations that are applicable to Nahawand can be applied to Nahawand Muraṣṣaʿ. By dwelling on Ṣabā Zamzama on D1, which is one of the secondary adjnās of this scale, we can also modulate to Ṣabā on D1 or even to Bayāt on D1. Other possible modulations are, to Nawā-Athar or Nakrīz on E♭1, to ʿAdjam on E♭1, or to Djahārkāh on F1.

The Progression of the Maqām

Nahawand Muraṣṣaʿ usually appears as a variation or an alteration of the "standard" Nahawand. Its progression usually starts from the first djins.

6. Maqām Sulṭānī-Yakāh

The Scale

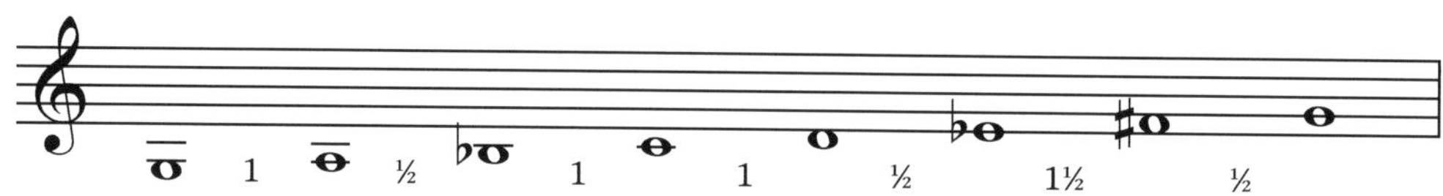

Intervals: 1–½–1–1–½–1½–½ (tones)

Analysis of the Scale

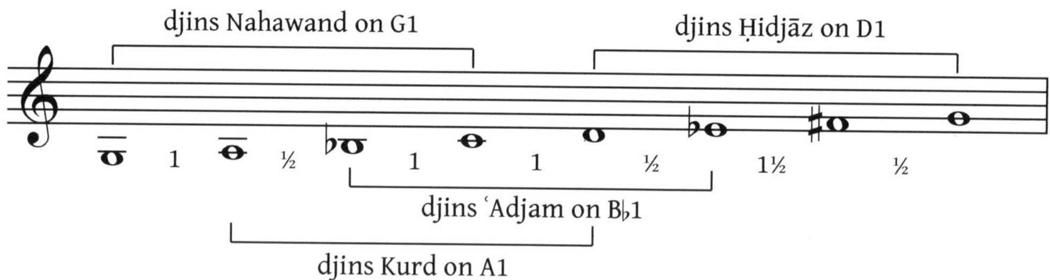

Adjnās

Primary adjnās:	djins Nahawand on G1 djins Ḥidjāz on D1 (disjunct adjnās)
Secondary adjnās:	djins Kurd on A1 djins ʿAdjam on B♭1

The scale of Sulṭānī-Yakāh corresponds to the second species of Nahawand.[1] However, it is differentiated from Nahawand by the transposition to G1 and by its unique melodic progression. Al-Ḥilū and Mashʿal do not refer to this scale. Al-Mahdī mentions it in his list of "Turkish maqāmāt," but he does not analyze it (19??: 71). I think that the reason why many Arab scholars do not refer to this maqām is that its scale is perceived to be just a transposition of the second species of Nahawand. The Arab *muwashshaḥ* (type of song) *Lamma Bada Yatathanna*, for example, has the same progressions as maqām Sulṭānī-Yakāh, but it is titled by Arab musicians as a song in maqām Nahawand.

1 See the section on maqām Nahawand above.

The Name

I COULD NOT find an explanation as to the origin of this name in my sources, but its meaning is "the place of the sultan." Yakāh, naturally, refers to the tonic of the scale – G1.

The Conventional Position

G1 (Yakāh)

Repositions, Transpositions, and Modulations

ANY OF THE repositions, transpositions, and modulations that are applicable to Nahawand can be applied to Sulṭānī-Yakāh.

The Progression of the Maqām

BECAUSE ITS TONIC is so low, the progression of Sulṭānī-Yakāh usually starts from its second or third djins and then descends. It starts with djins Nahawand on G2 and emphasizes djins Ḥidjāz on D1. From there it usually modulate to djins Ḥidjāz on G2, descends again to djins Ḥidjāz on D1, and by altering F♯1 to F♮1, it descends to the tonic with the scale of the first species of Nahawand.

CHAPTER 14

THE KURD FAMILY OF MAQĀMĀT

1. **Maqām Kurd**
2. **Maqām Ḥidjāz-Kār-Kurd**
3. **Maqām Lāmī**
4. **Maqām Ṭarz Nawīn**

THE SCALE OF maqām Kurd corresponds to the Phrygian mode of European music. As all other scales that belong to the Kurd family, it starts with djins Kurd (½–1–1 tones). Since it is a diatonic scale, it combines nicely with other Arab diatonic scales, such as ʿAdjam, Nahawand, Lāmī, and Nahawand Kabīr. Maqām Kurd is widely used in Turkey and the Arab world.

1. Maqām Kurd

The Scale

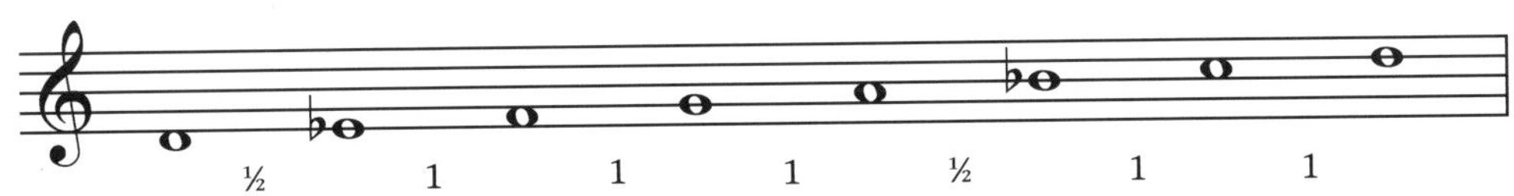

Intervals: ½–1–1–1–½–1–1 (tones)

Analysis of the Scale

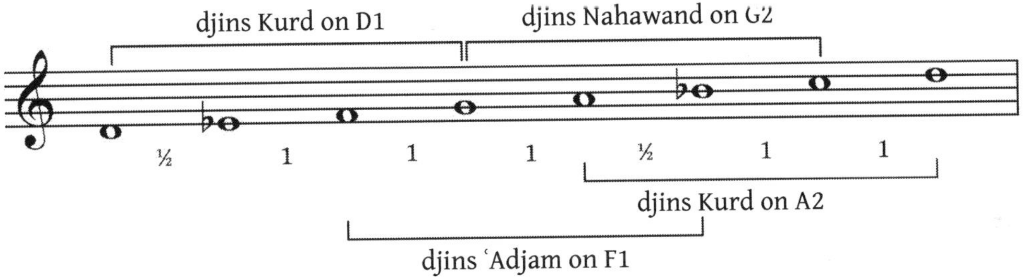

Adjnās

Primary adjnās: djins Kurd on D1
djins Nahawand on G2
(conjunct adjnās)

Secondary adjnās: djins ʿAdjam on F1
djins Kurd on A2

Some writers give a different analysis and maintain that the second primary djins of the scale of Kurd is djins Kurd on the fifth note (in Kurd on D1 it is the note A2), and therefore the adjnās are in disjunct sequence (for example, al-ʿAbbas1986: 123). These differences in analysis should not be considered significant contradictions. In both maqām Kurd and maqām Ḥidjāz-Kār-Kurd, the melodic progression employs both djins Nahawand on the fourth note of the scale as well as djins Kurd on the fifth note. However, after looking into the matter I came to prefer the above analysis, especially because it is the analysis common in Turkish music theory. It seems that in maqām Kurd, djins Nahawand stands out more as the second djins of the scale than djins Kurd.

The Name

MAQĀM KURD IS probably named so because of the structural importance of its second note, E♭1, which is named Kurd. This note distinguishes it from the scales of Bayāt and Nahawand. These three scales have a very similar structure – they differ only in their second note.[1] An example of a maqām that combines two of these similar scales can be found in the maqām Muḥayyar Kurdī. The ascending scale of Muḥayyar Kurdī is the scale of Muḥayyar, while when descending to the tonic, the scale changes to the scale of Kurd by altering B𝄳1 to B♭1.

Some musicians claim that the scale of Kurd is an "altered" version of the scale of Sīkāh or the scale of Bayāt. These scales contain quartertonal intervals, so when they were played on instruments that could produce only semitones, they were changed. According to al-Mahdī, the name Kurd is relatively new in the Arab maqām system, and in ancient times this maqām was called Bayātī Ifrandjī, which means "Western Bayātī" (19??: 36).

The Conventional Position

D1 (Dūkāh)

Repositions

KURD IS A diatonic scale, and can be considered the second reposition of the scale ʿAdjam ʿUshayrān. All the repositions possible with a diatonic scale can be applied to Kurd.

The third reposition up, or the fourth down, forms the scale of Nahawand on G.

The fourth reposition up, or the third down, forms the scale of Lāmī.

Transpositions

THE TRANSPOSITION OF the scale of Kurd to C1 is the scale of Ḥidjāz-Kār-Kurd, which of course has its own unique melodic progression and characteristics.

Modulations

KURD IS A diatonic scale, and therefore, any modulation applicable to ʿAdjam and other diatonic scales can be applied to Kurd. See the section about maqām ʿAdjam.

The scales of Kurd and Lāmī are very similar. They differ only in their fifth note. It is therefore easy to modulate from Kurd to Lāmī by altering A2 to A♭2 when descending. This alteration can be done either by descending directly to A♭2 or by passing through A𝄳2 in a chromatic progression.

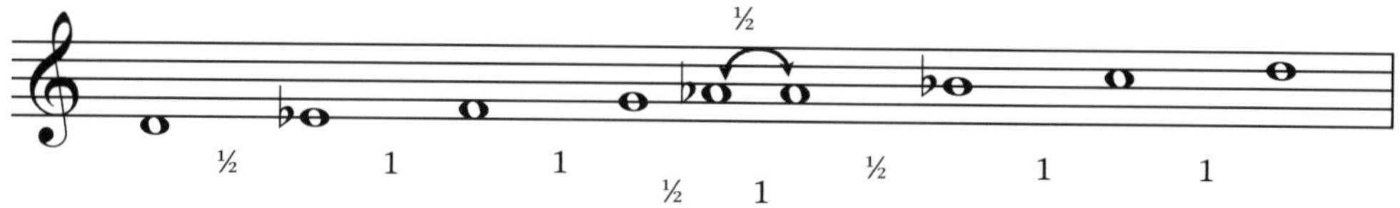

Other possible modulations are to Lāmī on G2, by altering A2 to A♭2 and D2 to D♭2, or to Bayāt or Rāst on G2. However, we must take care not to let the melodic progression sound like Lāmī and lose the distinctive characteristics of Kurd.

Modulating to Ṣabā on G2, on A2, or on D1 can also sound nice, as well as descending to Nahawand on G1 by using the F♯ below it as a leading note.

1 See the section on maqām Nahawand.

The Progression of the Maqām

IT IS IMPORTANT to note the differences between the progression of maqām Kurd and that of its transposition to C1, maqām Ḥidjāz-Kār-Kurd. The main difference between these two maqāmāt is that the progression of Kurd usually starts from its first djins and then ascends, while the progression of Ḥidjāz-Kār-Kurd starts from its higher adjnās (its second and even its third djins) and then descends to the tonic.

According to al-Ḥilū, maqām Kurd emphasizes djins Kurd on D1 and djins ʿAdjam on F1 (1972: 123). The progression starts from djins Kurd on D1, then ascends to G2 and descends back to the tonic. When ascending again, the melody alternates between djins Adjam on F1 and djins Nahawand on G2. The melody then ascends to the second djins and the octave area before descending back to the tonic D1.

2. Maqām Ḥidjāz-Kār-Kurd

The Scale

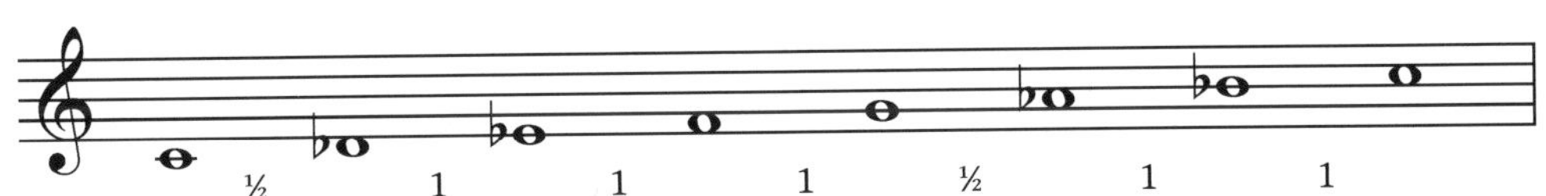

Intervals: ½–1–1–1–½–1–1 (tones)

Analysis of the Scale

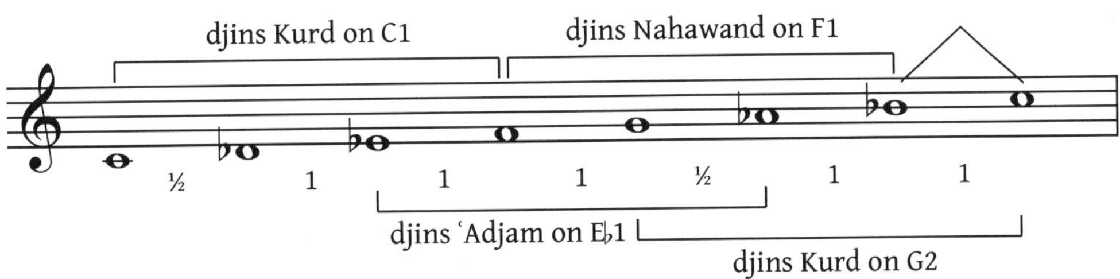

Adjnās

Primary adjnās: djins Kurd on C1
djins Nahawand on F1
(conjunct adjnās)

Secondary adjnās: djins ʿAdjam on E♭1
djins Kurd on G2

The Name

THE SCALE OF Ḥidjāz-Kār-Kurd is identical in its intervallic structure to the scale of Kurd: it is a transposition of Kurd from D1 to C1. When explaining the origin of the name of this maqām, al-Ḥilū says:

> Transposed scales are scales that were moved from their conventional tonic to a different one. However, sometimes, additional notes and intervals that cannot be found in the original scale are added to the transposed scale, and so, the transposed scale acquires new characteristics and a special shade. The Turks transposed the scale of Kurd to C, and since they used to start the progression of this new maqām with Ḥidjāz-Kār, they named it Ḥidjāz-Kār-Kurd. Since then, this new scale has been modified, but its name has remained with it. (al-Ḥilū 1972: 11)

Maqām Ḥidjāz-Kār-Kurd is very common in Turkey (where it is called "Kurdi'li Hicaz Kar"), but it became common in the Arab world only at the beginning of the twentieth century. Some Iraqi musicians that I interviewed maintain that the scale of Ḥidjāz-Kār-Kurd consists of djins Kurd on C1 and djins Ḥidjāz on G2 in a disjunct sequence (Salman; al-Nur). Al-Nur writes this scale like this:

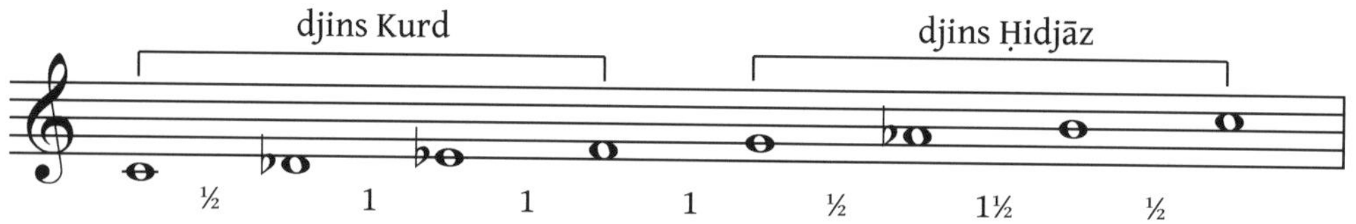

The above scale, however, is not the scale of Ḥidjāz-Kār-Kurd as it appears in literature. This scale can be considered a variation of the second species of Nahawand (which corresponds to the harmonic minor scale) with its second note lowered. Elias comments that the above scale is a transposition of the scale of Shāhnaz Kurdī from D1 to C1.

The conventional Position

C1 (Rāst)

Repositions

Any of the repositions that are applicable to Kurd can be applied to Ḥidjāz-Kār-Kurd.

Transpositions

The scale of Ḥidjāz-Kār-Kurd is a transposition of Kurd from D1 to C1.

Modulations

ANY OF THE modulations that are applicable to Kurd can be applied to Ḥidjāz-Kār-Kurd. However, since Ḥidjāz-Kār-Kurd is positioned on a different tonic, not all of these modulations are easy to perform on some instruments.

The Progression of the Maqām

THE PROGRESSION OF maqām Ḥidjāz-Kār-Kurd emphasizes djins Nahawand on the fourth note of the scale (F1) and djins Kurd on its tonic (C1).

One of the differences between the progression of maqām Ḥidjāz-Kār-Kurd and the progression of maqām Kurd is that in Ḥidjāz-Kār-Kurd the melody usually starts from the higher adjnās and then descends, while in Kurd it usually starts from the tonic and then ascends. At any rate, the fact that these two maqāmāt are played on different conventional positions changes their character, or "shade," and these differences in character can be recognized by ear even when the two maqāmāt are played on the same instrument.

According to al-Ḥilū, the progression of maqām Ḥidjāz-Kār-Kurd starts from the third djins of the scale, djins Kurd on C2, which is usually entered through B♭2, and then it may perhaps ascend to the fourth djins. When descending towards the first djins and the tonic of the scale, the notes C2 and F1 should be emphasized (1972: 117).

3. Maqām Lāmī 13 14

The Scale

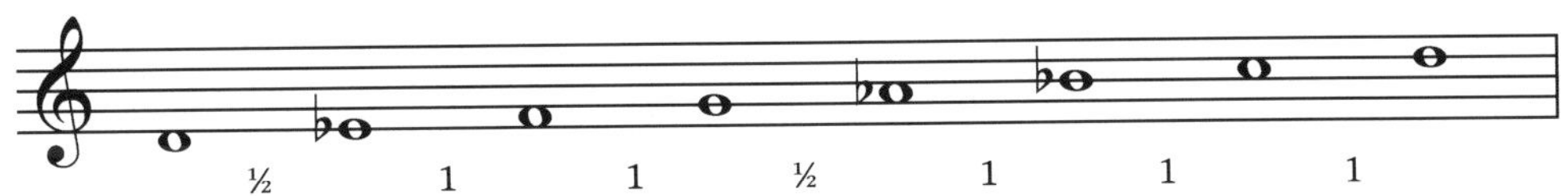

Intervals: ½–1–1–½–1–1–1 (tones)

Analysis of the Scale

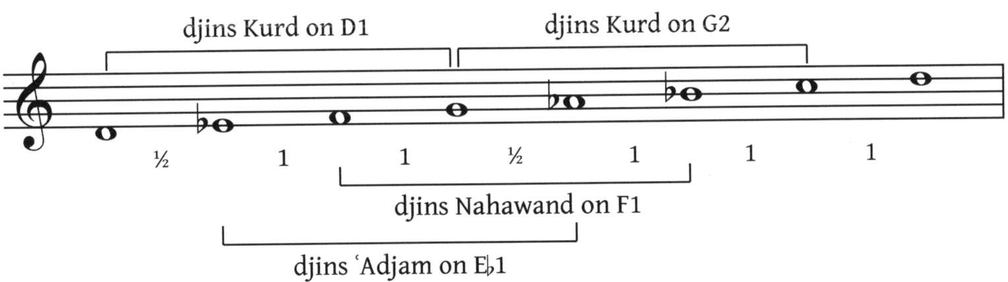

Adjnās

Primary adjnās: djins Kurd on D1
djins Kurd on G2
(conjunct adjnās)

Secondary adjnās: djins ʿAdjam on E♭1
djins Nahawand on F1

Maqām Lāmī originated in Iraq. Al-Mahdī writes that it is "essentially an Iraqi maqām" and that the first musician to implement this scale in the Iraqi maqām system (al-maqām al-ʿirāqī) was the singer (*qāriʾ*) Muḥammad al-Qubbāndjī (1901–1989) (Al-Mahdī 19??: 66).

This scale was not used in other Arab countries until the Egyptian singer and composer Muḥammad ʿAbd al-Wahhāb visited Iraq. After listening to this maqām, he used it for his song *Yali Zaraʿatū al-Burtuqāl* ("You Are the Orange-Tree Planters"), as well as for other songs of his.

Both Mashʿal and al-Ḥilū do not mention this maqām. When writing about the modal theory of the medieval scholar Ṣafī al-Dīn al-Urmawī, Shiloah mentions his twenty-seventh *dawr* (mode), which has the same intervals as the scale of Lāmī (1995: 115).

The Conventional Position

BOTH AL-MAHDĪ (19??: 66), who is Tunisian, and al-Nur, who is Iraqi, position the scale of maqām Lāmī on E1 (Būsalīk). Al-ʿAbbas, who is probably Iraqi since his book was published by the Iraqi ministry of education, positions it on D1 (Dūkāh).

Lāmī is the sixth reposition up, or the first down, of ʿAdjam. When it is positioned on E, it is the reposition of ʿAdjam on F; when it is positioned on D, it is the reposition of ʿAdjam on E♭.

Repositions

LĀMĪ IS A CYCLICAL diatonic scale, and therefore all other diatonic scales, such as the scales of ʿAdjam, Kurd, Nahawand Kabīr, and Nahawand, can be produced by repositioning the tonic within its scale. See the section about maqām ʿAdjam.

Transpositions

There are no distinct transpositions of Lāmī.

Modulations

Since it is a diatonic scale, modulations from Lāmī to other diatonic scales, such as ʿAdjam, Nahawand, and Kurd, are easy to perform. When playing Nahawand, it is nice to modulate to Lāmī on the fifth note of the scale; in Nahawand on C1, for example, this will be Lāmī on G2.

Another option is to embellish ʿAdjam with a modulation to Lāmī on its fifth note. If we ascend in Adjam on C1 to its octave note, C2, we can then descend to Lāmī on G2 by first altering D2 to D♭2.

Other possibilities are modulations to maqām Ṣabā on the tonic of Lāmī or on its fourth note and to Bayāt on its fourth note.

Al-Mahdī notes that there is a variant of Lāmī that is called maqām Qatar (19??: 66). It is composed of djins Lāmī on the tonic and djins Ḥidjāz on the third note of the scale in conjunct sequence:

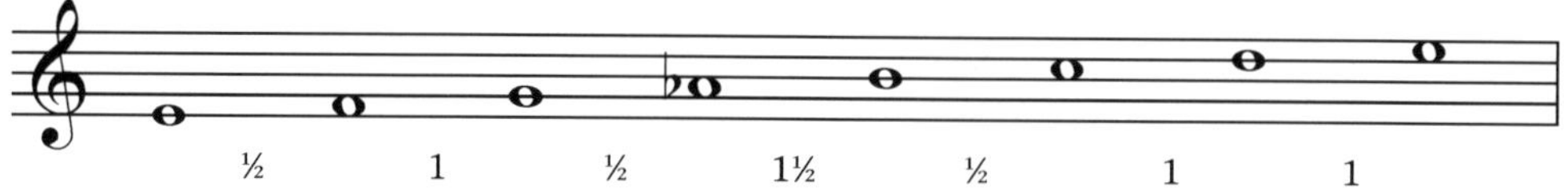

I do not know why al-Mahdī determines that this scale is a variant of the scale of Lāmī; it looks more like a transposition of the scale of Ṣabā Zamzama.[1]

1 See the sections on maqām Ṣabā and maqām Ṣabā Zamzama.

The Progression of the Maqām

THE PROGRESSION OF Lāmī usually starts from its ghammāz (G2) and emphasizes A♭2 and B♭2. Then the melody emphasizes F1 before descending to the tonic. Tracks 13 and 14 of the accompanying CD are two musical examples of Lāmī.

4. Maqām Ṭarz Nawīn

The Scale

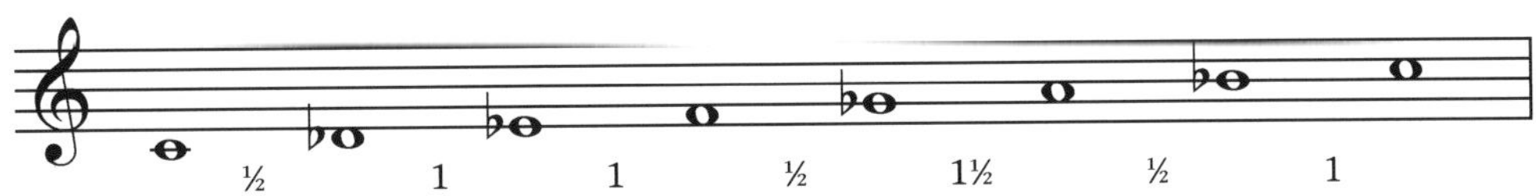

Intervals: ½–1–1–½–1½–½–1 (tones)

Analysis of the Scale

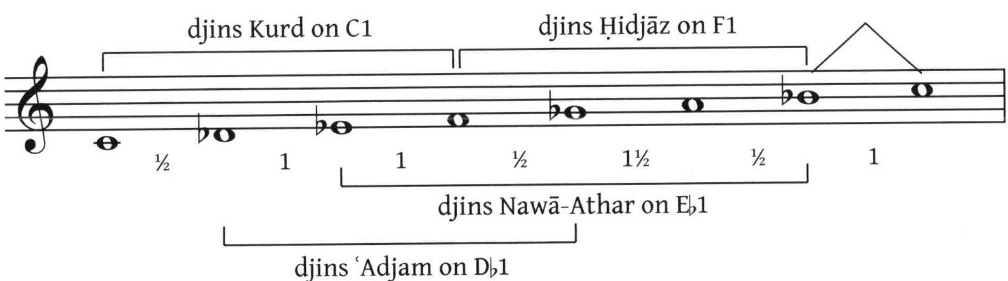

Adjnās

Primary adjnās: djins Kurd on C1
djins Ḥidjāz on F1
(conjunct adjnās)

Secondary adjnās: djins ʿAdjam on D♭1
djins Nawā-Athar on E♭1

The second octave of the scale of Ṭarz Nawīn is different from its first one. Al-Ḥilū says that the second octave of the ascending scale has djins Ḥidjāz on C2 and djins Nahawand on F2, while in the descending scale the second octave is composed of djins Ḥidjāz on F2 and djins Kurd on C2 (al-Ḥilū 1972: 116):

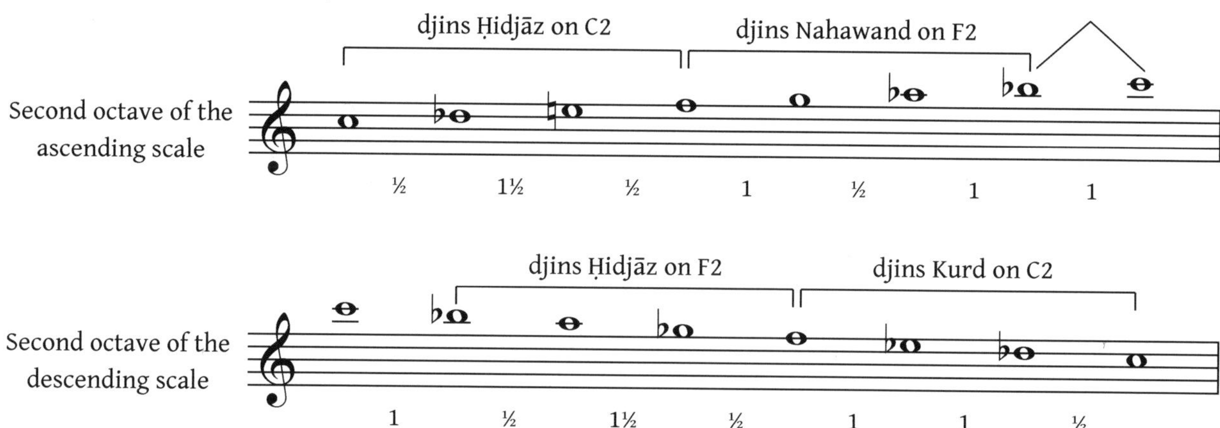

Therefore, the notes that are altered when ascending or descending are:

Ascending with E♮2 – descending with E♭2
Ascending with G♮3 – descending with G♭3
Ascending with A♭3 – descending with A♮3

Al-Mahdī mentions that the third djins of the scale is djins Ḥidjāz on C2, yet he does not talk about a fourth djins or about differences between the ascending and descending scales (19??: 46).

Even though the first djins of this scale is Kurd, the semitone between the fourth note and the fifth note while ascending causes this scale to sound very similar to the scale of Lāmī.

The Name

The words Ṭarz Nawīn mean "a new form" in Persian.

The Conventional Position

C1 (Rāst)

Repositions

The first reposition up forms the scale of Ṭarz Djadīd on D♭.[1]
The second reposition up forms the scale of Nakrīz on E♭.
The third reposition up forms the scale of Ḥidjāz-Humayūn on F.
The fourth reposition up forms the scale of Midmī on G.
The fifth reposition up forms the scale of Mustaʿār ʿIrāqī on A.
The sixth reposition up forms the scale of the second species of Nahawand on B♭.

Transpositions

There are no distinct transpositions of Ṭarz Nawīn.

1 This scale was presented by the Egyptian delegation to the Cairo Congress of Arab Music in 1932. According to al-Mahdī, Ṭarz Djadīd is composed of djins ʿAdjam on B♭1 (Qarār ʿAdjam) and djins Ḥidjāz on D1 (Dūkāh) (19??: 45).

Modulations

THE FIRST THREE intervals of Ṭarz Nawīn are the same as in Lāmī. It is therefore easy to modulate to Lāmī.

If we ascend to C2, we can modulate to Ḥidjāz-Kār-Kurd by altering A1 to A♭1 and G♭1 to G1 when descending.

It is easy to modulate to Nahawand on G2 by using F♯1 as a leading note.

Another possibility is to alter D♭1 to D♮1 and then modulate to Ṣabā Zamzama on D1 or to Ṣabā on D1 by also altering E♭1 to E𝄳1.

The Progression of the Maqām

THE FOREMOST MELODIC characteristic of maqām Ṭarz Nawīn is the emphasis of djins Ḥidjāz on F1. The progression starts from this djins and then ascends to Ḥidjāz on C2 (the third djins) and Nahawand on F2 (the fourth djins). When descending, the progression employs djins Ḥidjāz on F2, instead of Nahawand, and djins Kurd on C2, instead of Ḥidjāz. From C2, the melody descends through the second and first adjnās and establishes the tonic by using B♭1 as a leading note.

CHAPTER 15

THE NAWĀ-ATHAR FAMILY OF MAQĀMĀT

1. Maqām Nawā-Athar

2. Maqām Nakrīz

3. Maqām Ḥiṣār

DJINS NAWĀ-ATHAR is composed of the four intervals 1–½–1½–½ (tones), and is therefore a djins of five notes (a pentachord). The scale of Nawā-Athar is the third reposition up of the scale of Shadd-ʿArabān, which is a transposition of Ḥidjāz-Kār to G1. Some scholars who do not classify maqāmāt families according to the first djins of the scale, list Nawā-Athar, Nakrīz, and Ḥiṣār as belonging to the Ḥidjāz family (al-ʿAbbas 1986: 58). There is some logic to this classification, since all these scales contain at least one djins Ḥidjāz as one of their secondary or primary adjnās.

Al-Ḥilū, on the other hand, lists Nawā-Athar as belonging to the Ḥiṣār family, Nakrīz to the Nakrīz family, and Ḥiṣār to the Nawā-Athar family (1972: 114, 111, 130). I do not know which method of classification al-Ḥilū uses, but it seems that his classification is not systematic. In a similar way, al-Mahdī's explanations are incoherent. Al-Mahdī states that Nawā-Athar is composed of djins Nawā-Athar and djins Ḥidjāz; he classifies Nakrīz as belonging to the Nawā-Athar family, while when talking about maqām Ḥiṣār, he says that its first djins is Nakrīz (19??: 31, 47).

As we can see, there is some mix-up between the names Nakrīz and Nawā-Athar, which are attributed by different scholars to the same djins (1–½–1½–½ tones). In this book, we will name this djins "Nawā-Athar."

Similarly to the Ḥidjāz family, the scales of the Nawā-Athar family are considered to be very moving and emotional. The scale of Nakrīz has a peculiar feature: by repositioning its tonic, seven scales of recognizable maqāmāt can be formed; the scale of Nakrīz can therefore be considered a cyclical scalar system.

1. Maqām Nawā-Athar 

The Scale

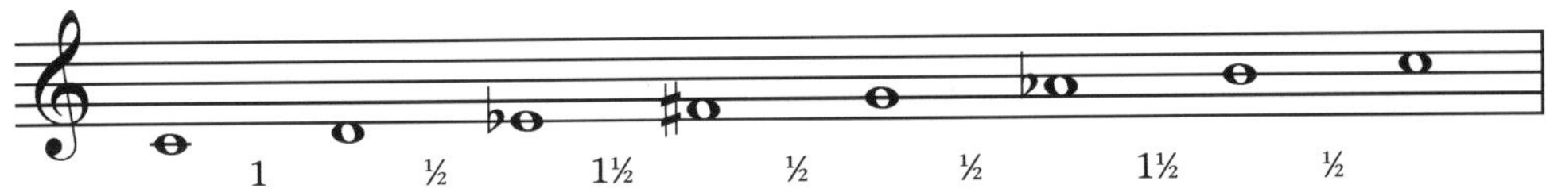

Intervals: 1–½–1½–½–½–1½–½ (tones)

Analysis of the Scale

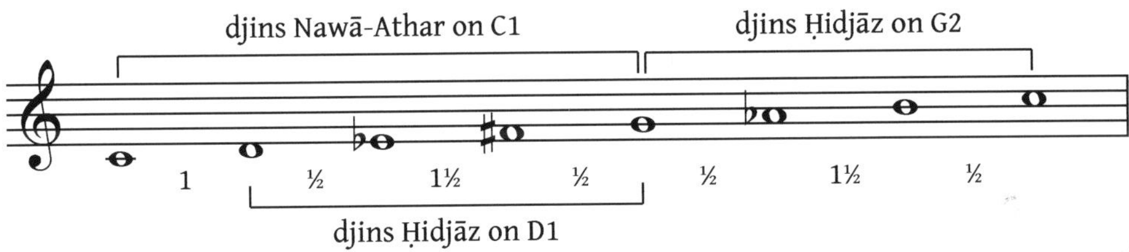

Adjnās

Primary adjnās: djins Nawā-Athar on C1
djins Ḥidjāz on G2
(conjunct adjnās)

Secondary adjnās: djins Ḥidjāz on D1

The Name

THIS MAQĀM IS called "Neveser" in Turkish. Al-Ḥilū names it Nawāthar and says it is a Persian name that means "the new style" or "the new influence" (1972: 214).

The Conventional Position

C1 (Rāst)

Repositions

THE FOURTH REPOSITION up, or the third down, forms the scale of Shadd-ʿArabān on G.

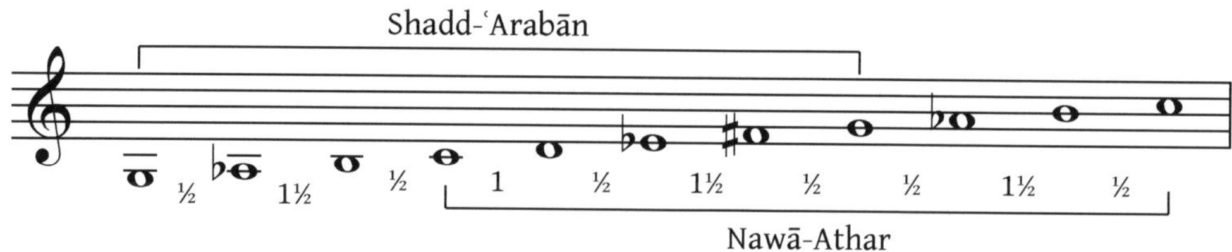

Transpositions

The transposition of Nawā-Athar to D1 is called Ḥiṣār.

Modulations

WE CAN MODULATE to Nakrīz by altering A♭2 to A♮2 and B2 to B♭2, that is, changing the second djins to djins Nahawand:

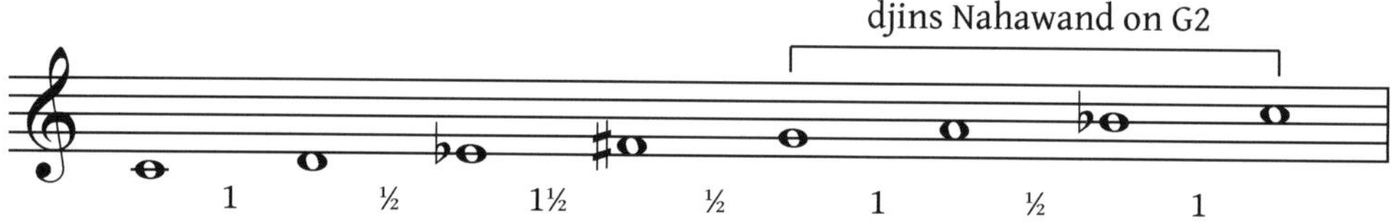

Each reposition of the scale of Nakrīz forms a new scale.[1] Therefore, there are many possibilities of modulating from Nawā-Athar to other scales.

We can easily modulate to scales of the Ḥidjāz family, because the scale of Nawā-Athar contains djins Ḥidjāz as both one of its primary adjnās and one of its secondary ones.

Modulating to Nahawand on C1, either of the first or the second species, is also very common. Other common modulations of Nawā-Athar include Bayāt on G2, Rāst on C1, and Ṣabā on G2 or C1.

The Progression of the Maqām

THE PROGRESSION STARTS from the first djins, Nawā-Athar on C1, and then ascends to the second djins, Ḥidjāz on G2. Sometimes the progression starts from the ghammāz (G2) and the second djins, ascends to the octave, and then descends. When descending back to the tonic, we should use the leading note, B1, in order to establish the tonic firmly.

Al-Ḥilū mentions that the progression should descend to djins Ḥidjāz on G1 (below the tonic) before returning to the tonic (1972: 114), but I am not sure that this is a typical progression of this maqām.

1 See the section on maqām Nakrīz below.

2. Maqām Nakrīz

The Scale

Intervals: 1–½–1½–½–1–½–1 (tones)

Analysis of the Scale

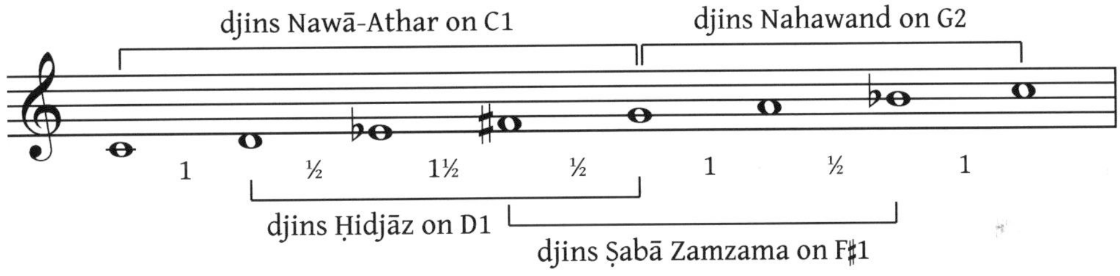

Adjnās

Primary adjnās: djins Nawā-Athar on C1
djins Nahawand on G2
(conjunct adjnās)

Secondary adjnās: djins Ḥidjāz on D1
djins Ṣabā Zamzama on F♯1

Al-Ḥilū thinks that when descending, B♭2 should be altered to B𝄳2 so the second djins changes to Rāst on G2; he claims that such a progression is integral to the maqām (1972: 111).

Al-Nur referred me to a song by Ṣalāḥ al-Kuwaytī (1908–1986), a famous Jewish violinist and composer who came to Baghdad from Kuwait in the 1920s and became an important figure of twentieth century Iraqi music. In this song, he uses the scale of Nakrīz with B𝄳2. Al-Nur himself uses the note B♮ in his samāʿī in maqām Nakrīz. He suggests that there are three species of Nakrīz: one with B♭, one with B𝄳, and one with B♮.

However, in his famous samāʿī in maqām Nawā-Athar, ʿAbd al-Munʿim al-Ḥarīrī, an Egyptian musician and composer, modulates to maqām Nakrīz in the second *khānah* (section) and uses B♭2 throughout this khānah.

The Name

According to al-Mahdī, Nakrīz is a Persian word that means "do not escape" (19??: 31).

The Conventional Position

C1 (Rāst)

Repositions

The first reposition up forms the scale of Ḥidjāz-Humayūn on D1.	½-1½-½-1-½-1-1 (tones)
The second reposition up forms the scale of Midmī on E♭1.	1½-½-1-½-1-1-½ (tones)
The third reposition up forms the scale of Mustaʿār ʿIrāqī on F♯1.	½-1-½-1-1-½-1½ (tones)
The fourth reposition up forms the scale of the second species of Nahawand on G2.	1-½-1-1-½-1½-½ (tones)
The fifth reposition up forms the scale of Ṭarz Nawīn on A2.	½-1-1-½-1½-½-1 (tones)
The sixth reposition up forms the scale of Ṭarz Djadīd on B♭2.	1-1-½-1½-½-1-½ (tones)

Transpositions

Not known

Modulations

MAQĀM NAKRĪZ IS closely related to maqām Nawā-Athar. Modulating between these two related maqāmāt, by altering between djins Nahawand and djins Ḥidjāz on G2, can sound very interesting. Therefore, we can also apply all the common modulations of Nawā-Athar to Nakrīz. Since so many scales can be formed by repositioning the tonic of Nakrīz, musicians can perform a variety of modulations. For example, by ascending to C2, descending to G2, and then using F♯1 as a leading note we can easily modulate to Nahawand on G2. From Nahawand on G2, we can easily modulate to Bayāt, Kurd, or Lāmī on G2. Another typical progression of Nakrīz is to modulate to Ṣabā on D2 and then descend to Nahawand on G2.

The Progression of the Maqām

WHEN PERFORMING MAQĀM Nakrīz, the second djins-- Nahawand on G2 – must be emphasized in the beginning of the progression in order to differentiate it from maqām Nawā-Athar.

Al-Ḥilū, on the other hand, suggests that the progression of the maqām starts from its tonic, with a slight emphasis of B𝄳1 (1972: 111). He claims that the progression of any maqām should start from its first djins, since it is the "basic" djins of the scale, and therefore the progression should start with it as well as end with it. However, in my opinion, though the first djins of a maqām is important, many times the traditional melodic progression of the maqām (sayr al-maqām) requires starting the progression from elsewhere on the scale – from the second djins, or even the third.

Al-Ḥilū adds that when descending, B♭2 should be altered to B𝄳2 so the second djins is Rāst on G2, and that the melody should pass through B𝄳1 before the progression ends on the tonic C1.

3. Maqām Ḥiṣār

The Scale

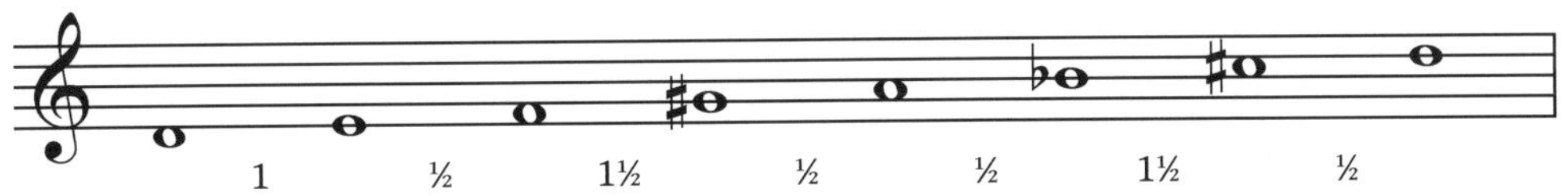

Intervals: 1–½–1½–½–½–1½–½ (tones)

Analysis of the Scale

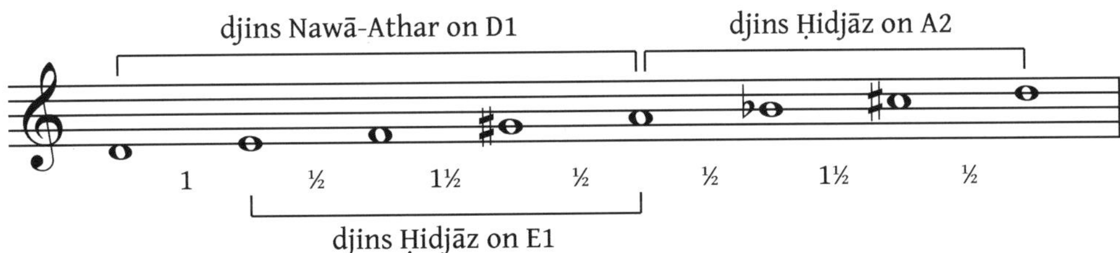

Adjnās

Primary adjnās: djins Nawā-Athar on D1
djins Ḥidjāz on A2
(conjunct adjnās)

Secondary adjnās: djins Ḥidjāz on E1

The scale of Ḥiṣār as it appears above is a transposition of the scale of Nawā-Athar to D1. The analysis of the primary adjnās of both of these scales is also identical.

Al-Ḥilū, however, thinks the first djins of maqām Ḥiṣār is "djins Ḥiṣār or Bayātī on D1 that consists of five notes" (1972: 130). The second djins of Ḥiṣār, in his analysis, is Ḥidjāz on A2. Al-Ḥilū, therefore, gives two alternatives for the second note of the scale – E♮1 and E𝄳1 – and his analysis of the scale of Ḥiṣār looks like this:

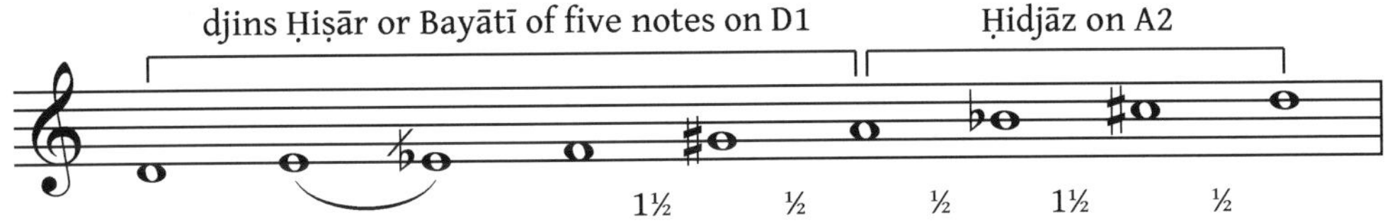

I must comment on al-Ḥilū's conception of the analysis of the Ḥiṣār: Nowhere else have I seen an Arab scholar using two different adjnās as the first primary djins of a scale, nor have I seen a djins Bayāt consisting of five notes.

Furthermore, playing the scale of Ḥiṣār with the second note as E𝄳1 forms a djins that consists of the intervals ¾–¾–1½ (tones), which seems like an "illogical" djins that has no connection with djins Bayāt.

In his list of adjnās, al-Ḥilū mentions two adjnās – djins Nawā-Athar and djins Ḥiṣār – as two distinct adjnās. Both of these adjnās appear as consisting of the same intervals. However, the former is positioned on C1, while the latter is positioned on D1:

I do not agree with the method of giving different names to adjnās that have an identical intervallic structure only because they are written on different conventional positions. Such a system is confusing and complicates the systematic classification of adjnās and maqāmāt.

Even al-Ḥilū himself has difficulties in defining the differences between these two adjnās. When talking about djins Ḥiṣār he writes: "that is, djins Nawā-Athar on D1" (ibid.). He also remarks later that djins Bayāt on D1 can be ignored – it is not considered a primary djins of the scale and appears only as a passing variation, and that the progression finishes on djins Ḥiṣār on D1. Furthermore, almost all scholars agree that djins Nawā-Athar consists of five notes, so al-Ḥilū's remark that djins Nawā-Athar consists of only four notes seems strange.

Al-Mahdī analyzes the scale of Nawā-Athar very briefly and says it consists of djins Nakrīz (his name for djins Nawā-Athar) on D1 and djins Ḥidjāz on A2 (19??: 47).

The Name

The origin of the name of this maqām is rather obscure. The word Ḥiṣār means "a siege" in Arabic, and it may be the origin of the name.

The Conventional Position

D1 (Dūkāh)

Repositions

All the repositions applicable to Nawā-Athar can be applied to Ḥiṣār.

Transpositions

The scale of Ḥiṣār is a transposition of Nawā-Athar to D1.

Modulations

All the modulations applicable to Nawā-Athar can be applied to Ḥiṣār.

The Progression of the Maqām

THE TYPICAL PROGRESSION of Ḥiṣār emphasizes its primary adjnās – djins Nawā-Athar on D1 and djins Ḥidjāz on A2. The progression starts by exposing the second djins, Ḥidjāz on A2, while using G♯2 as a leading note to A2. The progression then descends to the first djins, Nawā-Athar on D1. Ḥiṣār has some typical modulations that appear as part of its progression, for example, Kurd on A2 or Nahawand on G2.

CHAPTER 16

THE ḤIDJĀZ FAMILY OF MAQĀMĀT

1. Maqām Ḥidjāz

2. Maqām Ḥidjāz-Kār

3. Maqām Shadd-ʿArabān

4. Maqām Shāhnaz

5. Maqām Zandjarān or Zank-Kalā

6. Maqām Sūzdāl

DJINS ḤIDJĀZ (½–1½–½ tones) is one of the most important adjnās of Arab music. It is considered a very romantic, emotional, and even melancholic djins. It is the second djins in the scales of many maqāmāt, such as Sūznāk, Awshār, and Bayāt Shūrī. Djins Ḥidjāz can be considered a very "flexible" djins – it is easy to modulate to it and from it.

All the maqāmāt of the Ḥidjāz family are very romantic and emotional and many of them are composed of two adjnās of Ḥidjāz – both their first as well as their second djins is Ḥidjāz. The name Ḥidjāz is the name of a region in today's Saudi Arabia. It is interesting to note that this scale appears in many musical cultures under various names.

1. Maqām Ḥidjāz

The Scale

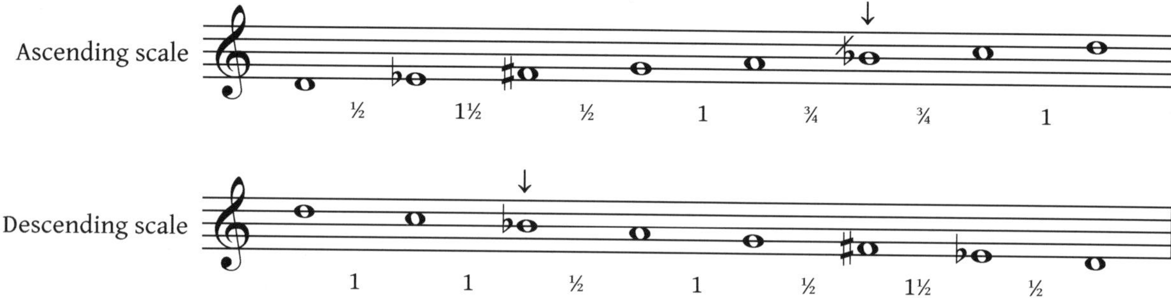

Intervals:

ascending scale: ½–1½–½–1–¾–¾–1 (tones)
descending scale: ½–1½–½–1–½–1–1 (tones)
(ascending with B𝄳2; descending with B♭2)

Analysis of the Scale

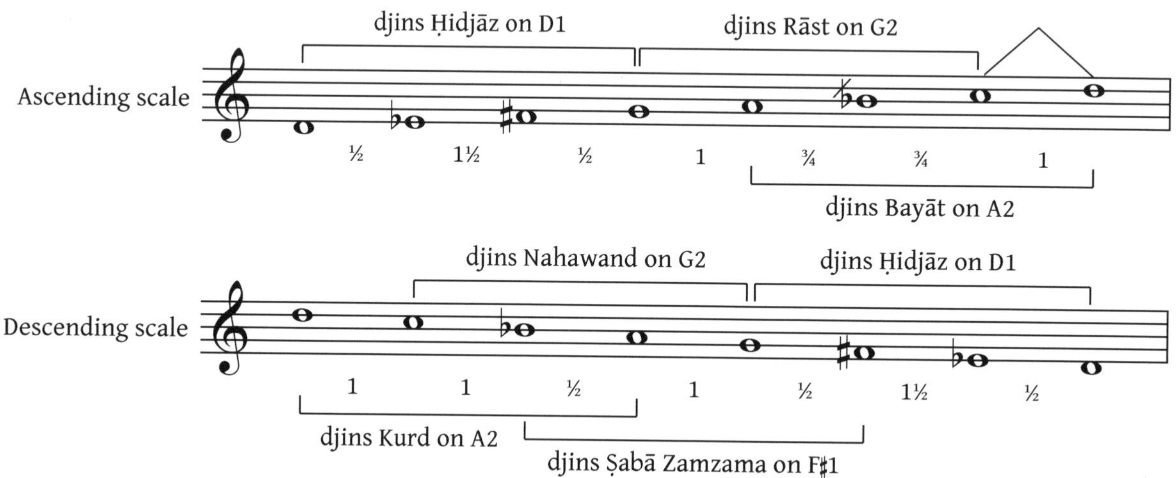

Adjnās

Primary adjnās:

In the ascending scale:	djins Ḥidjāz on D1 djins Rāst on G2 (conjunct adjnās)
In the descending scale:	djins Ḥidjāz on D1 djins Nahawand on G2 (conjunct adjnās)

Secondary adjnās

In the ascending scale:	djins Bayāt on A2
In the descending scale:	djins Kurd on A2 djins Ṣabā Zamzama on F♯1

As we can see in the above analysis, the scale of maqām Ḥidjāz ascends with B𝄳2, but descends with B♭2. Most Arab scholars write this scale in this way. Al-Ḥilū, on the other hand, suggests that the scale of Ḥidjāz consists of two octaves, and he adds variations that cannot be found in other theory books (1972: 120).

There are several variations to the analysis presented above. Some scholars, for example, divide the ascending scale into djins Ḥidjāz on D1 and djins Bayāt on A2 in a disjunct sequence:

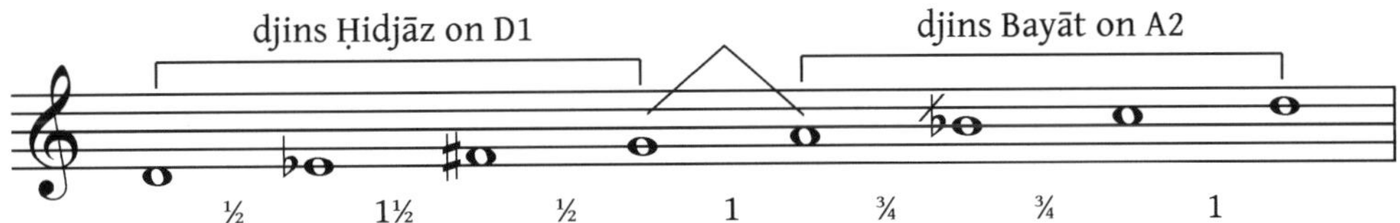

Sometimes the descending scale is not divided as above, into djins Ḥidjāz on D1 and djins Nahawand on G2 in a conjunct sequence, but into Djins Ḥidjāz on D1 and djins Kurd on A2 in a disjunct sequence:

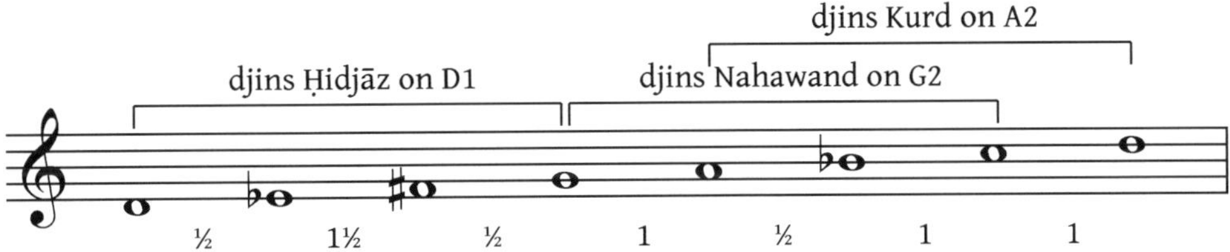

I think that the contradicting views on the analysis of Ḥidjāz presented above stem from the fact that the changes in the sixth note of the scale (B♭ or B𝄳) are not always a part of the structure of the maqām, but are sometimes the result of transitory embellishments. The real differences between the various forms of maqām Ḥidjāz are apparent in the various ways its primary and secondary adjnās are emphasized.

Yinon Muallem, a musician who learned and performed Turkish classical music, has explained to me that in Turkish music, there are four forms of the scale of Ḥidjāz, which acquire names according to the second djins of their scale:

The scale composed of djins Ḥidjāz on D1 and djins Rāst on G2 is called Ḥidjāz

The scale composed of djins Ḥidjāz on D1 and djins Nahawand on G2 is called Ḥidjāz-Humayūn

The scale composed of djins Ḥidjāz on D1 and djins Bayāt on A2 is called ʿUzzāl

The scale composed of djins Ḥidjāz on D1 and djins Ḥidjāz on A2 is called Zirgule'li Ḥidjāz

Elias comments that in Egypt, musicians distinguish between two main species of Ḥidjāz. The first one, Ḥidjāz with B𝄳, is called Ḥidjāz Miṣrī, because of the definite Arab, or "Egyptian" (*miṣrī*), flavor that the quartertone note gives to the scale; while Ḥidjāz with B♭ is called Ḥidjāz ʿAdjamī, because of the "foreign" (ʿ*adjamī*) flavor of this scale. It must be noted that there are several other scales that are conventionally positioned on D1 in which the notes B♭ and B𝄳 alternate.[1]

The many names associated with maqām Ḥidjāz are not essential to the study and analysis of this maqām, though it is interesting to observe the great importance given to this scale.

The Name

THE NAME ḤIDJĀZ is the name of a region in today's Saudi Arabia. Al-Mahdī, therefore, concludes that it is a "genuine" Arab scale (19??: 36). This maqām appears under many names in various Arab countries: in Tunisia, it is known as al-ʾIsbaʿayn; in Algeria, as al-Zayyidan; in other Maghrib countries, as Al-Ḥidjāz al-Kabīr; and in Iraq, as al-Mathnawī. Like many other maqāmāt of the Ḥidjāz family, maqām Ḥidjāz is one of the most important maqāmāt in the Arab and Turkish musical cultures.

The Conventional Position

D1 (Dūkāh)

Repositions

Repositions of Ḥidjāz with B𝄳 :

The third reposition up forms the scale of Sūznāk on G.

The fourth reposition up forms the scale of Bayāt Shūrī (or Qārdjighār) on A.

The fifth reposition up forms the scale of Huzām on B𝄳.

The sixth reposition up forms the scale of one of the species of Nakrīz on C.[2]

Repositions of Ḥidjāz with B♭:

The first reposition up forms the scale of Midmī on E♭. Midmī is an Iraqi maqām that is little known in the rest of the Arab world; its first djins is composed of 1½–½–1 (tones).

The second reposition up forms the scale of Mustaʿār ʿIrāqī on F♯. It is a different scale than the scale of Mustaʿār (al-Nur).

The third reposition up forms the scale of the second species of Nahawand on G.

The fourth reposition up forms the scale of Ṭarz Nawīn on A.

The fifth reposition up forms the scale of Ṭarz Djadīd on B♭.[3]

The sixth reposition up forms the scale of the second species of Nakrīz on C.

Transpositions

Not known

Modulations

DJINS ḤIDJĀZ IS a very flexible djins and it is easy to modulate from it as well as to it. It can be easily combined with other adjnās to form various scales, or its notes can be altered to form a different djins. There are many possibilities of modulations when using this djins.

As was shown above in the section about the repositions of the scale of Hidjas, it can be repositioned to form many scales; these can all be considered options for modulations.

We can alter the note C2 to C♯2 in order to modulate to Ḥidjāz-Kār on D1 (the Turkish Zirgule'li Ḥidjāz), or we can descend below the tonic D1 with djins Ḥidjāz on G1 and modulate to maqām Shadd-ʿArabān.

1 See for example the chapter on the Bayāt family and especially the sections on maqām Ḥusaynī and maqām Muḥayyar there.

2 See the section on Nakrīz.

3 See the section about repositions of the scale of Nahawand.

Descending below the tonic to B♭̸1 would result in a modulation to Huzām on B♭̸1 (Rāḥat al-Arwāḥ). From there, we can ascend back to the tonic D1, establish djins Ṣabā on it, and then descend back to B♭̸1 in order to modulate to maqām Bastah-Nikār.

The Progression of the Maqām

THE PROGRESSION OF maqām Ḥidjāz can start either from its tonic and first djins or from its higher adjnās – Nahawand on G2, Rāst on G2, or Bayāt on A2. When starting from its first djins, it is preferable to start with the note C1 and later even descend to djins Rāst on G1 before ascending to the second djins.

Track 17 on the accompanying CD demonstrates Ḥidjāz, while track 18 demonstrates Ḥidjāz-Humayūn.

2. Maqām Ḥidjāz-Kār

The Scale

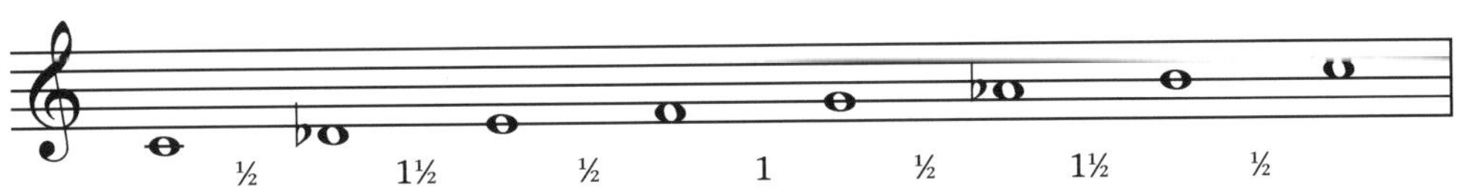

Intervals: ½–1½–½–1–½–1½–½ (tones)

Analysis of the Scale

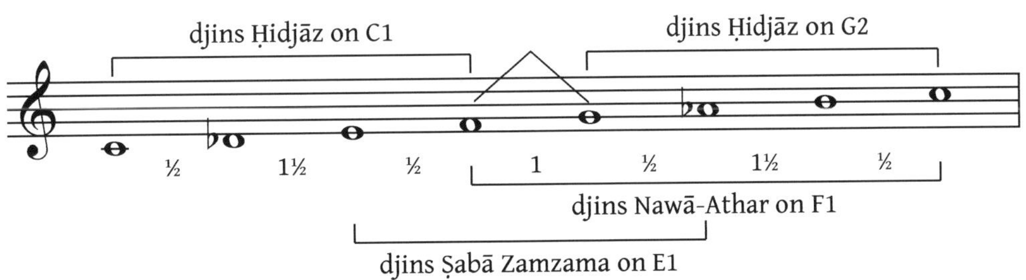

Adjnās

Primary adjnās:

- djins Ḥidjāz on C1
- djins Ḥidjāz on G2
- (disjunct adjnās)

Secondary adjnās

- djins Ṣabā Zamzama on E1
- djins Nawā-Athar on F1

Most Arab musicologists agree that the first djins of the second octave of maqām Ḥidjāz-Kār (that is the third djins, positioned on C2) is djins Nahawand; this is a unique characteristic that distinguishes it from other similar maqāmāt, such as Shadd-ʿArabān. Al-Ḥilū explains that the third djins should be either Nahawand or Ḥidjāz (1972: 112). Al-Mahdī also stresses the option of employing djins Nahawand instead of Ḥidjāz in the second octave before descending towards the first djins (19??: 32).

In a similar way, maqām Shāhnaz, which is a transposition of Ḥidjāz-Kār to D1, starts with djins Nahawand on the octave note (that is, as the third djins) and then descends towards the tonic.

The Name

THE NAME ḤIDJĀZ is the name of a region in today's Saudi Arabia. In Persian and Ottoman Turkish, the word *kār* means "work," "operation." The meaning of the name is therefore "making Ḥidjāz," or maybe "elaborating on Ḥidjāz." This scale acquired an important position in various Middle-Eastern musical cultures. In Iran, it is called Chargah. In Turkey, its transposition to D1 is called Shāhnaz or Zirgule'li Ḥidjāz, and its transposition to A1 is called Sūzdāl or Sūzdīl. According to al-Ḥilū, this scale was originally positioned on D1, but the Turks, or the Persians before them, transposed it to C1, and therefore it acquired unique characteristics and its melodic progression has changed a little (1972: 112).

The Conventional Position

C1 (Rāst)

Repositions

The second reposition up forms the scale of Ṣabā Zamzama on E1.
The third reposition up forms the scale of Nawā-Athar on F1.

Transpositions

WHEN THE SCALE of Ḥidjāz-Kār is transposed to G1, it is called Shadd-ʿArabān; when it is transposed to A1, Sūzdāl or Sūzdīl. In Turkey, its transposition to D1 is called Shāhnaz or Zirgule'li Ḥidjāz.

Modulations

AS WAS MENTIONED above, djins Ḥidjāz can be considered a very "flexible" djins – it is easy to modulate to it or from it. Since the scale of Ḥidjāz-Kār is composed of two adjnās of Ḥidjāz (on C1 and on G2), it is easy to perform modulations with it. If we descend to G1 with djins Kurd (C1–B♭1–A♭1–G1), we can modulate to scales of the Kurd family, such as Kurd and Lāmī, on G1. Another nice modulation is to descend from C1 to djins Ṣabā on A1 through B𝄳1. Modulating to Ṣabā on G2 might require some more skill, but can combine nicely with a descent on djins Ḥidjāz to the tonic C1.

The Progression of the Maqām

The progression of maqām Ḥidjāz-Kār must emphasize the two primary adjnās Ḥidjāz – on C1 and on G2. The progression must start from the octave note (C2), which can be emphasized by the leading note B2. It then ascends to the third djins of the scale, which may be either Ḥidjāz or Nahawand on C2, and descends through djins Ḥidjāz on G2 and djins Nahawand on F1 to the first djins. The leading note B1 should be used to emphasize the conclusion on the tonic C1.

A very common embellishment of Ḥidjāz-Kār is to alter G2 to G♭2 when descending. This is usually done by passing first through E1 and F1, emphasizing G♭2 and then descending to the tonic.

3. Maqām Shadd-ʿArabān

The Scale

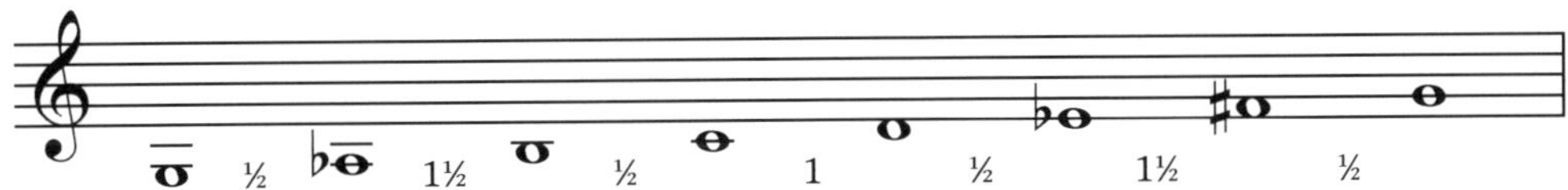

Intervals: ½–1½–½–1–½–1½–½ (tones)

Analysis of the Scale

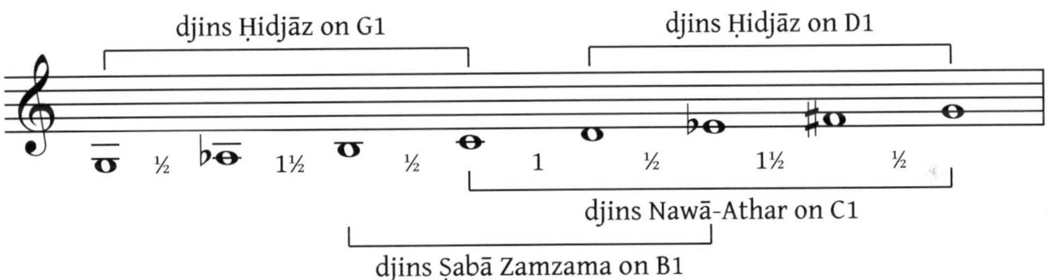

Adjnās

Primary adjnās:

djins Ḥidjāz on G1
djins Ḥidjāz on D1
(disjunct adjnās)

Secondary adjnās:

djins Ṣabā Zamzama on B1
djins Nawā-Athar on C1

One of the characteristics of maqām Shadd-ʿArabān is that when descending to the tonic G1, the F♯ is often altered to F♮ in order to form djins Nahawand on C1:

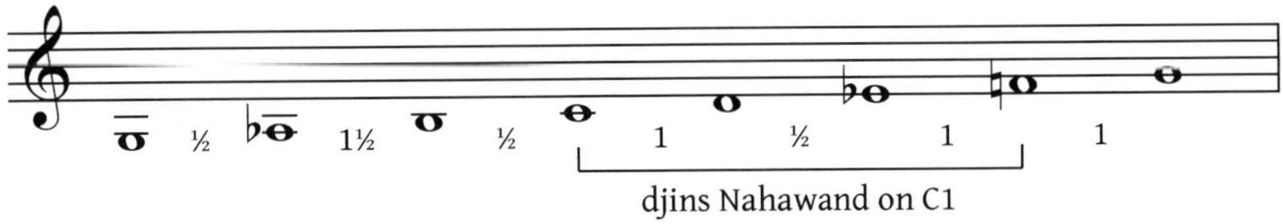

Another characteristic of Shadd-ʿArabān, which distinguishes it from maqām Ḥidjāz-Kār, is that its third djins (the first djins of the second octave) is Ḥidjāz and not Nahawand.

The Name

THE WORD "SHADD" (or "Shed") is a Turkish word. Its meaning is somewhat close to "transposition" and it refers to scales that are transposed from their conventional tonics to other tonics. The name "ʿArabān" is the name of a maqām that is rarely used anymore in Turkey today; its scale is similar to Ḥidjāz and its tonic is G2. The name of maqām Shadd-ʿArabān therefore, comes from the transposition of the scale of ʿArabān to G1. Al-Ḥilū suggests that the name "ʿArabān" comes from a mispronunciation of the name "ʿArabā," which was the old name of maqām Ḥidjāz among the Arabs (1972: 96).

The Conventional Position

G1 (Yakāh)

Repositions

THE SAME AS with the scale of Ḥidjāz-Kār:
The second reposition up forms the scale of Ṣabā Zamzama on B1.
The third reposition up forms the scale of Nawā-Athar on C1.

Transpositions

The scale of maqām Shadd-ʿArabān is a transposition of the scale of Ḥidjāz-Kār

Modulations

ANY OF THE modulations that are applicable to the scale of Ḥidjāz-Kār can be applied to Shadd-ʿArabān.

The Progression of the Maqām

THE PROGRESSION OF maqām Shadd-ʿArabān must emphasize both djins Nawā-Athar and djins Nahawand on C1. The progression starts from the third djins, then descends to the second djins – Ḥidjāz on D1 – and then alternates between djins Nawā-Athar and djins Nahawand on C1 by alternating between F♯1 and F♮1. The progression can then ascend to the fourth djins (the second djins of the second octave) which also alternates between Nahawand and Nawā-Athar on C2. From there, the progression descends back to the second djins (Ḥidjāz on D1, Nawā-Athar or Nahawand on C1) and from there to the tonic G1. The leading note F♯ (below G1) can be used to emphasize the conclusion on the tonic G1.

4. Maqām Shāhnaz

The Scale

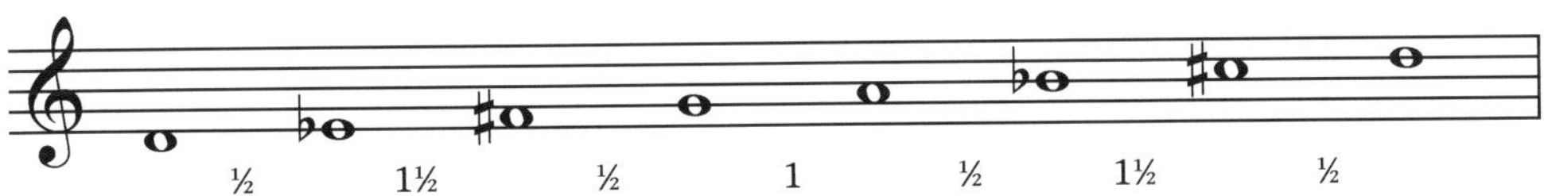

Intervals: ½–1½–½–1–½–1½–½ (tones)

Analysis of the Scale

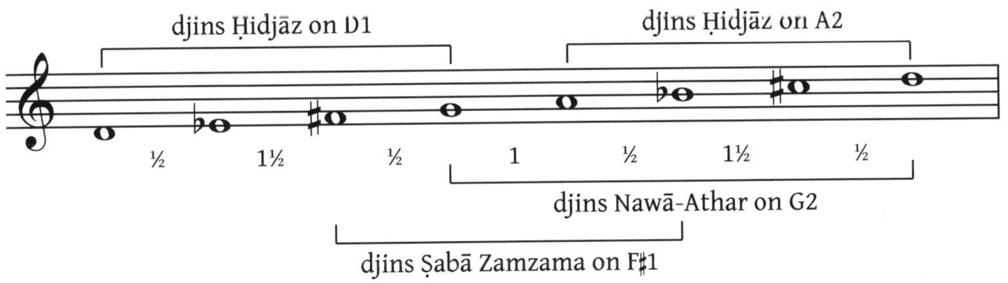

Adjnās

Primary adjnās:
- djins Ḥidjāz on D1
- djins Ḥidjāz on A2
- (disjunct adjnās)

Secondary adjnās:
- djins Ṣabā Zamzama on F♯1
- djins Nawā-Athar on G2

The Name

"Shāhnaz" is a Persian name that means "the sultan's delights." Shāhnaz is the name of the note D♯2, which is rarely used in the system of maqām scales. It may be that this unique note has given its name to this scale, which is a transposition of the scale of Ḥidjāz-Kār to D1.

The Conventional Position

D1 (Dūkāh)

Repositions

Any of the repositions that are applicable to the scale of Ḥidjāz-Kār can be applied to Shāhnaz.

Transpositions

The scale of Shāhnaz is a transposition of Ḥidjāz-Kār to D1.

Modulations

ANY OF THE modulations that are applicable to the scale of Ḥidjāz-Kār can be applied to Shāhnaz. However, since the tonic is D1 and not C1, some modulations to scales that are conventionally positioned on D1, such as Bayāt, may be easier.

The Progression of the Maqām

MANY WRITERS MENTION maqām Shāhnaz only in passing; it may be that it is considered merely a transposition of maqma Ḥidjāz-Kār. Salman sees Shāhnaz as a transposition of Ḥidjāz-Kār, but its third djins is djins Nahawand on D2. The progression of maqām Shāhnaz is essentially descending; it starts from djins Nahawand on D2 and then descends to the second and first adjnās. Usually, when descending, C♯2 is altered to C♮2 and B♭2 is altered to B♮2.

5. Maqām Zandjarān or Maqām Zank-Kalā

The Scale

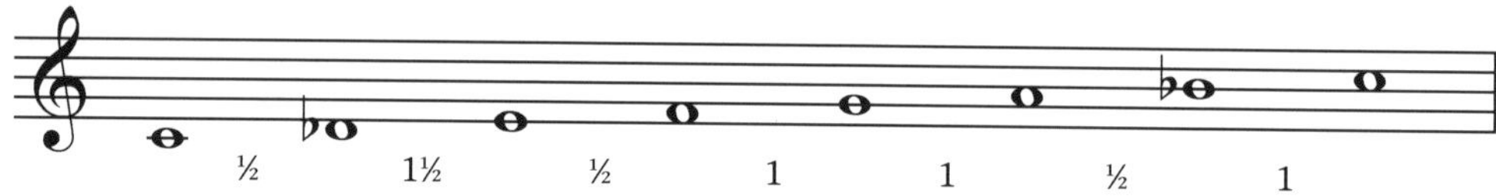

Intervals: ½–1½–½–1–1–½–1 (tones)

Analysis of the Scale

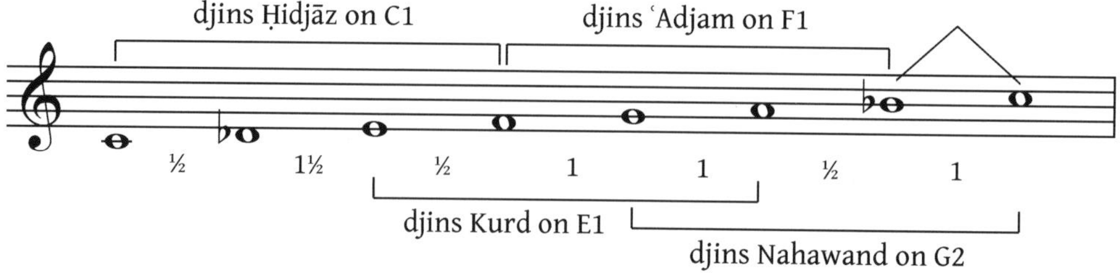

Adjnās

Primary adjnās:

djins Ḥidjāz on C1
djins ʿAdjam on F1
(conjunct adjnās)

Secondary adjnās:

djins Kurd on E1
djins Nahawand on G2

The Name

THIS SCALE, which is composed of the intervals ½–1½–½–1–1–½–1 (tones), is known throughout the Arab world as Zandjarān or Sandjarān. Nevertheless, both al-ʿAbbas and al-Mahdī do not mention any such name. Al-ʿAbbas calls this scale Zank-Kalā, while al-Mahdī calls it Zunkulāh (al-ʿAbbas 1986: 60; al-Mahdī 19??: 32). Both of them set this scale's conventional tonic as C1. Apparently, both of these names refer to the same scale. However, al-Mahdī adds other elements to the scale: djins Ṣabā on A2 and djins Ḥidjāz on C2:

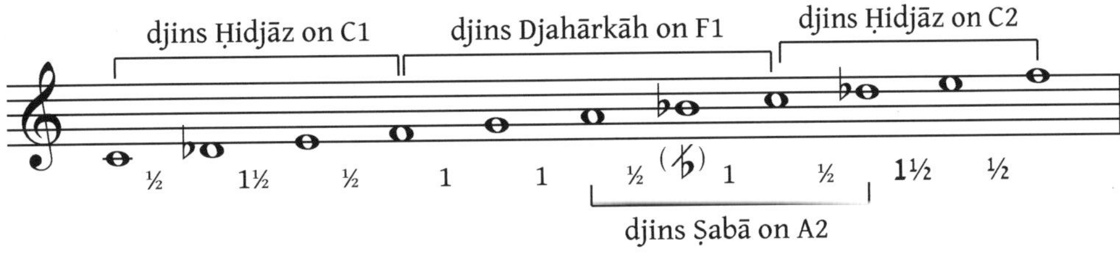

This interesting analysis of al-Mahdī may be a result of hearing some musical piece or improvisation in this maqām that modulated to Ṣabā on A2.

It might be that the confusion regarding the name and structure of this maqām is caused by the fact that this scale is rather new to Arab music. Al-Ḥilū, for example, does not mention this scale under any name. Al-ʿAbbas says that it is uncommon and rarely used and that its theoretical analysis is still not completely formulated (1986: 60). Al-Ḥanafī, in his biography of the Egyptian composer Sayyid Darwīsh (1892–1923), says that maqām Zandjarān is sometimes called Zankulāh, and that in the time of Darwīsh this maqām was not widely used (1955: 71). This fact may explain everything.

The Conventional Position

ALMOST ALL ARAB scholars set the conventional position of this maqām on C1 (Rāst). However, not all scholars agree on the family to which this maqām should be attributed. Al-ʿAbbas, for example, attributes it to the Ḥidjāz family of maqāmāt (1986: 60), while al-Mahdī attributes it to the family of Ḥidjāz-Kār (19??: 32). According to the classification into families that is used in the present book, there is no Ḥidjāz-Kār family of maqāmāt. There seems no doubt that this maqām belongs to the Ḥidjāz family, and it may be that al-Mahdī made a mistake in the distinction between Ḥidjāz and Ḥidjāz-Kār.

Repositions

THE THIRD REPOSITION up forms the scale of Shawq-Afzā on F1:

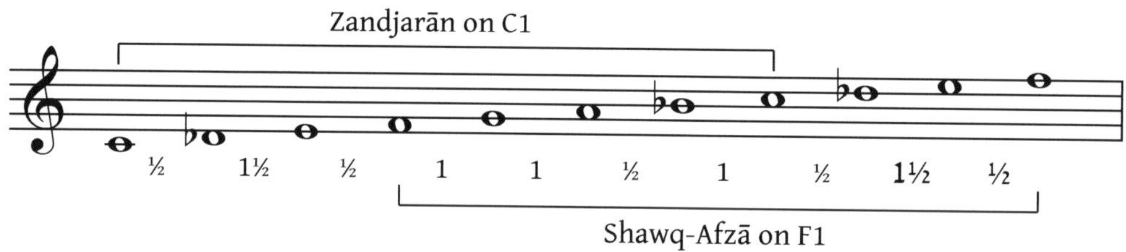

This reposition actually switches the order of adjnās: from djins Ḥidjāz + djins ʿAdjam in Zandjarān to djins ʿAdjam + djins Ḥidjāz in Shawq-Afzā.

The fourth reposition up forms the scale of Nahawand Muraṣṣaʿ on G2

The fifth reposition up forms the scale of Ṣabā Zamzama on A2

Transpositions

I DO NOT know of any distinct scales that are formed by the transposition of the scale of Zandjarān. It is often more convenient to play maqām Zandjarān on the tonic D1, because then it is possible to descend with the scale of Shawq-Afzā to G1. If we play Zandjarān on D1, djins ʿAdjam is positioned on G2 and then it is easy to modulate to maqām ʿAdjam on C1.

Modulations

IF WE REPOSITION the tonic to E1 and alter the note D♭ to D♮, we can modulate to maqām Lāmī. We can also modulate directly to Kurd on E1. Using djins Ḥidjāz, we can perform all the modulations that are applicable to the scale of Ḥidjāz. If we ascend to F2, we can descend from there using the scale of Nahawand on F. A very common modulation is performed by descending two notes below the tonic of Zandjarān, and modulating to the scale of Ṣabā on this new tonic. In the case of Zandjarān on C1, this would be Ṣabā on A1:

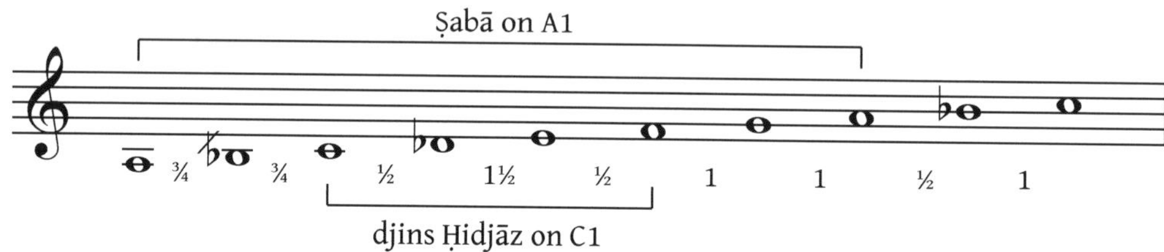

Such a modulation sounds very natural, because djins Ḥidjāz is a very important secondary djins in the scale of Ṣabā.

By repositioning the tonic to D♭1 and altering the note A2 to A♭2, we can modulate to the scale of Midmī, which is an Iraqi scale common in lullaby tunes:

The Progression of the Maqām

AS WITH MAQĀM Shawq-Afzā, the progression of maqām Zandjarān is essentially descending. The progression usually starts from the second djins by emphasizing djins ʿAdjam on F1 and then descends to the first djins – djins Ḥidjāz on C1 – before concluding on the tonic.

6. Sūzdāl or Sūzdīl

The Scale

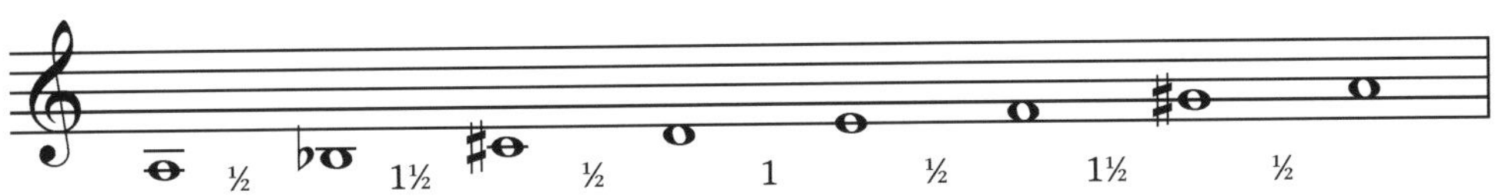

Intervals: ½–1½–½–1–½–1½–½ (tones)

Analysis of the Scale

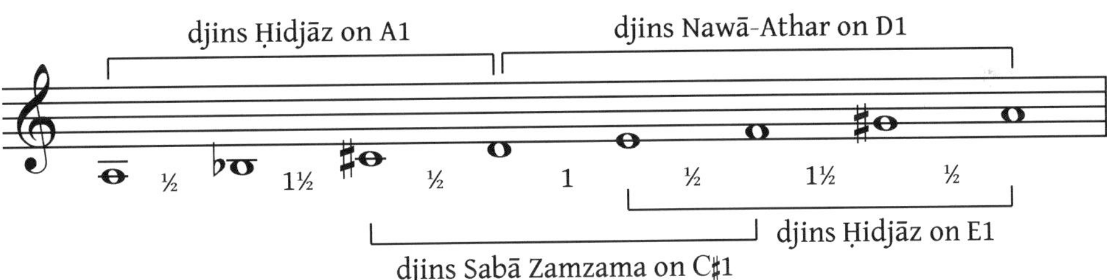

Adjnās

Primary adjnās:
- djins Ḥidjāz on A1
- djins Nawā-Athar on D1
- (conjunct adjnās)

Secondary adjnās:
- djins Ḥidjāz on E1
- djins Ṣabā Zamzama on C♯1

Al-ʿAbbas analyzes this scale as consisting of two disjunct adjnās – djins Ḥidjāz on A1 and djins Ḥidjāz on E1 (1986: 83):

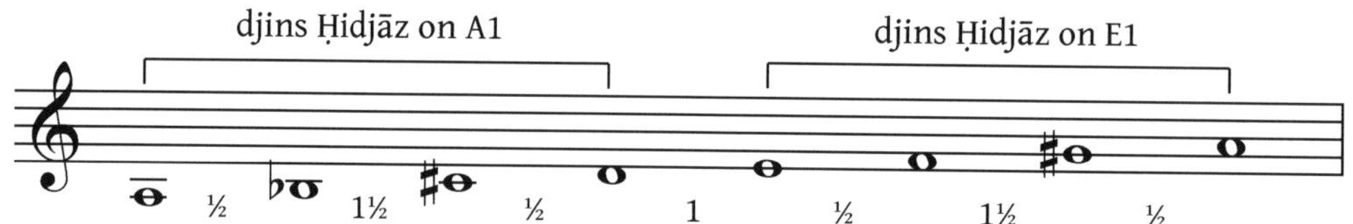

Al-Ḥilū, on the other hand, analyzes the scale as in the above analysis. He names the second djins "djins Ḥiṣār," which I corrected here to djins Nawā-Athar.[1] I give here al-Ḥilū's analysis because I think it is the more common one. Al-Mahdī presents an analysis that is similar to al-Ḥilū's (19??: 44). The scale of Sūzdāl is actually a transposition of the scale of Ḥidjāz-Kār. The main differences between these two scales is that in Sūzdāl, the second octave is identical to the first octave and that in Sūzdāl, djins Nawā-Athar on D1 is emphasized (al-Ḥilū 1972: 99). It should be noted that according to al-ʿAbbas's analysis, the ghammāz of the scale is its fifth note (E1) and according to al-Ḥilū's analysis, the ghammāz is the fourth note (D1).[2]

The Name

Sūzdāl comes from Persian; it means "burner of the heart" (al-Ḥilū 1972: 215).

The Conventional Position

A1 (ʿUshayrān)

Repositions

Any of the repositions that are applicable to the scale of Ḥidjāz-Kār can be applied to Sūzdāl.

Transpositions

The scale of Sūzdāl is a transposition of the scale of Ḥidjāz-Kār to the tonic A1.

Modulations

Any of the modulations that are applicable to scale of Ḥidjāz-Kār can be applied to Sūzdāl.

The Progression of the Maqām

THE MAIN MELODIC characteristic of this maqām is that djins Nawā-Athar on D1 and djins Ḥidjāz on A1 are emphasized. In this way, it is distinguished from maqām Ḥidjāz-Kār. The progression starts by exploring the higher notes of the second djins – Nawā-Athar on D1 – and then descends to the first djins.

---

1 Al-Ḥilū distinguishes between djins Nawā-Athar and djins Ḥiṣār according to their conventional tonics (C1 and D1) though he lists them both as composed of the intervals 1-½-1½-½ (tones). In my opinion, this kind of distinction is irrelevant and unpractical. See the section on maqām Ḥiṣār.

2 We should note that al-ʿAbbas's analysis is much closer to the analysis given by Turkish scholars than al-Ḥilū's.

CHAPTER 17

THE RĀST FAMILY OF MAQĀMĀT

1. Maqām Rāst

2. Maqām Sūznāk

3. Maqām Māhūr

4. Maqām Nayrūz

5. Maqām Nishābūrk

6. Maqām Dalanshīn

7. Maqām Yakāh

Maqām Rāst is the most important and fundamental maqām in most musical cultures of the Middle East, all the more so in the Arab musical culture. As Dalia Cohen states, the scale of Rāst functions as a scalar system: repositions of this scale form some of the most common and important scales in Arab music.

The scale of Rāst and the scales of the Rāst family clearly represent the system of dividing the octave into 24 quartertones. The first djins of these scales is djins Rāst, which is composed of the intervals 1-¾-¾ (tones). Djins Rāst and other important adjnās that contain quartertonal intervals, such as djins Bayāt, are often used as modulations and as temporary embellishment within pieces in other maqāmāt, even in maqāmāt that are essentially based on semitones.

The previous chapters of Part III dealt mainly with scales that are composed of semitones and their multiplications. The following chapters deal with scales that contain quartertonal (or microtonal) intervals such as the three-quartertone and the five-quartertone intervals. These scales are essentially Arab – since they contain quartertonal, or microtonal, intervals. They cannot be performed on European instruments that cannot produce quartertonal intervals, such as the piano and the guitar.

1. Maqām Rāst

The Scale

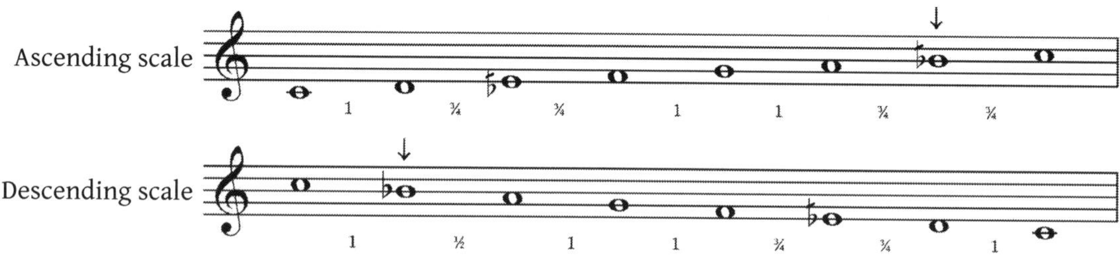

Intervals: ascending scale: 1-¾-¾-1-1-¾-¾ (tones)
descending scale: 1-¾-¾-1-1-½-1 (tones)
(ascending with B𝄳2; descending with B♭2)

Analysis of the Scale

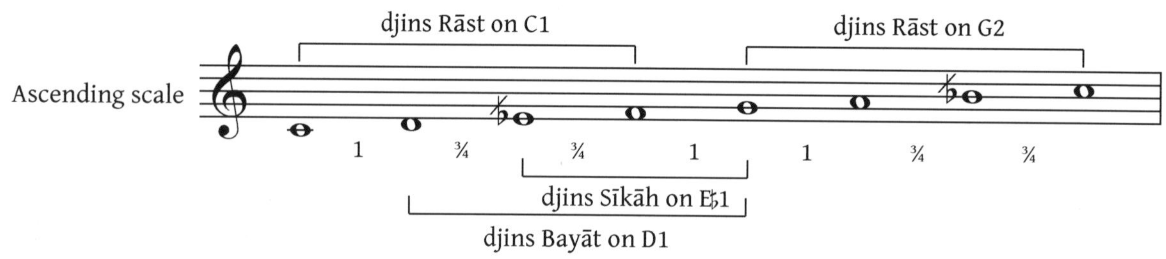

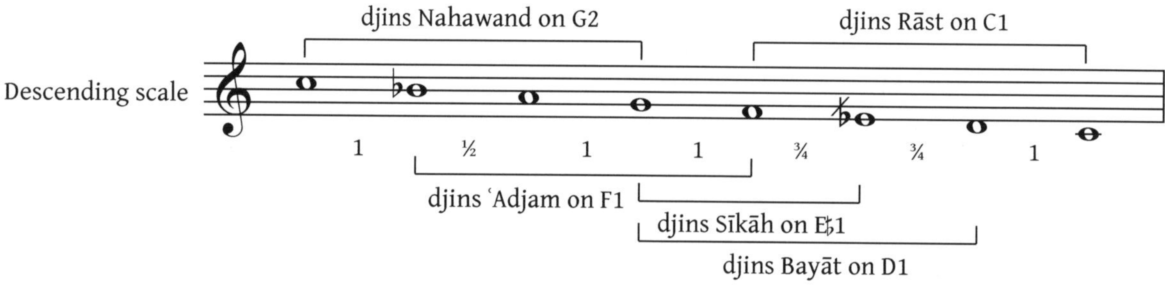

Adjnās

Primary adjnās:

In the ascending scale: djins Rāst on C1
djins Rāst on G2
(disjunct adjnās)

In the descending scale: djins Rāst on C1
djins Nahawand on G2
(disjunct adjnās)

Secondary adjnās:

In the ascending scale:	djins Bayāt on D1
	djins Sīkāh on E𝄳1
In the descending scale:	djins ʿAdjam on F1
	djins Sīkāh on E𝄳1
	djins Bayāt on D1

The above analysis, according to which the seventh note of the scale of Rāst is altered from B𝄳2 to B♭2 in the descending scale, appears in both al-ʿAbbas's and Mashʿal's analyses (1986: 36; 1959: 25). Al-Ḥilū, on the other hand, presents the scale without any alterations, but he adds a written passage in which he explains the alteration of B𝄳2 to B♭2, and thus the change from djins Rāst to djins Nahawand on G2 (1972: 107).

Al-Nur suggests that there are two species of Rāst, one with B𝄳 and another with B♭. As an example of the latter, he gives the song *Habīb al-Qalb* by the Egyptian composer Muḥammad ʿAbd al-Wahhāb. This song starts in maqām Rāst on the tonic C1. It ascends to the note B♭, and not B𝄳, and then descends to djins Ḥidjāz on G1. The resulting scale looks like this:

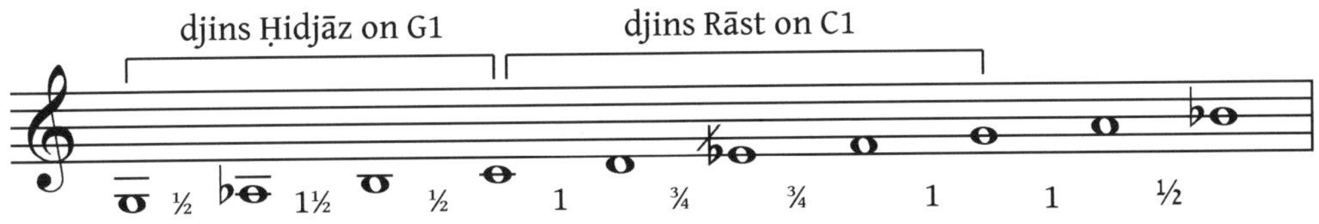

It is hard to know whether the notes A2 and B♭2 are structural notes of the scale or are merely passing embellishments. The above scale, however, is the scale of Ḥidjāz on G1, composed of djins Ḥidjāz and djins Rāst in a conjunct sequence.

I doubt whether the progression presented in ʿAbd al-Wahhāb's song can indicate the existence of two species of the scale of Rāst, as suggested by al-Nur. Elias also doubts such an analysis and thinks the whole progression represents an elaboration of maqām Rāst. It may be that we should refer to it as a transposition of the scale of Ḥidjāz to the tonic G1.

It is interesting to note that both in the scale of Rāst as well as in other scales that are formed by its repositions, alternating between the notes B𝄳2 and B♭2 is a common progression. In some maqāmāt, this alternation is an essential structural part of the scale, while in others it allows for interesting variations, developments, and modulations, such as the modulation to the scale of ʿAdjam ʿUshayrān on B♭1 in the maqāmāt Bayāt, Muḥayyar, and Sīkāh. Elias suggests that the alteration from B𝄳2 to B♭2 allows for a "smoother" descent with a "definite direction." My own conclusion is that the scale of maqām Rāst can employ both notes: B𝄳2 and B♭2 and that this fact does not suggest the existence of two species of Rāst.

The Name

RĀST IS A Persian word; it means "straight," "direct," or "correct." Maqām Rāst is the primary and most important scale in the Arab, Turkish, and Persian musical cultures.

The Conventional Position

THE CONVENTIONAL position of the scale of Rāst is the note C1, which is also named Rāst. Because of the importance of this scale and its constituent notes to the theory of Arab music, I give the Arab names of its notes below:

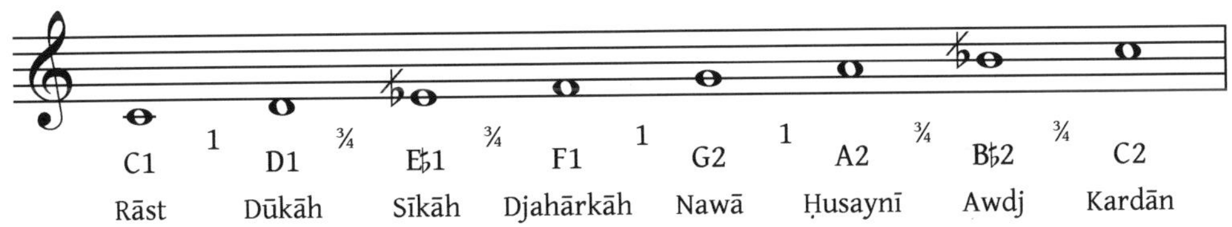

Some of the above notes, such as Sīkāh, Djahārkāh, Ḥusaynī, and Awdj give their name to distinct maqāmāt because they serve as their tonic notes or as important structural notes of their scales.

Repositions

ANY REPOSITION OF the tonic in the scale of Rāst to one of its constituent notes forms a distinct scale of a familiar maqām in Arab music. We should remember, however, that in these scales, the note B♮̸2 (Awdj) is not a "stable" note, as we have seen in the case of the scale of Rāst. In some repositions of Rāst, such as in the scale of Bayāt, B♭2 is a structural note of the scale. In other scales, such as Ḥusaynī, B♮̸2 is altered to B♭2 when the melody descends.

The first reposition up forms the scale of Bayāt, or Ḥusaynī, or Muḥayyar (depending on whether we employ B♭2 or B♮̸2) on D1. Conventionally, the scale of Bayāt employs B♭2, while the scales of Ḥusaynī and Muḥayyar employ B♮̸2. In practice, however, these two notes appear interchangeably in all three scales:

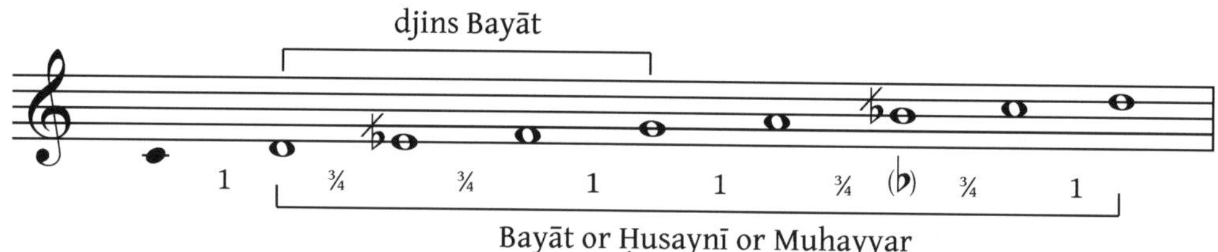

The second reposition up forms the scale of Sīkāh on E♮̸1:

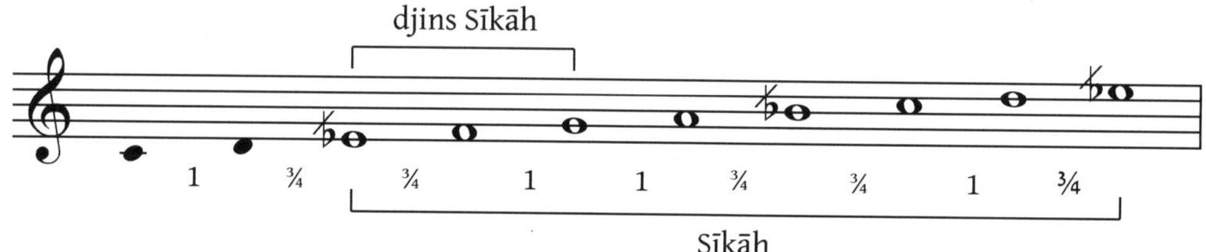

The third reposition up forms the scale of Djahārkāh on F1:

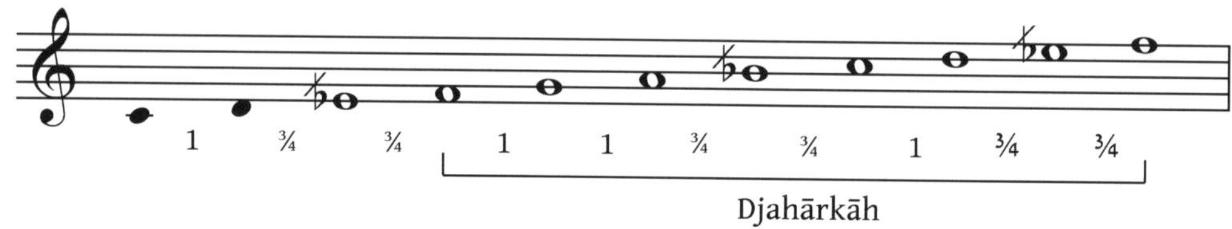

The fourth reposition up forms the scale of Nayrūz on G.
The fifth reposition up forms the scale of Ḥusaynī on A.
The sixth reposition up forms the scales of Awdj and ʿIrāq on B♮̸.

Transpositions

THERE ARE NO transpositions of Rāst that form distinct maqāmāt. In Egypt, however, there is a descending variant of maqām Rāst called maqām Kardān. Its progression starts with djins Rāst on C2 (the octave note) and then descends towards the tonic, C1.

Modulations

AS WAS NOTED above, maqām Rāst is the most important maqām of Arab music, and its scale is considered the most "natural" scale. The conventional position of Rāst is C1, which is the tonic of many other maqāmāt, such as Sūznāk,

Nahawand, Ḥidjāz-Kār, Nawā-Athar, Nakrīz, ʿAdjam, and many more. This allows for many modulations. The scales of Rāst and ʿAdjam are very close to one another and therefore alternating between the two can be done easily. It is also very common to modulate from Rāst to Sūznāk by changing the second djins to Ḥidjāz on G2. We can then employ this djins in order to modulate to Nawā-Athar, Nakrīz, or Ḥidjāz-Kār.

Modulating to Ḥidjāz on D1 can be done easily by employing djins Bayāt on A2, which is common to both scales. We can modulate to Bayāt on G2, or use repositions in order to modulate to Bayāt on D1 or Sīkāh on E𝄳1.

The Progression of the Maqām

THE MAIN MELODIC characteristic of this maqām is the emphasis of djins Rāst on C1 and djins Rāst on G2.

The progression of Rāst starts on the tonic C1 and then descends with djins Rāst to G1. The progression then ascends back to the tonic and from there ascends further to the second and third adjnās. When descending from the octave note, the note B𝄳2 is usually altered to B♭2. Many times, the progression descends to G1 before the conclusion on the tonic.

2. Maqām Sūznāk

The Scale

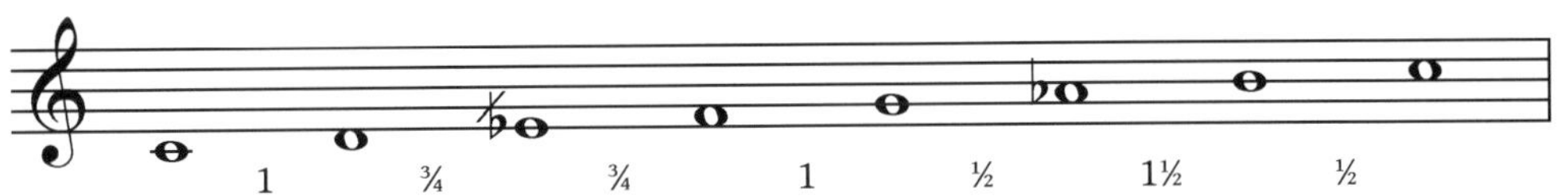

Intervals: 1–¾–¾–1–½–1½–½ (tones)

Analysis of the Scale

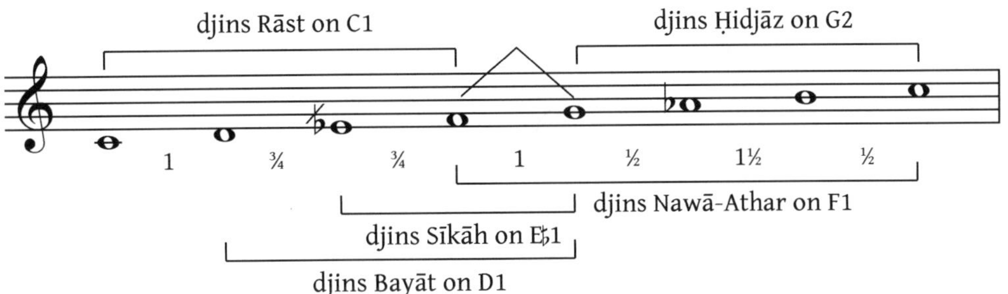

Adjnās

Primary adjnās: djins Rāst on C1
djins Ḥidjāz on G2
(disjunct adjnās)

Secondary adjnās: djins Bayāt on D1
djins Sīkāh on E𝄳1
djins Nawā-Athar on F1

There is some similarity between the scale of Sūznāk, which has djins Rāst on the tonic and djins Ḥidjāz on the fifth note of the scale, and the scale of Shawq-Afzā, which has djins ʿAdjam on the tonic and djins Ḥidjāz on the fifth note of the scale.

In Turkey, musicians and scholars distinguish between two species of the scale Sūznāk: (1) A scale named Sūznāk, which is identical to the Arab Sūznāk; and (2) A scale named Zirgule'li Sūznāk, which is similar to the scale of Ḥidjāz-Kār. Its progression usually starts with djins Ḥidjāz on C1 but typically concludes with djins Rāst on C1.

Some Arab musicians became aware of this variant of maqām Sūznāk and they introduce momentary alterations to djins Ḥidjāz on C1 when performing Sūznāk. The name of this innovated maqām in Arab theoretical literature is Balazar-Kūlā (al-Ḥilū 1972: 108)

The Name

In Persian, Sūznāk means "burner of the heart," or "the painful" (al-Ḥilū 1972: 213).

The Conventional Position

C1 (Rāst)

Repositions

The first reposition up forms the scale of Bayāt Shūrī on D1.
The second reposition up forms the scale of Huzām on E𝄳1.
The third reposition up forms the scale of Nakrīz on F1.
The fourth reposition up forms the scale of Ḥidjāz on G2.

Transpositions

Not known

Modulations

SINCE THE SCALE of Sūznāk is composed of djins Rāst and djins Ḥidjāz, it offers many possibilities for modulation.[1] By establishing djins Rāst on C1, we can descend to Ḥidjāz on G1. By altering the second djins of Sūznāk from Ḥidjāz to Bayāt, we can modulate to maqām Nayrūz, which is composed of djins Rāst and djins Bayāt on the fifth note of the scale. We can also modulate to the scale of Ṣabā on D1, on G2, or on A2. The scale that is formed of djins Rāst on the tonic and djins Ṣabā on the sixth note of the scale is called Dalanshīn.

The Progression of the Maqām

THE MAIN MELODIC characteristic of maqām Sūznāk is the emphasis of djins Ḥidjāz on G2. The progression may start from either the first or the second djins. As was mentioned above, in some Arab countries, musicians adopted the

1 See the modulations in the sections about maqām Rāst, maqām Ḥidjāz, maqām Nawā-Athar, and maqām Sīkāh.

Turkish variant of Zirgule'li Sūznāk, and they sometimes pass through djins Ḥidjāz on C1 when performing maqām Sūznāk.

3. Maqām Māhūr

The Scale

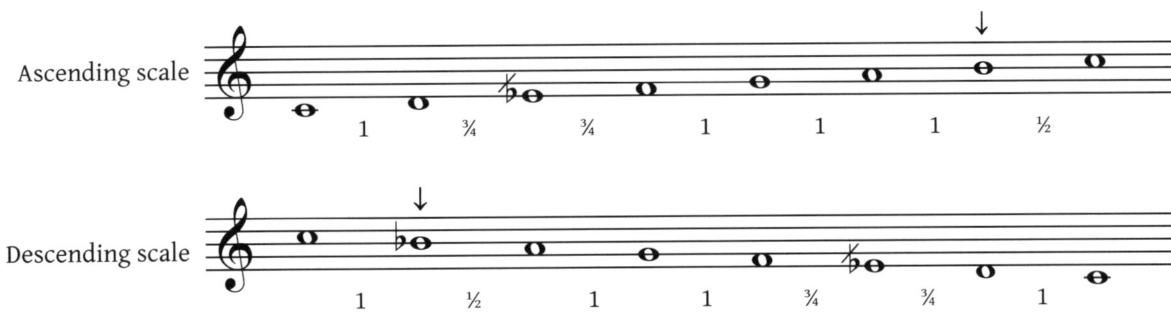

Intervals: ascending scale: 1–¾–¾–1–1–1– ½ (tones)
descending scale: 1–¾–¾–1–1–½–1 (tones)
(ascending with B♮2; descending with B♭2)

Analysis of the Scale

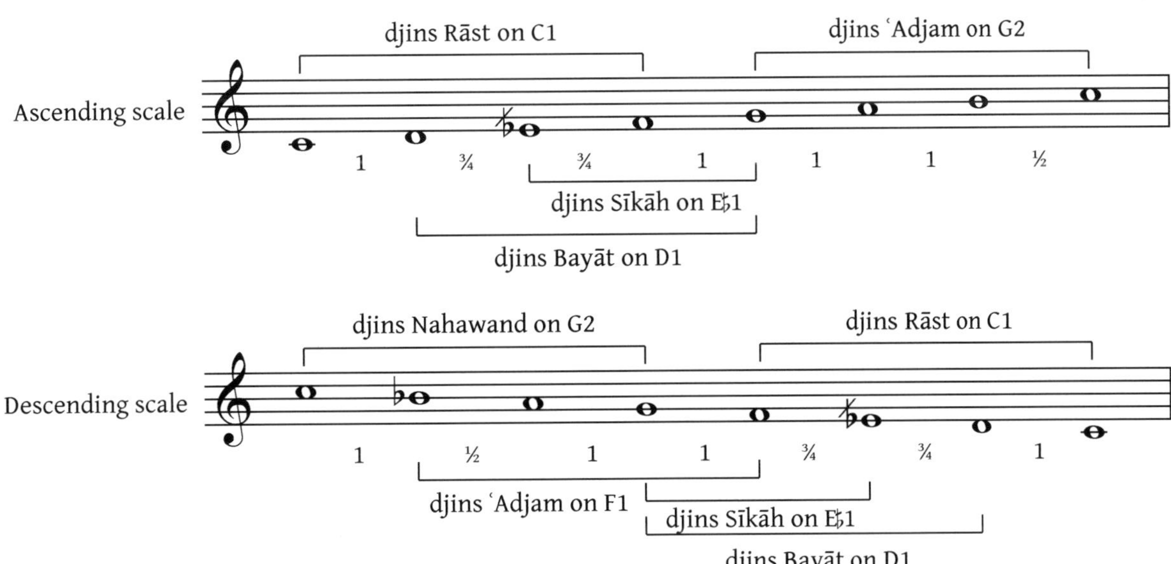

Adjnās

Primary adjnās:

In the ascending scale:	djins Rāst on C1 djins ʿAdjam on G2 (disjunct adjnās)
In the descending scale:	djins Rāst on C1 djins Nahawand on G2 (disjunct adjnās)

Secondary adjnās:

In the ascending scale:	djins Bayāt on D1 djins Sīkāh on E𝄳1
In the descending scale:	djins ʿAdjam on F1 djins Sīkāh on E𝄳1 djins Bayāt on D1

Al-Mahdī maintains that the scale of Māhūr corresponds to the major scale of European music, except for the fact that the seventh note (here B2) is lowered by a semitone when descending (19??: 28). He writes the scale of Māhūr like this:

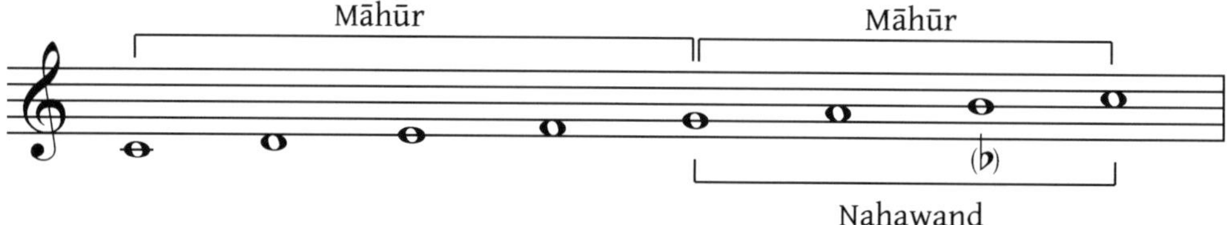

Al-Mahdī calls djins ʿAdjam "djins Māhūr" and does not distinguish between five-note adjnās and four-note adjnās. Mashʿal also calls the European major scale "Māhūr," but he names Māhūr on C1 "ʿAdjam" (1959: 18). Mashʿal does not distinguish between an ascending and a descending Māhūr scales. For Mashʿal, therefore, Māhūr and ʿAdjam are identical.

Abraham Salman maintains that the scale of Māhūr is almost identical to the scale of Rāst; the only difference is that in Māhūr, the third and the seventh notes – E𝄳1 and B𝄳2 – are flattened by only an eighth of a tone and not by a quartertone. Al-Nur, on the other hand, maintains that Māhūr is identical to Rāst, but its seventh note is altered from B𝄳2 to B♭2 in the descending scale.

These different and often contradicting opinions of various musicians and scholars of Arab music on the nature of maqām Māhūr serve to show the deep gap between theory and practice in Arab music. Indeed, we can say that all the above views are correct; they represent opinions of people from various musical backgrounds, with different musical training and education. In Arab music, theory is not always in line with practice.

We can conclude, however, that the scale of Māhūr is associated with the scales of Rāst and ʿAdjam, and variations and alterations borrowed from the latter scales can be applied to the former. An important feature of maqām Māhūr is that its melodic progression is essentially descending.

The Name

MĀHŪR IS A Persian name that means "the crescent moon." In literature, we can find two names for the note C2: Kardān and Māhūr. It may be, as suggested by Elias, that maqām Māhūr is named thus because its progression starts from its octave note – C2.

The Conventional Position

C1 (Rāst)

Repositions

Not known

Transpositions

Not known

Modulations

THE SCALE OF maqām Māhūr is formed of djins Rāst and djins ʿAdjam. These two adjnās belong to two important families of maqāmāt and offer a great range of possibilities for modulation. See the chapters on these families for more information on possible modulations.

The Progression of the Maqām

THE PROGRESSION OF maqām Māhūr starts from its octave note – C2. It then descends to the second djins – ʿAdjam on G2. When descending towards the first djins – Rāst on C1 – B2 should be altered to B♭2. Usually, B𝄳1 is used as a leading note before concluding on the tonic note – C1.

4. Maqām Nayrūz

The Scale

Intervals: 1–¾–¾–1–¾–¾–1 (tones)

Analysis of the Scale

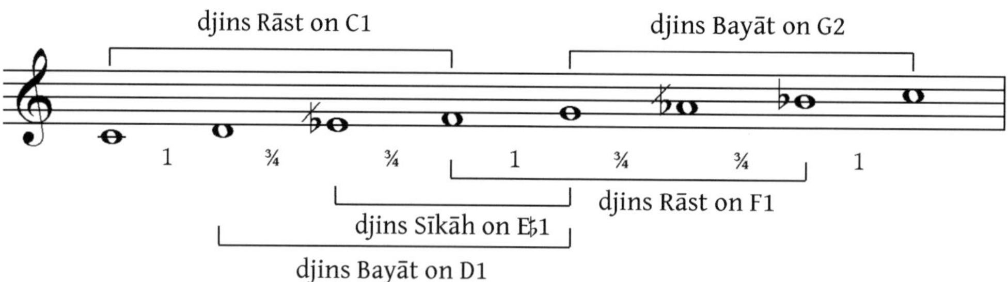

Adjnās

Primary adjnās: djins Rāst on C1
djins Bayāt on G2
(disjunct adjnās)
Secondary adjnās: djins Bayāt on D1
djins Sīkāh on E𝄳1
djins Rāst on F1

Both al-ʿAbbas and Mashʿal do not mention such a maqām, while al-Ḥilū mentions it in his list of maqāmāt, but does not analyze it. Al-Ḥilū calls this scale "Nawrūz, or Nayrūz, or Nawrūz ʿAdjam," and says that this is a unique scale positioned on the tonic ʿAdjam (B♭) (1972: 216). Since in Arabic, both B♭1 and B♭2 are called ʿAdjam (though B♭1 is sometimes called ʿAdjam ʿUshayrān or Qarār ʿAdjam) we cannot know to which tonic exactly al-Ḥilū refers.

Of all my sources, the only one that presents the scale of maqām Nayrūz is al-Mahdī. He also gives various names for this scale: Nayrūz, al-Nurūz, and Nayrāz-Rāst. Al-Mahdī's analysis of the scale presents also the third djins of the scale: djins Rāst when ascending and djins Nahawand when descending:

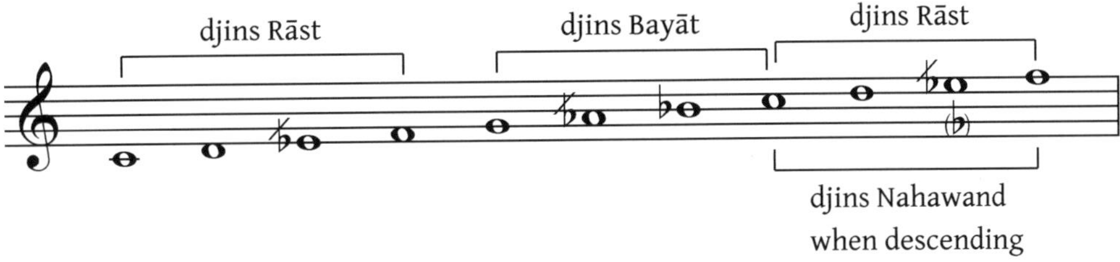

The Name

NAYRŪZ IS A Persian word that al-Ḥilū translates as "the new day" and al-Mahdī as "the holiday of spring." I have not been able to verify these translations.

The Conventional Position

C1 (Rāst)

Repositions

THE SCALE OF Nayrūz is formed by the fourth reposition of the scale of Rāst. The repositions of the scale of Nayrūz, therefore, are the same as the repositions of the scale of Rāst. We should remember, however, that the conventional position of maqām Nayrūz is on C1:

The third reposition up forms the scale of Rāst on F1.

The fourth reposition up forms the scale of Ḥusaynī (or Bayāt) on G2.

The fifth reposition up forms the scale of Sīkāh on A♭2.

Transpositions

THE TRANSPOSITION OF the scale of Nayrūz to D1 is named Nishābūrk.

The transposition of the scale of Nayrūz to G1 is named Yakāh. However, there is a difference between Nayrūz and Nishābūrk concerning the analysis of their primary adjnās. While the scale of Nayrūz is divided into djins Rāst on the tonic and djins Bayāt on the fifth note in a disjunct sequence, the scale of Nishābūrk is divided into djins Rāst on the tonic and djins Rāst on the fourth note in a conjunct sequence.

Modulations

MAQĀM NAYRŪZ belongs to the Rāst family of maqāmāt and any of the modulations that are applicable to the scale of Rāst can be applied to Nayrūz. We should note, however, that the scales that are formed by repositioning the scale of Nayrūz (which is positioned on C1) are not positioned on their conventional tonic, and therefore their range will be different.

The Progression of the Maqām

MAQĀM NAYRŪZ is an ascending maqām. Its progression starts from its tonic and its first djins – Rāst on C1 – and then ascends to its second djins – Bayāt on G2. The melody should not emphasize the second djins too much, because this might create the feeling of a modulation into Bayāt on G2 and obscure the first djins. Elias suggests that in order to return to djins Rāst on C1 from Bayāt on G2, it may be best to first ascend to djins Rāst on the octave note – C2 – and then descend to the tonic.

5. Maqām Nishābūrk

The Scale

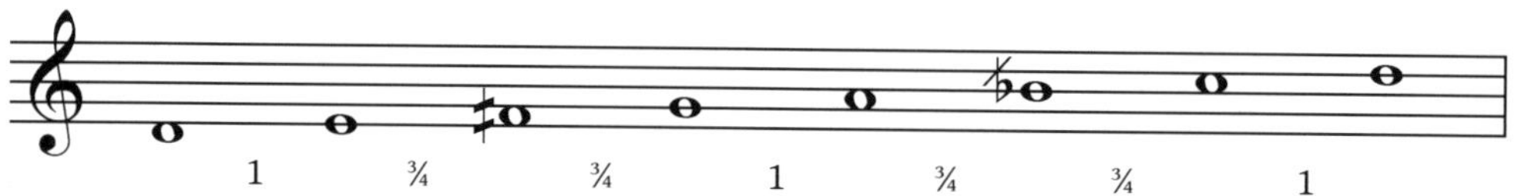

Intervals: 1-¾-¾-1-¾-¾-1 (tones)

Analysis of the Scale

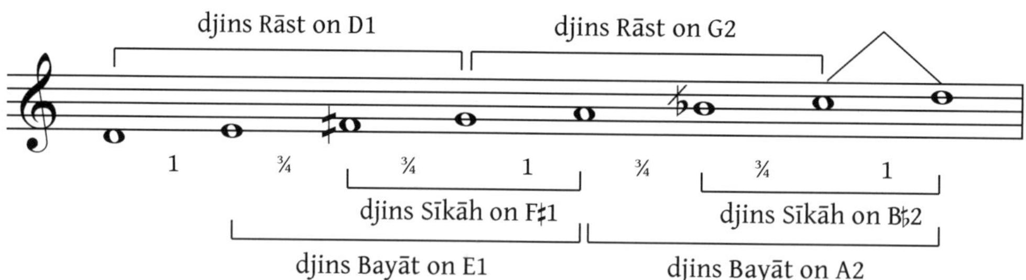

Adjnās

Primary adjnās: djins Rāst on D1
djins Rāst on G2
(conjunct adjnās)

Secondary adjnās: djins Bayāt on E1
djins Bayāt on A2
djins Sīkāh on F♯1
djins Sīkāh on B♭2

The intervals of the scale of Nishābūrk are identical to those of Nayrūz; therefore, we should perceive the scale of Nishābūrk as a transposition of Nayrūz. Both of these scales are formed by the fourth reposition of the scale of Rāst. It is recommended that the reader refer to the section on maqām Nayrūz when studying maqām Nishābūrk. Any of the repositions, transpositions, and modulations that are applicable to the scale of Nayrūz can be applied to Nishābūrk.

Regarding the progression of the maqām, we should notice the difference between the structure of the scale of Nayrūz and that of Nishābūrk. While the scale of Nayrūz is divided into djins Rāst on the tonic and djins Bayāt on the fifth note of the scale in a disjunct sequence, the scale of Nishābūrk is divided into djins Rāst on the tonic and djins Rāst on the fourth note in a conjunct sequence. The progression should emphasize the second djins accordingly. Some musicians think that the scale of Nishābūrk is a transposition of Rāst to D1; as we can see from the above analysis, this is not so.

The Name

According to al-Ḥilū, Nishābūrk is a Turkish and Persian scale. Nishabur (Neyshābūr) is a town in Iran (1972: 214).

The Conventional Position

BOTH AL-ḤILŪ and al-ʿAbbas position this scale on the tonic D1. Al-Ḥilū does not analyze it (1972: 215 – a list explaining the names of maqāmāt) but al-ʿAbbas gives an analysis (1986: 71). It seems that this maqām is not widely used, and scholars derive its analysis from written sources, maybe without even listening to it. I bring it here because it belongs to the Rāst family and because it serves as an interesting example of a scale composed of two adjnās Rāst in a conjunct sequence.

This maqām is analyzed and performed in various ways, and I did not find it important to expand extensively on its analysis nor to include an audio example of its performance in the accompanying CD.

6. Maqām Dalanshīn

The Scale

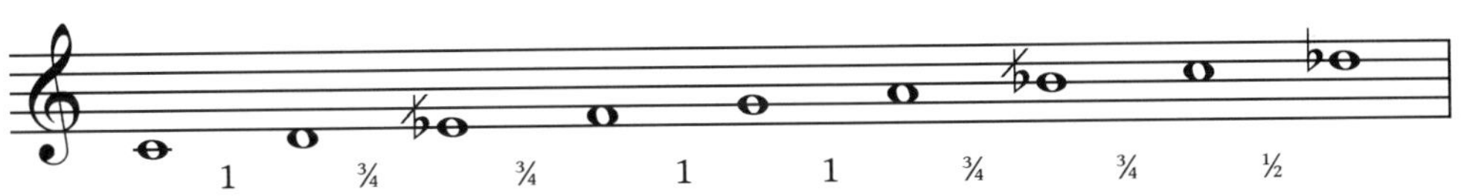

Intervals: 1–¾–¾–1–1–¾–¾–½ (tones)

Analysis of the Scale

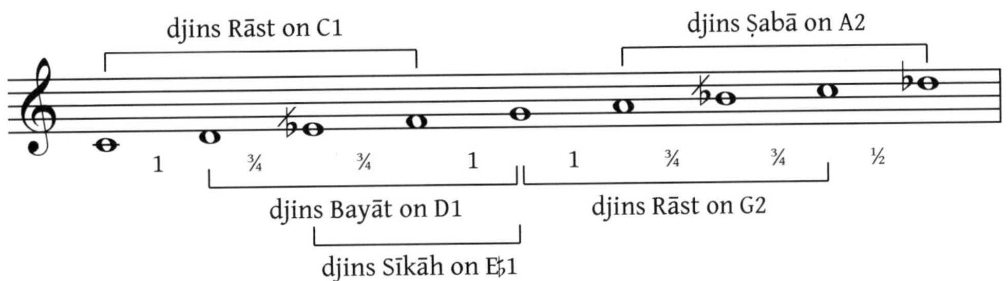

Adjnās

Primary adjnās:	djins Rāst on C1 djins Ṣabā on A2 (disjunct adjnās)
Secondary adjnās:	djins Bayāt on D1 djins Sīkāh on E𝄳1 djins Rāst on G2

The scale of Dalanshīn has a very peculiar structure: its second djins is positioned on the sixth note of the scale, and therefore, there is a gap of two whole tones between the two primary adjnās. Because of this structure, the scale stretches over at least nine notes. This scale is rarely used, and most scholars do not refer to it.

The Name

Dalanshīn means "dweller of the heart" in Persian.

The Conventional Position

C1 (Rāst)

Repositions

BECAUSE OF ITS non-cyclical structure and the interval of a semitone between C2 and D♭2 it is difficult to reposition this scale. The scale from C1 up to C2, however, is essentially the scale of Rāst, and any of the repositions that are applicable to the scale of Rāst can be applied to it.

Transpositions

Not known

Modulations

THE GREATER PART of this scale is identical to the scale of Rāst, and many of the modulations that are applicable to the scale of Rāst can be applied to Dalanshīn. When emphasizing djins Ṣabā on A2, we can apply the modulations that are applicable to the scale of Ṣabā.

The Progression of the Maqām

IN MY OPINION, maqām Dalanshīn is a compound maqām.[1] It seems that it is a relatively newer maqām and there is not a clear and definite tradition concerning its melodic progression. As with many compound maqāmāt, it would seem most natural to treat it as a descending maqām. In maqām Bastah-Nikār, for example, the progression must start from djins Ṣabā and then descend to djins Sīkāh in order to emphasize the maqām's unique characteristics. In Dalanshīn, however, the case does not seem to be the same, and there are various opinions concerning its proper melodic progression. Some suggest that the progression starts from the first djins and then ascends to Bayāt or Ṣabā on A2. When descending back towards the tonic, B𝄳2 should be altered to B♭2, and djins Nahawand on G2 should be emphasized before descending to the tonic. In the accompanying CD, the taqsīm in maqām Dalanshīn presents a descending progression: it starts with djins Ṣabā on A2 and then descends to djins Rāst on C1.

1 See Chapter 7 for an explanation on compound maqāmāt.

7. Maqām Yakāh

The Scale

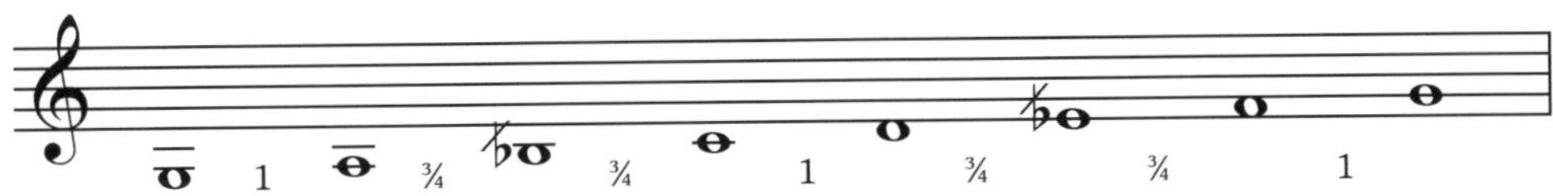

Intervals: 1–¾–¾–1–¾–¾–1 (tones)

Analysis of the Scale

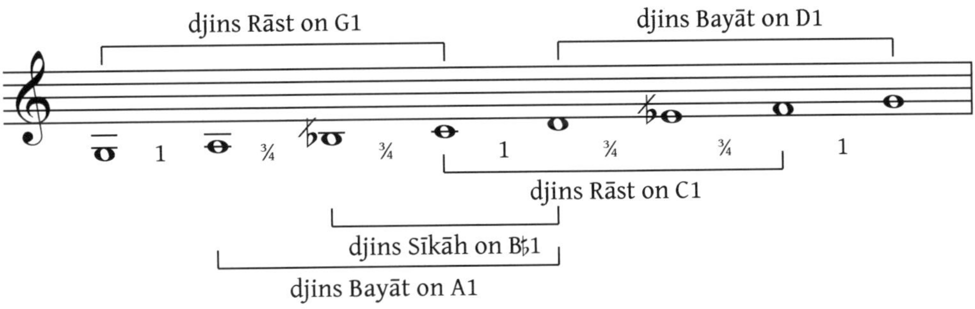

Adjnās

Primary adjnās: djins Rāst on G1
djins Bayāt on D1
(disjunct adjnās)

Secondary adjnās: djins Bayāt on A1
djins Sīkāh on B♮1
djins Rāst on C1

The scale of maqām Yakāh is a transposition of the scale of Nayrūz or the scale of Nishābūrk to the tonic G1 (Yakāh). The intervals of these three scales are identical (1–¾–¾–1–¾–¾–1 tones), but their conventional tonics differ. We must note the difference between Nayrūz and Nishābūrk concerning the analysis of their primary adjnās. While the scale of Nayrūz is divided into djins Rāst on the tonic and djins Bayāt on the fifth note of the scale in a disjunct sequence, the scale of Nishābūrk is divided into djins Rāst on the tonic and djins Rāst on the fourth note in a conjunct sequence. The scale of Yakāh is divided into adjnās exactly like Nayrūz, but maqām Yakāh has a different progression (sayr al-maqām) than Nayrūz. Since the scale of Yakāh is positioned on the lowest note in the Arab system of notes, the descent to the tonic at the end of the progression has to be adapted accordingly – there are no notes lower than G1 that can serve as leading notes or through which the melody can pass before concluding on the tonic.

The Name

Yakāh is the name of the note G1 in the Arab system of notes. Maqām Yakāh, therefore, is named after its tonic.[1]

The Conventional Position

G1 (Yakāh)

Repositions

Please refer to the repositions in the sections on maqām Nayrūz and maqām Nishābūrk.

Transpositions

THE TRANSPOSITION of the scale of Yakāh to C1 is named Nayrūz. The transposition of the scale of Yakāh to D1 is named Nishābūrk.

Modulations

Any of the modulations that are applicable to the scales of Nayrūz and Nishābūrk can be applied to Yakāh.

The Progression of the Maqām

YAKĀH IS A descending maqām. Its progression starts from its third djins – Rāst on G2 – then descends to its second djins – Bayāt on D1 – before descending to conclude on the first djins – djins Rāst on G1.

---

1 See Chapter 6 for more information about names of notes and specifically about older names for the note G1.

CHAPTER 18

THE BAYĀT FAMILY OF MAQĀMĀT

1. Maqām Bayāt (or Bayātī)

2. Maqām Bayāt Shūrī (Qārdjighār)

3. Maqām Ḥusaynī

4. Maqām Ḥusaynī ʿUshayrān

5. Maqām Nuhuft

6. Maqām Muḥayyar

MAQĀM BAYĀT IS one of the most famous and widespread maqāmāt in Arab music. In Turkish music, where it is also considered a fundamental maqām, it is usually named maqām ʿUshshāq.

Some scholars maintain that the scale of maqām Bayāt is derived from the first reposition of the Rāst scalar system; according to this view, the sixth note of the scale of Bayāt should be B𝄳2. Although thinking of the scale of Bayāt as a reposition of the scale of Rāst is quite widespread among scholars and musicians, I maintain that the sixth note of the scale of Bayāt is B♭2, and not B𝄳2. It is true that many times the progression of maqām Bayāt employs the note B𝄳2 as an embellishment or as part of various modulations, but this note is not essential to the presentation of the maqām.

The conventional position of Bayāt is on D1, and its structure is almost identical to the scales of Nahawand and Kurd. When these three scales are positioned on the tonic D1, they differ only in their second note: In Kurd it is E♭1, in Bayāt it is E𝄳1, and in Nahawand it is E♮1.

All the scales of the Bayāt family start with djins Bayāt (¾–¾–1 tones). Some scholars see other scales in the Bayāt family, such as Ḥusaynī and Bayāt Shūrī, as mere variations, or species, of the scale Bayāt. In the Turkish and Arab musical systems, however, many variations have become distinct maqāmāt.

1. Maqām Bayāt (or Bayātī)

The Scale

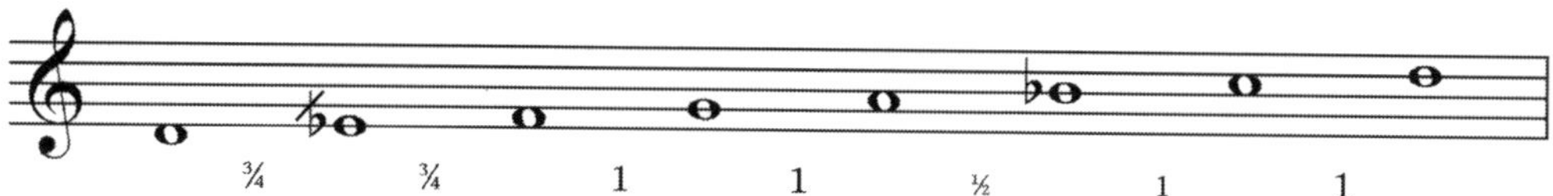

Intervals: ¾–¾–1–1–½–1–1 (tones)

As we can see from the above figure, the scale of maqām Bayāt ascends and descends with B♭2. This is the way it is presented by Al-ʿAbbas and Mashʿal, (1986: 39; 1959: 31). Al-Mahdī, however, maintains that the scale of Bayāt ascends with B𝄳2 and descends with B♭2 (19??: 86). As was stated in the introduction to this chapter, I agree with Al-ʿAbbas's and Mashʿal's version.

Al-Ḥilū presents the scale of Bayāt over two octaves and notates it with B♭ in both octaves (B♭2 and B♭3), both when ascending as well as when descending. However, he introduces another alteration: The note E𝄳3, which is the second note of the second octave of the scale, is altered to E♭3 when descending, thus forming djins Kurd, instead of djins Bayāt, on D2:

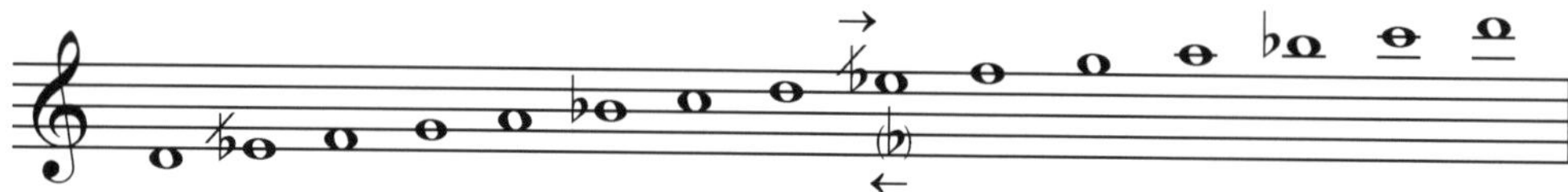

I do not see these differing analyses of the scale as contradicting, because the sixth note of the scale of Bayāt is a "flexible" note. When descending, it is usually B♭2; when ascending, it may be altered to B𝄳2, depending on the melodic context and the various adjnās and scales into which we can modulate from Bayāt. In my opinion, the scale of Bayāt essentially employs B♭2, and its intervals are therefore: ¾–¾–1–1–½–1–1 (tones).

Analysis of the Scale

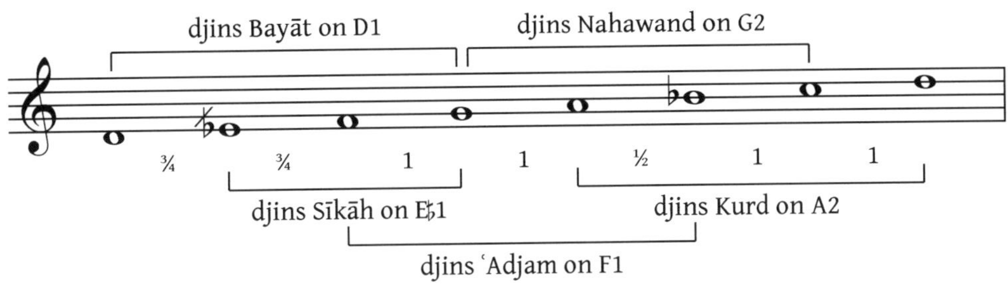

Adjnās

Primary adjnās:	djins Bayāt on D1 djins Nahawand on G2 (conjunct adjnās)
Secondary adjnās:	djins Sīkāh on E𝄳1 djins ʿAdjam on F1 djins Kurd on A2

The two primary adjnās are in conjunct sequence, because the second djins is positioned on the fourth note of the scale, which is the ghammāz, or dominant note, of the scale.

As was said before, the sixth note of the scale of Bayāt is sometimes altered from B♭2 to B𝄳2, usually when ascending:

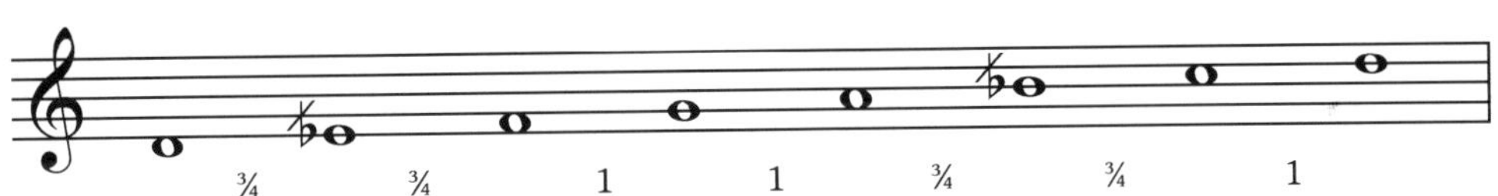

As a matter of fact, this alteration occurs in several other maqāmāt that share the same scale as above, but their ghammāz, structure of adjnās, and progression (sayr al-maqām) differ from those of Bayāt. If we take the above scale and emphasize its octave note (D2) and the third djins (djins Bayāt on D2) and then descend, it is maqām Muḥayyar. If we emphasize the fifth note, A2, as the ghammāz of the scale, it is called maqām Ḥusaynī.

In both maqām Muḥayyar and maqām Ḥusaynī, the sixth note is altered from B𝄳2 to B♭2 when descending.[1] Some scholars claim that there are two species of Bayāt, one with B♭2 and the other with B𝄳2. I do not see the point of such a distinction, and I think it is preferable to simply say that the scale of Bayāt can employ either of these notes.

The Name

ACCORDING TO AL-ḤILŪ, Bayāt is an Arab name (1972: 216). The meaning of the word is probably "sleep" or "slumber." This maqām is sometimes called Bayātī. Sometimes the name of this maqām appears attached to names of other maqāmāt that are derived from it or belong to its family, e.g., "Bayāt Muḥayyar" or "Muḥayyar Bayātī," and some scholars even define these scales, such as Muḥayyar, Ḥusaynī, and the Turkish ʿUshshāq as "species of Bayātī" (al-Mahdī 19??: 34). Maqām Bayāt is an ancient and important maqām, and is mentioned in *Kitāb al-Aghāni* (*Book of Songs*) by the medieval Arab scholar al-Iṣfahānī (d. 967) (ibid.).

1 These maqāmāt, which belong to the Bayāt family of maqāmāt, are discussed below.

The Conventional Position

D1 (Dūkāh)

Repositions

IF WE NOTATE the scale of Bayāt with B𝄳2, it can be considered a reposition of the scale of Rāst:

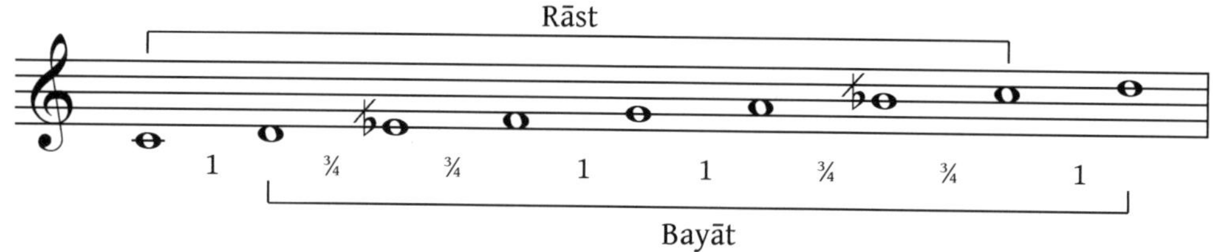

Therefore, any of the repositions that are applicable to the scale of Rāst can be applied to Bayāt.

Transpositions

Not known

Modulations

IN THE SECTION on maqām Nahawand, I explained how there are three scales that are almost identical in their intervals, but vary in their second note. These are the scales of Kurd, Bayāt, and Nahawand. When we place these three scales on the tonic D1, we can see that the second note is E♭1 in Kurd, E𝄳1 in Bayāt, and E♮1 in Nahawand. Since these scales are similar, it is easy to modulate between them, by ascending with one and descending with the other. When modulating to Nahawand on D1, it is advisable to use C♯1 as its leading note (ẓahīr).

It is also easy to modulate to maqām Rāst by ascending from the tonic to G2, and then descending to C1.

By altering the second djins to djins Ḥidjāz on G2, we can modulate to maqām Bayāt Shūrī. From there, by using djins Ḥidjāz on G2 as a "pivot," we can modulate to other maqāmāt that employ this djins, such as Ḥidjāz-Kār on C1 and Nawā-Athar on C1.

By ascending to the octave note, and then descending to djins Nahawand on G2, we can modulate to Nahawand on G2. As usual with Nahawand, it is advisable to use F♯1 as a leading note.

By altering G2 to G♭2, we can easily modulate to maqām Ṣabā.

Another easy modulation is to maqām Ḥidjāz-Humayūn, by altering djins Bayāt on D1 to djins Ḥidjāz on D1.

The Progression of the Maqām

The main melodic characteristics of maqām Bayāt is the emphasis of djins Nahawand on G2 and djins ʿAdjam on F1. According to al-Ḥilū, in the past, the progression of the maqām started from the note G2 and then descended to the first djins; al-Ḥilū claims that this kind of progression is essentially Turkish (1972: 118). Today, this type of progression is not compulsory, and the progression of maqām Bayāt may start from other notes, such as the tonic D1, the note A2, or the leading note C1 (ẓahīr al-maqām). For example, in the song in maqām Bayāt *Habībī Yisʿid*, a beautiful song composed by Zakariyyā Aḥmad for the singer Umm Kulthūm, the melody starts on B♭2.

After starting somewhere on the scale, the progression of maqām Bayāt emphasizes djins Nahawand on G2 and djins ʿAdjam on F1. The note B♭2 is also emphasized a lot, and may be used for modulating to maqām ʿAdjam ʿUshayrān. Before ending on the tonic D1, the melody usually passes through the leading note, C1.

There are two maqāmāt in Turkey that share the same tonic, scale, and dominant note; these are maqām ʿUshshāq and maqām Bayātī. They differ in their melodic progression, or sayr al-maqām: In maqām ʿUshshāq, the progression starts from the tonic area and the first djins, and then ascends. In maqām Bayātī, the progression starts from the second djins, Nahawand on G2, while emphasizing the sixth note, B♭2 (Bitmez; see also Signell 1977: 51ff.).

2. Maqām Bayāt Shūrī (Qārdjighār)

The Scale

Intervals: ¾–¾–1–½–1½–½–1 (tones)

Analysis of the Scale

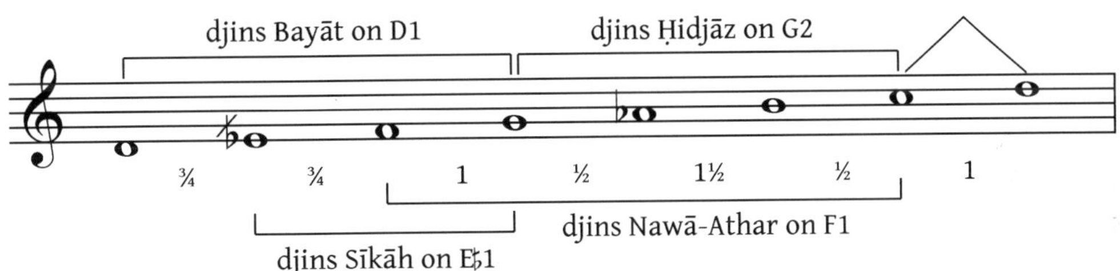

Adjnās

Primary adjnās: djins Bayāt on D1
djins Ḥidjāz on G2
(conjunct adjnās)

Secondary adjnās: djins Sīkāh on E𝄳1
djins Nawā-Athar on F1

The Name

This scale is named Bayāt Shūrī in Arab countries and Qārdjighār in Turkey.

The Conventional Position

D1 (Dūkāh)

Repositions

The first reposition up, or the sixth down, forms the scale of Huzām on E♭̸.
The third reposition up, or the fourth down, forms the scale of Ḥidjāz on G.
The sixth reposition up, or the first down, forms the scale of Sūznāk on C.

Transpositions

Not known

Modulations

IT IS EASY to modulate from Bayāt Shūrī to Bayāt by descending through djins Ḥidjāz on G2 to F1 and then ascending to A2 instead of A♭2 before descending to djins Bayāt on the tonic D1.

By using djins Ḥidjāz on G2, we can modulate to other maqāmāt that employ this djins, such as Ḥidjāz-Kār on C1 and Nawā-Athar on C1.

We can also modulate to maqām Sūznāk by repositioning the tonic from D1 to C1, or to maqām Huzām by repositioning the tonic to E♭̸1.

The Progression of the Maqām

THE PROGRESSION OF maqām Bayāt Shūrī starts from the octave note D1 and its second djins, Ḥidjāz on G2. Usually the melody also modulates to djins Nahawand on G2, by altering A♭2 to A♮2, and sometimes emphasizes djins Nawā-Athar on F1. The melody then descends to the first djins, Bayāt on D1, and concludes on the tonic.

3. Maqām Ḥusaynī

The Scale

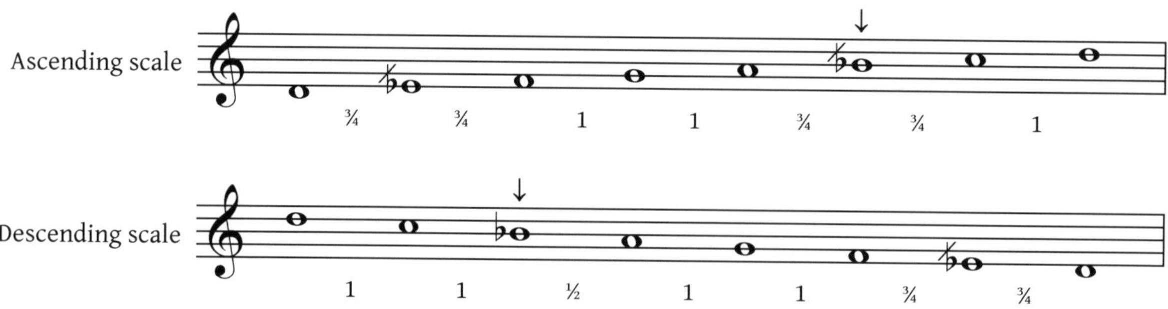

Intervals: ascending scale: ¾–¾–1–1–¾–¾–1 (tones)
descending scale: ¾–¾–1–1–½–1–1 (tones)
(ascending with B♭̸2; descending with B♭2)

As we can see from the above scales, the scale of maqām Ḥusaynī ascends with B♭̸2 and descends with B♭2, but this is not always so; the melody may sometimes descend with the note B♭̸2. The scale of maqām Ḥusaynī is identical to the scale of Muḥayyar, and in both of them the sixth note (B2) is "flexible" – it can alternate between B♮2 and B♭2, as in maqām Rāst. The uniqueness of maqām Ḥusaynī, however, is that its dominant note is the fifth note of the scale, A2.

Analysis of the Scale

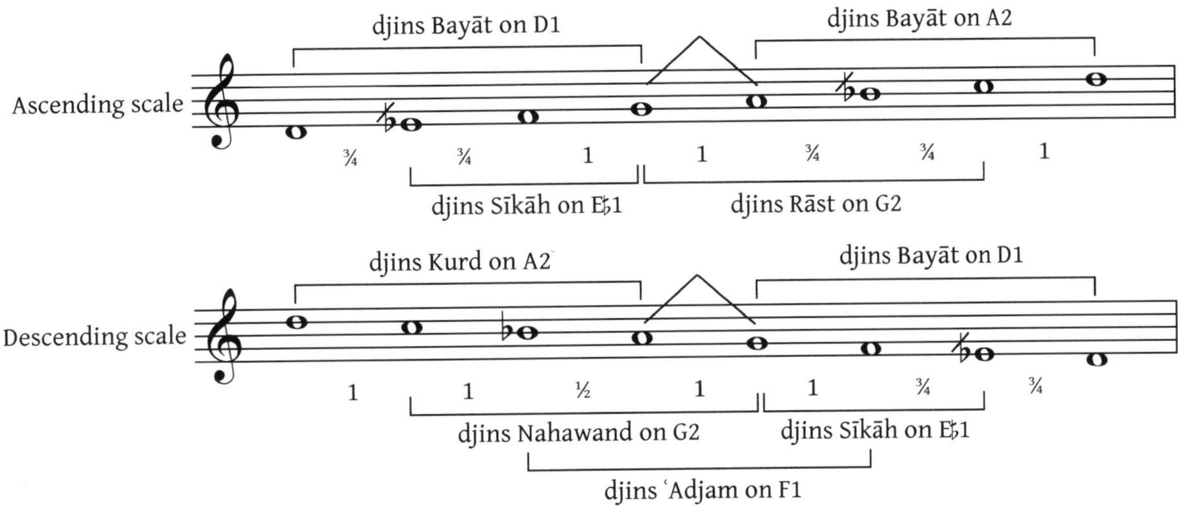

Adjnās

Primary adjnās:

In the ascending scale:	djins Bayāt on D1 djins Bayāt on A2 (disjunct adjnās)
In the descending scale:	djins Bayāt on D1 djins Kurd on A2 (disjunct adjnās)

Secondary adjnās:

In the ascending scale:	djins Sīkāh on E♮1 djins Rāst on G2
In the descending scale:	djins Sīkāh on E♮1 djins ʿAdjam on F1 djins Nahawand on G2

The differences between maqām Bayāt and maqām Ḥusaynī represent an interesting phenomenon in Arab music theory. Both Bayāt and Ḥusaynī share almost the same scale, but the dominant of maqām Bayāt is G2, while the dominant of maqām Ḥusaynī is A2. This difference causes these two maqāmāt to have different melodic characteristics and to differ in their melodic progression.

The Name

The name Ḥusaynī is an Arab name.

The Conventional Position

D1 (Dūkāh)

Repositions

THE ASCENDING SCALE of maqām Ḥusaynī can be considered a reposition of the scale of Rāst. Therefore, any of the repositions that are applicable to the scale of Rāst can be applied to Ḥusaynī.

Transpositions

Not known

Modulations

ANY OF THE modulations that are applicable to the scales of Bayāt and Rāst can be applied to Ḥusaynī.

The Progression of the Maqām

THE MAIN MELODIC characteristic of maqām Ḥusaynī is the emphasis of its dominant note, A2, and djins Bayāt that is positioned on it. The progression usually starts on this note and often returns to it, or "jumps" to it from various other notes of the scale, such as the tonic D1, and the note F1, or even E𝄳1. Emphasizing this note serves to distinguish this maqām from maqām Bayāt. In the conclusion, the progression usually descends while altering B𝄳2 to B♭2 and then continues to the first djins and the tonic note D1.

4. Maqām Ḥusaynī ʿUshayrān

The Scale

Intervals: ¾–¾–1–¾–¾–1–1 (tones)

Analysis of the Scale

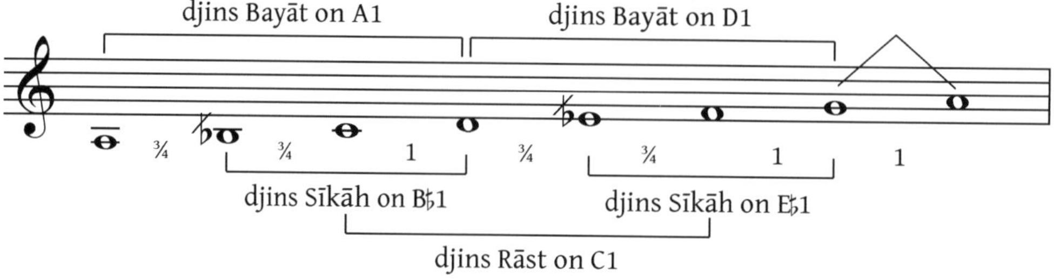

Adjnās

Primary adjnās: djins Bayāt on A1
djins Bayāt on D1
(conjunct adjnās)

Secondary adjnās: djins Sīkāh on B𝄳1
djins Rāst on C1
djins Sīkāh on E𝄳1

The scale of Ḥusaynī ʿUshayrān is the second reposition down, or the fifth up, of the scale of Rāst:

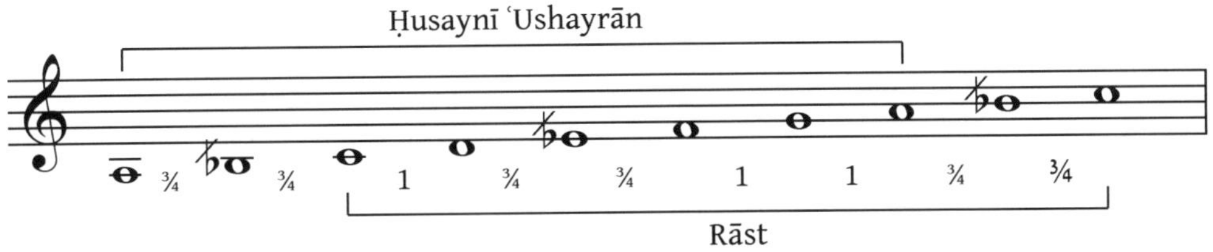

The scale of Ḥusaynī ʿUshayrān is composed of two conjunct adjnās: djins Bayāt on A1 and djins Bayāt on D1. As is the case with many maqāmāt in the Bayāt family, the ghammāz of the maqām is the fourth note of its scale.

Al-Ḥilū analyses the scale very similarly, but adds some of his own interpretations to it. While he agrees that the scale is composed of djins Bayāt on A1 and djins Bayāt on D1 in conjunct sequence, he says that the descending progression modulates to djins Nawā-Athar on C1 by altering E𝄳1 to E♭1 and F1 to F♯1 (1972: 98). Maqām Ḥusaynī ʿUshayran is not widely used, and it may be that al-Ḥilū only gives his interpretation to a single musical piece that he heard. In fact, modulating from djins Bayāt on D1 to djins Nawā-Athar on C1 forms the scale of Bayāt Shūrī on A1: djins Bayāt on A1 and djins Ḥidjāz on D1:

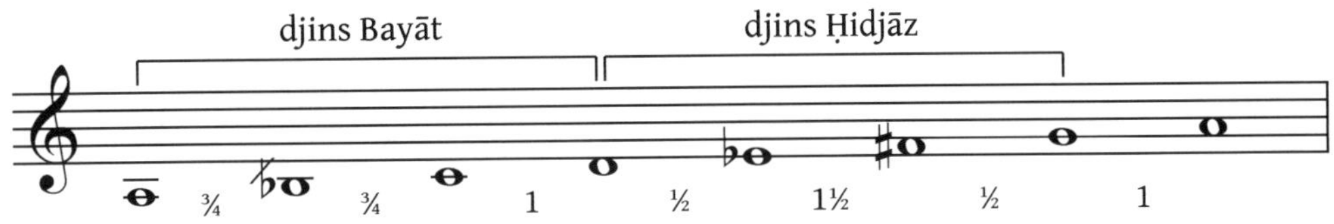

The Name

THE NAME Ḥusaynī ʿUshayrān is derived from the name of the tonic note of the maqām – A1. The note A2 is named Ḥusaynī, and the note A1, which is one octave lower, is called ʿUshayrān, and sometimes Ḥusaynī ʿUshayrān (al-Ḥilū 1972: 89).[1]

The Conventional Position

A1 (ʿUshayrān)

This scale should not be mistaken for a transposition of the scale of Bayāt. The intervals and structure of these two scales differ.

1 On names of notes, see Chapter 6.

Repositions

SINCE THE SCALE of Ḥusaynī ʿUshayrān is a reposition of the scale of Rāst, any of the repositions that are applicable to the scale of Rāst can be applied to it.

Transpositions

Not known

Modulations

Many of the modulations that are applicable to maqām Rāst can be applied to maqām Ḥusaynī ʿUshayrān.

The Progression of the Maqām

MAQĀM ḤUSAYNĪ ʿUSHAYRĀN is not widely used and is rarely analyzed by scholars. The only source I could find regarding its progression is al-Ḥilū (1972: 98).

Al-Ḥilū states that one of the essential melodic characteristics of this maqām is the emphasis of djins Nawā-Athar on C1. The progression starts from the third djins (djins Bayāt on A2), then descends to the second and first adjnās before concluding on the tonic.

5. Maqām Nuhuft

The Scale

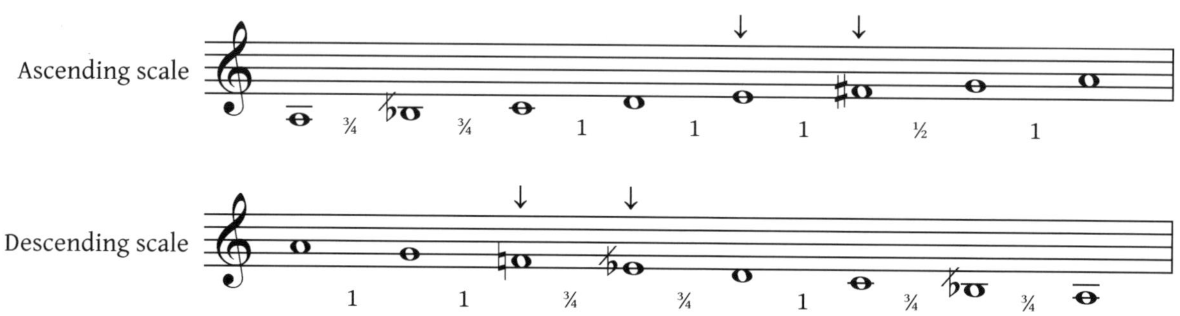

Intervals: ascending scale: ¾–¾–1–1–1–½–1 (tones)
descending scale: ¾–¾–1–¾–¾–1–1 (tones)

As we can see, in the descending scale, E1 is altered to E𝄳1 and F♯1 is altered to F♮1. The descending scale of maqām Nuhuft is therefore identical to the scale of Ḥusaynī ʿUshayrān.

Analysis of the Scale

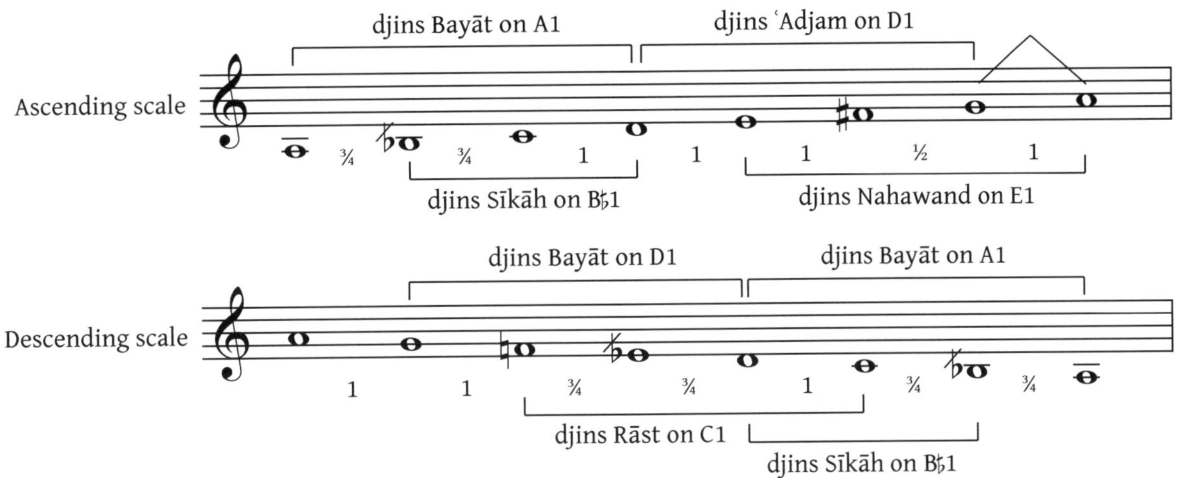

Adjnās

Primary adjnās:

In the ascending scale: djins Bayāt on A1
djins ʿAdjam on D1
(conjunct adjnās)

In the descending scale: djins Bayāt on A1
djins Bayāt on D1
(conjunct adjnās)

Secondary adjnās:

In the ascending scale: djins Sīkāh on B𝄳1
djins Nahawand on E1

In the descending scale: djins Sīkāh on B𝄳1
djins Rāst on C1

The above analysis is given by al-ʿAbbas (1986: 81). We can see again that in the Bayāt family, most scales have their ghammāz on the fourth note, and therefore the two adjnās that form the scale are connected in conjunct sequence on this note.

Mashʿal does not mention this scale, while al-Ḥilū (1972: 89) only mentions it in his list of maqāmāt that are positioned on the tonic A1, but does not give any analysis of it. Al-Mahdī gives only a short explanation: "It is composed of Bayātī [that is, djins Bayāt] on A1, followed by Djahārkāh on D1[1] or Ḥidjāz on D1" (19??: 44). Djins ʿAdjam and djins Djahārkāh are very similar, and therefore there is no real contradiction between al-ʿAbbas's analysis and al-Mahdī's.

Djins Ḥidjāz on D1, however, is not mentioned by al-ʿAbbas, and al-Mahdī does not distinguish here between an ascending and a descending scale. It may be that djins Ḥidjāz on D1 is an example of another variation of the scale and therefore, in maqām Nuhuft, the second djins can be Ḥidjāz, Bayāt, or ʿAdjam.

With djins Bayāt on D1, the scale is identical to the scale of Ḥusaynī ʿUshayrān. With djins Ḥidjāz on D1, the scale is a transposition of the scale of Bayāt Shūrī to the tonic A1.

1 In the source appears "C1," which is probably a mistake.

The Name

IN HIS LIST of maqāmāt, al-Ḥilū names this maqām "Nahaft or Nahaft al-ʿArab." According to him, this is a Persian word, meaning "low" – that is, a low voice or register – or "behind the veil" (1972: 212).

The note G1, which is named "Yakāh" nowadays, was named in the past "Nuhuft," while the name "Yakāh" was given to the note C1, which today is named "Rāst."

The Conventional Position

A1 (ʿUshayrān)

Repositions

IT IS HARD to apply repositions to such a "flexible" scale that undergoes so many changes when ascending or descending. Its only permanent djins is its first one – djins Bayāt on D1.

Transpositions

Not known

Modulations

TWO VARIATIONS OF the scale of Nuhuft are identical to the scales of Ḥusaynī ʿUshayrān and Bayāt Shūrī. Many of the modulations that are applicable to these scales can be applied to Nuhuft.

By descending to G1, we can modulate to maqām Rāst on G1.

Other common modulations are to ʿAdjam on G1 and to Nawā-Athar on C1.

The Progression of the Maqām

ACCORDING TO AL-ḤILŪ, the main melodic characteristics of maqām Nuhuft is the emphasis of djins Nawā-Athar on C1 and the emphasis of the note A2. The progression starts from the third djins (the first djins of the second octave), then descends to the second djins and emphasizes it, before descending to the first djins. The progression has to start from the note A2, because it is the central note of the scale. The descent from the third djins should be gradual (1972: 98).

If we emphasize the note A2 and djins Bayāt that is positioned on it, we actually modulate to maqām Ḥusaynī, and if we descend to djins Bayāt on D1, we reach the tonic of maqām Ḥusaynī. The progression of Maqām Nuhuft, therefore, is similar to the progression of maqām Ḥusaynī, only instead of concluding on D1, it descends further down to djins Bayāt on the tonic A2.

6. Maqām Muḥayyar

The Scale

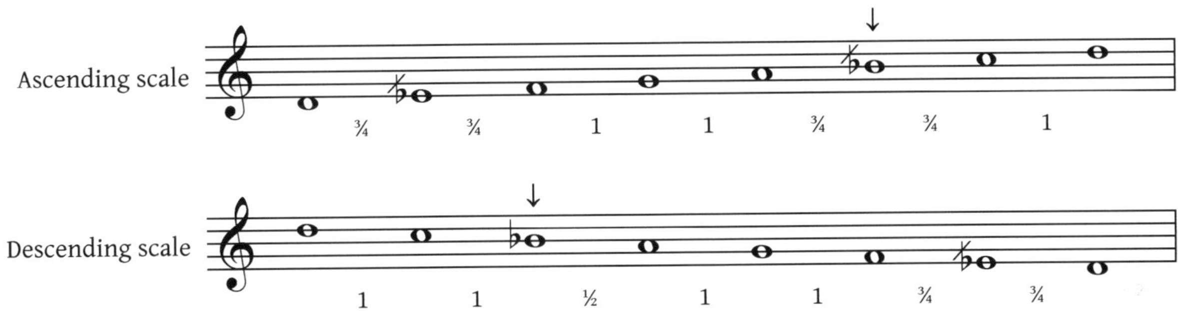

Intervals: ascending scale: ¾–¾–1–1–¾–¾–1 (tones)
descending scale: ¾–¾–1–1–½–1–1 (tones)
(ascending with B𝄳2; descending with B♭2)

Analysis of the Scale

SEE THE ANALYSIS of maqām Bayāt in the first section of this chapter.

I refer the reader to the analysis of the scale of maqām Bayāt, because most Arab scholars see maqām Muḥayyar as a variety of maqām Bayāt that differs from it in its melodic progression. No Arab source that I have used for this book sees maqām Muḥayyar as a distinct and independent maqām, nor devotes a separate analysis for it. Some do not mention it at all (for example, al-ʿAbbas 1986), while most others see it as a variety of maqām Bayāt.

Al-Ḥilū mentions it at the end of his analysis of maqām Bayāt, in a list of "scales that are similar to Bayāt," and gives a few words to explain its progression (1972: 119). Both Mashʿal and al-ʿAbbas (1959; 1986) do not mention it at all, while al-Mahdī (19??: 34) only mentions its name under a section called "species of Bayātī" and says that when maqām Bayāt emphasizes its third djins and its octave note, it is called Bayātī Muḥayyar. From all these accounts, we can conclude that Arab music theoreticians do not see maqām Muḥayyar as a distinct maqām, but only as a variety of maqām Bayāt. Some of these scholars refer also to maqām Ḥusaynī in a similar way (for example, al-Mahdī 19??: 34).

In Turkey, maqām Muḥayyar is a very important and distinguished maqām that has a large repertoire. This maqām may have been borrowed by the Arabs from the Turks, and lately, it is recognized in Arab countries as a distinct and independent maqām with its own unique characteristics.

Though the Turks also perceive maqām Muḥayyar as a "descending ʿUshshāq (Bayāt)," they analyze it differently than the analysis presented here. As with Ḥusaynī, the ghammāz of Muḥayyar is its fifth note, and therefore, its second djins is ʿUshshāq (as djins Bayāt is called in Turkish music theory) on A2 in the ascending scale and Kurd on A2 in the descending scale.

The Name

THE WORD "MUḤAYYAR" means "embarrassed" or "confused" in Arabic. In Iraq, this term is used when a person wants to express a doubt concerning quantity. For example, if you ask a merchant whether the piece of cloth you buy is enough for making a suit, he might reply "Muḥayyar" if he does not know.

Al-Mahdī says that in Iran, this scale is named "Baba-Ba" because it is attributed to a ruler with the same name (19??: 34).

Most likely, however, Maqām Muḥayyar is named so because the note D2, from which the progression of the scale starts, is named Muḥayyar.[1]

The Conventional Position

D1 (Dūkāh)

Repositions

See the repositions in the sections on maqām Bayāt and maqām Ḥusaynī.

Transpositions

Not known.

Modulations

See the modulations in the sections on maqām Bayāt and maqām Ḥusaynī.

The Progression of the Maqām

THE PROGRESSION OF maqām Muḥayyar starts from its third djins, Bayāt on D2 (the first djins of the second octave). From there the progression descends to djins Bayāt on A2, and modulates to djins Nahawand on G2 by altering B𝄳2 to B♭2. The progression then descends to djins Bayāt on the tonic D1.

1 On names of notes, see Chapter 6.

CHAPTER 19

THE SĪKĀH FAMILY OF MAQĀMĀT

1. **Maqām Sīkāh**
2. **Maqām Huzām**
3. **Maqām Awshār**
4. **Maqām ʿIrāq**
5. **Maqām Rāḥat al-Arwāḥ**
6. **Maqām Bastah-Nikār**
7. **Maqām Awdj**
8. **Maqām Mustaʿār**

THE NOTE SĪKĀH (literally meaning "the third position") is the third note of the scale of Rāst, which is the principal scale of Arab music and its most important one. The notes of Rāst are considered primary positions for various scales of Arab music.

The scales in the Sīkāh family all begin with djins Sīkāh, which is composed of only three notes and therefore, of two intervals (¾–1 tones), though some Arab theoreticians claim that it is composed of four notes. I do not agree with this concept, and throughout this book, I present djins Sīkāh as composed of three notes. There is no dispute, however, that the ghammāz of the scale of Sīkāh is its third note, and therefore, in all the maqāmāt of the Sīkāh family, the second djins is positioned on the third note of the scale.

Maqām Sīkāh is considered a very sentimental and romantic maqām, and so are other maqāmāt of the Sīkāh family. In many if these maqāmāt, other "emotional" adjnās, such as djins Ḥidjāz (in the maqāmāt Huzām and Rāḥat al-Arwāḥ) and djins Ṣabā (in maqām Bastah-Nikār) are combined with djins Sīkāh; together they form very expressive maqāmāt.

1. Maqām Sīkāh

31

The Scale

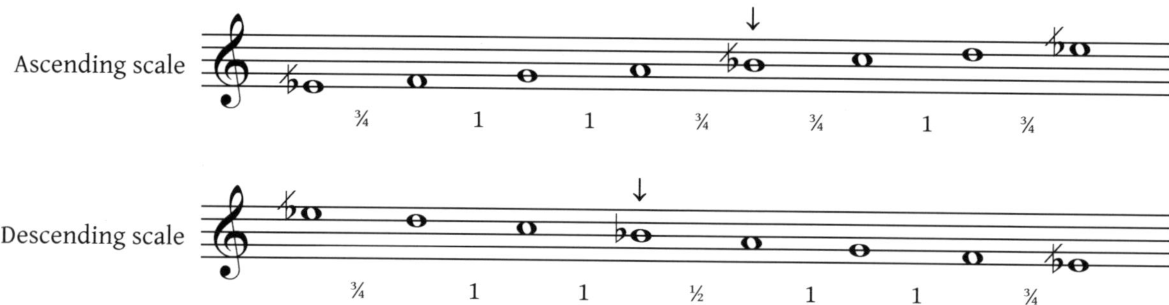

Intervals: ascending scale: ¾–1–1–¾–¾–1–¾ (tones)
descending scale: ¾–1–1–½–1–1–¾ (tones)
(ascending with B𝄳2; descending with B♭2)

Analysis of the Scale

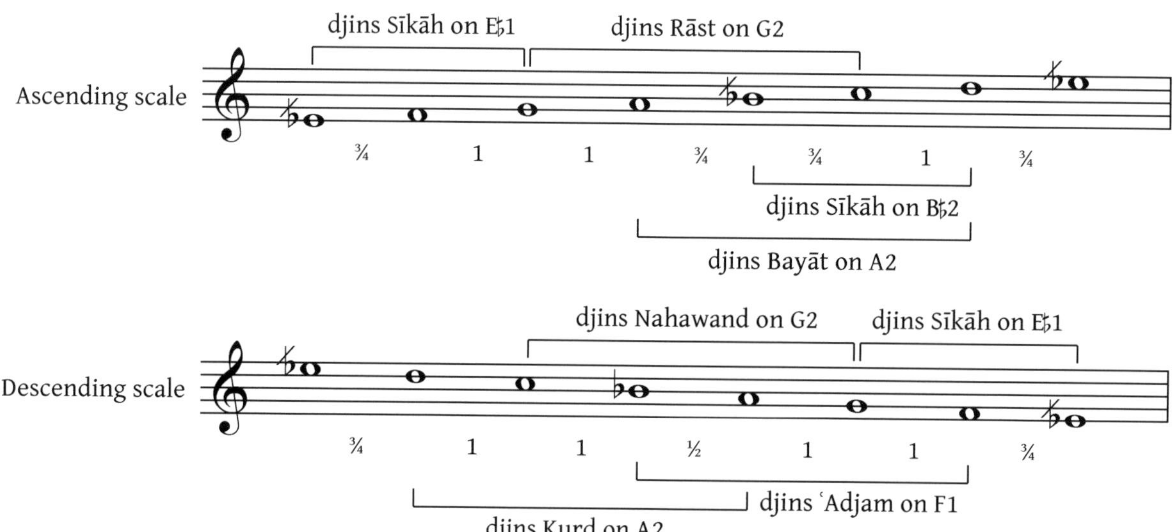

Adjnās

Primary adjnās:

In the ascending scale:	djins Sīkāh on E𝄳1 djins Rāst on G2 (conjunct adjnās)
In the descending scale:	djins Sīkāh on E𝄳1 djins Nahawand on G2 (conjunct adjnās)

Secondary adjnās:

In the ascending scale:	djins Bayāt on A2 djins Sīkāh on B𝄳2
In the descending scale:	djins ʿAdjam on F1 djins Kurd on A2

The above analysis is the one given by al-ʿAbbas (1986: 43). The ascending scale is the second reposition of the scale of Rāst. Mashʿal presents the scale of Sīkāh with the note B𝄳2 in both the ascending and the descending scales (1959: 33). In al-Mahdī's version, the analysis is as above, and the descending scale has djins Nahawand on G2. Al-Mahdī, however, presents the scale as consisting of ten notes (19??: 39):

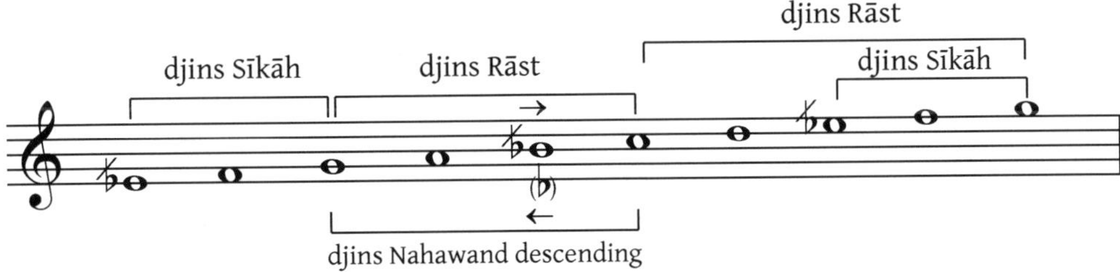

Al-Ḥilū presents the scale of Sīkāh as consisting of 13 notes. He also states that the second djins of the scale is djins Rāst when ascending and djins Nahawand when descending, but in his analysis, the second octave is composed of djins Rāst of five notes on C2 and djins Rāst of four notes on G3 (1972: 131):

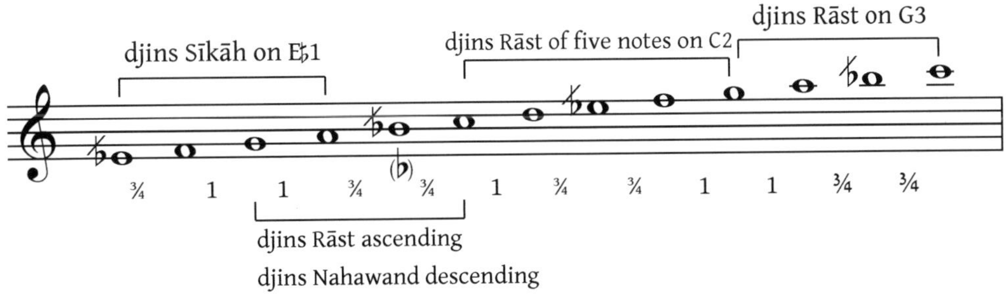

Both al-Ḥilū and Mashʿal (1959: 33) maintain that djins Sīkāh is composed of four notes. As we can see above in the scale taken from al-Ḥilū, the adjnās of the scale of Sīkāh in such an analysis are not disjunct or conjunct adjnās, but *overlapping adjnās*, because djins Sīkāh on E𝄳1 and djins Rāst on G2 overlap each other. In this book, I maintain that djins Sīkāh is composed of three notes.[1]

1 Al-Ḥilū's conception of two types of djins Rāst, one with four notes and one with five, does not comply with the general theory of Arab music. See the section on the Turkish conception of adjnās in Chapter 8.

The Name

THE NAME OF maqām Sīkāh is derived from the name of its tonic – the note Sīkāh. The name Sīkāh comes from the combination of two words of Persian origin: *sī*, which means "three," and the suffix *kāh*, from the Persian *gāh*, which means "a position." The name Sīkāh, therefore, means the third position on the scale of Rāst, which is the primary scale of Arab music.

The Conventional Position

E𝄳1 (Sīkāh)

Repositions

The scale of Sīkāh is the second reposition up of the scale of Rāst.

Transpositions

Not known

Modulations

THE SECOND DJINS in all the scales of the Sīkāh family is a "flexible" djins, which can be easily modulated. In maqām Sīkāh, the second djins is Rāst. By altering djins Rāst to djins Bayāt, we can modulate to maqām ʿIrāq on E𝄳1. By altering djins Rāst to djins Ṣabā, we can modulate to maqām Bastah-Nikār on E𝄳1.

By altering djins Rāst to djins Ḥidjāz, we can modulate to maqām Huzām. After establishing djins Ḥidjāz on G2, we can modulate to other maqāmāt that employ this djins, such as maqām Ḥidjāz-Kār, maqām Zandjarān, and maqām Sūznāk.

We can modulate to maqām ʿAdjam by altering djins Rāst on G2 to djins ʿAdjam and then descending through the scale of ʿAdjam to its tonic, C1.

The Progression of the Maqām

ACCORDING TO AL-ḤILŪ, the progression of maqām Sīkāh starts from its first djins, to which we enter by way of the notes C1 and D♯1. The note D♯1 serves as the leading note (ẓahīr) to the note E♭1; it helps establish and strengthen it as the tonic of the scale. The progression then ascends to the second djins, Rāst on G2, and the third djins, Rāst on C2.

The interval between D♯1 and E𝄳1 is a quartertone. Arab music theory does not recognize the interval of a single quartertone as an integral interval of a scale, that is, as an interval between two consecutive notes; it can only be combined to create larger intervals, such as the three-quartertone and the five-quartertone intervals. In the usage of D♯1 as a leading note in maqām Sīkāh, therefore, we witness a unique usage of the interval of one quartertone.

2. Maqām Huzām

The Scale

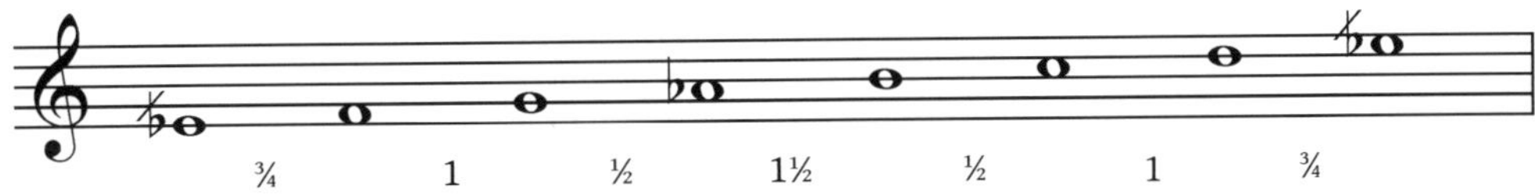

Intervals: ¾–1–½–1½–½–1–¾ (tones)

Analysis of the Scale

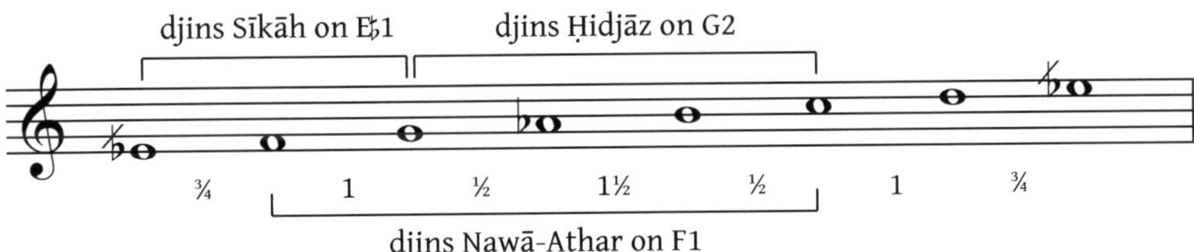

Adjnās

Primary adjnās: djins Sīkāh on E𝄳1
djins Ḥidjāz on G2
(conjunct adjnās)

Secondary adjnās: djins Nawā-Athar on F1

The Name

ACCORDING TO AL-ḤILŪ, Maqām Huzām was originally an Arab maqām and was named maqām Sīkāh. This maqām was adapted and modified by the Turks, who named it Huzām.

The Conventional Position

E𝄳1 (Sīkāh)

Repositions

THE FIRST REPOSITION up forms one of the variants of the scale of Nakrīz on F.[1]
The second reposition up forms the scale of Ḥidjāz on G.

Transpositions

The transposition of the scale of Huzām to B𝄳1 is named Rāḥat al-Arwāḥ.

Modulations

MANY OF THE modulations that are applicable to maqām Sīkāh can be applied to maqām Huzām.

We can also modulate to the scale of Bastah-Nikār by descending to djins Ṣabā on D1 and then descend to djins Sīkāh on B𝄳1.

By using djins Ḥidjāz on G2, we can modulate to other maqāmāt that employ this djins, such as Ḥidjāz-Kār on C1 and Nawā-Athar on C1.

The Progression of the Maqām

The main melodic characteristic of maqām Huzām is the emphasis of djins Ḥidjāz on G2. The progression starts from the first djins, Sīkāh on E𝄳, goes up to the second djins, Ḥidjāz on G2, and explores these two adjnās. It then goes up to the third djins, Rāst on C2, and then descends while altering the second djins to djins Nahawand on G2. When arriving at the tonic E𝄳1, we should support it with the notes C1 and D♯1 (the leading note).

We should remember that when altering the second djins to djins Nahawand, we form the scale of maqām Awshār, which is analyzed below.

3. Maqām Awshār

The Scale

Intervals: ¾–1–1–½–1–1–¾ (tones)

1 See the section on Nakrīz for more information on its variants.

Analysis of the Scale

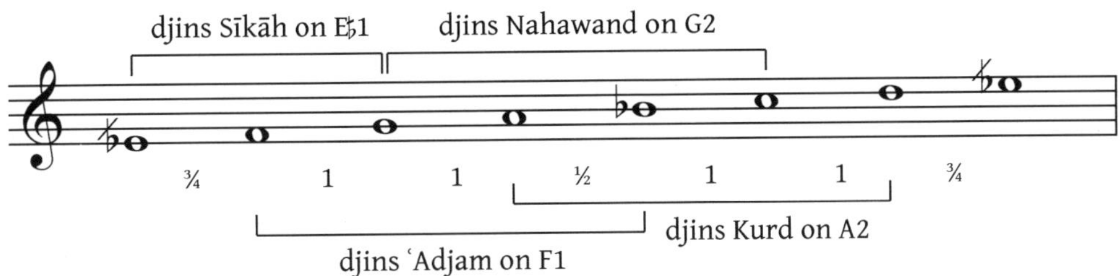

Adjnās

Primary adjnās: djins Sīkāh on E𝄳1
djins Nahawand on G2
(conjunct adjnās)

Secondary adjnās: djins ʿAdjam on F1
djins Kurd on A2

The Name

THE NAME OF maqām Awshār is probably Arabic, but its meaning is not completely clear. This scale is mentioned only by al ʿAbbas (1986: 45). Al-ʿAbbas is an Iraqi scholar and his book was published in Iraq. Indeed, Iraqi musicians are familiar with this maqām. Elias says that in Egypt, this maqām is known as maqām Shaʿār, but I could not find such a name in the literature available to me.

The Conventional Position

E𝄳1 (Sīkāh)
As with maqām Huzām, maqām Awshār can be considered a variant of maqām Sīkāh.

Repositions

The first reposition up forms the scale of Djahārkāh on F1.
The first reposition down forms the scale of Bayāt on D1

Transpositions

Not known

Modulations

BY REPOSITIONING THE tonic, we can modulate to maqām Djahārkāh or maqām Bayāt. If we alter B♭2 to B𝄳2, we can modulate to the scale of Sīkāh, which is a reposition of Rāst. From there, by descending to C1, we can modulate to maqām Rāst. This modulation can also be performed without altering B♭2 to B𝄳2. Modulations to other scales in the Sīkāh family can be performed easily.

The Progression of the Maqām

THE PROGRESSION STARTS by emphasizing the ghammāz of the scale, G2. The ghammāz is approached from the tonic and the second note, F1. The progression then explores djins Nahawand on G2, before descending to the tonic.

4. Maqām ʿIrāq

The Scale

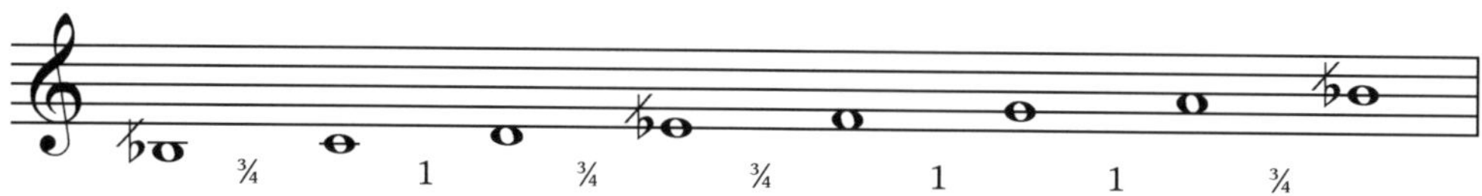

Intervals: ¾–1–¾–¾–1–1–¾ (tones)

Analysis of the Scale

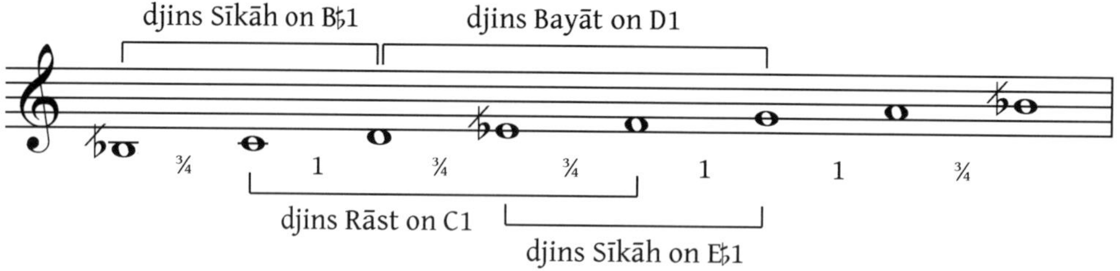

Adjnās

Primary adjnās: djins Sīkāh on B𝄳1
djins Bayāt on D1
(conjunct adjnās)

Secondary adjnās: djins Rāst on C1
djins Sīkāh on E𝄳1

All the sources that I consulted mention maqām ʿIrāq, and all of them represent the first octave of its scale as djins Sīkāh on the tonic and djins Bayāt on the third note of the scale, D1.

However, scholars differ in the way they analyze the scale in terms of adjnās. Both Al-ʿAbbas and al-Mahdī represent djins Sīkāh as consisting of three notes, and name the first djins of the scales of ʿIrāq and Rāḥat al-Arwāḥ "djins Sīkāh" (Al-ʿAbbas 1986: 44; al-Mahdī 19??: 41). In the scales of the Sīkāh family, the second djins is always positioned on the third note of the scale, and therefore, the adjnās in their analyses are in conjunct sequence.

Al-Ḥilū and Mashʿal, on the other hand, maintain that djins Sīkāh consists of four notes, and name the first djins of the scales of ʿIrāq and Rāḥat al-Arwāḥ "djins ʿIrāq" (al-Ḥilū 1972: 102; Mashʿal 1959: 71). Since they also place the second djins of all the scales of the Sīkāh family on the third note, the adjnās in their analyses are not conjunct adjnās, but overlapping ones. In order to examine their approach and comment on it, let us look at al-Ḥilū's analysis of the scale of ʿIrāq:

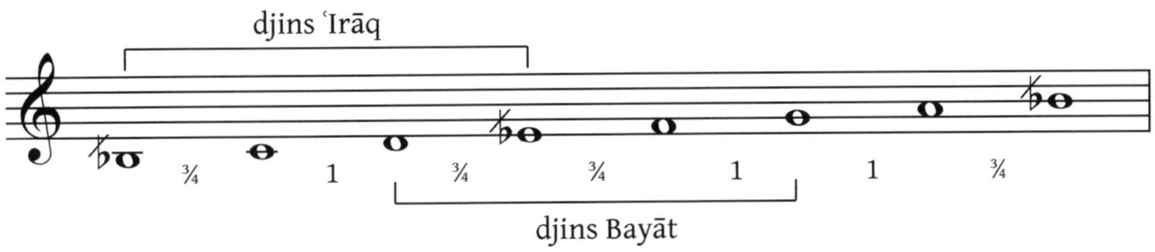

As we can see, djins ʿIrāq in this analysis consists of four notes, and its intervals are ¾–1–¾ (tones); that is, the whole djins extends over 2½ tones.

On the other hand, the scale of Rāḥat al-Arwāḥ is analyzed like this (al-Ḥilū 1972: 103):

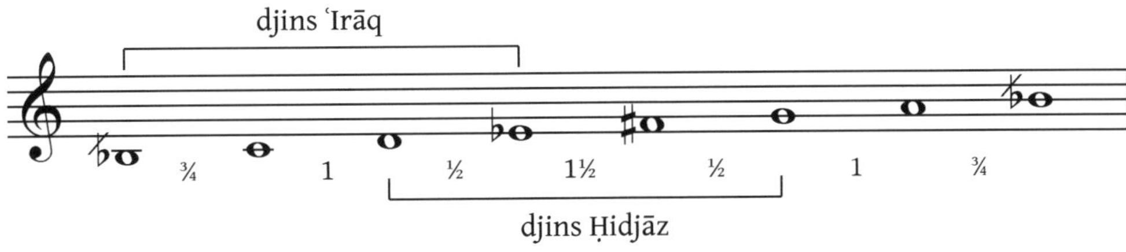

The intervals of djins ʿIrāq in this analysis are ¾–1–½ (tones); that is, the whole djins extends over 2¼ tones.

It seems illogical that two adjnās with different intervals are called by the same name. There are many inconsistencies in al-Ḥilū's analyses, not only when he discusses the above maqāmāt, but also when he discusses others. In short, I would say that I do not agree with al-Ḥilū's conception of djins Sīkāh as consisting of four notes, or with his differentiation between djins Sīkāh and djins ʿIrāq: Almost all scholars agree that the second djins in all scales is always positioned on the ghammāz and that the ghammāz in the scales of the Sīkāh family is always the third note of the scale. Therefore, I maintain that djins Sīkāh consists of three notes and that all the adjnās in the scales of the Sīkāh family are in conjunct sequence. Such an analysis agrees with the theory of adjnās analysis presented in this book.

Both al-Ḥilū and al-Mahdī maintain that the scale of ʿIrāq has a third djins – djins Rāst on G2. Al-Ḥilū even goes further to say that the scale of ʿIrāq consists of fourteen notes and presents a fourth djins – djins Sīkāh of five notes on E𝄳2; this is how his analysis looks like:

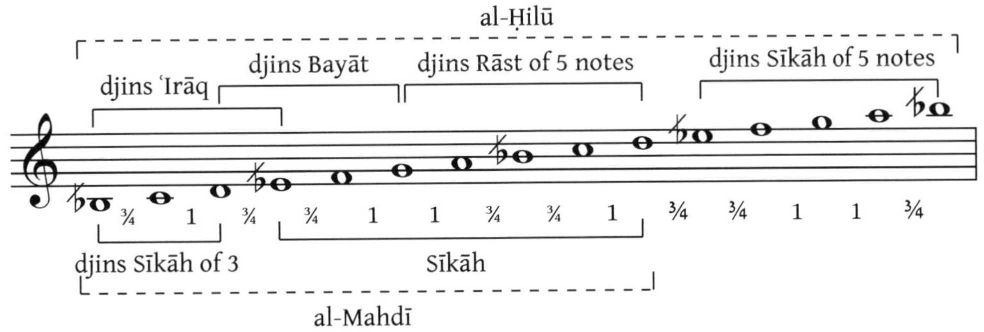

The Name

Maqām ʿIrāq is probably named after the tonic note of its scale, B𝄳1 (ʿIrāq).

The Conventional Position

B𝄳1 (ʿIrāq)

Repositions

The scale of ʿIrāq is the first reposition down of the scale of Rāst.

Transpositions

The scale of ʿIrāq is a transposition of one of the variants of the scale of Sīkāh.

Modulations

SINCE THE SCALE of ʿIrāq is formed of the adjnās Sīkāh and Bayāt, we can use the modulations that are applicable to their corresponding maqāmāt.

If we alter E𝄳1 to E♭1 and F1 to F♯1, we can modulate to Huzām on B𝄳1 (maqām Rāḥat al-Arwāḥ). We can modulate to maqām Bastah-Nikār by performing djins Ṣabā on D1 and then descending to djins Sīkāh on B𝄳1. We can further descend to A1, and from there, ascend to C1 in order to modulate to maqām Rāst, whose scale is the first reposition up of ʿIrāq.

The Progression of the Maqām

THE PROGRESSION OF maqām ʿIrāq starts from the note C1 and the first djins, while the note G1 is used to "support" the tonic, B𝄳1.

According to al-Ḥilū, the ascending scale and the descending one are identical in all four adjnās that he presents, except for the alteration of B𝄳2 to B♭2 in the descending scale.

5. Maqām Rāḥat al-Arwāḥ

The Scale

Intervals: ¾–1–½–1½–½–1–¾ (tones)

Analysis of the Scale

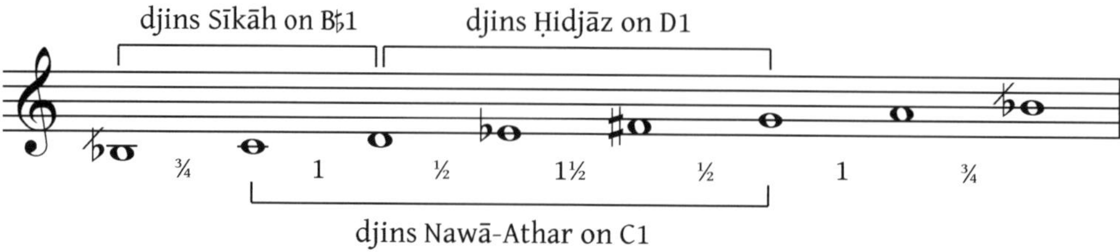

Adjnās

Primary adjnās: djins Sīkāh on B♭1
djins Ḥidjāz on D1
(conjunct adjnās)
Secondary adjnās: djins Nawā-Athar on C1

Al-Ḥilū, in his usual manner, maintains that the first djins of the scale of Rāḥat al-Arwāḥ consists of four notes, and names it "djins ʿIrāq." Since the second djins of this scale is Ḥidjāz on D1, the adjnās in his analysis are overlapping adjnās (al-Ḥilū 1972: 103).[1] Mashʿal, on the other hand, names the same four-note djins "djins Rāḥat al-Arwāḥ."

According to al-Ḥilū, the scale of Rāḥat al-Arwāḥ consists of fourteen notes. He positions djins Rāst of five notes on G2 and djins Ḥidjāz of five notes on D2:

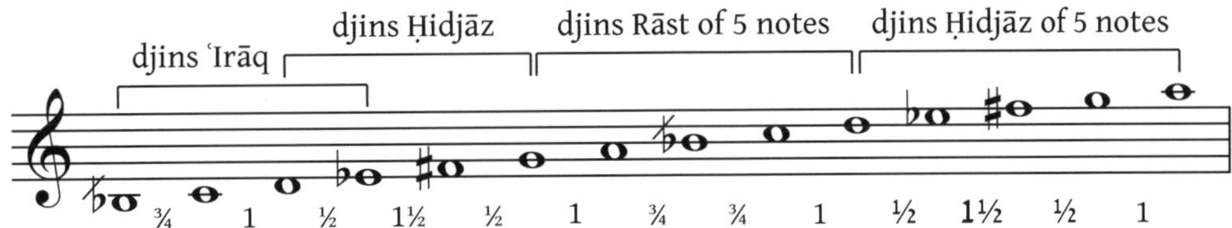

The Name

The name Rāḥat al-Arwāḥ means "the tranquility of the souls" in Arabic. However, it is probably of Persian origin.

The Conventional Position

B♭1 (ʿIrāq)

Repositions

Any of the repositions that are applicable to the scale of Huzām can be applied to Rāḥat al-Arwāḥ.

Transpositions

The scale of Rāḥat al-Arwāḥ is a transposition of Huzām to the tonic B♭1.

Modulations

Any of the modulations that are applicable to the scale of Huzām can be applied to Rāḥat al-Arwāḥ.

The Progression of the Maqām

The main melodic characteristic of maqām Rāḥat al-Arwāḥ is the emphasis of djins Ḥidjāz on D1. The progression starts from djins Ḥidjāz on D1, and then ascends to the third djins, which can be altered to Nahawand on G2. The third djins can then be modulated back to djins Rāst on G2 before descending to the tonic.

1 See the comment on al-Ḥilū's concepts in the section on maqām ʿIrāq.

6. Maqām Bastah-Nikār

The Scale

Intervals: ¾–1–¾ –¾–½–1½–¾ (tones)

Analysis of the Scale

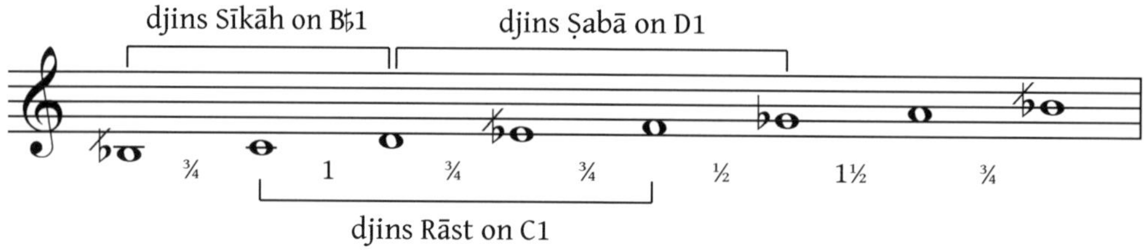

Adjnās

Primary adjnās:	djins Sīkāh on B𝄳1 djins Ṣabā on D1 (conjunct adjnās)
Secondary adjnās:	djins Rāst on C1

It is important to note that the above scale and its analysis cannot fully represent the unique melodic characteristics of maqām Bastah-Nikār. Though this can be said about the representation of any maqām, it is especially true concerning this maqām.

Let us examine this unique maqām closely. The second djins of Bastah-Nikār is djins Ṣabā, which is the first djins of maqām Ṣabā. The scale of Ṣabā is a unique scale. It can be perceived as the scale of Bayāt with a flattened fourth note:

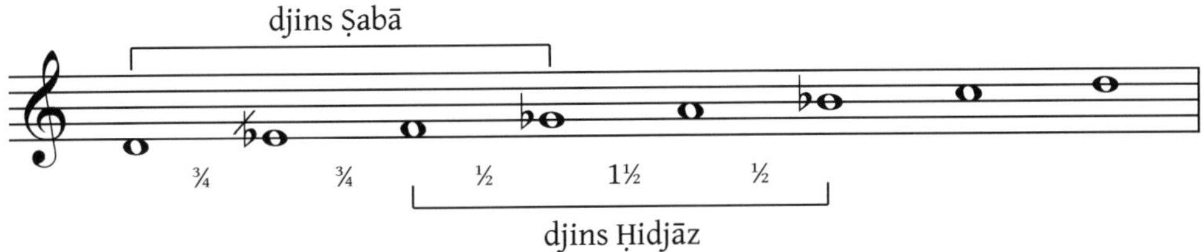

As we can see, the flattening of G2 to G♭2 forms djins Ḥidjāz on F1. This djins is an integral djins of the scale of Ṣabā, and therefore, it causes the alteration of B𝄳2 to B♭2. Al-Mahdī represents the scale of Bastah-Nikār like this (19??: 41):

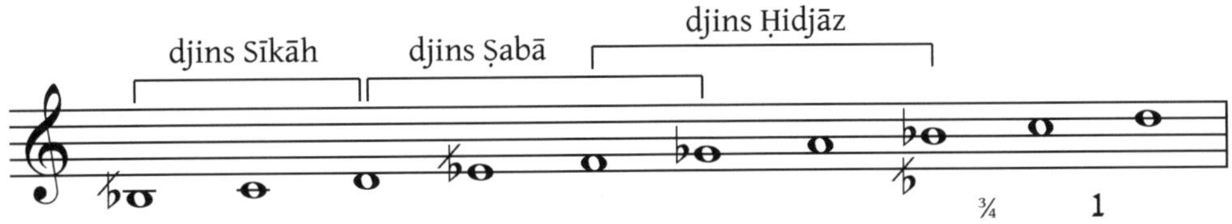

While the ascending scale has B𝄳2 as the tonic of djins Sīkāh, the descending scale has B♭2 in order to form djins Ḥidjāz on F1. From there, the scale descends to djins Ṣabā on D1 and djins Sīkāh on the tonic of the scale, B𝄳1.

The Name

Bastah-Nikār is a Persian name.

The Conventional Position

B𝄳1 (ʿIrāq). Nevertheless, it is sometimes positioned on E𝄳1 (Sīkāh).

Repositions

WE CAN SAY that the second reposition up of Bastah-Nikār forms the scale of Ṣabā on D1. However, the scale that is formed by such a reposition does not represent one of the unique characteristics of maqām Ṣabā: namely, that the octave note of Ṣabā is usually flattened by a semitone. In Ṣabā on D1, the octave note is D♭2, and therefore this scale spans five and a half tones instead of six. The reposition to Ṣabā would have to be "corrected" to accommodate this special characteristic.[1]

Transpositions

The scale of Bastah-Nikār is sometimes positioned on E𝄳1, but even then, it is still named Bastah-Nikār.

Modulations

AS IS EXPLAINED in the section on maqām Ṣabā, by employing djins Ḥidjāz on F1, we can use the modulations available for maqām Ḥidjāz, such as a modulation to Ḥidjāz-Kār on F1.

Modulating to other maqāmāt of the Sīkāh family that are positioned on B𝄳1 can be performed easily.

Modulating to maqām Bayāt or maqām Ḥidjāz on D1 can also be performed easily if when descending from A2, we alter G♭2 to G♮2. We can also modulate to Nahawand on G2 by using F♯1 as a leading note.

1 See the analysis of maqām Ṣabā in Chapter 20.

The Progression of the Maqām

Maqām Bastah-Nikār is a unique maqām and has some distinctive melodic characteristics. It is frequently used in Iraqi music, and many Iraqi songs are composed in this maqām. Its main melodic characteristic is the emphasis of djins Ṣabā on D1 before descending to djins Sīkāh on the tonic B𝄳1.

According to al-Ḥilū, the progression of the maqām starts from djins Ṣabā on D1, descends to djins Sīkāh on B𝄳1, and then ascends gradually (al-Ḥilū 1972: 104). We must note that when descending, B𝄳2 is altered to B♭2 in order to form djins Ḥidjāz on F1 before descending to djins Ṣabā on D1. Furthermore, as was said above, the octave note of the scale of Ṣabā is usually flattened by a semitone; this quality of maqām Ṣabā is discussed below, in the section about this maqām.

7. Maqām Awdj 36

The Scale

Intervals: ¾–1–¾–¾–1–1–¾ (tones)

Analysis of the Scale

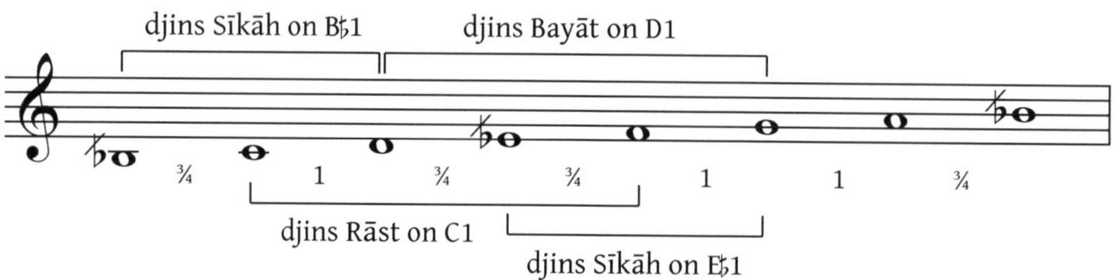

Adjnās

Primary adjnās:	djins Sīkāh on B𝄳1
	djins Bayāt on D1
	(conjunct adjnās)
Secondary adjnās:	djins Rāst on C1
	djins Sīkāh on E𝄳1

As we can see, the scale of maqām Awdj is positioned on the same tonic as the scale of maqām ʿIrāq (B𝄳1), its intervallic structure is the same as ʿIrāq, and so is the analysis of its scale in terms of adjnās. The difference between these two maqāmāt is that while the progression of maqām ʿIrāq starts from the tonic note B𝄳1 (the note ʿIrāq) and ascends, the progression of maqām Awdj starts from its second octave and the note B𝄳2, which is the octave note of its tonic B𝄳1, and then descends. Only after exploring the higher area of the scale, the progression descends and concludes on the tonic B𝄳1, just as with maqām ʿIrāq.

Basically, maqām Awdj is a Turkish maqām and the Arabs probably borrowed it from the Turks. The Turks interpret maqām Awdj the way it was analyzed above – as having the same scale as maqām ʿIrāq, but as differentiated from it by its descending melodic progression (sayr al-maqām). Al-Mahdī, gives such an analysis, but very shortly and concisely (19??: 45). Many Arab scholars, however, present contradicting opinions and misunderstandings when discussing maqām Awdj. Some of them view the scale of maqām Awdj as a transposition of the scale of ʿIrāq to B𝄳2. These scholars write the scale of Awdj like this:

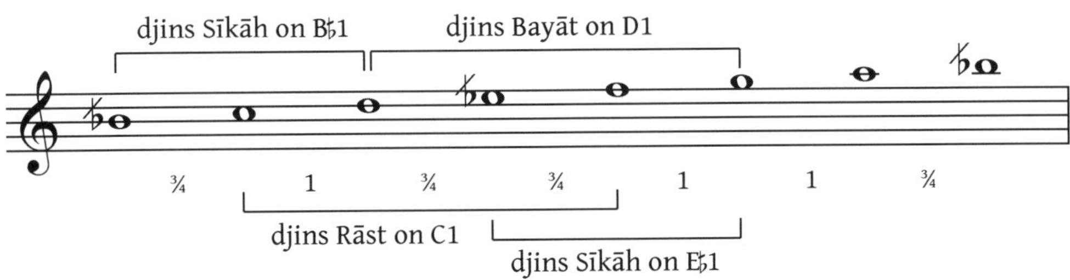

The analysis of the constituent adjnās in the above scale is the same as with the scale of maqām ʿIrāq. However, even those who position the scale of Awdj on B𝄳2 maintain that its melodic progression has to descend to the lower octave and conclude on B𝄳1.

I tend to agree with the Turkish interpretation of maqām Awdj for several reasons: Firstly, Maqām Awdj employs a second octave (above the note B𝄳2) as part of its melodic progression (sayr al-maqām). This does not mean that its scale should be positioned in that range. Moreover, more than a few maqāmāt have a descending melodic progression, which starts from the second octave and then descends to the first octave; however, in no other descending maqām is the tonic of the scale positioned in the second octave. Secondly, the tonic on which a scale is positioned is determined by the note that concludes the melodic progression of the maqām (called *qarār al-maqām*). All the musicians I interviewed agree that maqām Awdj concludes on B𝄳1, therefore, this note is the tonic of its scale. Finally, if we position the scale of Awdj on the tonic B𝄳2, the scale would stretch beyond the note G3, which is the upper limit of the two-octave range (diapason) used in Arab music.[1] Such an interpretation would contradict a fundamental conception in Arab music theory and in the method of analyzing maqāmāt and their scales as it is accepted by most scholars and as it is presented in this book.

Other scholars, like al-Ḥilū (1972: 105), present analyses of the scale of maqām Awdj that are very different from the analyses presented here. I did not find it necessary to refer to such analyses here.

The Name

THE NAME AWDJ is the name of the seventh note of the scale of Rāst (B𝄳2). It comes from Persian and Arabic and its meaning is "exalted" or "highest." It may be that the name was given to this maqām because its progression starts from this note, which is the octave note of its tonic.[2]

The Conventional Position

B𝄳1 (ʿIrāq)

1 See Chapter 6 for a discussion on range in Arab music.

2 Compare this with maqām Muḥayyar, which has the same scale as maqām Bayāt, but its progression starts and descends from its octave note Muḥayyar (D2).

Repositions

Any of the repositions that are applicable to the scale of ʿIrāq can be applied to Awdj.

Transpositions

Not known.

Modulations

Any of the modulations that are applicable to the scale of ʿIrāq can be applied to Awdj.

The Progression of the Maqām

THE PROGRESSION OF maqām Awdj starts from its third djins – djins Sīkāh on B𝄳2. After establishing this djins, the progression descends to the tonic. When descending, the fourth note, E𝄳1, is sometimes altered to E♭1. According to al-Nur, this is how it is played in Iraq.

8. Maqām Mustaʿār

The Scale

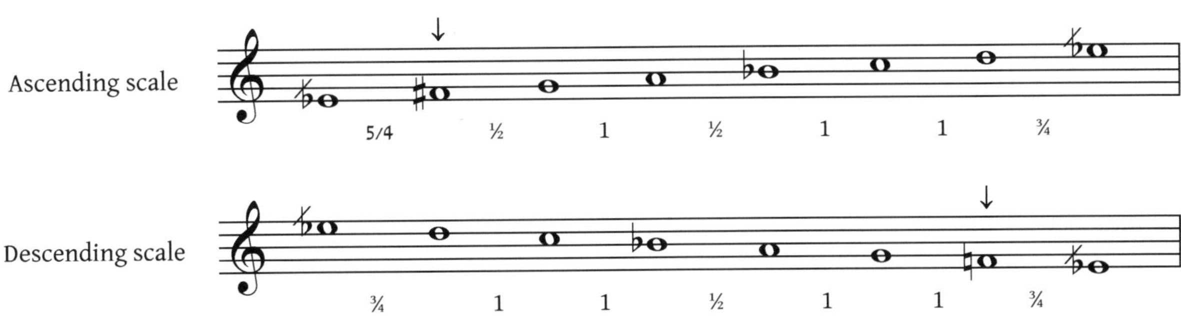

Intervals: ascending scale: 5/4-½-1-½ -1-1-¾ (tones)
descending scale: ¾-1-1-½-1-1-¾ (tones)

Analysis of the Scale

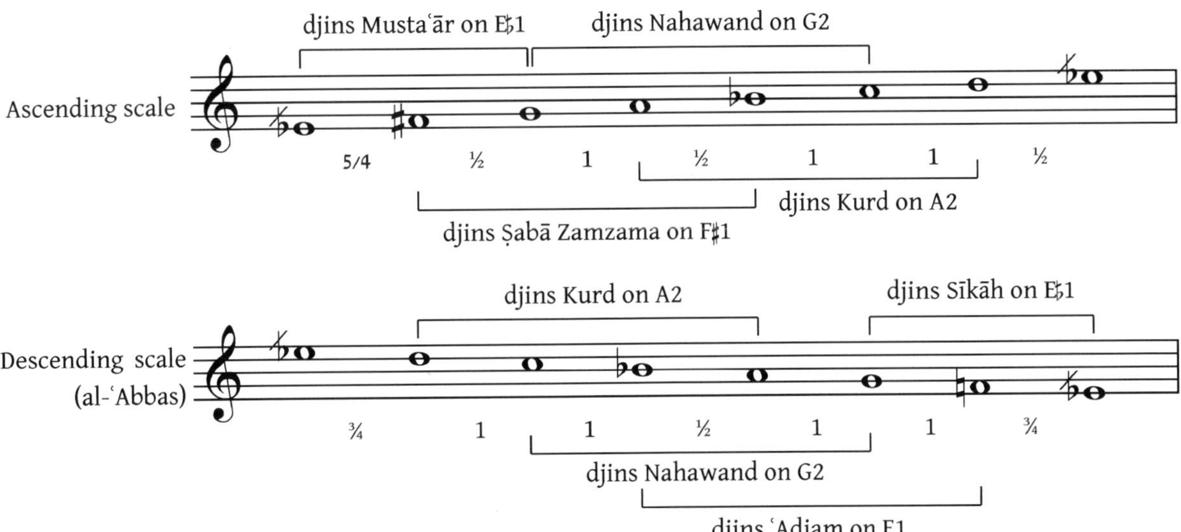

Adjnās

Primary adjnās:

In the ascending scale:	djins Mustaʿār on E𝄳1
	djins Nahawand on G2
	(conjunct adjnās)
In the descending scale:	djins Sīkāh on E𝄳1
	djins Kurd on A2
	(disnjunct adjnās)

Secondary adjnās:

In the ascending scale:	djins Ṣabā Zamzama on F♯1
	djins Kurd on A2
In the descending scale:	djins ʿAdjam on F1
	djins Nahawand on G2

In the descending scale, F♯1 is altered to F♮1, and so the first djins is altered to djins Sīkāh. Djins Mustaʿār is a unique djins: its intervals are 5/4–½ (tones) and it spans over 1¾ tone. The five-quartertone interval is a unique one, rarely to be found in other maqāmāt.

Al-Ḥilū does not mention either maqām or djins Mustaʿār, nor does he list any djins that includes an interval of 5/4 tones. Mashʿal presents the scale of Mustaʿār as the ascending scale above; in his interpretation, the scale does not change when descending (1959: 69).

Al-ʿAbbas lists Mustaʿār as belonging to the Sīkāh family of maqāmāt, but according to him, in the descending scale, djins Mustaʿār is altered to djins Sīkāh, as in the above scales (1986: 46). Therefore, the djins that concludes the progression of this maqām is Sīkāh. Since the concluding djins is the one that defines a maqām's melodic character, we can include maqām Mustaʿār in the Sīkāh family. If we accept Mashʿal's interpretation, maqām Mustaʿār would have to be an independent maqām, without a family. I could not find djins Mustaʿār mentioned in any other source.

Al-ʿAbbas maintains that in the descending scale, the second djins is Kurd on A2 and not Nahawand on G2. This approach contradicts the view that in the Sīkāh family, the second djins is always positioned on the third note. Positioning djins Nahawand on G1 conforms to the generally accepted analysis of the Sīkāh family.

I presented all the above views and interpretation so that readers can examine and consider them. In my opinion, Mashʿal's interpretation, in which the note F♯1 appears in both the ascending and the descending scales, is the most commonly accepted in the Arab world. This is how it is played in Iraq, where it is a common and widespread maqām.

Another example of a scale with the five-quartertone interval can be found in the Turkish maqām Pesendide, which was devised by Sultan Selim the Third. It can be perceived as the scale of Rāst with the fourth note altered from F1 to F♯1:

The progression of this maqām starts from its third djins and descends through F♯1 to E𝄳1. From there, the melody descends through djins Rāst to G1 (C1–B𝄳1–A1–G1), and then ascends back to E𝄳1 before concluding on the tonic C1. However, the note E𝄳1 (Sīkāh) is higher in Turkish music than in Arab music, and sometimes even E♮1 is used.

The Name

THE NAME MUSTAʿĀR comes from Arabic and its meaning is "borrowed," or even, "faked." It can be assumed that this name was given to this maqām because of the unique alteration of djins Sīkāh by sharpening F1 to F♯1.

The Conventional Position

E𝄳1 (Sīkāh)

Repositions

It is difficult to form repositions from the scale of Mustaʿār because of the interval of 5/4 tones. In Arab music, no other scale employs such an interval. There is, however, a unique Iraqi scale called Mukhālaf, which does not span a complete octave. It consists of only five notes and is written like this:

This "partial" scale is analyzed in the next chapter, but I give it here to show that though it uses the five-quartertone interval, it cannot be considered a reposition of Mustaʿār.

Transpositions

Not known

Modulations

THE SCALE OF Mustaʿār employs the adjnās Nahawand, Kurd, and Sīkāh. We can use various modulations that can be applied to their corresponding maqāmāt. See the sections on these maqāmāt for possible modulations.

The Progression of the Maqām

THE PROGRESSION OF maqām Mustaʿār starts from the tonic, E𝄳1, but ascends immediately to G2 and djins Nahawand positioned on it. The melody then passes through the notes F♯1 and E𝄳1, goes back to djins Nahawand on G2, and then descends to the first djins to a cadence on the tonic (G1–F♯1–E𝄳1).

CHAPTER 20

MAQĀMĀT THAT DO NOT BELONG TO A FAMILY

1. Maqām Ṣabā

2. Maqām Ṣabā Zamzama

3. Maqām Mukhālaf

Several maqāmāt cannot be easily associated with a certain family. This chapter deals with these maqāmāt. When examining maqām Mukhālaf, it becomes obvious that it cannot be listed under any family of maqāmāt. Concerning the maqāmāt Ṣabā and Ṣabā Zamzama, however, the answer is not as clear.

The scales of Ṣabā and Ṣabā Zamzama are very similar; they differ in only one detail: the first djins of Ṣabā is formed of the intervals ¾–¾–½ (tones), while the first djins of Ṣabā Zamzama is formed of the intervals ½–1–½ (tones). This means that when we position these two scales on their conventional tonic, D1, they differ in their second note: in Ṣabā the second note of the scale is E𝄳1, while in Ṣabā Zamzama, the second note is E♭1. Because of this slight difference, we distinguish between two similar adjnās – djins Ṣabā and djins Ṣabā Zamzama. Djins Ṣabā appears in several scales, but, as the first djins of a scale, it appears only in the scale of Ṣabā. Similarly, Djins Ṣabā Zamzama can be found in some scales as a secondary djins, but, as a primary djins, it appears only in the scale of Ṣabā Zamzama.

Because of the correspondence between their two first adjnās, it may have been proper to list the maqāmāt of Ṣabā and Ṣabā Zamzama under one family – the Ṣabā family. Though the progression of Ṣabā Zamzama starts with djins Ṣabā Zamzama (½–1–½ tones), when descending to the tonic, this djins is modulated to djins Ṣabā (¾–¾–½ tones). In view of the fact that the actual melodic character of a maqām is determined by its concluding djins, that is, the djins that descends to the tonic and concludes the musical piece, it may be reasonable to view Ṣabā Zamzama as a scale that belongs to the Ṣabā family, but which has received a distinct status because of its unique melodic progression (sayr al-maqām). In my opinion, the scale of Ṣabā Zamzama is not the scale of a distinct maqām: it is a transitory development of the progression of maqām Ṣabā, which serves as an embellishment.

Maqām Ṣabā is a unique maqām. Its structure and progression exhibit distinctive characteristics that cannot be found in other maqāmāt. We will discuss these characteristics, and the issues concerning the analysis of maqām Ṣabā, in the section about this maqām. Maqām Ṣabā is considered melancholic; it is usually used for sad songs, such as laments and songs about unrequited love. The scale of Ṣabā preserves its uniqueness also when it is used in the contexts of other scales, such as in the case of maqām Bastah-Nikār.

I added maqām Mukhālaf to this chapter for two purposes: Firstly, it serves as an example of a scale that is unique to a specific musical culture, in this case, to the Iraqi culture. Secondly, it shows that there are some unique scales, especially in Iraqi music, that do not span a complete octave, but only a part of it – in this case, a pentachord.

1. Maqām Ṣabā 38

The Scale

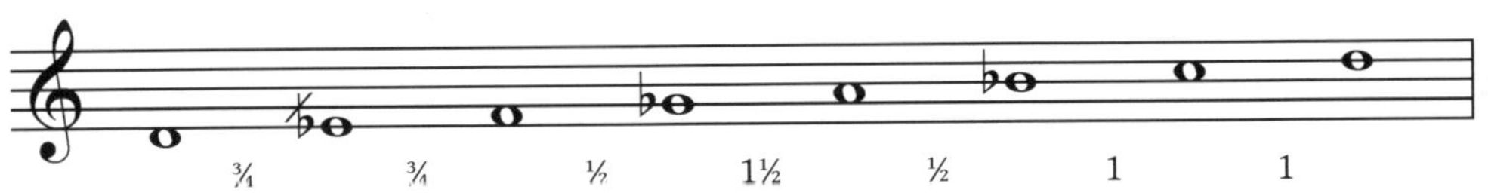

Intervals: ¾–¾–½–1½–½–1–1 (tones)

Analysis of the Scale

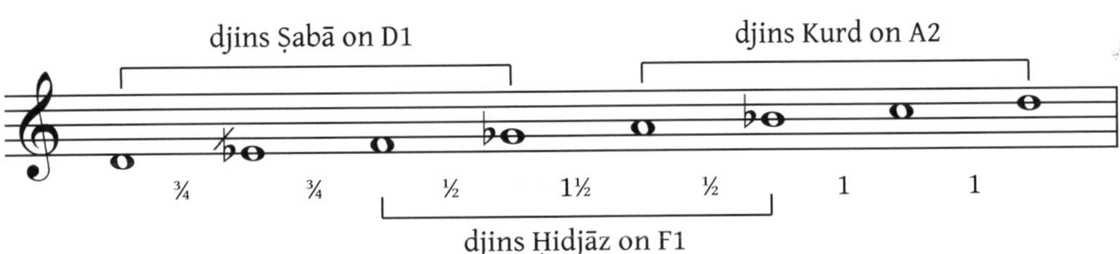

Adjnās

Primary adjnās:	djins Ṣabā on D1 djins Kurd on A2 (disjunct adjnās)
Secondary adjnās:	djins Ḥidjāz on F1

The above analysis is taken from al-ʿAbbas, who maintains that the scale of maqām Ṣabā does not change when ascending or descending (1986: 49). The second djins of the scale, Kurd, is positioned on the fifth note of the scale, A2, and therefore, according to this analysis, the ghammāz of Ṣabā is its fifth note.

The scale in Mashʿal's analysis is composed of the same notes as in al-ʿAbbas's analysis, but he maintains that the second djins of the scale is djins Ḥidjāz on F1, and the adjnās here are therefore overlapping (1959: 61).[1]

1 See Chapter 8 for an explanation about overlapping adjnās.

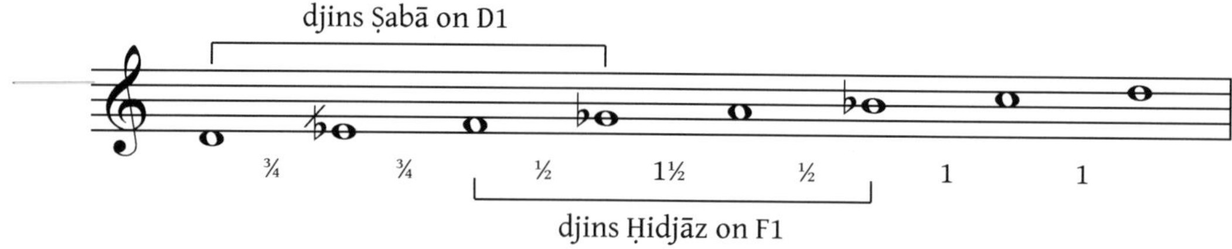

Mashʿal, therefore, suggests that the ghammāz of the scale of Ṣabā is its third note. If he is right, we cannot rule against the possibility of overlapping adjnās, because djins Ṣabā cannot contain only three notes (since then it cannot be differentiated from djins Bayāt).

Al-Ḥilū, like Mashʿal, maintains that djins Ṣabā consists of four notes and that the second djins is djins Ḥidjāz on F1 (1972: 122). Al-Ḥilū describes the progression of the maqām like this: After starting from djins Ṣabā on the tonic, the melody continues to djins Ḥidjāz on F1. From here, the progression goes to the third djins, Ḥidjāz on C2. It must be noted that in order to perform djins Ḥidjāz on C2, the octave note D2 must be flattened to D♭2. Following is al-Ḥilū's analysis of the scale of Ṣabā:

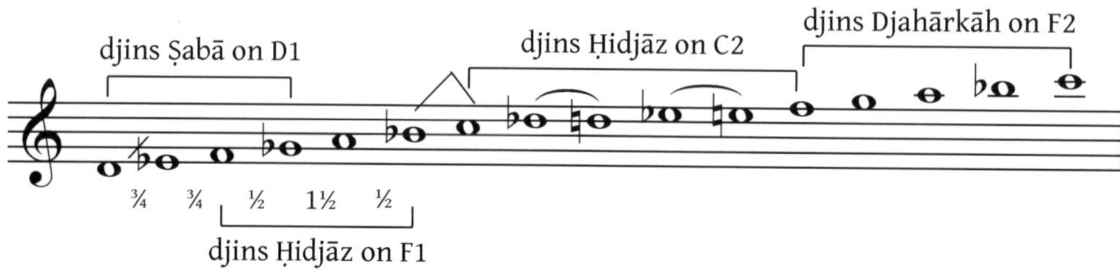

It seems to me that the three analyses above ignore a unique feature of maqām Ṣabā that cannot be found in any other maqām, namely, that the octave note of the scale of Ṣabā is flattened from D2 to D♭2. The scale of Ṣabā, therefore, spans a diminished octave, that is, only 5½ tones instead of six tones. For this reason, the analysis of the scale of Ṣabā should look like this:

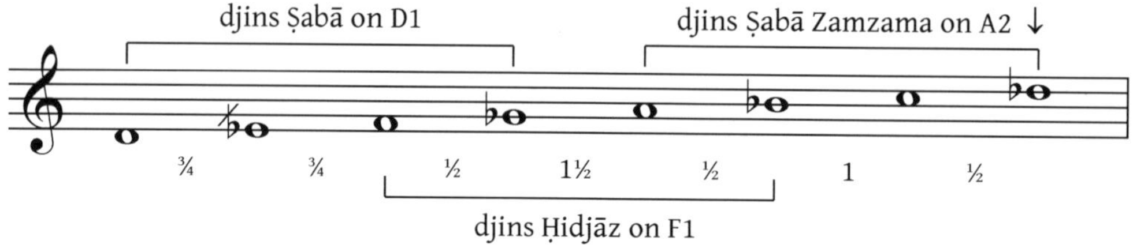

According to this analysis, those who analyze the scale as formed by disjunct adjnās, like al-ʿAbbas, need to position djins Ṣabā Zamzama on the fifth note, and not djins Kurd. Such a perception can solve many problems in the analysis of this unique scale. We can determine that the ghammāz of the scale is its fifth note, A2, and that the scale is formed of disjunct adjnās. It is true that djins Ḥidjāz on F1 is an important djins that must be emphasized in the progression of the maqām, but in many cases, secondary adjnās acquire a prominent role in the melodic progression of the maqām. In my opinion, djins Ṣabā Zamzama on A2 is not less prominent than djins Ḥidjāz on F1 in the progression of maqām Ṣabā.

This analysis also does not contradict the placing of djins Ḥidjāz on C2. Actually, such a progression forms the scale of Ḥidjāz-Kār on F1, which is characteristic of maqām Ṣabā. However, if we want to ascend to the second octave without placing djins Ḥidjāz on C2, we must ascend with D♮2 and only flatten it to D♭2 when descending again. This note alteration forms an integral part of the progression of maqām Ṣabā, and it does not affect the above perception concerning the diminished octave of the scale and the analysis of its adjnās.

Al-Mahdī presents an interesting analysis of maqām Ṣabā. According to him, djins Ṣabā consists of four notes. Like others, he also maintains that the second djins of Ṣabā is djins Ḥidjāz on F1, and forms his analysis accordingly.

Nevertheless, it seems that al-Mahdī does not recognize the concept of overlapping adjnās. When talking about the Sīkāh family of maqāmāt, for example, he maintains, like me, that djins Sīkāh consists of three notes, and he positions the second adjnās of the scale of the Sīkāh family on the third note of the scale. From such an approach, it is apparent that he holds that the note of the scale on which the second djins is positioned is the ghammāz of the scale. However, in his analysis of the scale of Ṣabā, al-Mahdī does not state that djins Ṣabā consists of three notes, but he also does not suggest the possibility of overlapping adjnās. Moreover, in the written explanation he contradicts his own scale analysis and says that the scale of Ṣabā is composed of djins Bayāt of three notes on D1 and djins Ḥidjāz of four notes on F1. The following figure presents the two contradicting approaches in al-Mahdī's analysis of the scale of Ṣabā:

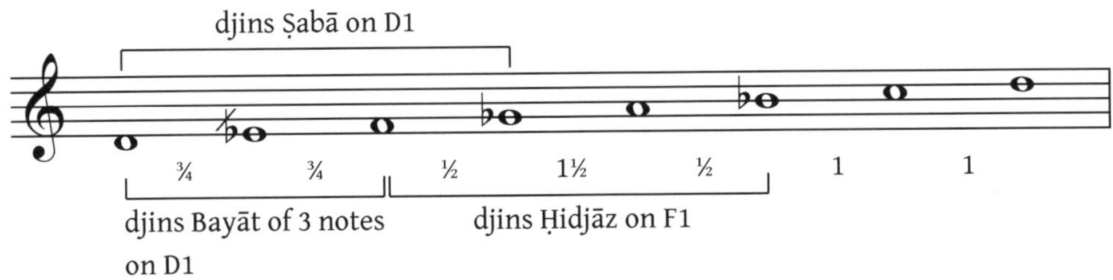

Al-Mahdī's idea of a djins Bayāt consisting of only three notes seems strange, and he does not refer to the diminished octave note D♭2, which is so characteristic of maqām Ṣabā. When examining various analyses of the scale of Ṣabā , it becomes apparent that scholars are perplexed and puzzled by this unique scale.

Djins Ṣabā is a unique djins: it spans only two tones though it consists of four notes. Though it can be said to be similar to djins Bayāt, the flattened fourth note, G♭2, makes the melodic character of djins Ṣabā considerably different from the one of djins Bayāt.

Al-Ḥilū is aware that the note D♭2 brings up some questions regarding the analysis of the scale of Ṣabā (1972: 122). In his analysis, he does not mention djins Kurd on A2, but divides the scale into djins Ṣabā on D1, djins Ḥidjāz on F1, and djins Ḥidjāz on C2. Such an analysis results in the formation of the scale of Ḥidjāz-Kār on F1. This is how the scale of Ṣabā looks like according to al-Ḥilū's analysis:

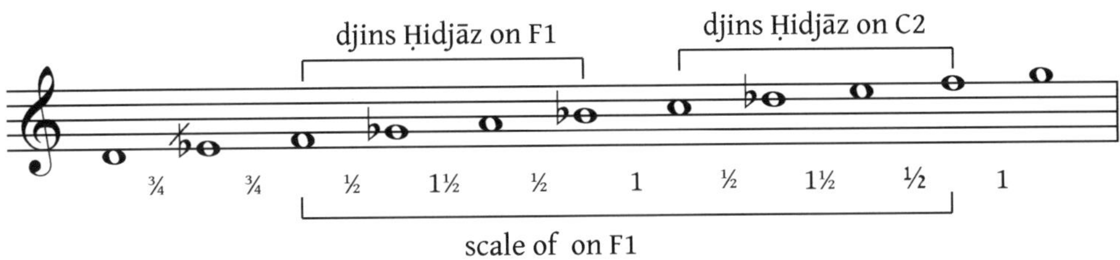

The Name

THE WORD ṢABĀ is an Arabic word meaning "to long for" or "to pine for." Al-Mahdī says that "its name in Iraq is al-Manṣūrī and it is attributed to the Abbasid caliph Djaʿfar al- Manṣūr or to Manṣūr Zalzal, who was the most famous ʿūd player in the Abbasid kingdom" (19??: 38). Maqām Ṣabā is considered a melancholic and emotional maqām, and is used for lamentations and sad love songs about unrequited love.

The Conventional Position

D1 (Dūkāh)

Repositions

THE SCALE OF Ṣabā is a complex scale: it is not a cyclical scale, and therefore, it is not possible to form scales by repositioning its tonic.

Transpositions

Not known

Modulations

IT IS EASY to modulate form djins Ṣabā on D1 to djins Bayāt or djins Ḥidjāz by altering G♭2 to G♮2.

If we descend from djins Ṣabā on D1 to djins Sīkāh on B𝄳1 we can modulate to maqām Bastah-Nikār. After we establish djins Sīkāh on B𝄳1, we can modulate to other maqāmāt of the Sīkāh family on this tonic.

Maqām Ṣabā is strongly associated with maqām ʿAdjam ʿUshayrān. Modulations between these two maqāmāt are very common.

The Progression of the Maqām

The third note of the scale of Ṣabā, F1, is an important note that should be emphasized, and many times, the progression of maqām Ṣabā starts on this note. From here, the progression descends to the tonic D1 before ascending again to explore the scale of Ḥidjāz-Kār on F1, which consists of djins Ḥidjāz on F1 and djins Ḥidjāz on C2, and which requires the flattening of D2 to D♭2. The descending progression explores djins Ṣabā on D2 and then descends back to djins Ḥidjāz on C2 and djins Ḥidjāz on F1, before concluding on djins Ṣabā on the tonic D1.

2. Maqām Ṣabā Zamzama

The Scale

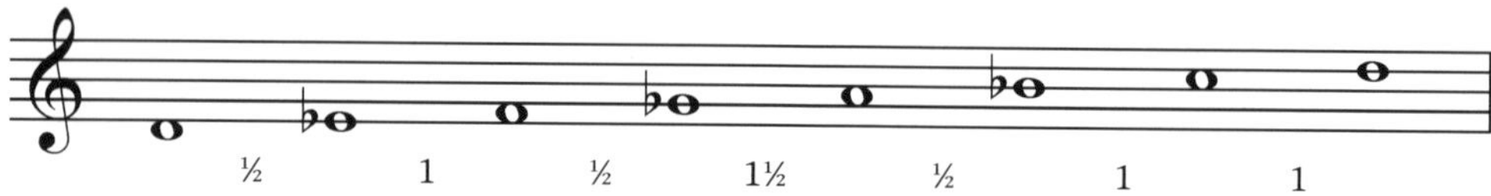

Intervals: ½-1-½-1½-½-1-1 (tones)

Analysis of the Scale

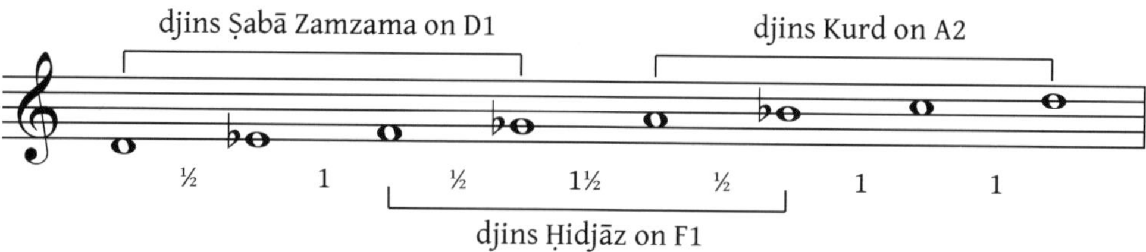

Adjnās

Primary adjnās: djins Ṣabā Zamzama on D1
djins Kurd on A2
(disjunct adjnās)

Secondary adjnās: djins Ḥidjāz on F1

Maqām Ṣabā Zamzama is almost identical in its structure and characteristics to maqām Ṣabā. This maqām can be thought of as a variant of maqām Ṣabā, but some scholars list these two maqāmāt separately, and therefore, I have decided to do the same.

Al-Ḥilū notes in the section devoted to the analysis of the scale of Ṣabā that "there is a scale named Ṣabā Zamzama, which is identical to the scale of Ṣabā, but when descending in Ṣabā Zamzama, E𝄳 is altered to E♭" (1972: 122). Al-Ḥilū, therefore, suggests that the progression of maqām Ṣabā Zamzama starts as in maqām Ṣabā, and only in the descending progression, E𝄳1 is altered to E♭1.

Some scholars distinguish between three variants of maqām Ṣabā:

(1) Maqām Ṣabā Zamzama, or "Ṣabā Kurdī," which is named so because the second note of the scale is the note E♭1 (Kurd);

(2) Maqām Ṣabā, in which the second note of the scale is E𝄳1; and

(3) Maqām Ṣabā Būsalīk, in which the second note is E♮1 (Būsalīk).

The progressions of these maqāmāt start with djins Ṣabā and only in their conclusions, when descending to the tonic, does the second note change to E♭1 (Kurd) or to E♮1 (Būsalīk).

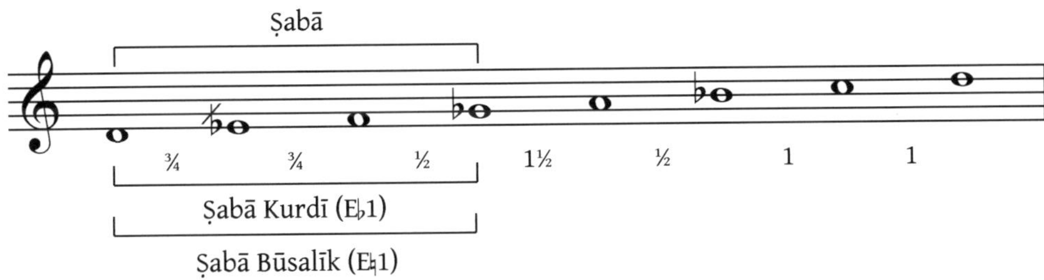

It must be noted that in the scale of Ṣabā Būsalīk there are two consecutive semitones:

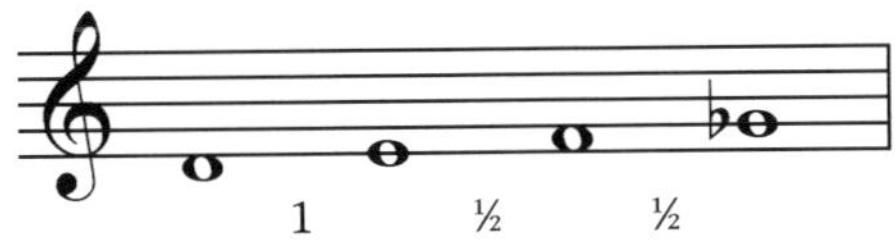

Djins Ṣabā Būsalīk is a unique djins that appears only in the context of maqām Ṣabā. As far as I know, maqām Ṣabā Kurdī and maqām Ṣabā Būsalīk are rarely used, though al-Mahdī lists the names of some musical pieces that are written in these maqāmāt (19??: 38). Elias notes that in Arab music, maqām Ṣabā Zamzama is more commonly used than maqām Ṣabā Būsalīk. He adds that in Ṣabā Zamzama, the octave note is flattened to D♭2, as in Ṣabā, while in Ṣabā Būsalīk, it stays D♮2.

The Name

The word *zamzama* is a Persian word meaning "the echo of a sound or a note."

The Conventional Position

D1 (Dūkāh)

Repositions, Transpositions, Modulations, and the Progression of the Maqām

BECAUSE OF THE similarities between maqām Ṣabā and maqām Ṣabā Zamzama, I refer the reader above, to the section about maqām Ṣabā, for more information.

3. Maqām Mukhālaf

The Scale

AS WE CAN discern from the above notation, the notes that form Mukhālaf do not cover a complete octave, and therefore, it is better to define it not as a scale, but as a pentachord. It includes the unconventional five-quartertone interval, and its structure is different from the prevailing structure of most scales of maqāmāt, such as the ones we have examined so far.

Mukhālaf is a melodic progression that is unique to the Iraqi musical culture, and its name is unmistakably an Iraqi name. The expression *Mukhālaf* is frequently used in Iraq and its meaning is "different" or "uncommon." Al-Mahdī mentions "maqām al-Mukhālaf" and states that this maqām is unique for Iraq. He does not notate it but explains it verbally. His explanation, however, differs from the scale notated above (19??: 65).

Of all other scholars, only al-ʿAbbas, who is Iraqi and whose book was published in Iraq, presents the notation of Mukhālaf as above (1986: 33). Al-ʿAbbas calls it "ʿaqd al-Mukhālaf," and indeed, the term *ʿaqd* is another name for a five-note djins in Arab music theory.

I have presented here the discussion on maqām Mukhālaf in order to present a unique and distinctively Iraqi maqām, and in order to show that in some cultures, melodic motifs that do not form a complete scale can be developed into a maqām.

BIBLIOGRAPHY AND SOURCES

List of English Sources

al-Faruqi, Lois Ibsen. c1981. *An Annotated Glossary of Arabic Musical Terms.* Westport, Conn.: Greenwood Press.

Arnon, Yoram. 2008. "Improvisation as Verbalization: The Use, Function, and Meaning of Pauses in the Turkish Taksim." *Dutch Journal of Music Theory*, Vol. 13, No. 1, pp. 36–47.

Karolyi, Otto. 1998. *Tradional African and Oriental Music.* London: Penguin Books.

Kojaman, Yeheskel. 2001. *The Maqam Music Tradition of Iraq.* London: Yeheskel Kojaman.

Marcus, Scott Lloyd. 1989. *Arab Music Theory in the Modern Period.* PhD Dissertation, University of California, Los Angeles.

Sadie, Stanely, ed. 1988. *The Grove Concise Dictionary of Music.* London: Macmillan.

Shiloah, Amnon. 1995. *Music in the World of Islam: A Socio-Cultural Study.* Detroit: Wayne State University Press

Signell, Karl L. 1977. *Makam: Modal Practice in Turkish Art Music.* Seattle: Asian Music Publications.

Touma, Habib Hassan, 1996. *The Music of the Arabs.* Portland, Oregon: Amadeus Press.

List of Arabic Sources

al-ʿAbbas, Ḥabīb Ẓahir. 1986. *Naẓariyyāt al-Mūsīqā al-ʿArabiyya (The Theory of Arab Music).* Baghdad: Maʿhad al-Dirāsāt al-Naghamiyya al-ʿIraqi.

Abū al-Madjd, Ṣabrī. 1963. *Zakariyyā Aḥmad.* Cairo: Egyptian Ministry of Education.

al-Ḥanafī, al-Duktūr Muḥammad Aḥmad. 1955 [?]. *Sayyid Darwīsh.* Cairo [?]: Egyptian Ministry of Education.

al-Hāshimī, Aḥmad. 1938. *Mīzān al-Dhahab fī Ṣināʿat Shiʿr al-ʿArab (The Golden Poetic Meter of Arab Poetry).* Cairo.

al-Ḥilū, Salīm. 1965. *Al-Muwashshaḥāt al-Andalusiyya Nashʾatuhā wa-Taṭwwuruhā (The Muwashshaḥāt of Andalusia).* Beirut: Manshūrāt Dār Maktabat al-Hayāt.

al-Ḥilū, Salīm. 1972. *Al-Mūsīkā al-Naẓariyya (The Theory of Music).* Beirut: Manshūrāt Dār Maktabat al-Hayāt.

al-Mahdī, Ṣāliḥ. 19??. *Maqāmāt al-Mūsīqā al-ʿArabiyya (The Maqāmāt of Arab Music).* Tunis: Nashr al-Maʿhad al-Rashīdī lil-Musīqa al-Tunisiyya.

al-Mahdī, Ṣāliḥ. 1990. *Iīqāʿāt al-Mūsīqā al-ʿArabiyya wa-Ashkāluhā (The Rhythms of Arab Music and Their Forms).* Tunis: Al-Mu ʾassasa al-Wataniyya lil-Tardjama wal-Taḥqīq wal-Dirāsāt "Bait al-Ḥikma."

Mash'al, Abd al-Ḥamīd. 1959 [?]. *Mūsīqā al-Ghinā' al-'Arabī (The Music of Arab Singing).* Cairo [?].

Qūdjamān, Y. 1978. *Al-Mūsīqā al-Fannīyya al-Mu'āṣira fi al 'Irāq (The Contemporary Art Music of Iraq).* London: Act.

al-Radjab, al-Ḥadjdj Hāshim Muḥammad. 1983. *Al-Maqām al-'Irāqī (The Iraqi Maqām).* Baghdad: Manshūrāt Maktabat al-Muthanna.

Shafīq, Ibrāhīm. 1982 [?]. *Turāthunā al-Mūsīqī (Our Musical Heritage).* Cairo [?]: The Egyptian High Commission of Music.

'Ubadyā, Ibrāhīm. 1999. *Fī Dunyā al-Maqāmāt wal-Ghinā' al-Sha'bī al-'Irāqī (In the World of Iraqi Maqāmāt and Folk Singing).* Tel Aviv: The Association of Iraqi Academicians in Israel.

List of Hebrew Sources

Cohen Dalia. 1990. *Akustika VeMuzika (Acoustics and Music).* Jerusalem: Academon.

Cohen, Dalia. 1986. *Mizraḥ UMa'arav BaMuzika (East and West in Music).* Jerusalem: Magnes.

Elias, Taiseer. 2007. *Ḥukiyut Smuya Be'Iltur Muzika Aravit Kelit (Takasim) BeIsra'el Be'Emtsa'ut Ekronot Shel Skhemot Tiv'iyot VeNilmadot (The Latent Regularity in Improvisation of Instrumental Arab Music [Taqāsīm]) in Israel, in Terms of Learned and Natural Schemata).* PhD Dissertation. Available at the Jewish National and University Library, The Hebrew University Library at Mount Scopus, and the Library of the Jerusalem Academy of Music and Dance.

Eliyahu, Peretz. 1998. *Te'oryat HaMuzika HaMizraḥit (The Theory of Eastern Music).* A collection of lectures delivered at Bar Ilan University, edited by David Muallem.

Sharoni, Avraham. 1987. *HaMilon HaMakif Aravi-Ivri (The Comprehensive Arabic-Hebrew Dictionary).* Tel Aviv: Ministry of Defense.

Personal Communications and Interviews

al-Nur, Selim (Shlomo Ziv-Li): Weekly workshops held over a period of four years; conversations and interviews.

Bar-Yosef, Amatzia: Comments on the manuscript and conversations.

Bitmez, Mehmet Emin: Consultations regarding Turkish classical music.

Cohen, Dalia: Guidance and counseling.

Elias, Taiseer: Meetings and conversations; comments on the manuscript; lectures at the Bar Ilan University.

Maayani Ami: Comments on the manuscript.

Mualem, Yinon: Conversations and interviews.

Salman, Abraham: Conversations and interviews.

GLOSSARY OF TERMS

ab'ād. Plural of ***bu'd.*** See **interval.**

accidentals (pp. 47; 61). Conventional signs affixed to note names that indicate the sharpening (raising) or flattening (lowering) of the note's pitch by a certain interval; for example, the signs *sharp* (♯), *flat* (♭), *natural* (♮), *half-sharp* (𝄲), *half-flat* (𝄳). See also **flatten; sharpen.**

adjnās munfarida. See **disjunct adjnās.**

adjnās mutadākhila. See **overlapping adjnās.**

adjnās muttaṣila. See **conjunct adjnās.**

adjnās. Plural of ***djins.***

'adjz (p. 26). Literally, "back." A term used in Arab poetry. See ***bayt.***

alteration or **note alteration** (pp. 46–49; 87–88). The practice of sharpening (raising) or flattening (lowering) single notes in a scale. In Arab music, note alterations serve several functions: (1) as an integral part of the melodic progression of the maqām; (2) as a way to change notes in the scale in order to perform a modulation to another scale; and (3) as a passing embellishment in the context of the performed maqām. See also **accidentals; modulation.**

bashraf (p. 27). A classical instrumental genre in which a recurring refrain, named *taslīm*, separates several stanzas, or musical passages, named *khānāt* (singular: *khānah*). Unlike the *samā'ī*, the bashraf is based on one rhythmic pattern in all of its sections. See also ***khānah; samā'ī.***

bayt; ṣadr; 'adjz (p. 26). Terms used in Arab poetry, which is mostly metered and rhymed. *Bayt* is a unit of the poem divided into two parts: the first is named *ṣadr* ("front") and the second *'adjz* ("back"). Both parts are composed in the same meter, while the second one ends with a rhyme.

bu'd. See **interval.**

cents (p. 64). An accurate method for measuring the exact microtonal intonation of intervals and notes by which the semitone is divided into 100 units called cents. Using the cent measuring system, Arab scholars have tried to establish the accurate intonations of notes, especially quartertonal notes, whose intonations are not identical in all maqāmāt or in all musical cultures. See also **intonation; comma.**

chromatic scale (p. 39). A scale of all 12 consecutive semitones in an octave.

comma (pp. 63–65). A method for measuring the microtonal intonations of intervals and notes by which the whole tone is divided into nine units called commas. See also **intonation; cents.**

conjunct adjnās (Arabic: *adjnās muttaṣila*) (pp. 77–78). The sequence of adjnās in which the second djins of the scale is positioned on the last note of the first djins. See also ***djins***; **disjunct adjnās; overlapping adjnās.**

conventional position or **conventional tonic** (pp. 84–87). A term unique to Arab music theory. The conventional position of a maqām is the note on which the scale of the maqām is traditionally positioned – the "natural" tonic of the maqām. When a maqām is transposed to a position different from its conventional one, its new tonic should be stated; for example, "Rāst on G2," "Bayāt on A1." See also **tonic;** ***qarār; taṣwīr.***

conventional tonic. See **conventional position.**

diapason (p. 60). The range or compass of notes – from the lowest to the highest – of an instrument, a voice, or (as it is used in this book) of a musical system; i.e., the diapason of Arab classical music is two octaves – from G1 to G3.

diatonic scale (pp. 39–41; 70). A scale derived from the diatonic scalar system. In diatonic scales used in European music, five whole tones are separated by two semitones to form two groups of two and three whole tones. For example, the major scale: 1–1–½–1–1–1–½ tones. See also **diatonic system.**

diatonic system or **diatonic scalar system** (p. 39–41; 70). A cyclical scalar system by which the octave is divided into five whole tones and two semitones. In the European diatonic system, the five whole tones are separated by the two semitones to form two groups of two and three whole tones. There are two other forms of diatonic scalar systems: (1) five tones divided into two groups of four and one whole tones, separated by two semitones; (2) one group of five consecutive whole tones with two consecutive semitones next to them. See also **diatonic scale.**

disjunct adjnās (Arabic: *adjnās munfarida*) (p. 77). The sequence of adjnās in which there is an interval of a second between the first djins and the second djins of the scale. Disjunct adjnās usually lie at both ends of the scale. See also ***djins***; **overlapping adjnās; conjunct adjnās.**

dīwān (p. 36). The Arabic term for the interval, or range, of an octave between the tonic note and the octave note of a musical scale. See also **octave;** ***djawāb.***

Djāhiliyya (p. 30). "The age of ignorance." The historical period before the rise of Islam (622 AD). The origins of Arab classical music can be traced back to this period.

djālghī baghdād (p. 98). An ensemble unique to the musical culture of Iraq. It consisted of two melodic instruments (the *djūzah* and the *sanṭūr*) two percussion instruments (the *darbūkah* and the *riqq*) and a singer (called *qāri'*). The djālghī baghdād ensemble performed the genre known as *al-maqām al-'irāqī*, an ancient musical genre that comprises all the scales and modes unique to Iraqi musical culture.

djawāb or ***djawāb al-maqām*** (p. 44). The Arabic word for the octave note of the scale. See also **octave;** ***dīwān.***

djins (plural: ***adjnās***) (p. 72; Chapter 8). Literally, "species" or "type." In Arab music theory, a djins is a small group of consecutive notes that may consist of three notes (*trichord*), four notes (*tetrachord*), or five notes (*pentachord*). In Arab music, a scale is formed by combining two primary adjnās and therefore, combinations of different adjnās form a variety of scales. See also **tetrachord; trichord; pentachord; primary adjnās.**

djūzah (pronounced *djōzah*). A bowed instrument similar to the *kamāndjah*, unique to the Iraqi musical culture and a regular member of the *djālghī baghdād* ensemble. Its body is made of a coconut shell. See also ***kamāndjah; djālghī baghdād.***

dominant (p. 44). The second most important note of the scale after the tonic. In European classical music, the dominant is always the fifth note of the scale; in Arab music, the dominant (named *ghammāz*) can be the third, fourth, or fifth. See also ***ghammāz.***

duration (p. 24). The length of time of a sound event. A term related to the time parameter in music and represented mainly by meter and rhythm.

equal temperament (p. 63). A tuning system used in European music by which the octave is divided into 12 identical semitones.

European modes (pp. 42–43). The seven modes formed by repositioning the tonic in the diatonic scalar system. See also **mode.**

first djins (pp. 72; 74–75). The lower djins of the two primary adjnās in the scale. See also ***djins***; **primary adjnās.**

first octave (pp. 59–60). (1) The first octave of a scale in Arab music. (2) The first octave in the two-octave range of Arab music. See also ***dīwān.***

flat (p. 47). Indicates the lowering, or *flattening*, of a note by a semitone. Represented by the accidental ♭. For example, the note E♭ ("E-flat") is a semitone lower than the note E. See also **accidentals.**

flatten (p. 47). To flatten a note is to lower its pitch by a certain interval; for example, flattening the note A by a semitone gives the note A♭. See also **accidentals.**

frequency (pp. 34–35). The number of vibrations in a given time produced by an object (for example, a string). If an object's frequency is constant, it produces regular airwaves with a specific length, which the ear and the brain interpret as musical sound.

ghammāz or ***ghammāz al-maqām*** (pp. 44–45; 74–75). The dominant note of a maqām, on which the second djins of the scale is positioned. In Arab music theory, the ghammāz can be the third, fourth, or fifth note of the scale. See also **dominant.**

half-flat (p. 61). Indicates the lowering, or *flattening*, of a note by a quartertone. Represented by the accidental 𝄳. For example, the note E𝄳 ("E-half flat") is a quartertone lower than the note E. See also **accidentals.**

half-sharp (p. 61). Indicates the raising, or *sharpening*, of a note by a quartertone. Represented by the accidental 𝄲. For example, the note F𝄲 ("F-half-sharp") is a quartertone higher than the note F. See also **accidentals.**

harmony (p. 95). Mainly the organization of several notes simultaneously, by combining several melodic lines or by adding chords to accompany the melody. Harmony is almost completely irrelevant to Arab music, which is primarily monophonic. See also **polyphony; monophony.**

heptatonic scale (pp. 38–39; 57). A scale that consists of seven consecutive notes in the framework of an octave. It is the type of scale prevalent in both European music and Arab music.

interval (Arabic: *bu'd*; plural: *ab'ād*) (pp. 36–38). The distance between two notes. An interval can be measured by counting the two notes plus the notes that are between them, for example, the interval between D1 and A2 is called a *fifth*, because they are five notes apart (D1–E1–F1–G2–A2); or by measuring the distance in tones, for example, the interval between B𝄳1 and C1 is three quartertones. See also **second.**

intonation (p. 63). The adjustment of the exact pitches of notes and intervals, especially when talking about subtle, microtonal alterations. See also **comma; cents.**

kamāndjah (p. 26). A bowed string instrument common throughout the Middle East, which is played vertically and placed on the player's thighs or knees. It is believed to be the predecessor of the European violin. See also ***djūzah.***

khānah (plural: *khānāt*). The stanzas, sections, or musical passages, that make up the main melodic development in certain classical instrumental pieces (such as the *bashraf* and the *samā'ī*) and are separated by a recurring refrain, called *taslīm*. See also ***bashraf*; *samā'ī.***

layālī (p. 27). In Arab music, a vocal improvisational genre similar to the instrumental *taqsīm*. Its name, literally meaning "nights," comes from the words the singer recites while improvising, *Yā laylī, yā 'aynī*, "O my night, O my eye." See also ***taqsīm***; ***mawwāl.***

leading note (p. 44). In European music theory, the seventh note of the major scale, the harmonic minor scale, or the melodic minor scale – the note that "leads" to the tonic or octave note. It is always a semitone below the note to which it leads. The corresponding Arab term is *ẓahīr*. In Arab music, however, the ẓahīr can be a semitone, a three-quartertone, a whole tone, or rarely a quartertone below the note to which it leads. See also ***ẓahīr*.**

maqām (plural: *maqāmāt*) (pp. 56–57). The term *maqām* is used in two contexts: (1) It may refer to the whole system of scales and modes of Arab music, i.e., the Arab *maqām system*. (2) It corresponds to the term *mode*, and represents one specific group of notes (*sullam al-maqām*, the scale of the maqām) together with the manner in which these notes are combined to form a melody (*sayr al-maqām*, the progression of the maqām), e.g., "maqām Nahawand." See also **mode; scale; *sayr*; *sullam al-maqām*.**

al-maqām al-'irāqī (p. 31). An ancient musical genre that comprises all the scales and modes unique to Iraqi musical culture. See also ***djālghī baghdād*.**

***maqām system*.** See ***maqām*.**

***maqāmāt*:** Plural of ***maqām*.**

mawwāl (p. 27). In Arab music, a vocal improvisational genre similar to the instrumental *taqsīm*. Its text is usually in vernacular Arabic. See also ***layālī*; *taqsīm*.**

melodic progression. See ***sayr*.**

microtonal intervals (pp. 59; 71). Intervals that are based on the division of the octave into more than 12 semitones, that is, they are based on units that are smaller than the semitone. Because of the division of the octave into 24 parts, Arab music features microtonal intervals called *quartertones* as well as their multiplications, such as the three-quartertone interval and the five-quartertone interval. See also **quartertonal intervals.**

microtonal notes. Notes based on **microtonal intervals.**

mīzān (p. 25). The term used for rhythmic patterns in Arab music. It is close to the terms *rhythm* and *meter* in European music theory.

mode (p. 42). From the Latin word *modus*, meaning "way," "method." In the context of European music theory, the term *mode* may stand for something between "scale" and "melody type." In Arab music, the concept of *maqām* can be considered close to the concept of mode, although it has a wider and more intricate meaning. See also **European modes.**

modulation (pp. 51–53; 90–94). The practice of moving from one scale, mode, or *maqām* to another. See also **alteration.**

monophony or **monophonic texture** (p. 95). Music that features only one core melodic line for all instruments and voices, as opposed to harmony and polyphony. Monophony is one of the main characteristics of Arab music. See also **harmony; polyphony.**

musical scale. See **scale.**

musical sound. See **note; tone.**

muwashshaḥ (p. 27). An ancient vocal musical genre still performed today. Its origins can be traced back to the medieval Arab culture of al-Andalus (Andalusia), Spain.

natural notes (p. 47). Notes that are neither sharpened nor flattened; namely, the notes of the white keys on the keyboard or the notes of the C major scale, C–D–E–F–G–A–B.

natural (p. 47). Indicates that any sharpening or flattening of a note that appeared previously in the notation is cancelled and the note returns it to its natural pitch. Represented by the accidental ♮. For example, when the note A♮ ("A natural") appears after the note A♯, the note is flattened back to the natural note A. See also **accidentals; natural notes.**

nāy. A flute-like wind instrument used throughout the Middle East, made of a tube (usually a reed) with finger holes. The nāy is completely open on both ends and sound is produced by resting the mouth on the rim of one end and blowing sideways.

nīm (p. 62). A term related to the Arab system of note names. When the word *nīm* comes before an Arab note name, it indicates the lowering of the note's pitch by a quartertone. For example, lowering the note Ḥiṣār (A♭2) by a quartertone gives the note Nīm Ḥiṣār (G♯2). See also ***tīk***.

note alteration. See **alteration.**

note (pp. 34–35). In the sense used in this book, a musical sound or tone – a sound with a distinct pitch whose frequency can be measured accurately. Music is formed of notes. Also means the name or the graphic sign used for a musical sound (as on the staff, for example). See also **tone.**

octave (pp. 36, 44). The word *octave* has two meanings: (1) the *octave note* is the eighth note in a heptatonic scale (Arabic: *djawāb al-maqām*); (2) the *octave interval* is the interval between two notes that are eight notes apart, counting both of them. A *perfect octave* equals six whole tones. Musical scales are usually presented and analyzed in the framework of an octave. See also ***djawāb; dīwān.***

overlapping adjnās (Arabic: *adjnās mutadākhila*) (p. 78). A disputable form of adjnās sequence presented by some scholars, in which the second djins of the scale is positioned on one of the middle notes of the first djins, and so the two adjnās "overlap." See also ***djins***; **disjunct adjnās; conjunct adjnās.**

pentachord. A group of five consecutive notes. A term often used in the context of Arab music theory. See also ***djins***; **tetrachord; trichord.**

polyphony (p. 54). A musical texture in which two or more melodic lines are performed simultaneously. Polyphony is almost completely irrelevant to Arab music, which is primarily monophonic. See also **monophony; harmony.**

primary adjnās (p. 79). The adjnās that form the scale of a maqām and are positioned on the *qarār* (tonic) and *ghammāz* (dominant) of the scale. See also **secondary adjnās.**

progression or **melodic progression.** See ***sayr***.

qānūn. A trapezoidal, zither-like plucked instrument common throughout the Arab world and in Turkey. It has about 26 courses of three strings, each course tuned to one note. By using small metal levers that can shorten the string, the player can produce microtonal notes.

qarār or ***qarār al-maqām*** (pp. 44; 57). The Arabic word for the tonic of a scale – the note on which the scale is positioned and the last note in the progression of the maqām. See also **tonic;** ***djawāb.***

qaṣīda (pp. 26–27). A poetical genre written in literary Arabic.

qiṭʿah mūsīqiyyah (p. 96). An instrumental musical genre that developed in the second quarter of the twentieth century. At that time, Arab composers started to break free from the confines of traditional music, which was mainly vocal, and the classical instrumental forms such as the *samāʿī* and the *bashraf*, and began composing instrumental pieces in a newer, more modern style.

quartertonal intervals (pp. 59; 71). Microtonal intervals that are derived from the division of the octave into 24 quartertones; mainly, the quartertone, the three-quartertone, and the five-quartertone intervals. This term is offered in this book as an alternative to the use of the term *microtonal* when discussing Arab music theory. See also **microtonal intervals.**

quartertonal notes (p. 59). Notes derived from the division of the octave into 24 quarter notes; for example B𝄳, F𝄲. See also **quartertonal intervals.**

quartertone (pp. 58–59). The quarter of a tone. The 24th part of an octave and the smallest interval used in classical Arab music. See also **interval; second.**

range. See **diapason.**

reposition (pp. 50–51; 83–84). The practice of moving, or *repositioning*, the tonic of a scale to one of its other notes, without changing the scale's intervals, in order to create a new scale. It is sometimes termed *scalar transposition, diatonic transposition*, or *tonic shifting*. See also **modulation; transposition.**

ṣadr (p. 26). Literally, "front." A term used in Arab poetry. See ***bayt.***

salṭanā (pp. 96–97). Literally, "control," or "dominion." It signifies the performer's control over the "spirit" or "essence" of the maqām and the intricacies and nuances of its performance – the right intonation of its quartertonal intervals, its melodic progression and its various modulations. In a vocal performance, the accompanying instrumental ensemble helps the singer attain salṭanā.

samāʿī (pp. 24–25; 27). A classical instrumental genre in which a recurring refrain, named *taslīm*, separates several stanzas, or musical passages, named *khānāt* (singular: *khānah*). The first three khānāt and the taslīm are based on a rhythmic pattern in $\frac{10}{8}$, also called samāʿī, while the last khānah features another meter, usually $\frac{3}{4}$ or $\frac{6}{8}$. See also ***khānah; bashraf.***

sayr or ***sayr al-maqām*** (pp. 57; 105). The *melodic progression* of the maqām: the way, or manner, in which the notes of the scale of the maqām are formed into a melody that represent the maqām. See also ***maqām; sullam al-maqām.***

scalar system (pp. 39–42; 66–69). A system of notes arranged by pitch from which scales and modes are derived and formed. In European music, the prevalent scalar system is the diatonic system – a cyclical system from which all scales are derived. In Arab music, we find several scalar systems, some of which are not cyclical, as well as stand-alone scales. See also **diatonic system.**

scale or **musical scale** (pp. 36; 39). A group of consecutive notes arranged in the framework of an octave.

second djins (pp. 72; 74–75). The upper djins of the two primary adjnās in the scale. See also ***djins*; primary adjnās.**

second octave (pp. 59–60). (1) The second octave of a scale in Arab music. (2) The second octave in the two-octave range of Arab music. See also ***dīwān.***

second (pp. 36–38). The interval between two consecutive notes in a scale. See also **interval.**

secondary adjnās (p. 79). Adjnās that are not the primary adjnās comprising the scale, that is, they are not positioned on the qarār (tonic) and ghammāz (dominant) of the scale, but on other notes. See also **primary adjnās.**

semitone (pp. 34; 39). Half of a tone. The twelfth part of an octave and the smallest interval used in classical European music. See also **tone; interval; second.**

sharp (p. 47). Indicates the raising, or *sharpening*, of a note by a semitone. Represented by the accidental ♯. For example, the note A♯ ("A-sharp") is a semitone higher than A. See also **accidentals.**

sharpen (p. 47). To sharpen a note is to raise its pitch by a certain interval; for example, sharpening the note A by a semitone gives the note A♯ . See also **accidentals.**

sullam al-maqām (p. 57). The group of notes employed by a certain maqām and represented by its scale. It should be differentiated from *sayr al-maqām* (the *melodic progression* of the maqām) – the way, or manner in which these notes are formed into a melody that represent the maqām. See also ***maqām; sayr;* scale.**

system of scales. See **scalar system.**

takht (p. 98). Literally, "a bench," "a counter." Especially in Egypt, a term used for small ensembles that consist of five to six instruments, while each instrument has only one representative. The Iraqi *djālghī baghdād* is similar in concept, but is not named *takht*. See also ***djālghī baghdād.***

taqāsīm. Plural of ***taqsīm.***

taqsīm (pp. 96–98). An improvisational instrumental genre with an unmetered, or "free," rhythm, usually performed by a solo instrumentalist. The taqsīm's melody is not pre-composed or written but is improvised (or "composed") by the player at the time of performance according to certain conventional aesthetic rules. The taqsīm is probably the most important instrumental genre of Arab music.

taqsīm ʿalā al-waḥdah (p. 97). Literally, "rhythmic taqsīm." Unlike the standard *taqsīm*, which is usually played solo, in the taqsīm ʿalā al-waḥdah the improvising performer is accompanied by a regular rhythm or a repeating melodic pattern.

ṭarab (p. 99). A state of spiritual exultation or ecstasy that a listener may experience when enjoying a superb musical performance.

taṣwīr (pp. 86–87). The practice of shifting the scale of a maqām from its conventional position and transposing it to another tonic and tessitura. The transposed maqām is then named *taṣwīr*, which means "an imitation" or "a copy." See also **transposition; reposition; conventional position; tessitura.**

tessitura. The range of notes in which the greater part of the activity of a melody, a musical piece, a mode, or a scale takes place. See also **diapason.**

tetrachord (pp. 42–44). From the Greek *tetra*, "four," and *chordē*, "string." A group of four consecutive notes. European diatonic scales can be divided into two tetrachords. See also ***djins*; trichord; pentachord.**

tīk (p. 62). A term related to the Arab system of note names. When the word *tīk* comes before an Arab note name, it indicates the raising of the note's pitch by a quartertone. For example, raising the note Ḥiṣār (A♭2) by a quartertone gives the note Tīk Ḥiṣār (A𝄳2). See also ***nīm*.**

tone (pp. 34–35). In English, the word tone has several meanings and usages, the three most important ones are: (1) a musical sound, a note; (2) the quality of a musical sound, e.g., "this singer has a beautiful tone"; (3) the interval equivalent to a sixth of the octave or to the sum of two semitones, sometimes called a *whole tone*. See also **note; semitone; interval.**

tonic or **tonic note** (p. 44). The first note of a musical scale, that is, the note on which the scale is positioned. It is the most important note of the scale. See also ***qarār*.**

transposition (pp. 49–50; 84–87). The practice of shifting a scale, a melody, or a complete musical piece from one tonic to another, without changing its intervallic structure. See also **reposition; *taṣwīr***

trichord. A group of three consecutive notes. A term often used in the context of Arab music theory. See also ***djins*; tetrachord; pentachord.**

ʿūd (p. 26). A plucked string instrument with a pear-shaped body common throughout the Middle East and the Mediterranean. It is the predecessor of the European lute.

uṣūl (p. 25). Literally, "rules," "foundations," "behavior." *Uṣūl* is the term used for the system of rhythmic patterns of Arab and Turkish music. These rhythmic patterns have a significant role in defining and shaping the various musical forms and genres.

whole tone. See **tone.**

ẓahīr or ***ẓahīr al-maqām*** (p. 44). In Arab music theory, a term similar to the European term *leading note* – the note below the tonic or below the octave note of a scale. It pulls and "leads" towards these notes and helps to strengthen them. Unlike the European *leading note*, which is always a semitone below the note it leads to, the *ẓahīr* can be a semitone, a three-quartertone, a whole tone, or rarely a quartertone below the note to which it leads. See also **leading note.**

Made in the USA
Middletown, DE
27 December 2020

30174642R00130